The European Tour Yearbook 2003

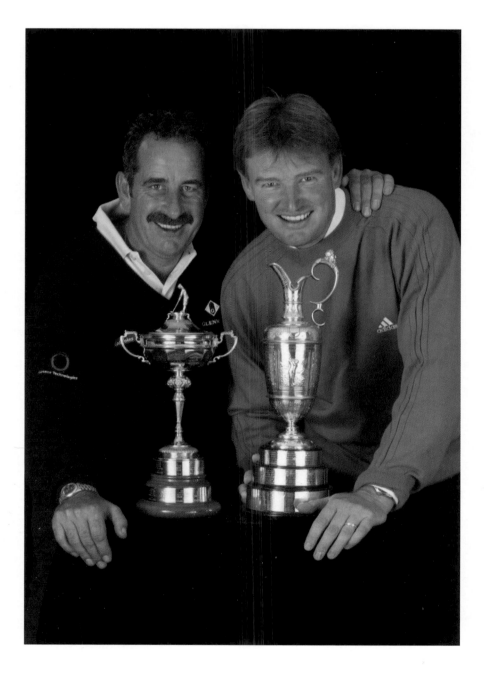

OFFICIAL  PUBLICATION

Executive Editor
Mitchell Platts

Production Editor
Vanessa O'Brien

Editorial Consultants
Scott Crockett
Chris Plumridge

Picture Editors
David Cannon
Stephen Munday
Andrew Redington

Art Director
Tim Leney
TC Communications Plc

Produced By
London Print & Design Plc

The European Tour Yearbook 2003
is published by The PGA European Tour,
Wentworth Drive, Virgina Water, Surrey GU25 4LX.

Distributed through Aurum Press Ltd.
25 Bedford Avenue
London WC1B 3AT

Colour reproduction through Essex Colour.

Printing and binding by Mohn Media.
© PGA European Tour.

Gut Lärchenhof Golf Club,
Cologne, Germany

Introduction from The European Tour

In winning The 34th Ryder Cup Matches, Sam Torrance and his twelve superb Team Members deservedly earned worldwide recognition for Europe in another outstanding year when we had good reason to also celebrate the victory by Ernie Els in the 131st Open Golf Championship and congratulate Retief Goosen in retaining his leadership of the Volvo Order of Merit.

Many observers believed we would be treated to a marvellous match at The De Vere Belfry, played in the highest traditions of the game, with Sam Torrance and Curtis Strange, two outstanding Captains, determined that whatever the result, golf would be the winner. This was most certainly the case with Sam enjoying a special moment, following a career which was launched in the same year as the official birth of The European Tour in 1971, as his Squad regained the prized trophy in a magnificent encounter.

Retief Goosen, challenged all the way by Padraig Harrington and Ernie Els, became the fifth golfer since the start of the Tour to retain the Number One position in the Volvo Order of Merit - following Peter Oosterhuis, Severiano Ballesteros, Sandy Lyle and, of course, Colin Montgomerie who compiled a record seven successive titles - and, furthermore, he won the Johnnie Walker Classic in Perth, Australia.

In winning the Open Golf Championship at Muirfield, Ernie Els fulfilled a dream and he also took the total number of Major Championship victories by European Tour Members to 27 since Severiano Ballesteros won the Open Golf Championship in 1979. Ernie also won the Heineken Classic, the Dubai Desert Classic and the Cisco World Match Play Championship on The European Tour International Schedule. We also offer our congratulations to Thomas Levet and Sergio Garcia. Thomas tied Ernie for the Open Golf Championship, along with Stuart Appleby and Steve Elkington, and Sergio finished in the top ten of each of the four Major Championships in addition to winning the Canarias Open de España on The European Tour International Schedule.

The continued progress made by Sergio (aged 22) and that of Justin Rose (aged 22), who won no less than four times around the world including the dunhill championship and the Victor Chandler British Masters on The European Tour International Schedule, and Adam Scott (aged 22), who won the Qatar Masters and the Diageo Scottish PGA Championship, provided ample evidence that the future is in good hands. Indeed Adam and Justin were two of four multiple winners on The European Tour International Schedule - the others were Ernie Els and Tiger Woods - and there were no fewer than 14 first time winners including Graeme McDowell, who claimed a remarkable victory in the Volvo Scandinavian Masters in only his fourth European Tour event. Nick Dougherty, a member of

the winning 2001 Great Britain and Ireland Walker Cup team, became The 2002 Sir Henry Cotton Rookie of the Year.

The leading 15 players led by Lee S James from the 2002 European Challenge Tour will now, having secured their cards, face the opportunity to challenge for similar honours with the knowledge that a record of no fewer than 125 Members earned in excess of £100,000 on the 2002 Volvo Order of Merit. Five years ago that figure was 65. They will also be joining a Tour on which players from no fewer than 14 countries enjoyed tournament victories with a total of 22 countries hosting Tour competition. The international pedigree of The European Tour was further enhanced with players from no less than 11 countries winning on the European Challenge Tour, which visited 18 countries. Japan's Seiji Ebihara finished Number One on the 2002 European Seniors Tour, which visited 14 countries, ahead of England's Denis Durnian, Jamaica's Delroy Cambridge, England's John Morgan, Ireland's Christy O'Connor Jnr, America's Steve Stull, Canada's John Irwin, Scotland's John Chillas, Ireland's Denis O'Sullivan and England's Nick Job.

We have placed ourselves at the forefront of the internationalisation of golf. We lead the challenge to unite nations and embrace the game at all levels. We recognise we must continue to bring forward fresh and powerful initiatives to enhance the popularity of golf, and we trust this is reflected in The 15th Edition of The European Tour Yearbook which we hope you enjoy reading.

KENNETH D SCHOFIELD CBE
Executive Director, The European Tour

contents

The 34th Ryder Cup Matches · The De Vere Belfry · Sutton Coldfield · England

out of the shadows

come heroes

I t was, quite simply, sport at its very best and for its own sake; when the virtues of courage, self-belief, determination and skill combined to reach a level of excellence amongst the best golfers in the world for no other reason than to determine which of them played the better golf.

In the process it inspired the main characters of this drama to heights of achievement perhaps even they never suspected lurked within themselves. It not only set a measure of behaviour for all other sports to follow but also gave 35,000 enthusiastic fans that last day the joy of knowing they had witnessed a piece of history as they departed The 34th Ryder Cup Matches on The Brabazon Course at The De Vere Belfry.

From left to right: Ian Woosnam, Sam Torrance, Mark James and Joakim Haeggman

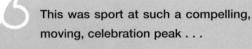

> **This was sport at such a compelling, moving, celebration peak . . .**
>
> *Sue Mott (Daily Telegraph)*

But above all it was the spirit of the game, best illustrated afterwards by the tributes and unabashed praise from the American campaigners towards their European opponents, who prevailed by $15^{1}/_{2}$–$12^{1}/_{2}$, that defined precisely the hard but fair-minded manner in which this Match had been conducted and in so doing set a glorious standard by which all future contests will be judged.

Darren Clarke and David Duval

Over eighteen holes, anything is possible.

Every two years, the greatest European and American golfers do battle for the world's most coveted golf trophy – The Ryder Cup.

It's a competition that rouses a rare passion. And when there is passion on a golf course – anything is possible. In 2006 The Ryder Cup will be played at The K Club. At AIB, we're delighted to play our part in making it possible.

AIB, proud partner to The 2006 Ryder Cup in Ireland.

RYDER CUP 2006
Ireland
AIB
PROUD PARTNER

Be with AIB.

The Opening Ceremony

USA Captain Curtis Strange

This truth, now realised, must be valued and preserved because it is the cornerstone of golf in its original form in which the primary objective is to determine who plays better on the day. In an age of such evenly-balanced talents there is no wider significance than this nor thoughts of global supremacy. Such days are gone because it is in the marginal subtleties and nuances of play that the difference between winning and losing is to be found.

> Paul McGinley is a wonderful gentleman. I never met him before. I told him afterwards that I'd made a new friend this week.
>
> *Jim Furyk*

In such a context, the role of Sam Torrance, the charismatic European Captain, cannot be overstated. He came with a pedigree that made him an obvious talisman because he had already earned his place in Ryder Cup history with *that* winning last green putt at The De Vere Belfry in 1985 when Europe won the Cup for the first time in 28 years and restored a balance of power between the two sides that has remained constant ever since.

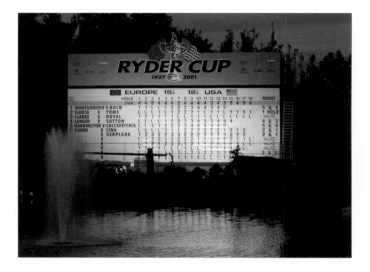

He had experienced the joys and sorrows in team golf since his Ryder Cup debut in 1981 and had gained an exhaustive inside knowledge of the strengths and pitfalls of collective play. He also knew how The Brabazon Course should be prepared to give his twelve men - four of them newcomers - their best chance, whether that meant narrow fairways to restrict the more powerful American hitters or slower than usual greens to puzzle those more comfortable on a faster surface. The tee on the 311 yard tenth hole was pushed back to heighten the risk of trying to drive the green thereby reducing long hitters to taking short irons to lay up short

> The swirling galleries were thoroughly well behaved, and especially mannerly to the visiting Americans. When a US player would miss a critical putt, there would be an audible gasp for the man's misfortune then applause and plenty of celebration for their own team's jolly good play.
>
> *The Washington Post*

> The best sport is almost too dramatic to bear. It leans towards the excruciating, the harrowing. For The Ryder Cup to turn that screw as early as the opening day settles the debate about where to find golf's most consuming theatre. On days like this, you can keep the individualism of the Open or the Masters.
>
> Here was the magic and magnetism they talk about: the man subsumed by the team, to glorious effect. Under the gaze of 35,000 live spectators, an event that had threatened to get lost in a Spaghetti Junction of moral writhing reclaimed its place in sport's list of unmissable attractions.
>
> *Paul Hayward (Daily Telegraph)*

of the pond in front of the putting surface. From Sam's point of view, it was simply a case of levelling the playing field.

Moreover he switched the playing format for the first day so that the fourball Matches opened proceedings and in consequence allowed his players the freedom to play attacking golf and not be constrained by the disciplines of foursomes play that on past occasions, had sometimes caused a tentative start. It was a perfect ploy - and one approved by his Vice Captain Ian Woosnam and 'backroom boys' Joakim Haeggman and Mark James - as the home side emerged from the morning session with a 3-1 lead, their best start since Great Britain and Ireland led 3-1 at the Old Warson Country Club, St Louis, in 1971.

He led with Thomas Björn and Darren Clarke because, as he explained, they were "birdie machines" and they did not let him down. They faced Paul Azinger, a seasoned and respected campaigner, and Tiger Woods, unquestionably the best golfer in the world, and yet it may have occurred to Tiger that both the opponents had got the better of him in earlier encounters – Björn

> Curtis Strange took it in the eye magnificently. His speech from the abyss of defeat was filled with grace and closed, magnificently, the book on the disfigurement brought by the appalling excesses of Brookline Country Club three years ago.
>
> *Jim Lawton (The Independent)*

in the 2001 Dubai Desert Classic and Clarke in the 2000 World Golf Championships – Accenture Match Play.

Clarke opened with three successive birdies but the Americans parried and struck back superbly, finishing with a 63, only to realise it was not good enough because the Europeans had taken 62

Phil Mickelson and David Toms

Tiger Woods and Jesper Parnevik

Padraig Harrington

> It was just a beautiful week. It was the best thing for golf to have it played this way.
>
> The fans were partisan, which is the way it should be, but they were fair. And they were respectful. And they liked seeing good golf shots, and they were courteous the entire week. We are certainly appreciative of that.
>
> *Tiger Woods*

Thomas Björn

strokes to win by a one hole margin. In the second match the inspired pairing of Sergio Garcia with Lee Westwood was to transform the Englishman's performance as they formed a formidable alliance. Their exuberance and skill quickly earned another European point by a 4 and 3 margin against David Duval and Davis Love III.

By this time Europe's most experienced partnership of Bernhard Langer, playing in his tenth Ryder Cup Match, and Colin Montgomerie, had taken command against Jim Furyk and Scott Hoch who had little defence against opponents who were eight under par when they triumphed by 4 and 3.

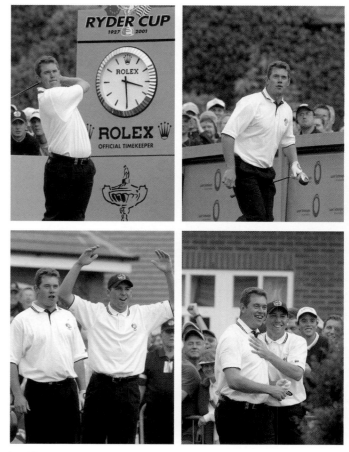

Lee Westwood and Sergio Garcia

...am Torrance back in the swing of things 24 hours later on Patrons Day with Richard Hills, The Ryder Cup Director, holding the prized trophy

Ireland

A Natural Home for the RYDER CUP 2006

It says much for the loyalty and commitment to the team of both Langer and Montgomerie that both required physiotherapy treatment for neck and back ailments respectively before and sometimes between matches to keep going. Montgomerie maintained this ritual for the full five appearances while Langer felt obliged to take a rest yet still managed to set a record of 11 foursomes wins in his career to better Nick Faldo's previous record.

> " I thank Curtis and his men for the way The Ryder Cup has been contested, with a passion and intensity but also with the traditions, like courtesy and sportsmanship, which are the bedrock of our great game.
>
> *Sam Torrance* "

Paul Azinger

> " Sam Torrance heard Professor David Purdie, a gynaecologist, speak at the Association of Golf Writers' Dinner in July. He was impressed by his use of language, and used some of his lines to rally his troops. On Saturday night he told them 'They have one Tiger, but we have 12 lions.' For those at the back of the order who might have felt like they were being thrown away, he said 'Always remember - from out of shadows, heroes emerge.
>
> *Derek Lawrenson (Daily Mail)* "

The defeat of Swedish newcomer Niclas Fasth and Ireland's Padraig Harrington by Phil Mickelson and 2001 US PGA Champion David Toms hid the story of a determined counter-attack when the Europeans trailed three down after 11 holes yet narrowly missed clinching a half point on the last green. Sam's men were encouraged by their confident start but smart enough to contain their jubilation.

True enough, by the afternoon foursomes, it was clear the American squad was in determined mood and Hal Sutton together with Scott Verplank put the next US point on the board by beating Björn and Clarke 2 and 1. Garcia and Westwood maintained their ebullient form against Mark Calcavecchia and Woods to win 2 and 1, but Paul McGinley and Harrington succumbed to Stewart Cink and Jim Furyk by 3 and 2.

View From men's and women's performance golfwear.
Available exclusively at Marks & Spencer.

With the last pair of Langer and Montgomerie three up at one stage against Mickelson and Toms, honours looked to be set even in the second session until the Americans levelled the match with three magnificent birdies then halved the last hole in dramatic style to snatch a half point. Mickelson prompted a few raised eyebrows when he took a wedge - and a divot - on the 18th green to move the ball 100 feet from the front edge to within twelve feet of the flag. His Captain Curtis Strange said afterwards: "I question your choice of club. But it worked!" Mickelson replaced his divot seamlessly, too.

The second day took on the shape and form of a dog fight with everyone engaged in their own skirmishes and nobody quite sure

> The sheer uplifting magnificence of The Ryder Cup left Britain a happier place on Monday morning. The manner of the victorious team, delirious but respectful, and the demeanor of the losing team, gutted but gracious, was a sight of the finest order. The Ryder Cup was, quite simply, one of the most involvingly thrilling sports events of the year-going-on-decade.
>
> *Sue Mott (Daily Telegraph)*

what had happened until it was all over and the dust had settled. In the morning foursomes session newcomers Pierre Fulke, from Sweden, and Phillip Price, from Wales, looked set for a remarkable debut when they went one up after twelve holes against Mickelson and Toms but three successive birdies from the Americans brought the European duo back to reality and a 2 and 1 loss.

But Garcia and Westwood were still in commanding mood and produced a standard of play strong enough to defeat Cink and Furyk by 2 and 1 and elicit a fulsome tribute from Cink: "You can have peace of mind playing with Sergio," said the American. "When you hit a bad shot you can rely on him to make up for the mistake."

There was, however, a sense of dèja vu for Langer and Montgomerie as they saw a leading margin slip away against Hoch and Verplank. Then Bernhard commented to his partner: "We're still level. Let's win this thing." Langer obliged with a seven iron to eight feet on the long 17th and Montgomerie holed for a winning birdie to give Europe the lead again and, after halving the last hole, the point.

Woods had reason to smile as he scored his first point of the contest with partner Love III by a 4 and 3 margin over Björn and Clarke, who could not quite maintain their earlier consistency. Even so, Europe still held an overall lead of $6^{1}/_{2}$-$5^{1}/_{2}$ points going into the afternoon fourball series.

THE DE VERE BELFRY,
RYDER CUP HOST VENUE
1985, 1989, 1993 & 2002

memories are made of this...

When the victorious 34th Ryder Cup Matches teed off on the 27th September 2002 history was made,
as The De Vere Belfry became the only venue to have ever staged the prestigious event four times.

the course

One of the world's greatest arenas for match play golf, rewarding the brave yet always threatening disaster for error. The final hole across water defines its challenge and underlines the eternal truth that the match isn't over until the last putt drops.

Bernhard Langer and Colin Montgomerie

L'esprit Moët & Chandon

BRUT IMPÉRIAL

MOËT & CHANDON

CHAMPAGNE

moët.com

Official Supplier to the PGA European Tour

By now the Americans sensed a revival and Fasth, paired with fellow countryman Jesper Parnevik, had his first taste of the vagaries of Ryder Cup golf when he scored five birdies to help his side into a three hole lead after seven but still lost out by one hole to Calcavecchia and Duval who, incidentally, was one of the few players who threw caution to the wind - or perhaps had enough nerve - to drive the tenth green and win the hole with a birdie to start the fightback.

Meanwhile Harrington and Montgomerie, with Langer rested, formed a formidable partnership and scored a confident win over Mickelson and Toms by 2 and 1 after taking a three hole lead by the turn. With Garcia and Westwood one up with two to play against Love III and Woods, another European point seemed inevitable especially when the young Spaniard laced a three wood into the 17th green.

Niclas Fasth

Pierre Fulke

But the American stars are at their most lethal when seemingly counted out and Love III coolly chipped in for his birdie while Garcia three putted so that the match was all square playing the last. All hopes of even a half point for Europe vanished when Westwood's par putt refused to drop and the Americans gained a dramatic one hole victory.

> " I wouldn't have Darren Clarke for a friend if it wasn't for The Ryder Cup
>
> *Davis Love III* "

Clarke and McGinley had been two down with five to play against Furyk and Hoch, fought back valiantly, but still came to the 18th one down. This was to be a pivotal moment. If Clarke and McGinley lost then the United States would lead entering the singles. McGinley drove into the fairway; Clarke into a bunker. It was Clarke's turn but, by the side of the fairway, Langer touched Torrance on the shoulder and whispered: "I think it would be better if Paul played first."

Phillip Price

Colin Montgomerie

Torrance considered Langer's opinion, and said to McGinley: "If you don't mind, we would like you to play first." McGinley found the green, and the pressure was instantly switched to their opponents. Europe won the hole, halved the match and so after two days of pulsating drama the fourballs and the foursomes had been tied 8-8.

With everything to play for, the differing mind-set of opposing captains presented an intriguing study. Lead in strength from the top, or load the bottom of the draw with established stars to knock over supposedly weaker players, or at worst carry out salvage work if the top of the draw gets into trouble? The risk of this strategy is that the Match could be over before the anchormen have a chance to take effect. In any case, the Americans needed only to halve the match to retain the trophy as holders.

Accordingly, skipper Curtis Strange decided on a safety first policy and consigned Azinger, Furyk, Love, Mickelson and Woods, in that order, to the tail-end of the US batting list. For Sam and his "twelve lions", there was never any other choice but to go for it with the established campaigners leading the way.

Sam remembered another truth from his years of Ryder Cup golf and explained: "I am a great believer in momentum in these

> This Ryder Cup was the most sporting event that most of us sport writers and other professional hangers-on can remember, and the audience deserve mention in the same paragraph as the Sydney Olympic audience of two summers ago.
>
> *Paul Hayward (Daily Telegraph)*

matches. All my players going out late will be well aware of what's happening on the course." That indeed is the blessing - or the curse - of the leaderboard in such moments. Torrance instructed his men not to study any leaderboard, unless it was a sea of European blue, and he told them all: "You've nothing to fear. Make today the best day of your life. You were born to do this job. This is what we practise for. This is what we live for. Now go, go and do it."

HOW EXACTLY DO YOU TELL YOUR DOCTOR YOU'RE HAVING ERECTION PROBLEMS?

"Hello Doctor, I'm having erection problems."

Or: "Hello Doctor, I'm having difficulty maintaining an erection."

Yes, it is difficult to say but your doctor will understand.

Erection problems are common, affecting at least one in every ten men. But not talking only makes matters worse.

Remember that erection problems don't just affect the man – there's a relationship with a wife or partner which is affected too. And the longer this goes on, the more likely they are to drift apart.

Talking to your doctor gives you the best chance of sorting things out. Erection problems have a variety of causes and are often due to other medical conditions such as hypertension or diabetes.

So it is a health problem which should be checked out. Remember, you're not alone. You're one of many people with a problem that can usually be solved. So talk to your partner. And talk to your doctor. There are solutions to your problem that can make you both feel better.

- -

Please send me more information on men's health.   10932j

Title ☐☐☐☐ First name ☐☐☐☐☐☐☐☐☐☐☐

Last name ☐☐☐☐☐☐☐☐☐☐☐☐☐☐

Address ☐☐☐☐☐☐☐☐☐☐☐☐☐☐

☐☐☐☐☐☐☐☐☐☐☐☐☐☐☐

☐☐☐☐☐☐☐☐☐ Postcode ☐☐☐☐☐☐

E-mail ☐☐☐☐☐☐☐☐☐☐☐☐☐☐☐

For information post coupon to: informED, Freepost (PY917).
PO Box 36, Plymouth PL1 1BR   Or call 0870 129 0100
Email: info@informED.org.uk   www.informED.org.uk

The Impotence Association   *the*MEN'S HEALTH FORUM

SUPPORTED WITH AN EDUCATIONAL GRANT FROM PFIZER LIMITED.

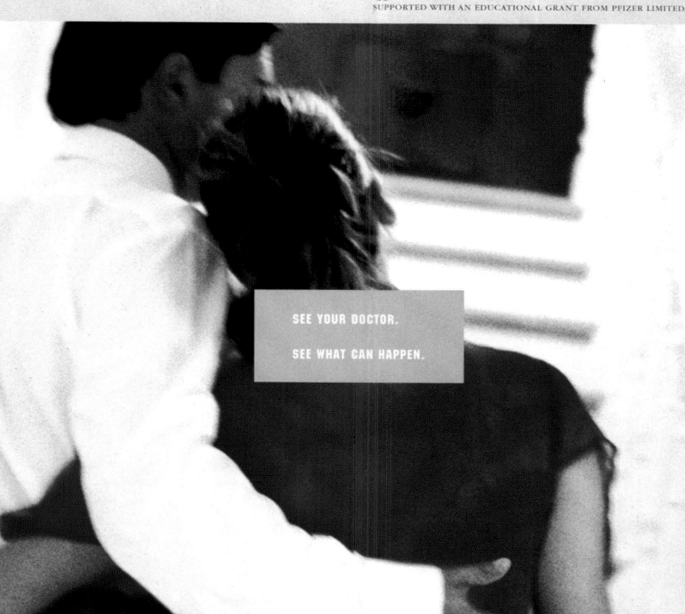

SEE YOUR DOCTOR.

SEE WHAT CAN HAPPEN.

shot of the week

PAUL McGINLEY Europe

At 4.52pm Paul McGinley faced a putt of nine feet on the last green well aware it could secure The 34th Ryder Cup Matches. It was virtually identical to one he had holed two years earlier in a Tour event and the memory served him well as once again he found the same unerring line.

So it was that Sam played to his considered strengths right from the top of the batting order with Montgomerie - who established himself as Europe's "rock" to whom team mates looked for example and encouragement - leading the charge with a resounding 5 and 4 win over Hoch to personally earn $4^1/_2$ points from five encounters during which he played 82 holes and was never behind.

The value of his singles point was not simply arithmetical but more importantly sent a message to his team mates via the scoreboard, and the explosive cheers of the fans, that they, too, could seize the moment. The scoreboard, with its mass of blue numbers denoting European advantage, showed that the message had got through and that the opposition was on the back foot. The mood was infectious.

> Nobody in this scribbling business should forget how lucky we are to be paid witnesses at great sporting occasions. Rarely can that good fortune have been so firmly underlined as in the concluding stages of The 34th Ryder Cup Matches last Sunday afternoon when the 35,000 people squeezed into The De Vere Belfry scurried from one drama to another to be delivered an experience they will never forget.
>
> *Kevin Mitchell (The Observer)*

Harrington went four up on Calcavecchia with a putt of 50 feet on the ninth as he eased to a 5 and 4 win. Langer put together four birdies in six holes against Sutton en route to a 4 and 3 win. Not all the drama followed the script however. Garcia looked to be marching irrepressibly towards yet another victory but his opponent Toms had other ideas and the irrepressible Spaniard was brought back to level terms then drove into the lake on the last to lose by one hole.

Despite the heat of the contest there was time for moments of chivalry between rivals that neither will forget. One such occured on the last green when Duval holed from 14 feet then conceded Clarke's missable putt for a half point. At that moment the prospect of a European victory was becoming an exciting reality especially when Björn beat Cink by 2 and 1, and despite Westwood's loss by 2 and 1 to Verplank.

The time now was 4.08pm on a gloriously, hot and sunny afternoon. Europe led $12^1/_2$-$10^1/_2$ with two points required for

The victorious European Team

victory. The next 46 minutes would seem like a lifetime to Torrance but as he would say later, it was the stirring culmination of the greatest week of his career – "I wish I could bottle it and take a sip every day for the rest of my life."

By now the eyes of the world were focused on the four European rookies – Fasth, Fulke, McGinley and Price – from whom two points were required to make the 12th match between Parnevik and Woods meaningless. Coincidentally Parnevik had told the four rookies at dinner on the Saturday night: "For two days we have been a team, but I remember in the singles in my first Ryder Cup it was a very lonely experience. It is going to feel like that for you tomorrow, so be wary, and prepare."

Then, on the way to the tee, Torrance had told Price, the World Number 119, as he prepared to face Mickelson, the World Number

> The Sam Torrances are here to remind us that it really can be about such time-honoured concepts as honour and pure competition.
>
> *Bob Ryan (Boston Globe)*

Two: "You can have him, Phillip." Price nodded: "You're right." So it came to pass that Price played the golf of his life, scored a decisive 3 and 2 win and by 4.36pm, victory was a finger-touch away.

This was the point, too, at which it became obvious that Strange's plan was going wrong as the men he had hoped to rely on began to struggle. Fasth withstood the most incredible pressure from Azinger, one the world's best match players, who sensationally holed from a bunker on the last hole knowing that if he lost his

Paul McGinley

The two Captains, Sam Torrance and Curtis Strange, brought courtesy and sportsmanship

match, the US squad would have lost the entire contest because only three matches remained on the course from which to salvage points. But even the half point Azinger earned simply gave the United States squad some breathing space and delayed what now seemed inevitable. Europe led 14-11 and another half point would see Sam Ryder's elegant golden chalice in Sam Torrance's eager hands.

It would require ten more minutes before the European emotions could be released. The Irish have made a habit of making the 18th green their own in Ryder Cups - Eamonn Darcy at Muirfield Village in 1987, Christy O'Connor Jnr at The De Vere Belfry in 1989 and Philip Walton at Oak Hill in 1995. Now it was the turn of Paul McGinley.

Two down after three, McGinley never looked anything other than composed. He was determined this would be his day; Europe's day. McGinley said: "Myself, Phillip Price and Pierre Fulke talked at breakfast about it coming down to one of us. One of us was going

to be there, to finish it as it was unlikely that the first six Matches would all be won. It was going to come down to whether we were going to win the Cup or not."

Two down on no less than four occasions, McGinley holed from six feet to win the 13th. Then he sank a 15 footer on the 17th to halve the match. At the 18th McGinley pulled his second left meaning he would need to carry a large mound with his recovery with little room in which to stop his ball before the pin; Furyk was in Azinger's bunker. McGinley played first, a superb shot in the circumstances as he was left with a nine foot, slightly uphill putt. Next Furyk. All held their breath as the ball brushed the hole. Now McGinley needed to hole for the half and the match. "I said to myself 'Don't miss it'." McGinley explained. "I knew the line. I had said earlier in the week that I would just love the opportunity to be in the position to strike the winning putt." McGinley struck the putt; the ball never wavered from the intended line and disappeared dead-centre into the cup.

All around the celebrations began; players, caddies, wives and partners hugged and danced for joy as the spectators sent wave upon wave of thunderous cheers flowing down from the huge grandstands.

The week had begun with Torrance stating that the Captaincy had been: "the greatest honour of my career." As McGinley's putt disappeared from view the Scot, seated on the bank to the right of the green, momentarily gazed down at the grass and gave silent thanks that the 'greatest honour' had indeed produced the perfect result.

Even though what followed in the last two Matches was incidental to the outcome, it underlined the spirit in which these Matches had been played. Fulke and Love III were on level terms and waiting in the middle of the last fairway for the celebrations to clear from the green so they could play their second shots. The Swede then offered to concede the point but Love III declined and settled for a half point each and declared later: "Pierre's a top guy because of that move."

"

I don't think I have ever been gripped by a sport other than football the way I was on Sunday. I was delighted for Sam. It was an epic achievement, especially when you consider that the whole thing was delayed for a year after September 11. Sam showed on Sunday what he is made of. He was never in panic mode, and that was exceptional. He was always in control.

Sir Alex Ferguson

"

Inevitably Tiger made the last gesture when he conceded Parnevik's missable putt on the last green so their match was halved which meant that every European player had contributed to the score sheet.

Sam Torrance with his wife, Suzanne, and their son, Daniel

This was The Ryder Cup which, as Torrance correctly pointed out, brought passion and intensity and traditions, like courtesy and sportsmanship, to the fore. This was The Ryder Cup where true sportsmanship was gloriously advertised both on and off the fairways. The Europeans were intoxicated by victory, but remained respectful to their opponents; the Americans were magnanimous in defeat. The spectators, too, played their part in elevating this contest to one of the most thrilling sporting events of the decade, for they cheered politely for the Americans and vigorously for the Europeans. They were partisan, but fair. Courteous and respectful. As Curtis Strange said: "The hardest, but fairest that I have ever seen."

Afterwards the American Captain could only reflect: "We got a European butt-whipping. I thought we played pretty good golf, but they did what they had to do."

For Sam Torrance, it was a lifetime's achievement but even in his moment of triumph he disregarded his own inspirational role and instead praised his team: "All I did was lead them to the water and they drank copiously," he said. "Out of the shadows come heroes."

Michael McDonnell

Make it a fourball

Make it happen

As one of the world's largest companies we continue to take pride in our involvement with Scotland's greatest home-grown game.

From the world's oldest open competition to the champions of tomorrow, we are dedicated to supporting all aspects of the game.

We are delighted to supply banking services to players, spectators, officials and exhibitors as Official Bank to The European Tour.

www.rbs.co.uk

THE 34TH RYDER CUP MATCHES

THE DE VERE BELFRY • SUTTON COLDFIELD • ENGLAND • September 27 – 29 • 2002 • Par 72 • 7118 yards • 6509 metres

Captains: Sam Torrance (Europe), Curtis Strange (USA)

EUROPE   **USA**

Day One

Fourballs: Morning

D Clarke & T Björn (1 hole)	1	T Woods & P Azinger	0
S Garcia & L Westwood (4&3)	1	D Duval & D Love III	0
C Montgomerie & B Langer (4&3)	1	S Hoch & J Furyk	0
P Harrington & N Fasth	0	P Mickelson & D Toms (1 hole)	1
	3		**1**

Foursomes: Afternoon

D Clarke & T Björn	0	H Sutton & S Verplank (2&1)	1
S Garcia & L Westwood (2&1)	1	T Woods & M Calcavecchia	0
C Montgomerie & B Langer (halved)	½	P Mickelson & D Toms (halved)	½
P Harrington & P McGinley	0	S Cink & J Furyk (3&2)	1
	4½		**3½**

Day Two

Foursomes: Morning

P Fulke & P Price	0	P Mickelson & D Toms (2&1)	1
L Westwood & S Garcia (2&1)	1	S Cink & J Furyk	0
C Montgomerie & B Langer (1 hole)	1	S Verplank & S Hoch	0
D Clarke & T Björn	0	T Woods & D Love III (4&3)	1
	6½		**5½**

Fourballs: Afternoon

N Fasth & J Parnevik	0	M Calcavecchia & D Duval (1 hole)	1
C Montgomerie & P Harrington (2&1)	1	P Mickelson & D Toms	0
S Garcia & L Westwood	0	T Woods & D Love III (1 hole)	1
D Clarke & P McGinley (halved)	½	S Hoch & J Furyk (halved)	½
	8		**8**

Day Three

Singles

C Montgomerie (5&4)	1	S Hoch	0
S Garcia	0	D Toms (1 hole)	1
D Clarke (halved)	½	D Duval (halved)	½
B Langer (4&3)	1	H Sutton	0
P Harrington (5&4)	1	M Calcavecchia	0
T Björn (2&1)	1	S Cink	0
L Westwood	0	S Verplank (2&1)	1
N Fasth (halved)	½	P Azinger (halved)	½
P McGinley (halved)	½	J Furyk (halved)	½
P Fulke (halved)	½	D Love III (halved)	½
P Price (3&2)	1	P Mickelson	0
J Parnevik (halved)	½	T Woods (halved)	½
Europe	**15½**	**USA**	**12½**

Individual Player Performances

Europe

	P	W	L	H	Pts
Thomas Björn	4	2	2	0	2
Darren Clarke	5	1	2	2	2
Niclas Fasth	3	0	2	1	½
Pierre Fulke	2	0	1	1	½
Sergio Garcia	5	3	2	0	3
Padraig Harrington	4	2	2	0	2
Bernhard Langer	4	3	0	1	3½
Paul McGinley	3	0	1	2	1
Colin Montgomerie	5	4	0	1	4½
Jesper Parnevik	2	0	1	1	½
Phillip Price	2	1	1	0	1
Lee Westwood	5	3	2	0	3

Individual Player Performances

USA

	P	W	L	H	Pts
Paul Azinger	2	0	1	1	½
Mark Calcavecchia	3	1	2	0	1
Stewart Cink	3	1	2	0	1
David Duval	3	1	1	1	1½
Jim Furyk	5	1	2	2	2
Scott Hoch	4	0	3	1	½
Davis Love III	4	2	1	1	2½
Phil Mickelson	5	2	2	1	2½
Hal Sutton	2	1	1	0	1
David Toms	5	3	1	1	3½
Scott Verplank	3	2	1	0	2
Tiger Woods	5	2	2	1	2½

steely and determined

Volvo Order of Merit Winner

Retief Goosen

Volvo Order of Merit Winner

Catching up with Retief Goosen is easy. Well, in one sense it is. Few men move more slowly or more gracefully than the South African whether on the golf course or the pavement. Where others march or swagger, Goosen appears to glide, each movement considered, deliberate. Clearly, if he ever studied dance it would be at the school of Fred Astaire and not John Travolta.

As he ambles gently through life he takes with him that trademark slow-burn grin of his. You know the one, the gentle smile he pulls out whether he eagles a hole or bogeys it, before wandering carefully off to unwrap the next challenge and to consider his response.

Now this challenge is to cruise into 2003 and try to make it a stunning three European Number One titles in succession. When he topped the Volvo Order of Merit in 2001, Goosen did so largely via his spectacular success in the US Open Championship, enhancing that effort with victories in The Barclays Scottish Open at Loch Lomond and the Telefonica Open de Madrid.

This time he had just one victory to his credit, in the Johnnie Walker Classic, so it is his overwhelming consistency throughout the rest of a long and testing season that has carried him to the highest plateau for the second time. It is this ability to achieve form and then to maintain it that marks Retief Goosen out as a very special golfer. His surge to the top is, as ever, based on a now unshakeable confidence in his own ability. "Last year I didn't know if I had it within me to stay strong towards the end of a Major, now I know I did," he said. "Winning the US Open is one way towards a great confidence boost. So, of course, is achieving Number One in Europe.

"Doing it for a second time just adds another layer to that confidence. I'd worked on my swing with my coach Sam Frost and that was fine, then Jos Vanstiphout, my sports psychologist, met up with me and he helped me win the mental game. My wife Tracy has also been a great support. So everything just seems to have come together for me at the right time."

Since that wonderful week in Oklahoma in the summer of 2001 Goosen has turned himself into one of the world's genuinely outstanding performers. There was even a time, in the first quarter of 2002, that he was, arguably, the very best on the planet. Until Tiger took the Masters Tournament and the US Open Championship, of course.

Retief celebrates a South African victory with David Frost and Ernie Els

Mel Pyatt (left), President & CEO, Volvo Event Management, and Ken Schofield (right), Executive Director of The European Tour, presented Retief Goosen with the 2002 Volvo Order of Merit Trophy

2001 US Open Champion

Certainly Goosen's victories around the world and his clinching of his first Harry Vardon Trophy made him one of the most successful. However, he then began the final round of the 2002 Masters Tournament in a tie for the lead with Woods and so had to play those 18 holes in his company, an experience that seemed to affect him as much as anybody else at Augusta National.

Is there, therefore, still a part of Goosen that simply does not believe enough? Reassuringly, he bristles a little at such a suggestion. "Firstly, I like Tiger," he said. "He's a great guy, very friendly. Sometimes the 25,000 people who want to see him play can be a problem if you are his partner, but apart from that I was fine on that last day. The problem was that all week I didn't really play well. I was pulling a lot of my iron shots but putting great. When I dropped shots over those first few holes, three putting the first and fourth, it was because my approaches were so poor.

"Those irons left me in impossible positions. There was just no way I could get down in two from where I put my ball. It might look easy on television but, believe me, I was in exactly the wrong places.

"But I'm pleased and proud of my second place. The best I'd managed at Augusta before was 33rd so that was a heck of an improvement. And I never stopped fighting. Even going down the 15th I turned to my caddie and told him we could still win.

"If I could eagle and Tiger missed his birdie and then I got another birdie at the 16th, it would have put pressure on him and then who knows what might have happened. Even on the 18th I still figured I had a chance because that's no gimme four now. But Tiger hit a good drive and that was that."

The contrast between these two stars could hardly be more defined. Where Tiger has been constructed as meticulously as a Michelangelo statue, Retief is more or less self-taught. Where Woods demonstrates his delight with natural abandon, Goosen celebrates so modestly one is left uncertain that he is actually celebrating at all.

Incredibly, he has not even had a proper holiday since his Oklahoma triumph although he has bought a new house in Sunningdale, England, and another in Orlando in America. Where Woods is comfortable in the company of the Hollywood A-list, Goosen is happier at home, wearing jeans and "probably painting something". This, of course, is more likely to be a fence than anything in oils or watercolour.

Does anything get him going? "Yeah, of course I get excited about things but I don't pump fists. I prefer to stay level," he says in his trademark quiet tone. "As a junior I was pretty heavy tempered and I can remember breaking a few clubs. Believe me, I had to work hard to improve my temperament.

"It's like my driving. I used to be the longest in Europe off the tee but I had a swing like John Daly's to achieve it and I wanted more consistency. I've got that now even if I'm maybe 30 yards shorter than I was. And mentally I'm much better.

"In fact the next five years should be the best of my career although I know the nature of this game so I'm not setting any goals. My aim is simple, to play my best and to try to win every week I'm competing. I don't see how anybody peaks just for a Major to be honest. Not really."

As ever, it is different strokes for different folks but it is good to talk to this modest, although steely and determined golfer who insists he will continue to remain loyal to the European circuit even if he did up his US PGA Tour commitment by four events in 2002 to 15.

"You know, it was really nice of The European Tour to make me an Honorary Member," he said. "I was touched by that gesture. Yeah, I'll continue to play a lot over here. The purses are improving and so are the courses we're playing so why not. It's a great Tour."

Bill Elliott

Retief after winning The 1996 Great North Open at De Vere Slaley Hall

Retief with his wife Tracy

charge of the young brigade

The Year in Retrospect

Professional golf, as with any other major sport, has a voracious appetite. So it is that The European Tour International Schedule remains a great and generous creature, because this insatiable desire for fresh and impressive talent is met each year.

New young stars press forward in their eagerness to take that first, difficult step out of the chorus line and into the unblinking glare of the global spotlight that is reserved exclusively for winners.

This challenge to the next generation to prove they, too, have what it takes has been met with impressive regularity over the four decades that the Tour has been circumnavigating the planet, but never in that time has the charge of the young brigade been quite so remarkable as it was during 2002 when no less than 14 professionals recorded their maiden European Tour victories.

Unquestionably this is a hugely impressive statistic as well as a reassuringly healthy one. Here is hard evidence not only of a genuine strength in depth, but of the existence of the necessary raw material that will allow the Tour to continue regenerating itself for many years to come.

In this sense, at least, the 2002 season may even, at this early stage of hindsight, be seen as some sort of particularly relevant landmark.

So step forward, in chronological order, and accept our congratulations - Tim Clark (Bell's South African Open), Justin Rose (dunhill championship), Richard S Johnson (ANZ Championship), Kevin Sutherland (World Golf Championships - Accenture Match Play), Arjun Atwal (Caltex Singapore Masters), Alastair Forsyth (Carlsberg Malaysian Open), Carl Pettersson (Algarve Open de Portugal), Malcolm Mackenzie (Novotel Perrier Open de France), Anders Hansen (Volvo PGA Championship), Miles Tunnicliff (The Great North Open), Søren Hansen (Murphy's Irish Open), Graeme McDowell (Volvo Scandinavian Masters), Rich Beem (US PGA Championship) and Adam Mednick (North West of Ireland Open).

Of this illustrious group, three deserve further, and sustained, applause. Few players have ever entered the paid ranks with quite the fanfare of trumpets that accompanied Justin Rose in 1998. Few have then suffered as much as this young player as he struggled to make the transition from gifted amateur to consistent professional.

Yet once again the Englishman, aged 22, proved that while form is temporary, class is permanent, as he followed up his maiden victory in the dunhill championship with further success in the Victor Chandler British Masters on The Marquess Course at Woburn Golf and Country Club. His rise up both the Volvo Order of Merit and

Nick Dougherty

the Official World Golf Ranking in 2002 offered his many supporters a glow of satisfaction that was only reduced by the untimely death, after a long illness, of his father, mentor and coach, Ken, in September.

Acclaim, too, for Denmark's Anders Hansen who became the first golfer ever to record his maiden Tour victory in an event as formidable and challenging as the Volvo PGA Championship at Wentworth Club. "Amazing, I can't believe it," he said immediately afterwards. Quite so.

Then there is Northern Ireland's Graeme McDowell who celebrated participating in only his fourth European Tour event, the Volvo Scandinavian Masters, by winning at the delightful Kungsängen course in Stockholm. McDowell, an outstanding amateur, had arrived on Tour with much to commend him but even so, this was a prodigious achievement. "I've never been happier," he said. He was a challenger, too, for the Sir Henry Cotton Rookie of the Year Award but that prestigious accolade

went deservedly to Nick Dougherty. Aged 20, Dougherty enjoyed several good tournements, including finishing runner-up in the Qatar Masters, and he eventually took 36th place in the Volvo Order of Merit. By the way across the Atlantic another Englishman, Luke Donald, aged 23, challenged for Rookie honours on the US PGA Tour following his win in the Southern Farm Bureau Classic.

Of course, happiness of one sort or another, embroidered The European Tour each week and while the next generation began to make their mark, the men who have illuminated the top table in recent years continued to dine grandly. No sooner had the year begun - Jarmo Sandelin and José Maria Olazábal had launched The 2002 European Tour International Schedule by winning the BMW Asian Open and the Omega Hong Kong Open respectively - than Retief Goosen won the Johnnie Walker Classic at Lake Karrinyup Country Club in Perth, Australia, to suggest that not only was he enjoying the stature of European Number One, but that he quite fancied retaining the accolade which, of course, is what he did.

Sam Torrance

Anders Hansen

A week later Down Under, fellow South African Ernie Els emphasised his presence on Tour with victory in the Heineken Classic at Royal Melbourne Golf Club in Victoria. Els would, after also capturing the Dubai Desert Classic at the Emirates Golf Club, eclipse this win when he lifted the Claret Jug after an unforgettably dramatic Open Golf Championship at Muirfield in July, a Championship that once again underlined the abiding strength lurking on The European Tour. In East Lothian, Els, who later won The Cisco World Match Play Championship, had to overcome the deliciously unpredictable challenge of Frenchman Thomas Levet in sudden death after Australians Stuart Appleby and Steve Elkington had fallen by the wayside following the initial four hole play-off.

The Major Championships, of course, remain the eternal yardstick of progress, prowess and ability. In that sense it is fitting that Tiger Woods won the Masters Tournament at Augusta National and the US Open Championship at Bethpage State Park, a rightful endorsement of the American's sublime brilliance. Woods also triumphed in the Deutsche Bank - SAP Open TPC of Europe at St Leon-Rot, Heidelberg, Germany, and the WGC - American Express Championship at Mount Juliet in Ireland. Yet it is in the

four great events - the Major Championships - that the continued relevance of European players on the world stage can best be judged.

Consider for a moment these facts: Sergio Garcia was the only player to finish in the top ten of each of the 2002 Major Championships - he also won the Canarias Open de España - and Padraig Harrington would have achieved the same distinction but for a three putt towards the end of the US PGA Championship.

At Augusta, a record 25 European Tour Members were invited to stroll amongst the azaleas, 18 of whom made the halfway cut and of those, 14 finished in the top 20. Indeed nine ended in the top ten, and in descending order they were; Retief Goosen, José Maria Olazábal, Padraig Harrington, Ernie Els, Vijay Singh, Sergio Garcia, Miguel Angel Jiménez, Angel Cabrera and Adam Scott.

Another record number of Members, this time 29, qualified for the US Open Championship two months later. From that, 20 made the halfway cut before Garcia finished fourth, Nick Faldo tied for fifth and Harrington shared eighth. In the Open Golf Championship, Levet's play-off challenge would have been at least matched by Harrington had the Irishman not whacked an over-exuberant drive into a fairway bunker as he pursued a birdie at the final hole,

Graeme McDowell

while of the 36 Members who teed up in the US PGA Championship at Hazeltine National Golf Club, five finished prominently, Singh leading the way in eighth while José Coceres, a resurgent Pierre Fulke, Ricardo Gonzalez and Garcia were among those to tie for tenth place.

The excitement of youth, and the glow of the future, was also amplified by the progress of Australia's Adam Scott, aged 22 like Garcia and Rose, who won the Qatar Masters at Doha and the Diageo Scottish PGA Championship at The Gleneagles Hotel. The Aussies have always had a special affinity for The European Tour and that was further underlined by the victories of Craig Parry in the WGC - NEC Invitational and Stephen Leaney in the Linde German Masters.

As the season unfolded so Diego Borrego (Madeira Island Open), Angel Cabrera (Benson and Hedges International Open), Darren Clarke (The Compass Group English Open), Michael Campbell (Smurfit European Open), Eduardo Romero (The Barclays Scottish Open), Tobias Dier (The TNT Open), Paul Lawrie (The Celtic Manor Resort Wales Open), Thomas Björn (BMW International Open), Robert Karlsson (Omega European Masters), Alex Cejka (Trophée Lancôme), Steen Tinning (Telefonica Open de Madrid), and Ian Poulter (59th Italian Open Telecom Italia) all enjoyed moving centre-stage before those two leading lights, Bernhard Langer and Colin Montgomerie, brought the curtain down at Valderrama by tying the Volvo Masters Andalucia.

Special mention must be made of Eduardo Romero. The genial Argentine may be 48 but is playing better than ever. His victory at Loch Lomond in The Barclays Scottish Open was a high point of the year, a victory that reflected the belief that age is not necessarily a barrier to ambition. It was a win, in front of his family, that had Romero admitting he was so happy he felt he could fly.

Back home, the 150 Buenos Aires street orphans this generous and decent man cares for, flew high alongside him that weekend. Romero almost took off again in the dunhill links championship at St Andrews, Carnoustie and Kingsbarns in October, but a couple of down-to-earth missed putts meant he had to settle for second place behind Harrington, who capped another year of wondrous consistency with a victory.

It is no accident that the Dubliner's triumph came a week after he had been a pivotal member of the European Ryder Cup Team that had overcome the United States at The De Vere Belfry. "I am still lost somewhere over the moon," was the basis of his emotional state in Scotland seven days later.

Carl Pettersson

No wonder. We all were. The 34th Ryder Cup Matches were simply breathtaking. They may have been delayed by a year and the form of some players might have slipped in the run-up, but Sam Torrance's insistence that the occasion would raise everyone's game proved absolutely spot on. Indeed everything this inspirational Captain did or said hit the mark during a week that brought glory to Europe and sporting sanity back to Samuel Ryder's great idea.

If the quality of golf was sublime, the behaviour of the galleries was exemplary. "The toughest and fairest I've ever seen," said United States Captain Curtis Strange.

The detail of this grand occasion and the vital contribution made by every European is outlined elsewhere but special mention must be made of three players. After a year during which his back proved a frustrating liability at times, Colin Montgomerie was simply superb, his golf over the three days better than anything this magnificent player has shown us to date. It was his commitment to the cause that proved inspirational to his team.

Then there was the winning putt from Paul McGinley, the Irishman slaying several demons with one stroke when he holed out on the final green before discovering his reward was an early bath in the adjoining lake. McGinley, by the way, had, with Harrington, been the top points scorer in The Seve Trophy earlier in the year at Druids Glen although on that occasion Harrington holed the putt that secured Great Britain and Ireland's $14^1/_2$-$11^1/_2$ victory over Continental Europe.

Finally, at The De Vere Belfry, there was Phillip Price, the quiet and modest Welshman. Written off in some quarters before a ball was struck, Price's singles victory over World Number Two Phil Mickelson was, perhaps, the individual achievement of the year.

Back row: (left to right) Paul McGinley, Darren Clarke, Lee Westwood, Colin Montgomerie, Jesper Parnevik, Joakim Haeggman, Padraig Harrington, Thomas Björn, Phillip Price Front row: (left to right) Ian Woosnam, Pierre Fulke, Niclas Fasth, Sam Torrance, Sergio Garcia, Bernhard Langer, Mark James

Both startling and enormously pleasing, it was also vivid testimony to the team spirit to be found at the core of the European camp. Strength in depth is one thing but deep friendship is another. And possibly more important.

Yes, The European Tour is strong but it is also a circuit where real friendships grow out of the shared need for success, or to simply earn a living, on top of the necessary routine of global travel. As someone else suggested soon afterwards, never underestimate the determination of a quiet man. I may have, indeed you may have, but Price's team-mates at The De Vere Belfry never did. Not for a moment. That's The European Tour for you.

So a week that had been studded with concern about security ended with the grand, old trophy returning to this side of the Atlantic. This, of course, is great. What is even better, however, is that The 34th Ryder Cup Matches rebuilt the foundations of the competition. For this, both Captains deserve praise.

Strange never conducted himself with less than commendable grace while Torrance was what he is anyway, a thoroughly nice bloke with an impish sense of humour, an essentially soft man who masquerades as a hard case. The crowd, meanwhile, cheered and applauded but by the end of the week they deserved the applause themselves. Stoic and enthusiastic to the last, these fans withstood, with great good humour, the understandable security scans.

Mostly they roared on Europe and acknowledged politely the good play of the Americans. It was the crowd that turned a great week into a fantastic one; the crowd that reclaimed an honourable Ryder Cup; the crowd that every player and both Captains declared the finest they had ever played before; and the crowd that washed away finally any lingering bad taste about Brookline.

People power was never more eloquently expressed. As a result, The European Tour has never looked in better shape.

Bill Elliott

BMW Asian Open Westin Resort · Ta Shee · Taiwan

rapid testimony

The rise and rise of players successfully graduating from the European Challenge Tour to The European Tour has been well documented, and the BMW Asian Open, the curtain-raising event on The 2002 European Tour International Schedule, provided further evidence that the system continues to proliferate champions.

Jarmo Sandelin

Michael Campbell

José Maria Olazábal

Jarmo Sandelin was not winning for the first time on The European Tour, indeed this was the fifth success for a student of the European Challenge Tour class of 1994. The Swede has often spoken of the important part that the European Challenge Tour has played in his career, helping lay the foundations for an impressive curriculum vitae which includes Ryder Cup and World Cup appearances.

In Taiwan, as the blue touch paper was ignited on another enthralling season, so came rapid testimony that players from the European Challenge Tour, not to mention a galaxy of new faces, would emerge seeking centre-stage stardom.

Sebastien Delagrange, of France, certainly wasted little time in emphasising his credentials. The 27 year old from Paris, who now resides in Boulogne, posted a first round 68 at the Westin Resort to lead by one from Gary Clark, with whom he had played alongside and against during the 2001 European Challenge Tour season, Tony Johnstone and Jamie Spence. Delagrange had teed-up at 06.40 local time and he would have equalled the course record if he had not dropped shots at each of his last two holes, the eighth and ninth.

Delagrange won twice on the 2001 European Challenge Tour whilst casting admiring glances at compatriots Gregory Havret (Atlanet Italian Open) and Thomas Levet (Victor Chandler British

Masters) as they triumphed on The European Tour International Schedule. Those victories by Havret and Levet, of course, further stirred his own ambition, but he still found time to summarise the importance of the European Challenge Tour.

"It's a good stepping stone to The European Tour, and something you must do," he said. "The European Challenge Tour has been good to me. If it hadn't been there I wouldn't have been able to progress to The European Tour." Clark gave good support to Delagrange both on and off the course as he commented: "The standard has been getting better and better on the European Challenge Tour. It's always moving forward and creating good players. It is more of a Tour than it's ever been, and it's tough."

Clark, unlike Delagrange, has been on The European Tour before, although this was his first time back in four years, and he first came to prominence when he collected a bronze medal as one of four amateurs to make the cut at the 1995 Open Golf Championship at St Andrews. The others were Gordon Sherry, eventual silver medallist Steve Webster and…Tiger Woods!

The resilience of Clark and Delagrange was to be tested over the next three days and for both, the challenge on this occasion proved insurmountable, although other new challengers did ascend the leaderboard including Thailand's Thongchai Jaidee, who was to eventually tie for second place with José Maria Olazábal, and the Korean Charlie Wi. This was to be an important result for Jaidee for it moved him to the top of the Davidoff Tour Order of Merit where he stayed following the season-ending Omega Hong Kong Open the following week where, incidentally, Mark Foster, Number One in the European Challenge Tour Rankings, was to finish fourth and Andrew Marshall, another graduate, tied sixth.

During his amateur days, Jaidee served in the army as a paratrooper. He also represented Thailand at football in his teens. He turned professional in 1999, shortly before his 30th birthday, and in 2001 became the first Thai player to compete in the US Open Championship in which he played all four rounds.

The BMW Asian Open, the richest tournament in Asia with a prize fund of 1,720,395 euro (£1,006,243), was jointly sanctioned by The European Tour and the Davidoff Tour. BMW, sponsors of the BMW International Open since 1989, regarded the move into Asia as a logical expansion in their global support of professional golf.

the course

The course at the Westin Resort, Ta Shee, is long on the scorecard, but does not play as long because the fairways can be really fast. Even so it is a tough course where par is a virtue when the wind blows in certain directions.

shot of the week

JARMO SANDELIN Sweden

Jarmo Sandelin had secured the lead but now he had to secure the title, and he took a giant stride forward with a two at the 208 yard 11th where he struck a superb five iron to six feet.

Gary Clark

Most certainly it provided the stage for Sandelin to remind all of his mercurial talent. He posted a second round of 66 to take the lead on six under par 138, one ahead of Miguel Angel Jiménez, but after a third round 72, he moved into the closing day sharing third place with Levet one behind joint leaders Carl Pettersson and Jiménez. Even so Sandelin, determined to swiftly put behind him a disappointing season in 2001, was confident. "I felt very focused before teeing-up in the final round, and when I get that feeling I know I have a chance," he said.

This positive attitude was essential because Sandelin, whose last win at the German Open in 1999 sealed his place in Europe's Team for The 33rd Ryder Cup Matches at The Country Club, Brookline, USA, had to contend with dropping a shot at the first hole. His response, however, was immediate with four birdies in the next five holes and another at the ninth taking him to the turn in 32 as he put daylight between himself and his rivals.

Olazábal had already set the clubhouse target with a 67 for 279, a total equalled by Jaidee, who also scored 67, when Sandelin, following a superb two at the 11th, moved into the closing stretch. He showed his steely courage by finishing with two pars to take the title by one shot as Swedish compatriot Pettersson,

who came through the 2000 European Tour Qualifying School, claimed a share of fourth place with Barry Lane.

This, however, was Sandelin's week. Ten years earlier he had called friends from a European Challenge Tour event in Italy as he needed $2,000 to pay his hotel bill and get to the next tournament. He now flies those friends three or four times each year to play golf, eat and drink in Monaco, where he is a resident. You see times have changed, and for the better, as a cheque for 273,702 euro (£169,631) proved beyond all doubt.

Mitchell Platts

Barry Lane

final results

Westin Resort · Ta Shee · Taiwan
November 22-25 · 2001 · Par 72 · 7104 yards · 6492 metres

Pos.	Name		Rd1	Rd2	Rd3	Rd4	Total	Par	Prize Money Euro	£
1	Jarmo SANDELIN	Swe	72	66	72	68	278	-10	273702.30	169631.61
2	José Maria OLAZÁBAL	Sp	70	70	72	67	279	-9	146818.30	90993.11
	Thongchai JAIDEE	Thai	74	70	68	67	279	-9	146818.30	90993.11
4	Barry LANE	Eng	70	73	69	69	281	-7	76211.73	47233.50
	Carl PETTERSSON	Swe	72	68	69	72	281	-7	76211.73	47233.50
6	Miguel Angel JIMÉNEZ	Sp	70	69	70	73	282	-6	55020.15	34099.66
	Michael CAMPBELL	NZ	72	73	71	66	282	-6	55020.15	34099.66
8	Brian DAVIS	Eng	72	70	69	72	283	-5	37953.31	23522.20
	Vijay SINGH	Fiji	71	69	73	70	283	-5	37953.31	23522.20
	Stephen DODD	Wal	72	69	70	72	283	-5	37953.31	23522.20
11	Charlie WI	R.Kor	76	68	68	72	284	-4	29082.28	18024.23
	Rolf MUNTZ	Hol	72	70	73	69	284	-4	29082.28	18024.23
	Stephen SCAHILL	NZ	70	71	74	69	284	-4	29082.28	18024.23
14	Steve WEBSTER	Eng	76	71	70	68	285	-3	25861.59	16028.16
15	Søren KJELDSEN	Den	75	68	71	72	286	-2	23827.47	14767.48
	Jyoti RANDHAWA	Ind	71	75	71	69	286	-2	23827.47	14767.48
	Ted OH	R.Kor	72	73	72	69	286	-2	23827.47	14767.48
18	Anders FORSBRAND	Swe	76	66	78	67	287	-1	19589.71	12141.05
	Jamie SPENCE	Eng	69	72	72	74	287	-1	19589.71	12141.05
	Thomas LEVET	Fr	71	70	69	77	287	-1	19589.71	12141.05
	Philip GOLDING	Eng	73	73	70	71	287	-1	19589.71	12141.05
	Gary EVANS	Eng	70	74	72	71	287	-1	19589.71	12141.05
	Adrian PERCEY	Aus	74	70	71	72	287	-1	19589.71	12141.05
	Kim FELTON	Aus	74	70	72	69	287	-1	19589.71	12141.05
	Unho PARK	Aus	71	71	72	73	287	-1	19589.71	12141.05
26	Nick FALDO	Eng	73	70	74	71	288	0	15690.98	9724.75
	Kyi Hla HAN	Myan	71	78	69	70	288	0	15690.98	9724.75
	Tony JOHNSTONE	Zim	69	75	74	70	288	0	15690.98	9724.75
	Gregory HAVRET	Fr	77	71	71	69	288	0	15690.98	9724.75
	Christian CÉVAËR	Fr	75	68	76	69	288	0	15690.98	9724.75
	James KINGSTON	SA	76	69	70	73	288	0	15690.98	9724.75
	Ter-Chang WANG	Taiwan	73	73	69	73	288	0	15690.98	9724.75
33	Klas ERIKSSON	Swe	74	74	71	70	289	1	13487.35	8359.01
	Arjun ATWAL	Ind	76	70	73	70	289	1	13487.35	8359.01
	Hendrik BUHRMANN	SA	72	75	68	74	289	1	13487.35	8359.01
36	Johan RYSTRÖM	Swe	78	65	74	73	290	2	12639.80	7833.73
	Stephen A LINDSKOG	Swe	74	72	71	73	290	2	12639.80	7833.73
38	Neil REILLY	Eng	76	71	72	72	291	3	11792.25	7308.45
	Søren HANSEN	Den	77	72	71	71	291	3	11792.25	7308.45
	Sebastien DELAGRANGE	Fr	68	77	72	74	291	3	11792.25	7308.45
41	Jean-Francois REMESY	Fr	74	75	72	71	292	4	10436.17	6467.99
	Kwang-Soo CHOI	R.Kor	75	73	71	73	292	4	10436.17	6467.99
	Yu-Shu HSIEH	C.Tai	79	70	67	76	292	4	10436.17	6467.99
	Jonathan LOMAS	Eng	80	69	68	75	292	4	10436.17	6467.99
	Des TERBLANCHE	SA	74	71	72	75	292	4	10436.17	6467.99
46	Raphaël JACQUELIN	Fr	73	71	77	72	293	5	8741.07	5417.42
	Henrik BJORNSTAD	Nor	74	72	74	73	293	5	8741.07	5417.42
	Craig COWPER	Eng	77	70	70	76	293	5	8741.07	5417.42
	Wei-Tze YEH	Taiwan	74	75	76	68	293	5	8741.07	5417.42
	Yuan-Chi CHEN	C.Tai	75	73	73	72	293	5	8741.07	5417.42
51	Elliot BOULT	NZ	73	75	73	73	294	6	7215.48	4471.91
	Patrik SJÖLAND	Swe	77	72	74	71	294	6	7215.48	4471.91
	Gregory HANRAHAN	USA	71	76	75	72	294	6	7215.48	4471.91
	Shinichi AKIBA	Jpn	74	72	74	74	294	6	7215.48	4471.91
55	Francis QUINN	USA	75	74	71	75	295	7	6028.91	3736.52
	Aaron MEEKS	USA	77	71	74	73	295	7	6028.91	3736.52
	Wen Teh LU	Taiwan	74	74	74	73	295	7	6028.91	3736.52
58	Scott DRUMMOND	Scot	76	73	76	71	296	8	5096.60	3158.71
	Arjun SINGH	Ind	74	73	72	77	296	8	5096.60	3158.71
	Gary CLARK	Eng	69	75	76	76	296	8	5096.60	3158.71
	Chun-Hsing CHUNG	Tai	74	71	77	74	296	8	5096.60	3158.71
62	Mark JAMES	Eng	77	72	76	72	297	9	4333.81	2685.95
	Malcolm MACKENZIE	Eng	74	73	78	72	297	9	4333.81	2685.95
	Lee THOMPSON	Eng	75	73	76	73	297	9	4333.81	2685.95
	Chie-Hsiang LIN	Taipei	77	72	72	76	297	9	4333.81	2685.95
	David GLEESON	Aus	73	74	75	75	297	9	4333.81	2685.95
67	Marc FARRY	Fr	76	69	75	78	298	10	3655.77	2265.72
	Ian POULTER	Eng	71	77	72	78	298	10	3655.77	2265.72
	Tobias DIER	Ger	74	73	75	76	298	10	3655.77	2265.72
70	Simon DYSON	Eng	73	74	77	75	299	11	2929.87	1815.84
	James STEWART	Scot	76	71	78	74	299	11	2929.87	1815.84
72	Mike CUNNING	USA	78	71	77	74	300	12	2535.50	1571.42
	Rafael PONCE	Equa	72	77	76	75	300	12	2535.50	1571.42
	Nico VAN RENSBURG	SA	71	76	75	78	300	12	2535.50	1571.42
	Craig KAMPS	SA	75	74	77	74	300	12	2535.50	1571.42
76	Chien-Soon LU	Taipei	75	73	75	78	301	13	2525.00	1564.91
	Dominique NOUAILHAC	Fr	80	67	76	78	301	13	2525.00	1564.91
	Rodrigo CUELLO	Phil	74	73	76	78	301	13	2525.00	1564.91
79	Danny ZARATE	Phil	77	70	80	78	305	17	2519.00	1561.19
80	Min-Nan HSIEH	C.Tai	73	76	78	79	306	18	2516.00	1559.33

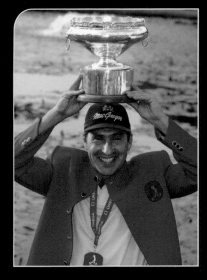

Omega Hong Kong Open Hong Kong Golf Club · Hong Kong

straight up

1	**José Maria OLAZÁBAL** Sp	262	-22
2	Henrik BJORNSTAD Nor	263	-21
3	Adam SCOTT Aus	264	-20
4	Mark FOSTER Eng	265	-19
5	Carl PETTERSSON Swe	266	-18
6	Anders FORSBRAND Swe	267	-17
	Andrew MARSHALL Eng	267	-17
	Mark PILKINGTON Wal	267	-17
9	Brian DAVIS Eng	268	-16
	Simon DYSON Eng	268	-16
	Jarmo SANDELIN Swe	268	-16
	Yeh WEI-TZE Taiwan	268	-16

José Maria Olazábal

The week might have begun with Adam Scott mixing cocktails at the Pro-Am dinner but come Sunday night in Hong Kong it was José Maria Olazábal who was uncorking the champagne.

Indeed, the Omega Hong Kong Open proved an effervescent ending to a relatively flat period for the two time Masters Champion and provided good reason to believe that 2002 would be another vintage phase in his outstanding career.

Granted, a tournament success had been achieved in 2001 at the Novotel Perrier Open de France, but even with that trophy in his hands the Spaniard admitted victory had been achieved largely by character and determination over technical frailty.

Uncertainty from the tee had been the problem, a year-long struggle which saw Olazábal finish 35th on the 2001 Volvo Order of Merit, his poorest finishing position in 14 full seasons on The European Tour International Schedule. Olazábal, however, is no quitter and, as he proved in his ultimately successful two year quest to find a solution to the dogged rheumatoid polyarthritis problem, will not rest until the demon has been defeated.

Mark Foster

In 1996, the medical cure came via Munich doctor Hans-Wilhelm Muller Wohlfahrt. In late 2001, the technical cure came via swing doctor Pete Cowen. Urged by caddie Phil Morbey to go for a session with the renowned coach at the Volvo Masters Andalucia three weeks beforehand, the Spaniard heeded the advice and the results were instantaneous.

A final round 67 the previous Sunday gave him a share of second place in the BMW Asian Open in Taiwan which prompted the comment: "My driving was very good - I wish it could be like this every week." For Olazábal, the request was about to be granted.

Seven birdies in an impressive first round 65 at the Hong Kong Golf Club moved the Spaniard into a share of second place with Ireland's Paul McGinley and local professional James Stewart, the trio one shot adrift of Scott. The young Australian's cocktail-shaking had drawn admiring glances the night before and although not quite in Tom Cruise's league, Scott proved to be Top Gun on the course with seven birdies and an eagle in an excellent 64.

Anders Forsbrand

Scott started The 2001 European Tour season in style with victory in his first event, the Alfred Dunhill Championship in South Africa, and remained on course to do the same in 2002 with a second round 67.

It was good enough for a share of third spot but the day belonged to the local challengers. Asian golf continues to go from strength to strength and only the week before Thongchai Jaidee finished alongside Olazábal in the BMW Asian Open in the year he became the first Thai golfer to play and make the cut in the US Open Championship.

This time the spotlight fell on Taiwan's Yeh Wei-Tze who moved into the lead, one shot clear of Myanmar's Zaw Moe, courtesy of a sparkling 63. Yeh won the 2000 Benson and Hedges Malaysian Open but this was his best ever round on The European Tour International Schedule.

Into the weekend when Moe slipped out of contention and Yeh's closing rounds of 72-67 gave him a top ten finish, it looked likely that the title and the 128,848 euro (£80,170) first prize would be heading for the pocket of one of the growing pride of young lions on The European Tour.

Henrik Bjornstad

the course

A composite course made up of holes from the club's New and Eden Courses, the Hong Kong Golf Club layout was not the longest played on The European Tour but its tree-lined fairways allied to ditches which ran parallel to many of the holes made accuracy from the tee paramount. Most greens featured big run-off areas which made it vital for the approach shot to be on the correct side of the green. An errant approach left a very difficult recovery pitch shot.

Paul McGinley

Adam Scott

Henrik Bjornstad, aged 22, led the way with a course record 61 in the third round which gave him the lead going into the last day, but also in close order were 2001 Challenge Tour winner Mark Foster (26), Sweden's Carl Pettersson (24) and Scott (21).

The prospect of a youthful champion, and possibly the first player from Norway to triumph on The European Tour International Schedule, loomed as Bjornstad and Scott tussled for the lead over the closing stretch. But both had reckoned without the resilience of the old warhorse Olazábal.

Two behind with three to play he rolled in respective 15 foot birdie putts at the 16th and 17th to draw level before producing an

shot of the week

JOSÉ MARIA OLAZÁBAL Spain

Without question, José Maria Olazábal's approach to the 18th in the final round. Having made his intentions clear with birdies at the 16th and 17th, the Spaniard was faced with a demanding second shot at the last to keep the momentum going. Once again, Olazábal proved why he is revered as one of the top iron players in the game, punching a majestic five iron under the branches of a nearby tree and over the water guarding the green to within six inches of the pin for a certain birdie. Sensational.

approach shot of pure genius to within six inches of the hole at the last. The guaranteed birdie three moved Olazábal into the lead and moments later it was enough to see him crowned Champion as Bjornstad could do no better than par to take second while Scott's errant tee-shot saw him make bogey five and finish third.

Once the dust had settled a delighted Olazábal admitted: "The last two weeks I've played as well as in 1994." High praise indeed for that year saw him lift the Volvo PGA Championship at Wentworth Club and the NEC World Series of Golf in addition to his first Masters Tournament triumph at Augusta National.

He went on: "The improvement in my driving has been excellent. Once you start hitting more fairways you are able to control the ball and go for the flags - that's the difference."

Scott Crockett

Simon Yates   Yeh Wei-Tze

final results

Hong Kong Golf Club · Hong Kong
November 29 - December 2 · 2001 · Par 71 · 6697 yards · 6124 metres

Pos.	Name		Rd1	Rd2	Rd3	Rd4	Total	Par	Prize Money Euro	£
1	José Maria OLAZÁBAL	Sp	65	69	64	64	262	-22	128848.10	80170.30
2	Henrik BJORNSTAD	Nor	66	69	61	67	263	-21	88791.13	55246.54
3	Adam SCOTT	Aus	64	67	66	67	264	-20	49441.17	30762.68
4	Mark FOSTER	Eng	66	65	67	67	265	-19	39863.08	24803.12
5	Carl PETTERSSON	Swe	67	64	68	67	266	-18	31881.34	19836.82
6	Anders FORSBRAND	Swe	67	64	68	68	267	-17	23899.61	14870.52
	Andrew MARSHALL	Eng	68	66	68	65	267	-17	23899.61	14870.52
	Mark PILKINGTON	Wal	69	68	62	68	267	-17	23899.61	14870.52
9	Brian DAVIS	Eng	70	67	64	67	268	-16	15481.44	9632.67
	Jarmo SANDELIN	Swe	68	70	66	64	268	-16	15481.44	9632.67
	Simon DYSON	Eng	67	64	70	67	268	-16	15481.44	9632.67
	Yeh WEI-TZE	Taiw	66	63	72	67	268	-16	15481.44	9632.67
13	Gary EVANS	Eng	70	66	65	68	269	-15	12214.34	7599.86
	Michael CAMPBELL	NZ	66	69	68	66	269	-15	12214.34	7599.86
	Thongchai JAIDEE	Thai	67	70	67	65	269	-15	12214.34	7599.86
16	Lian-Wei ZHANG	PRC	67	67	68	68	270	-14	10510.24	6539.55
	Andrew PITTS	USA	68	67	70	65	270	-14	10510.24	6539.55
	Thomas LEVET	Fr	70	67	66	67	270	-14	10510.24	6539.55
	Simon YATES	Scot	66	66	70	68	270	-14	10510.24	6539.55
20	Christian CÉVAÉR	Fr	68	69	67	67	271	-13	9632.48	5931.18
21	Mårten OLANDER	Swe	68	65	71	68	272	-12	8814.12	5484.21
	Thavorn WIRATCHANT	Thai	70	66	68	68	272	-12	8814.12	5484.21
	Des TERBLANCHE	SA	70	63	69	70	272	-12	8814.12	5484.21
	Stephen SCAHILL	NZ	68	68	69	72	272	-12	8814.12	5484.21
	Stephen A LINDSKOG	Swe	66	70	68	68	272	-12	8814.12	5484.21
26	Mark MOULAND	Wal	67	71	65	70	273	-11	7267.66	4521.99
	Jean-Francois REMESY	Fr	67	68	68	70	273	-11	7267.66	4521.99
	Thammanoon SRIROJ	Thai	69	69	66	69	273	-11	7267.66	4521.99
	Nick O'HERN	Aus	67	68	67	71	273	-11	7267.66	4521.99
	Paul McGINLEY	Ire	65	66	74	68	273	-11	7267.66	4521.99
	Aaron MEEKS	USA	71	66	68	68	273	-11	7267.66	4521.99
	Rolf MUNTZ	Hol	69	65	67	72	273	-11	7267.66	4521.99
	Wen-Chong LIANG	Jpn	69	66	73	65	273	-11	7267.66	4521.99
34	Anthony KANG	Kor	71	64	69	70	274	-10	5860.88	3646.68
	Johan RYSTRÖM	Swe	67	67	73	67	274	-10	5860.88	3646.68
	Boonchu RUANGKIT	Thai	69	68	68	69	274	-10	5860.88	3646.68
	Zaw MOE	Myan	66	64	71	73	274	-10	5860.88	3646.68
	Robert COLES	Eng	70	69	70	65	274	-10	5860.88	3646.68
	Patrik SJÖLAND	Swe	66	73	68	67	274	-10	5860.88	3646.68
	Matthew CORT	Eng	66	67	71	70	274	-10	5860.88	3646.68
41	Barry LANE	Eng	66	69	73	67	275	-9	4663.62	2901.74
	Anthony WALL	Eng	66	67	72	70	275	-9	4663.62	2901.74
	Arjun ATWAL	Ind	70	69	68	68	275	-9	4663.62	2901.74
	Jean VAN DE VELDE	Fr	71	66	69	69	275	-9	4663.62	2901.74
	Gregory HAVRET	Fr	71	67	66	71	275	-9	4663.62	2901.74
	Arjun SINGH	Ind	70	67	67	71	275	-9	4663.62	2901.74
	Jonathan LOMAS	Eng	72	67	67	69	275	-9	4663.62	2901.74
	Gerald ROSALES	Phil	70	66	67	72	275	-9	4663.62	2901.74
49	Peter FOWLER	Aus	67	66	71	72	276	-8	3865.44	2405.11
	Sushi ISHIGAKI	Jpn	70	67	71	68	276	-8	3865.44	2405.11
51	Chris WILLIAMS	Eng	66	71	68	72	277	-7	3386.54	2107.13
	Jyoti RANDHAWA	Ind	70	67	71	69	277	-7	3386.54	2107.13
	Ter-Chang WANG	Taiw	67	69	71	70	277	-7	3386.54	2107.13
	Jamie DONALDSON	Wal	72	66	70	69	277	-7	3386.54	2107.13
55	Søren HANSEN	Den	68	70	71	69	278	-6	2748.00	1709.83
	Christophe POTTIER	Fr	68	70	71	69	278	-6	2748.00	1709.83
	Stephen DODD	Wal	71	65	72	70	278	-6	2748.00	1709.83
	Chih-Bing LAM	Sing	71	67	65	75	278	-6	2748.00	1709.83
59	Klas ERIKSSON	Swe	72	66	69	72	279	-5	2069.55	1287.69
	Philip GOLDING	Eng	69	70	68	72	279	-5	2069.55	1287.69
	Emanuele CANONICA	It	71	67	70	71	279	-5	2069.55	1287.69
	Simon KHAN	Eng	68	69	71	71	279	-5	2069.55	1287.69
	Gregory HANRAHAN	USA	69	69	69	72	279	-5	2069.55	1287.69
	Tobias DIER	Ger	68	72	71	69	279	-5	2069.55	1287.69
	Gary RUSNAK	USA	71	68	67	73	279	-5	2069.55	1287.69
	James STEWART	Scot	65	71	71	72	279	-5	2069.55	1287.69
	Pablo DEL OLMO	Mex	67	69	72	71	279	-5	2069.55	1287.69
	Chang-Ting YEH	C.Tai	70	68	67	74	279	-5	2069.55	1287.69
69	Kwang-Soo CHOI	Kor	69	65	72	74	280	-4	1324.55	824.14
	Vivek BHANDARI	Ind	70	69	73	68	280	-4	1324.55	824.14
	Wen Teh LU	Taiw	71	68	71	70	280	-4	1324.55	824.14
	Danny ZARATE	Phil	68	70	71	71	280	-4	1324.55	824.14
	Kim FELTON	Aus	69	68	68	75	280	-4	1324.55	824.14
	Amandeep JOHL	Ind	73	66	72	69	280	-4	1324.55	824.14
75	Justin HOBDAY	SA	71	67	69	74	281	-3	1182.50	735.76
	Francis QUINN	USA	70	69	71	71	281	-3	1182.50	735.76
77	Jamie SPENCE	Eng	72	67	70	73	282	-2	1178.00	732.96
78	Charlie WI	Kor	69	70	74	71	284	0	1175.00	731.09
79	Gaurav GHEI	Ind	74	63	79	71	287	3	1172.00	729.23
80	Søren KJELDSEN	Den	69	64	RETD		133	-9		

Bell's South African Open The Country Club · Durban · South Africa

mission accomplished

1	**Tim CLARK** SA	269	-19
2	Steve WEBSTER Eng	271	-17
3	James KINGSTON SA	275	-13
	Jonathan LOMAS Eng	275	-13
5	Simon DYSON Eng	276	-12
	Alastair FORSYTH Scot	276	-12
	Retief GOOSEN SA	276	-12
	David PARK Wal	276	-12
9	Martin MARITZ SA	277	-11
	Doug McGUIGAN Scot	277	-11
	Roger WESSELS SA	277	-11

Tim Clark

Tim Clark was a man on a mission when he teed up alongside another 301 hopefuls for the 18 hole pre-qualifying ritual two days prior to the playing of the 2002 Bell's South African Open at The Country Club in Durban. As a native of Umkomaas, a pretty coastal town in Natal about 90 minutes from the asphalt sprawl of Durban, he had a deep appreciation of the special demands and nuances of playing the 6733 yard course where he had enjoyed considerable success in his youth.

After all, as a promising young amateur, he had carried off three successive Natal Junior titles before he left his teens, and a framed card of 66 on the walls of the vast clubhouse at The Country Club paid tribute to the fact that he held the amateur record.

A serious wrist injury early in 2001 had curtailed his season to a handful of rounds and he reasoned that, on medical grounds, an invitation to the Bell's South African Open might be forthcoming. It was not to be, so there was nothing else for it. Clark had to swallow his disappointment, put it to the back of his mind, and set about the daunting task of pre-qualifying, anathema to any touring professional worth his salt.

Ernie Els

Steve Webster

Clark duly produced a sparkling 66 at Mount Edgecombe to win the qualifying competition and secure one of the precious 12 spots available for the Championship, jointly sanctioned by The European Tour and the Sunshine Tour, which was hailed a success by The European Tour, the Sunshine Tour and the South Africa Golf Association, with all three bodies recognising the significant role played by the Royal and Ancient Golf Club.

Peter Dawson, Secretary of the R&A, explained: "We had an approach from the South African Golf Association last November. They told us they were worried that the Championship would not go ahead in 2002 and asked us for assistance. We did not wish to see that happen, so were pleased to help out financially.

"This was done on a one-off basis to ensure the continuity of the Championship and we were delighted when Bell's also came in with a sponsorship agreement which helped guarantee that the 2002 Bell's South African Open at Durban Country Club went ahead with a prize fund worthy of the status of the Championship."

Jonathan Lomas

Meanwhile Clark recalled: "I suppose it was a motivation, not getting an invite and feeling that I perhaps deserved a spot in the Championship. But then again, I knew the event was going to be at The Country Club in Durban a long time beforehand and I set my mind on playing because I knew I had a good chance to play well around that course. It wasn't nice to think I might not be playing over a course I knew intimately and where I felt I could do well.

"I just had to put it out of my mind and not worry about it when I went to the pre-qualifying. If I had, I wouldn't have made it. I had to forget about it and play golf."

The first part of his mission duly completed, the 26 year old local man, at the time Number 401 on the Official World Golf Ranking, then tackled the infinitely more demanding part of his assignment.

the course

At 6733 yards long, The Country Club at Durban could never be considered a monster by today's standards. However the layout, constructed in 1922, is a delightful test, meandering through undulating terrain, bordered by high bushes which shelter the course from the worst excesses of the warm winds blowing in from the Indian Ocean. Deservedly rated one of the best courses in South Africa.

shot of the week

RETIEF GOOSEN South Africa

Retief Goosen chipped in for an eagle at the 14th at The Country Club in the second round, but pulled off an even better stroke on Saturday. Tight against a thick collar of greenside rough at the par five eighth, he dug out his three wood and played an exquisite shot from 18 feet for a superb eagle three.

He had to try to win the world's second oldest Open Golf Championship, first played in 1893, from a field which included three Major Champions in Ernie Els, Retief Goosen and Paul Lawrie as well as a host of other gifted professional golfers from all corners of the globe.

However it should not have come as a great surprise that Clark went on to win the biggest title of his four year professional career. He is the same height, 5ft 7in, as his fellow countryman and sporting idol, Gary Player. Stockier, certainly, and with the clipped short stride and swaggering gait of Ian Woosnam. But, in common with those two great champions, he possesses a conviction in his own ability to get the job done. And get it done he did.

Rounds of 66 and 70 had left him nicely poised on eight under par, three behind leader James Kingston. As a native of Natal Province, he was fully conversant with the capricious, warm gusts which blow off the nearby Indian Ocean and he was confident of a strong showing over the weekend.

A third round 68 moved him out in front on 12 under par, two shots clear of his playing partner for Sunday afternoon and the new Championship favourite, Goosen, the reigning US Open Champion, the Volvo Order of Merit winner in 2001 and someone who had become virtually deified in South Africa following those notable achievements, and the determined Lomas.

Yet a close inspection of Clark's curriculum vitae revealed several interesting facts. For instance, between August 20 and September 16, 2000, Clark had annexed two titles on the Buy.Com Tour in the United States. In winning the Boise Open he shot rounds of 66-67-69-67 to win by six strokes. In the Fort Smith Classic, his rounds were 67-66-65-66 for a two shot victory. On both occasions he had led going into the final round. Impressive stuff.

Clark finished third on the money list to earn his US PGA Tour card. However, disaster struck during his third start, the AT&T Pebble Beach National Pro-Am. After an opening 79 he withdrew with a major problem in his right wrist. Due to wear and tear he had damaged the tendons so badly that reconstructive surgery was necessary in March. His season was over.

In Durban, he was still feeling the odd twinge despite a lengthy recuperation period at home, but with a two stroke advantage under his belt, Clark simply tightened his grip. Goosen shot a 70 for a share of fifth place, while the lesser known South African fired a seven under par 65 to win by two - four birdies in each half, one three putt bogey at the 11th being his only error.

England's Steve Webster, with a magnificent closing 64, managed to get within one shot of the leader with four to play, but Clark kicked on again, making twos at the 12th and 15th with a birdie four sandwiched in between at the 14th. The Championship was over, the local boy had made good, and there were no prouder onlookers than his parents Dave and Pat as Clark received the glittering prize. In that instant he knew one thing for certain - he would never have to endure the pre-qualifying scramble ever again. Mission accomplished.

Gordon Simpson

Bell's South African Open

Mark McNulty

final results

The Country Club · Durban · South Africa
January 10-13 · 2002 · Par 72 · 6733 yards · 6158 metres

Pos.	Name		Rd1	Rd2	Rd3	Rd4	Total	Par	Prize Money Euro	£
1	Tim CLARK	SA	66	70	68	65	269	-19	128052.90	79249.97
2	Steve WEBSTER	Eng	68	70	69	64	271	-17	92909.08	57500.00
3	Jonathan LOMAS	Eng	68	67	71	69	275	-13	47747.19	29550.00
	James KINGSTON	SA	66	67	74	68	275	-13	47747.19	29550.00
5	David PARK	Wal	71	68	73	64	276	-12	26135.73	16175.00
	Retief GOOSEN	SA	67	70	69	70	276	-12	26135.73	16175.00
	Alastair FORSYTH	Scot	66	71	70	69	276	-12	26135.73	16175.00
	Simon DYSON	Eng	67	73	69	67	276	-12	26135.73	16175.00
9	Roger WESSELS	SA	68	71	68	70	277	-11	15565.64	9633.34
	Doug McGUIGAN	Scot	71	69	71	66	277	-11	15565.64	9633.34
	Martin MARITZ	SA	72	64	72	69	277	-11	15565.64	9633.34
12	Jean HUGO	SA	68	71	68	71	278	-10	13411.22	8300.00
13	Dean VAN STADEN	SA	71	70	69	69	279	-9	12199.37	7550.00
	Ernie ELS	SA	73	69	68	69	279	-9	12199.37	7550.00
15	Des TERBLANCHE	SA	66	74	74	66	280	-8	10785.53	6675.00
	Andrew BUTTERFIELD	Eng	66	69	74	71	280	-8	10785.53	6675.00
	André CRUSE	SA	71	68	71	70	280	-8	10785.53	6675.00
	Jamie DONALDSON	Wal	69	73	66	72	280	-8	10785.53	6675.00
	Chari SCHWARTZEL (AM)	SA	71	67	73	69	280	-8		
20	Grant MULLER	SA	72	66	75	68	281	-7	9177.80	5680.00
	Andrew McLARDY	SA	75	67	72	67	281	-7	9177.80	5680.00
	Philip GOLDING	Eng	70	71	69	71	281	-7	9177.80	5680.00
	Marc CAYEUX	Zim	67	75	68	71	281	-7	9177.80	5680.00
	Ashley ROESTOFF	SA	66	71	73	71	281	-7	9177.80	5680.00
25	Michael KIRK	SA	69	69	76	68	282	-6	8402.21	5200.00
26	Malcolm MACKENZIE	Eng	71	69	72	71	283	-5	7444.27	4607.14
	Mark MOULAND	Wal	70	71	73	69	283	-5	7444.27	4607.14
	Mark MCNULTY	Zim	73	71	73	66	283	-5	7444.27	4607.14
	Arjun ATWAL	Ind	70	67	76	70	283	-5	7444.27	4607.14
	Jeremy ROBINSON	Eng	71	70	71	71	283	-5	7444.27	4607.14
	Christian CÉVAËR	Fr	69	70	73	71	283	-5	7444.27	4607.14
	Paul LAWRIE	Scot	68	70	76	69	283	-5	7444.27	4607.14
33	Warren BENNETT	Eng	70	74	68	72	284	-4	6220.87	3850.00
	Marco GORTANA	SA	73	67	74	70	284	-4	6220.87	3850.00
	Russell CLAYDON	Eng	73	70	73	68	284	-4	6220.87	3850.00
	Nicolas VANHOOTEGEM	Bel	72	72	72	68	284	-4	6220.87	3850.00
	Donald GAMMON	SA	73	70	72	69	284	-4	6220.87	3850.00

Pos.	Name		Rd1	Rd2	Rd3	Rd4	Total	Par	Prize Money Euro	£
	Carl PETTERSSON	Swe	64	77	73	70	284	-4	6220.87	3850.00
39	Jeev Milkha SINGH	Ind	69	69	74	73	285	-3	5332.17	3300.00
	Jamie SPENCE	Eng	71	69	74	71	285	-3	5332.17	3300.00
	Andrew MARSHALL	Eng	71	71	75	68	285	-3	5332.17	3300.00
	Amandeep JOHL	Ind	72	71	71	71	285	-3	5332.17	3300.00
	Nick DOUGHERTY	Eng	69	71	72	73	285	-3	5332.17	3300.00
44	Gavin LEVENSON	SA	75	69	71	71	286	-2	4605.06	2850.00
	Anthony WALL	Eng	73	70	72	71	286	-2	4605.06	2850.00
	Tjaart VAN DER WALT	SA	70	73	69	74	286	-2	4605.06	2850.00
	Chris WILLIAMS	Eng	72	71	74	69	286	-2	4605.06	2850.00
48	Desvonde BOTES	SA	68	70	79	70	287	-1	4120.31	2550.00
	Hendrik BUHRMANN	SA	69	74	73	71	287	-1	4120.31	2550.00
50	Magnus PERSSON ATLEVI	Swe	73	70	74	71	288	0	3797.15	2350.00
	Mark HILTON	Eng	70	74	73	71	288	0	3797.15	2350.00
52	Andrew PITTS	USA	71	72	75	71	289	1	3393.20	2100.00
	Darren FICHARDT	SA	69	71	79	70	289	1	3393.20	2100.00
	Michael HOEY (AM)	N.Ire	72	72	76	69	289	1		
	Mikael LUNDBERG	Swe	76	68	71	74	289	1	3393.20	2100.00
56	Hennie WALTERS	SA	73	71	74	72	290	2	2827.67	1750.00
	Michael ARCHER	Eng	68	75	79	68	290	2	2827.67	1750.00
	Simon HURD	Eng	70	70	77	73	290	2	2827.67	1750.00
	Bradley DAVISON	SA	71	71	73	75	290	2	2827.67	1750.00
60	Sean PAPPAS	SA	75	65	76	75	291	3	2302.53	1425.00
	David GILFORD	Eng	72	71	75	73	291	3	2302.53	1425.00
	Mårten OLANDER	Swe	70	73	73	75	291	3	2302.53	1425.00
	Schalk VAN DER MERWE	SA	70	72	76	73	291	3	2302.53	1425.00
	Keith HORNE	SA	74	70	75	72	291	3	2302.53	1425.00
	Trevor DODDS	Nam	73	71	73	74	291	3	2302.53	1425.00
66	Stephen DODD	Wal	73	71	74	74	292	4	2019.76	1250.00
67	Steve VAN VUUREN	SA	70	74	75	74	293	5	1898.58	1175.00
	Simon LILLY	Eng	73	71	78	71	293	5	1898.58	1175.00
69	Simon KHAN	Eng	74	70	74	76	294	6	1737.00	1075.00
	Derek CRAWFORD	Scot	73	73	79	71	294	6	1737.00	1075.00
71	Didier DE VOOGHT	Bel	71	71	77	77	296	8	1615.81	1000.00
72	Michael GREEN	SA	73	69	75	82	299	11	1535.02	950.00
73	Miguel Angel MARTIN	Sp	74	70	80	W/D	224	8	1413.84	875.00
	David DRYSDALE	Scot	72	70	W/D		142	-2	1413.84	875.00

From the front nine to the backyard,
you can count on us.

With over 88 years of experience, Toro is the most trusted supplier of turf equipment and irrigation systems to golf courses, parks and individual lawns around the world. Our commitment to providing innovative, high quality products and systems to help grow and maintain turf is legendary. We care about preserving the tradition of golf. We also care about providing the right solution to you. Make Toro the preferred name at your home today.

www.toro.com

TORO. **Count on it.**

paradise found

1	**Justin ROSE** Eng	268	-20
2	Mark FOSTER Eng	270	-18
	Retief GOOSEN SA	270	-18
	Martin MARITZ SA	270	-18
5	Paul McGINLEY Ire	271	-17
	Mark MOULAND Wal	271	-17
	Anthony WALL Eng	271	-17
8	Sandeep GREWAL Eng	272	-16
9	Ernie ELS SA	273	-15
10	Alan McLEAN Scot	274	-14
	Roger WESSELS SA	274	-14

Justin Rose

ometimes a heavy price must be paid for being a child prodigy. Michael Jackson and Wolfgang Amadeus Mozart, had he still been around, would probably concur. Tiger Woods, who made the seamless transition from infant marvel to adult genius, may not. However, ask Justin Rose the same question and he would more than likely side with the eccentric pair of musical virtuosos.

Thrust into the limelight with almost indecent haste, the journey from gifted amateur to Champion on The European Tour became a tortured trek through numerous metaphorical minefields until, finally, on January 20, 2002, he reached the Elysian Fields. Paradise found in Johannesburg, the city of his birth 21 years and six months earlier, and more specifically amid the rarified atmosphere of Houghton Golf Club.

Born in the area of Sandton, where Rose and most of his comrades in arms resided during the week of the dunhill championship, his family had emigrated to Hook in leafy Hampshire when Justin was but a five year old with a set of plastic clubs purchased by his father, Ken.

The aforementioned Rose Snr was to play a pivotal role in his younger son's career and it was a source of deep regret to Justin that Ken was too ill to return to his country of origin to witness in person the cathartic moment when Rose Jnr finally bloomed.

The bond between father and son had been a fundamental element of Justin's progress from cheeky chappie with cut-down clubs to teenage sensation and, ultimately, to mature professional Champion on The European Tour. The pair were inseparable. It was a union which created the occasional critical reaction from inside and outside the sport. Pushy parents are not usually welcomed. Justin Rose, however, never considered his dad to be a hindrance.

"I don't honestly believe my dad ever put a foot wrong in terms of my career," said Rose after triumphing at Houghton with a four round score of 268, 20 under par, in the elated company of his elder brother, Brandon, and his grandparents. "I never made a decision - any decision - without consulting him. Whether it was entering a tournament or buying a car, I asked dad for his opinion. I don't feel he ever made the wrong choice."

When Justin was a boy, Ken Rose was always in attendance, never fussy, but ready to shield his offspring. Protective rather than pushy. When Justin attempted, unsuccessfully, to qualify for the 1995 Open Golf Championship at St Andrews, dad was there to handle the inevitable media scrum. When Justin became, at 17, the youngest participant in Walker Cup history, Ken threw a protective arm around his son.

Mark Foster

the course

Houghton Golf Club, immaculately prepared, played shorter than usual due to the cloudless skies and hot sun. It was impossible to fault the layout, while the greens met with the universal approval of the players from The European and Sunshine Tours. A glorious setting for another wonderful Championship.

James Kingston

When, in 1998, and still an amateur, he entered the world's consciousness by finishing tied fourth in the Open Golf Championship at Royal Birkdale, Ken acted as chaperone, surrogate manager, father and, more importantly, friend to the youngster who had fame unexpectedly thrust on his slender shoulders.

"Dad always did the best by me," insisted Rose after finishing two strokes ahead of Mark Foster, the 2001 Challenge Tour Rankings winner, Retief Goosen, the 2001 Volvo Order of Merit winner, and South African Martin Maritz. "People can say what they like about him. I know there were negative comments and so did he.

"He once said to me: 'Okay, go out on your own without me there and see what happens. Maybe they're right. Maybe I am a negative influence.' Well, I did that and came home and said: 'No, they're wrong.' As far as I am concerned, his advice is what always mattered."

The public image of Justin Rose is still indelibly etched on the brain - baby-faced youth with a grin wider than the Mersey, eyes raised to the heavens, after sinking *that* chip on the 72nd hole at Royal Birkdale. Then reality set in. After a bizarre, almost surreal, press conference to announce his arrival as a professional golfer the following week in Holland, he embarked on a career which consisted of 21 consecutive missed cuts.

The wonder boy had toppled off his pedestal without earning so much as a penny, cent, franc, deutschemark or euro.

"You know, with hindsight, I feel all those missed cuts prepared me for this moment," he explained. "I felt under terrible pressure to make my first cut. It felt as if I was trying to win a tournament every week, just aiming to achieve that goal. Coming down the stretch at Houghton, I believe all experiences helped me to pull through.

"Actually, dad was on my bag the day it happened at the Compaq European Grand Prix in 1999. That was a buzz. Contrary to popular opinion, he didn't caddie for me that often, just a few times when I asked him to. It's funny, but a couple of days before winning at Houghton I said to someone that winning would be the only way to stop people remembering me just for that one week at Birkdale."

During the dark days, Ken Rose, a gentle, courteous man, never lost faith in his son. Neither did Justin doubt himself. Vindication came not once, but twice, in the dunhill championship. In 2001, he

shot of the week

JUSTIN ROSE England

A stroke of genius from the eventual Champion. At the 16th hole in the heat of battle on Sunday afternoon, Rose put his second shot into a greenside trap on the 511 yard hole but produced a truly wonderful escape. He propelled his 35 yard bunker shot to within six inches of the hole for a crucial birdie, which paved the way for victory.

Anthony Wall

shot 20 under par and missed out by a stroke to Adam Scott, a meritorious performance which set him on the way to securing his card for 2002. When the 2002 dunhill championship dawned, he would not be denied again.

"I always believed, deep down, I had the talent to do it," he said. "Family support was the thing which helped me through all those missed cuts, but I never lost the self belief and nor did the people close to me. My brother and grandparents still live in Johannesburg. They are my number one fans. To win in front of them was awesome. I just wish my mum and dad had been here and that would have been the full set. This win is for Dad, more than anybody. I owe most to him."

Nobody threw the dunhill championship at Rose. He won it, fair and square. Ernie Els, South Africa's favourite son, gave it his best shot but came unstuck with a double bogey at the 14th hole on the final day. Els finished ninth, as his close friend and rival, Goosen, threw down the gauntlet to Rose by closing with a 65 for 270, 18 under par.

The clubhouse target duly set, Rose focused on the task in hand. With four holes to play, he stood at 17 under, the same mark as the impressive Foster, aiming to take the next career step after his victory on the 2001 Challenge Tour Rankings. Rose didn't flinch.

He hit a five iron to three feet to birdie the 15th then played a sublime bunker shot to six inches for a birdie four at the next.

Victory was close, but not certain, when he then hit a crisp chip to 18 inches for a birdie at the last – something he failed to do in 2001 when it cost him a play-off.

"I was determined," he said. "Coming down the stretch the nerves were jangling a little but I kept saying to myself: 'Justin, you're a winner. You're going to win this week. It's your turn.'"

QED. It was, indeed, Justin Rose's turn. The young Englishman hosted a private reception for 80 specially invited guests in Johannesburg that night and footed the entire bill himself.

Gordon Simpson

final results

Houghton Golf Club · Johannesburg · South Africa
January 17-20 · 2002 · Par 72 · 7284 yards · 6542 metres

Pos.	Name		Rd1	Rd2	Rd3	Rd4	Total	Par	Prize Money Euro	£
1	Justin ROSE	Eng	71	66	66	65	268	-20	128173.50	79000.00
2	Mark FOSTER	Eng	69	67	65	69	270	-18	63140.34	38916.66
	Retief GOOSEN	SA	68	67	70	65	270	-18	63140.34	38916.66
	Martin MARITZ	SA	72	64	63	71	270	-18	63140.34	38916.66
5	Mark MOULAND	Wal	68	69	67	67	271	-17	28744.41	17716.67
	Anthony WALL	Eng	68	67	71	65	271	-17	28744.41	17716.67
	Paul McGINLEY	Ire	66	71	66	68	271	-17	28744.41	17716.67
8	Sandeep GREWAL	Eng	70	64	68	70	272	-16	19956.13	12300.00
9	Ernie ELS	SA	68	72	63	70	273	-15	17522.46	10800.00
10	Roger WESSELS	SA	68	66	69	71	274	-14	15210.47	9375.00
	Alan MCLEAN	Scot	71	70	69	64	274	-14	15210.47	9375.00
12	Arjun ATWAL	Ind	72	64	70	69	275	-13	12432.02	7662.50
	Mark PILKINGTON	Wal	68	68	73	66	275	-13	12432.02	7662.50
	Andrew COLTART	Scot	68	69	69	69	275	-13	12432.02	7662.50
	Jamie DONALDSON	Wal	67	72	68	68	275	-13	12432.02	7662.50
16	Grant MULLER	SA	69	69	69	69	276	-12	10708.17	6600.00
	Jean-Francois REMESY	Fr	67	70	73	66	276	-12	10708.17	6600.00
	Richard BLAND	Eng	73	68	67	68	276	-12	10708.17	6600.00
19	Darren FICHARDT	SA	73	67	66	71	277	-11	9572.45	5900.00
	Ian GARBUTT	Eng	70	72	69	66	277	-11	9572.45	5900.00
	Doug McGUIGAN	Scot	74	67	67	69	277	-11	9572.45	5900.00
22	David HOWELL	Eng	71	69	70	68	278	-10	8152.81	5025.00
	Mark MCNULTY	Zim	73	70	69	66	278	-10	8152.81	5025.00
	Andrew MARSHALL	Eng	69	72	66	71	278	-10	8152.81	5025.00
	Justin HOBDAY	SA	73	70	66	69	278	-10	8152.81	5025.00
	James KINGSTON	SA	67	71	71	69	278	-10	8152.81	5025.00
	Bradley DREDGE	Wal	69	72	67	70	278	-10	8152.81	5025.00
	Daren LEE	Eng	70	68	68	72	278	-10	8152.81	5025.00
	Carl PETTERSSON	Swe	68	70	74	66	278	-10	8152.81	5025.00
30	Wallie COETSEE	SA	70	69	69	71	279	-9	6652.05	4100.00
	Paul EALES	Eng	73	68	69	69	279	-9	6652.05	4100.00
	Stephen DODD	Wal	66	71	72	70	279	-9	6652.05	4100.00
	Christian CÉVAËR	Fr	70	67	68	74	279	-9	6652.05	4100.00
	Simon HURD	Eng	70	70	70	69	279	-9	6652.05	4100.00
	Simon DYSON	Eng	73	65	73	68	279	-9	6652.05	4100.00
36	Mark ROE	Eng	67	72	73	68	280	-8	5516.33	3400.00
	Jonathan LOMAS	Eng	71	71	70	68	280	-8	5516.33	3400.00
	Rolf MUNTZ	Hol	71	71	70	68	280	-8	5516.33	3400.00
	Donald GAMMON	SA	70	71	68	71	280	-8	5516.33	3400.00
	Gary CLARK	Eng	70	72	68	70	280	-8	5516.33	3400.00
	Alastair FORSYTH	Scot	68	72	70	70	280	-8	5516.33	3400.00
	Nick DOUGHERTY	Eng	70	71	72	67	280	-8	5516.33	3400.00
	Jaco VAN ZYL	SA	70	69	71	70	280	-8	5516.33	3400.00
44	Sammy DANIELS	SA	69	71	71	70	281	-7	4218.37	2600.00
	Mårten OLANDER	Swe	71	67	73	70	281	-7	4218.37	2600.00
	Maarten LAFEBER	Hol	69	71	70	71	281	-7	4218.37	2600.00
	David LYNN	Eng	72	71	66	72	281	-7	4218.37	2600.00
	André CRUSE	SA	72	71	70	68	281	-7	4218.37	2600.00
	Christopher HANELL	Swe	71	70	69	71	281	-7	4218.37	2600.00
	Sam WALKER	Eng	70	67	71	73	281	-7	4218.37	2600.00
	Michael KIRK	SA	72	68	70	71	281	-7	4218.37	2600.00
52	Charlie WI	R.Kor	74	68	69	71	282	-6	3407.15	2100.00
	Tim CLARK	SA	69	69	73	71	282	-6	3407.15	2100.00
54	Malcolm MACKENZIE	Eng	71	66	73	73	283	-5	2855.51	1760.00
	Sven STRÜVER	Ger	69	69	73	72	283	-5	2855.51	1760.00
	Paul BROADHURST	Eng	74	67	68	74	283	-5	2855.51	1760.00
	Gary EMERSON	Eng	70	71	71	71	283	-5	2855.51	1760.00
	Stephen SCAHILL	NZ	69	71	70	73	283	-5	2855.51	1760.00
59	Marco GORTANA	SA	72	71	69	73	285	-3	2352.55	1450.00
	Marc CAYEUX	Zim	68	74	68	75	285	-3	2352.55	1450.00
	Stephen GALLACHER	Scot	69	69	71	72	285	-3	2352.55	1450.00
	Matthew CORT	Eng	71	69	72	73	285	-3	2352.55	1450.00
	David DIXON	Eng	71	71	69	74	285	-3	2352.55	1450.00
64	David GILFORD	Eng	69	73	72	72	286	-2	2068.62	1275.00
	Jaco OLVER	SA	73	69	72	72	286	-2	2068.62	1275.00
66	Titch MOORE	SA	71	71	74	71	287	-1	1865.82	1150.00
	Greg OWEN	Eng	67	74	70	76	287	-1	1865.82	1150.00
	David PARK	Wal	70	73	70	74	287	-1	1865.82	1150.00
69	Philip GOLDING	Eng	72	71	69	76	288	0	1663.01	1025.00
	David HIGGINS	Ire	72	69	74	73	288	0	1663.01	1025.00
71	Hendrik BUHRMANN	SA	67	74	81	69	291	3	1215.50	749.18
	Bradley DAVISON	SA	70	73	77	71	291	3	1215.50	749.18
73	Joachim BACKSTROM	Swe	73	69	80	74	296	8	1211.00	746.40
74	Brian DAVIS	Eng	70	69	73	RETD	212	-4	1211.00	746.40

Photography • Design • Printing • New-media • Data management

Competing with the best in Europe

Books
Magazines
Catalogues
Brochures
Point of sale

Johnnie Walker Classic   Lake Karrinyup Country Club · Perth · Australia

different class

Retief Goosen

Johnnie Walker's ten year involvement with The European Tour is a sponsorship without frontiers. From its beginnings in Jamaica's Tryall Bay, it has reached out to embrace The Ryder Cup Matches on both sides of the Atlantic, and in more recent years, travelled extensively throughout Asia.

The decision to stop off in Western Australia for the first time - the 1997 Johnnie Walker Classic was played at Hope Island in Queensland - was inspired. The tree-lined Lake Karrinyup layout provided the sternest of golfing tests while nearby Perth possessed wonderful entertainment facilities which the sponsors used to generously dispense samples of their famous product.

Most inspired of all, however, was the golf produced in the third round by South Africa's Retief Goosen, which spreadeagled a high class field, broke several records and left him with a challenge which only existed on paper during the final day. To fully appreciate Goosen's nine under par 63 it only has to be compared with the efforts of the 155 other competitors, of whom just six managed to return an under par total over four rounds.

Lee Westwood

Simon Dyson

They struggled against two key elements. To the million or so citizens of Perth, The Freemantle Doctor, a southerly wind which blows in off the Indian Ocean around noon on most days, is heaven sent. It takes the raw heat out of cloudless skies, but it was to prove the undoing of many afternoon starters at Lake Karrinyup.

On several of the course's doglegs, drives hit with precision and power were suddenly blown off course by gusts that were not evident standing on the tees. Even those who found the fairways on the first two days, before extra watering was applied, then struggled with their approach shots to firm greens.

The exceptions tended to be among the early starters. On the opening day the name of Thailand's Thongchai Jaidee was found at the top of the leaderboard after he shot a five under par 67. Named the Davidoff Tour's Golfer of the Year at the lavish Saturday night Gala Dinner, Jaidee, who before turning professional spent eleven years handling high winds as an army paratrooper, struggled himself during the second afternoon.

shot of the week

RETIEF GOOSEN South Africa

Retief Goosen's second to the 18th green in the third round. From 224 yards out, uphill and into a stiff breeze, he hit a two iron with a controlled draw which worked the contours of the green to set up his ninth and final birdie of the round from 15 feet.

Although he managed to hand in a level par 72 it was overshadowed by Goosen's first significant move of the tournament, sweeping three shots clear with only three holes of his second round to play.

Despite dropping shots at both the 16th and 17th, where he left approach iron shots short of the greens into the wind, Goosen, with a six under par total of 138, held a one shot lead, and he was never to be overtaken. At the other end of the field the halfway cut reflected the testing conditions with those on seven over par or better staying for the weekend.

So to the dawning of the third day when, surely, despite the absence of Colin Montgomerie who withdrew with a bad back, the likes of Jaidee, one behind, and Ernie Els, Pierre Fulke and Sergio Garcia, all within striking distance, would test the resilience of Goosen. This did not happen because Goosen, on third round day, was in a different class.

Indeed he played such flawless golf for 18 holes, it moved sections of the local media to describe the round as one of the greatest

performances in Australian golfing history. Goosen was, quite simply, invincible. He stormed clear with four birdies in an outward nine of 32 and five more to come home in 31.

His 63 set a course record and with a 15 under par total of 201 he moved 13 shots ahead of Els and Garcia, who scored 71 and 72 respectively. The total also surpassed the previous 54 hole record lead on The European Tour of ten shots set by Tony Jacklin in the 1974 Scandinavian Enterprise Open and equalled by Ken Brown in the 1984 Glasgow Open and by Tiger Woods in the 2000 US Open Championship. Goosen said: "Given the conditions, and the way the course was set up, it was probably the best round I have ever played."

That evening, at a Johnnie Walker function, Jos Vanstiphout, the Belgian sports psychologist who councils the South African, among others, was asked what he had said or done to bring about such a score. "Me?" he said. "Look, I may be good, but I'm not God."

So the reigning US Open Champion achieved his first success in Australia, eventually winning by eight shots from Fulke, who closed with a flawless 66. Moreover Goosen continued an impressive

sequence of 13 top ten finishes, including three victories, from his last 16 events on The European Tour International Schedule.

Even so there was a story within a story because with the talk of 2002 producing a new class of potential stars it was interesting to note that apart from Garcia (aged 22) finishing third, Simon Dyson (24), Raphaël Jacquelin (27) and Anthony Wall (26) shared fifth place; Nick Dougherty (19) enjoyed his first top ten finish; and Jamie Donaldson (26), David Howell (26), Søren Kjeldsen (26) and Justin Rose (21) all enjoyed top 20 finishes.

Then again, as one golf writer recalled, back in the 1920s Walter Hagen used to stroll on to the first tee and drawl: "Waal, who's gonna be second?" If ever there was a case of Retief Goosen being first, and the rest nowhere then it was the Johnnie Walker Classic at Lake Karrinyup Country Club.

Graham Otway

Thomas Levet

the course

Lake Karrinyup Country Club is uniquely difficult. It is not extraordinarily long at 6974 yards, but the bunkers are huge and placed to perfection. A variety of trees encroach, the greens are firm, water hazards lurk - a tough test indeed.

Retief Goosen

final results

Lake Karrinyup Country Club • Perth • Australia
January 24-27 • 2002 • Par 72 • 6974 yards • 6375 metres

Pos.	Name		Rd1	Rd2	Rd3	Rd4	Total	Par	Prize Money Euro	£
1	Retief GOOSEN	SA	70	68	63	73	274	-14	243640.50	150000.00
2	Pierre FULKE	Swe	72	70	74	66	282	-6	162427.00	100000.00
3	Sergio GARCIA	Sp	69	73	72	69	283	-5	91511.37	56340.00
4	Ernie ELS	SA	72	71	71	72	286	-2	73092.15	45000.00
5	Raphaël JACQUELIN	Fr	75	72	72	68	287	-1	52333.98	32220.00
	Anthony WALL	Eng	71	75	69	72	287	-1	52333.98	32220.00
	Simon DYSON	Eng	71	74	70	72	287	-1	52333.98	32220.00
8	Mathias GRÖNBERG	Swe	73	73	71	71	288	0	34645.68	21330.00
	Nick DOUGHERTY	Eng	74	76	68	70	288	0	34645.68	21330.00
10	Nick FALDO	Eng	71	73	74	71	289	1	26203.54	16132.50
	Wayne RILEY	Aus	77	70	69	73	289	1	26203.54	16132.50
	Peter FOWLER	Aus	71	77	70	71	289	1	26203.54	16132.50
	Thongchai JAIDEE	Thai	67	72	78	72	289	1	26203.54	16132.50
14	Trevor IMMELMAN	SA	75	72	70	73	290	2	21489.09	13230.00
	Craig PARRY	Aus	78	69	71	72	290	2	21489.09	13230.00
	Jamie DONALDSON	Wal	73	75	70	72	290	2	21489.09	13230.00
17	David HOWELL	Eng	75	71	71	74	291	3	18565.41	11430.00
	Søren KJELDSEN	Den	77	73	69	72	291	3	18565.41	11430.00
	Steve ALKER	NZ	75	65	77	74	291	3	18565.41	11430.00
	Justin ROSE	Eng	78	71	68	74	291	3	18565.41	11430.00
21	Scott GARDINER	Aus	75	76	69	72	292	4	16957.38	10440.00
22	Santiago LUNA	Sp	74	75	75	69	293	5	15641.72	9630.00
	Thomas LEVET	Fr	75	70	76	72	293	5	15641.72	9630.00
	Peter LONARD	Aus	79	68	74	72	293	5	15641.72	9630.00
	Wei-Tze YEH	Taiwan	71	76	72	74	293	5	15641.72	9630.00
	James MCLEAN	Aus	78	70	72	73	293	5	15641.72	9630.00
27	Craig JONES	Aus	71	72	74	77	294	6	12588.09	7750.00
	Greg TURNER	NZ	74	73	76	71	294	6	12588.09	7750.00
	Nick O'HERN	Aus	73	76	72	73	294	6	12588.09	7750.00
	Charlie WI	RepKr	70	76	73	75	294	6	12588.09	7750.00
	Jarrod MOSELEY	Aus	76	72	72	74	294	6	12588.09	7750.00
	Roger WESSELS	SA	74	76	73	71	294	6	12588.09	7750.00
	Niclas FASTH	Swe	72	72	78	72	294	6	12588.09	7750.00
	Adam CRAWFORD	Aus	74	72	73	75	294	6	12588.09	7750.00
	Brett RUMFORD	Aus	71	77	73	73	294	6	12588.09	7750.00
36	Jean-Francois REMESY	Fr	73	76	73	73	295	7	9940.53	6120.00
	Mark ALLEN	Aus	77	74	71	73	295	7	9940.53	6120.00
	Ian GARBUTT	Eng	74	77	72	72	295	7	9940.53	6120.00
	David LYNN	Eng	78	72	72	73	295	7	9940.53	6120.00
	Prayad MARKSAENG	Thai	77	73	70	75	295	7	9940.53	6120.00
	Brendan JONES	Aus	79	72	70	74	295	7	9940.53	6120.00
42	Steve WEBSTER	Eng	75	72	75	74	296	8	7747.77	4770.00
	Richard GREEN	Aus	73	72	75	76	296	8	7747.77	4770.00

Pos.	Name		Rd1	Rd2	Rd3	Rd4	Total	Par	Prize Money Euro	£
	Robert KARLSSON	Swe	76	72	74	74	296	8	7747.77	4770.00
	Markus BRIER	Aut	73	75	75	73	296	8	7747.77	4770.00
	Michael CAMPBELL	NZ	69	80	74	73	296	8	7747.77	4770.00
	Christopher HANELL	Swe	74	74	72	76	296	8	7747.77	4770.00
	Ed STEDMAN	Aus	74	74	71	77	296	8	7747.77	4770.00
	Masanori KOBAYASHI	Jpn	82	69	74	71	296	8	7747.77	4770.00
	Hirokazu KUNIYOSHI	Jpn	75	73	76	72	296	8	7747.77	4770.00
51	Anders FORSBRAND	Swe	78	69	79	71	297	9	5408.82	3330.00
	Scott LAYCOCK	Aus	73	78	74	72	297	9	5408.82	3330.00
	Steen TINNING	Den	78	72	72	75	297	9	5408.82	3330.00
	Anthony KANG	RepKr	74	75	76	72	297	9	5408.82	3330.00
	Jonathan LOMAS	Eng	76	72	75	74	297	9	5408.82	3330.00
	David CARTER	Eng	73	76	76	72	297	9	5408.82	3330.00
	Carl PETTERSSON	Swe	74	73	72	78	297	9	5408.82	3330.00
58	Andrew BONHOMME	Aus	73	73	76	76	298	10	4020.07	2475.00
	Anthony PAINTER	Aus	73	76	75	74	298	10	4020.07	2475.00
	Jarmo SANDELIN	Swe	77	73	74	74	298	10	4020.07	2475.00
	Ter-Chang WANG	Taiwan	72	79	72	75	298	10	4020.07	2475.00
	Dean ROBERTSON	Scot	72	78	76	72	298	10	4020.07	2475.00
	Lee WESTWOOD	Eng	72	74	76	76	298	10	4020.07	2475.00
64	Andrew COLTART	Scot	74	77	73	75	299	11	3362.24	2070.00
	John BICKERTON	Eng	76	75	74	74	299	11	3362.24	2070.00
	Daniel CHOPRA	Swe	71	77	72	79	299	11	3362.24	2070.00
67	Barry LANE	Eng	75	74	73	78	300	12	2923.69	1800.00
	Gary EMERSON	Eng	72	79	72	77	300	12	2923.69	1800.00
	Adam SCOTT	Aus	72	76	77	75	300	12	2923.69	1800.00
70	James KINGSTON	SA	74	76	76	75	301	13	2348.93	1446.15
	Scott HEND	Aus	77	73	73	78	301	13	2348.93	1446.15
	Nathan GATEHOUSE	Aus	76	74	76	75	301	13	2348.93	1446.15
73	David ARMSTRONG	Aus	77	74	75	76	302	14	2185.50	1345.53
	Tobias DIER	Ger	75	71	77	79	302	14	2185.50	1345.53
75	Peter SENIOR	Aus	75	75	76	77	303	15	2173.50	1338.14
	David SMAIL	NZ	75	75	74	79	303	15	2173.50	1338.14
	Craig SPENCE	Aus	71	80	76	76	303	15	2173.50	1338.14
	Lucas PARSONS	Aus	75	76	75	77	303	15	2173.50	1338.14
	Terry PRICE	Aus	80	70	78	75	303	15	2173.50	1338.14
	Martin DOYLE	Aus	74	75	78	76	303	15	2173.50	1338.14
81	Stephen GALLACHER	Scot	72	75	81	77	305	17	2163.00	1331.68
82	Arjun ATWAL	Ind	77	74	81	74	306	18	2158.50	1328.90
	Kenny DRUCE	Aus	79	72	78	77	306	18	2158.50	1328.90
84	Vivek BHANDARI	Ind	78	73	81	80	312	24	2154.00	1326.13
85	Aaron BADDELEY	Aus	75	72	WD		147	3		

gettyimages NEWS AND SPORT

Live photographic coverage from every European Tour, PGA Tour and Australasian Tour event as well as many LPGA, Evian Ladies European Tour, The European Challenge Tour, The European Seniors Tour and Major International Amateur Events.

David Cannon

| Ross Kinnaird | Andrew Redington | Stuart Franklin | Warren Little | Stephen Munday |

Heineken Classic Royal Melbourne Golf Club · Victoria · Australia

master craftsman

1	**Ernie ELS** SA	271	-17
2	Peter FOWLER Aus	276	-12
	David HOWELL Eng	276	-12
	Peter O'MALLEY Aus	276	-12
5	Michael CAMPBELL NZ	277	-11
6	Nick FALDO Eng	278	-10
	Stephen LEANEY Aus	278	-10
	Greg NORMAN Aus	278	-10
9	Greg OWEN Eng	280	- 8
	Craig PARRY Aus	280	- 8

Ernie Els

Big smile, easy swing, rolling gait and the gifted touches of a master craftsman. From the very beginning of the Heineken Classic, out along the Melbourne sand-belt of golf courses, it was clear that the Ernie Els Show was in town. One of South Africa's favourite sons led the tournament from start to finish, leaving rivals in his wake and spectators in awe of his languid supremacy as he won by five shots at 17 under par from Australians Peter Fowler and Peter O'Malley and Englishman David Howell.

Els may have turned the tournament into a one-man exhibition, but there were other side-shows at the superbly conditioned Royal Melbourne course, a composite of the East and West where the original designer, Dr Alister Mackenzie, remains revered for his foresight and originality.

Tournament Officials presented an intriguing mix of the young and old in the order of world golf. On the first two days there was the imaginative grouping of three of the game's emerging young lions, Aaron Baddeley, Justin Rose and Adam Scott. Not far behind them were men who had figured in their schoolboy dreams, John Daly, Nick Faldo and Greg Norman.

Peter O'Malley

In the middle were the current grandees, unquestionably led by Els. He emphatically laid down his intentions with a first round 64 that gave him a two shot lead over the young Welshman, Mark Pilkington. Rose, understandably still tired from the exertions of his maiden European Tour victory in South Africa a fortnight earlier, missed the cut, but Baddeley and Scott acquitted themselves well.

While Faldo finished joint sixth with Norman and another Australian, Stephen Leaney, the progress of Els was no less than imperious, overshadowed only briefly in the second round by a record-breaking 62 from New Zealander Richard Lee who, when asked who was in his entourage, replied: "Just me, a Visa card and my golf bag."

Lee eventually finished tied for 14th for which he earned 17,809 euro (£10,934). Changed days indeed for the 28 year old who once had to phone a friend to send him money to get him home from Tour.

Peter Fowler

the course

A rolling parkland course of 6981 yards, a composite of the East and West of Royal Melbourne, finishing with seven par fours. The course was praised by all the players for the condition of the fairways and the firmness of the greens.

Greg Norman

It was not only Els who was geared up for battle. Norman, himself, was into the fight. When he birdied the eighth, ninth and tenth and the roars rolled across the fairways, it sounded like a bull elephant bellowing for a scrap. Els, however, was unmoved. He simply eagled the tenth and kept on strolling towards his first win on The European Tour International Schedule since Loch Lomond in 2000.

Norman eventually succumbed with two bogeys in the final four holes but left the impression that there might be more 'Shark Attacks' left. He was thrilled to be invited to the Masters Tournament and during his Heineken Classic rounds of 69-67-73-69 there were moments that took the spectators back to his days of winning no less than 78 tournaments with enormous galleries following every shot.

This time he was happy to pay tribute to the winner. He said: "Ernie sits rightly in the top five in the world. He plays very consistent, steady golf because he plays a lot. He has always got a

Els's rounds of 64-69-69-69 comprised a kind of golf that was both economical and exciting. There were times, in the final round, when Howell and Norman almost drew alongside but they were never able to overtake and one could not help reflect on the South African's pre-tournament comments when he said: "This is definitely a second shot golf course, an approach shot course. I feel excited playing on courses like this. The courses down here are brilliant."

His comfort with the surroundings translated into his play and by the time the fourth round had been completed he had the trophy in one hand, the 221,385 euro (£135,932) cheque in the other, and was looking ahead towards bigger things. Suddenly Tiger Woods, winner of three Major Championships in 2000, was in his sights as he said: "Tiger is not as dominant now. It's a strange, old game of highs and lows. I feel I am getting to my highs. I have a lot of golf left. To win by five shots against a very good field will give me a lot of confidence."

Standing close by was the Belgian sports psychologist Jos Vanstiphout who sent the South African out to the words of an old Finnish proverb: "The fighter who is afraid of a fight gets beaten immediately."

shot of the week

ERNIE ELS South Africa

David Smail's first round hole-in-one was overshadowed by Ernie Els's magnificent eight iron to the heart of the green at the par five tenth in the final round. He holed a ten footer for eagle and said: "That gave me the right cushion at the right time."

Mark Pilkington

good routine on the golf course. He is very smooth. I know Ernie does get upset with himself at times but he does not show it. He keeps it inside very nicely. I think that is a huge asset."

One man who learned a lot from the tournament was Pilkington. He was going along serenely with the prospect of a good cheque when he found himself in a bush at the 15th on the Saturday. He took a drop under penalty, somewhat hurriedly, as he was aware that Els and Norman were already on the tee with their huge gallery swarming. Although Pilkington's playing partner, O'Malley, agreed with the drop, some spectators did not and brought the matter to the attention of Officials. At the end of the round the players and European Tour Chief Referee John Paramor returned to the scene and Pilkington was penalised two shots. He never fully recovered and fell back through the field to finish tied 39th, his salutory lesson well learned.

James Mossop

David Howell

John Daly

final results

Royal Melbourne Golf Club · Victoria · Australia
January 31 - February 3 · 2002 · Par 72 · 6981 yards · 6395 metres

Pos.	Name		Rd1	Rd2	Rd3	Rd4	Total	Par	Prize Money Euro	£
1	Ernie ELS	SA	64	69	69	69	271	-17	221385.80	135932.09
2	Peter FOWLER	Aus	69	70	70	67	276	-12	89169.28	54750.43
	David HOWELL	Eng	68	70	70	68	276	-12	89169.28	54750.43
	Peter O'MALLEY	Aus	68	68	70	70	276	-12	89169.28	54750.43
5	Michael CAMPBELL	NZ	68	72	68	69	277	-11	49196.85	30207.13
6	Nick FALDO	Eng	67	73	69	69	278	-10	39767.45	24417.43
	Greg NORMAN	Aus	69	67	73	69	278	-10	39767.45	24417.43
	Stephen LEANEY	Aus	70	66	72	70	278	-10	39767.45	24417.43
9	Craig PARRY	Aus	68	71	71	70	280	-8	31977.95	19634.64
	Greg OWEN	Eng	73	70	68	69	280	-8	31977.95	19634.64
11	Anthony WALL	Eng	72	70	69	70	281	-7	24598.42	15103.56
	Scott LAYCOCK	Aus	73	68	71	69	281	-7	24598.42	15103.56
	Trevor IMMELMAN	SA	69	69	77	66	281	-7	24598.42	15103.56
14	Barry LANE	Eng	67	73	68	74	282	-6	17809.26	10934.98
	Jarrod MOSELEY	Aus	70	70	71	71	282	-6	17809.26	10934.98
	Fredrik JACOBSON	Swe	71	73	72	66	282	-6	17809.26	10934.98
	Adam SCOTT	Aus	67	72	70	73	282	-6	17809.26	10934.98
	Richard LEE	NZ	75	62	71	74	282	-6	17809.26	10934.98
19	Greg TURNER	NZ	72	72	70	69	283	-5	12760.43	7834.97
	David SMAIL	NZ	69	71	74	69	283	-5	12760.43	7834.97
	Mark ALLEN	Aus	70	70	72	71	283	-5	12760.43	7834.97
	Philip GOLDING	Eng	72	67	70	74	283	-5	12760.43	7834.97
	Jarmo SANDELIN	Swe	75	66	72	70	283	-5	12760.43	7834.97
	Scott HEND	Aus	71	72	68	72	283	-5	12760.43	7834.97
	Eddie LEE (AM)	NZ	67	75	71	70	283	-5		
26	Steen TINNING	Den	71	72	68	73	284	-4	9790.17	6011.22
	Joakim HAEGGMAN	Swe	72	68	73	71	284	-4	9790.17	6011.22
	Peter LONARD	Aus	67	71	72	74	284	-4	9790.17	6011.22
	Patrik SJÖLAND	Swe	68	71	73	72	284	-4	9790.17	6011.22
	Aaron BADDELEY	Aus	70	71	73	70	284	-4	9790.17	6011.22
31	Mark FOSTER	Eng	70	73	70	72	285	-3	7302.66	4483.87
	Sven STRÜVER	Ger	73	68	73	71	285	-3	7302.66	4483.87
	Steve CONRAN	Aus	76	68	70	71	285	-3	7302.66	4483.87
	Andre STOLZ	Aus	71	72	72	70	285	-3	7302.66	4483.87
	Gary ORR	Scot	70	71	70	74	285	-3	7302.66	4483.87
	Niclas FASTH	Swe	73	68	69	75	285	-3	7302.66	4483.87
	Daren LEE	Eng	73	70	70	72	285	-3	7302.66	4483.87
	John BICKERTON	Eng	76	68	73	68	285	-3	7302.66	4483.87
39	Miguel Angel MARTIN	Sp	73	71	71	71	286	-2	5288.66	3247.27
	Marc FARRY	Fr	68	74	69	75	286	-2	5288.66	3247.27
	Jamie SPENCE	Eng	72	72	73	69	286	-2	5288.66	3247.27
	Gavin COLES	Aus	73	67	77	69	286	-2	5288.66	3247.27
	Mark PILKINGTON	Wal	66	70	75	75	286	-2	5288.66	3247.27
	John DALY	USA	71	73	71	71	286	-2	5288.66	3247.27
	Wei-Tze YEH	Taiwan	74	66	76	70	286	-2	5288.66	3247.27
	Carl PETTERSSON	Swe	71	68	74	73	286	-2	5288.66	3247.27
47	Robert KARLSSON	Swe	70	70	75	72	287	-1	3587.27	2202.60
	Ian GARBUTT	Eng	71	70	75	71	287	-1	3587.27	2202.60
	Gary EVANS	Eng	75	68	72	72	287	-1	3587.27	2202.60
	Stephen GALLACHER	Scot	72	70	71	74	287	-1	3587.27	2202.60
	Alastair FORSYTH	Scot	70	71	71	75	287	-1	3587.27	2202.60
	Douglas LABELLE	USA	70	70	74	73	287	-1	3587.27	2202.60
53	Stephen COLLINS	Aus	71	72	72	73	288	0	2767.32	1699.15
	Terry PRICE	Aus	70	73	73	72	288	0	2767.32	1699.15
	Jamie DONALDSON	Wal	72	72	71	73	288	0	2767.32	1699.15
56	Jeev Milkha SINGH	Ind	69	73	74	73	289	1	2595.13	1593.43
	Marcus NORGREN	Swe	72	71	75	71	289	1	2595.13	1593.43
	Richard BACKWELL	Aus	71	71	73	74	289	1	2595.13	1593.43
	Thomas LEVET	Fr	74	70	69	76	289	1	2595.13	1593.43
	Gregory HAVRET	Fr	71	72	74	72	289	1	2595.13	1593.43
	Soren HANSEN	Den	72	69	73	75	289	1	2595.13	1593.43
	Stephen SCAHILL	NZ	71	72	73	73	289	1	2595.13	1593.43
	Robert ALLENBY	Aus	70	68	71	80	289	1	2595.13	1593.43
64	Costantino ROCCA	It	72	70	75	73	290	2	2459.84	1510.36
	Richard GREEN	Aus	70	72	73	75	290	2	2459.84	1510.36
	Andrew COLTART	Scot	71	70	74	75	290	2	2459.84	1510.36
67	Marcus CAIN	Aus	69	72	74	76	291	3	2373.75	1457.49
	Alex CEJKA	Ger	70	73	77	71	291	3	2373.75	1457.49
	Markus BRIER	Aut	72	70	77	72	291	3	2373.75	1457.49
	Paul SHEEHAN	Aus	73	71	77	70	291	3	2373.75	1457.49
71	Lian-Wei ZHANG	PRC	70	74	75	73	292	4	2287.65	1404.63
	Soren KJELDSEN	Den	74	70	77	71	292	4	2287.65	1404.63
	Simon DYSON	Eng	74	69	78	71	292	4	2287.65	1404.63
74	Raphaël JACQUELIN	Fr	71	70	75	77	293	5	2213.86	1359.32
	Matthew ECOB	Aus	72	72	75	74	293	5	2213.86	1359.32
	Mark WILSON	USA	71	72	75	75	293	5	2213.86	1359.32
77	Andrew TSCHUDIN	Aus	69	75	80	74	298	10	2164.66	1329.11

ANZ Championship The Lakes Golf Club · Sydney · Australia

wise decision

1	Richard S JOHNSON Swe	46 pts
2	Scott LAYCOCK Aus	44 pts
	Craig PARRY Aus	44 pts
4	André STOLZ Aus	43 pts
5	Stephen GALLACHER Scot	39 pts
6	Ian GARBUTT Eng	38 pts
7	Jonathan LOMAS Eng	37 pts
8	Trevor IMMELMAN SA	36 pts
	Thomas LEVET Fr	36 pts
	Greg TURNER NZ	36 pts

Richard S Johnson

Had you been looking for a potential winner before the start of the ANZ Championship, it is unlikely you would have settled on Richard S Johnson. The 25 year old Swede, Stanley to his friends, had dug deep to finish 112th on the 2001 Volvo Order of Merit, and was languishing just inside the top 400 of the Official World Golf Ranking. He had played hardly any golf for three months and had missed the cut by two shots in his first outing of the year in the Heineken Classic at Royal Melbourne a week earlier. Yet when The European Tour International Schedule hit Sydney for the third successive joint venture with the PGA Tour of Australasia in 2002, it proved to be his week.

In this age of burly long hitters, Richard, whose grandfather came from New Jersey, is a bantamweight with a big punch. If he was relatively unknown at the start of the Championship, Richard (pronounced Reekard) was a personality by the time it ended.

With 46 points in the modified stableford event, a format being used for the first time outside America where it was introduced at The International at Castle Pines, Colorado, in 1986, Johnson outpointed the stylish Scott Laycock and the experienced pre-tournament favourite Craig Parry, who had chased Stuart Appleby home earlier in the season at the Holden Australian Open Championship at The Grand Golf Club.

Taking full advantage of late slips by his rivals, Johnson, who had been working throughout the winter on building up his physique, muscled his way to becoming the 16th Swedish winner on The European Tour in the past 15 years and according to what the record books showed was the 45th victory by a Swedish player on The European Tour International Schedule since Ove Sellberg's breakthrough win in the 1986 Epson Grand Prix of Europe Match Play Championship. Johnson had spent recent winters with relatives in sunny Australia and, in the weeks leading up to the ANZ Championship, he had been practising on Queensland's Sunshine Coast. So there were many who wanted to call this a "home" win!

Johnson, an all-rounder with a big heart and keen competitive edge, only turned to golf after deciding his first love – skateboarding – was just too dangerous. Good enough to have competed in the Swedish Skateboard Championships, he opted to give golf a chance after suffering seven broken ribs, a broken hand and a broken foot. "To be any good at skateboarding you have to be crazy to do the stunts," said Richard. "I was not crazy enough!" He made a wise decision.

Yet after the first round at The Lakes Golf Club he was hardly hitting the headlines. He amassed only three points and was trailing leader Jonathan Lomas by 17 points. Lomas, who finished tied 51st

at the Johnnie Walker Classic and missed the cut at the Heineken Classic, had eight birdies, equal to 16 points, and a five point eagle on his card. A solitary bogey cost him a point and his 20 point tally represented a 64, just one outside the course record. That 20 point total equalled the record collected in one round at The International and was only equalled once more during the week in Sydney, by Sweden's Jarmo Sandelin in round two.

The real story of the first day, however, was the fact that the round was played at all. One month's rain had been dumped on Sydney

shot of the week

CRAIG PARRY Australia

When Craig Parry stepped on to the tee at the 208 yard 15th on the second day he was hot under the collar. He had just three putted the 14th. He pulled out his four iron, however, and hit the shot of the tournament straight into the hole for the fourth ace of his career and five valuable points.

Greg Turner

On day three Stolz moved to the 39 point mark, two ahead of Parry, who was attempting to add to his triumph a few weeks earlier over Tiger Woods in the Telstra Hyundai New Zealand Open. Johnson continued his charge, too, and with the help of another 16 points - the best third round score - ended the day four behind and tied third with late entrant Stephen Gallacher, of Scotland.

"I've played some of my best golf but everyone else is playing so well," said Johnson wistfully before adding prophetically, "But anything can happen." Parry admitted he would have to play very well on the final day to beat Stolz and in the end did but he had not banked on Johnson beating all of them. A final 11 point round gave the Swede 46 points and a two point victory over the consistent Laycock and Parry with Stolz fourth, Gallacher fifth and England's Ian Garbutt, who closed with a 19 points, sixth. Immelman, who had been trying to complete a hat-trick of South African successes following triumphs in the previous two weeks on The European Tour International Schedule by Ernie Els and Retief Goosen, managed to collect only seven points over the weekend and finished tied eighth with Thomas Levet, of France, and Greg Turner, of New Zealand.

in the previous five days. Few courses would have been playable but The Lakes is built on Sydney's sandbelt. The course drained so quickly and the greenkeeping staff, headed by Peter Brown, did such an expert mopping up job that Tournament Directors Trevor Herden and Miguel Vidaor did not even have to impose a preferred lies rule.

By the end of the second day the Australian André Stolz, who also carries a Swiss passport, had taken the lead – adding 19 points to the 11 he had scored on day one - for a total of 30. Lomas's putter, which had worked so well on Thursday, took Friday off and the 1996 Chemapol Trophy Czech Open winner added only one more point. Stolz, winner of the 2000 ANZ Tour Championship, led talented South African Trevor Immelman by one point with Parry, who had a hole-in-one at the 15th, a further point behind and still the favourite. Johnson recovered from his indifferent first round by scoring 16 points to be 11 behind the leader.

Johnson, who earned 195,079 euro (£118,675) - more in one week than he had amassed previously in any entire season - headed to Queensland on holiday with girlfriend Linda; Parry flew out to America; Stolz went to caddie for his wife Cathy in the ALPGA Championship; and tournament organiser Steve Frazer sat down to assess the success or otherwise of the stableford format designed, ostensibly, to reward attacking golf.

His conclusion was that against all the odds, notably the unsettled weather and the uncertain international situation after September 11, he had come through the week as successfully as the new Champion.

Renton Laidlaw

Stephen Gallacher

the course

The Lakes Golf Club, just a 20 minute drive from Sydney's Central Business District and close to the International Airport, had to be remodelled in 1968 by Bruce Devlin and Robert Van Hagge after a new freeway was built through the middle of the original layout. The redesigned course, further refined by, among others, Jack Newton, remains an excellent test with the lakes, formerly the reservoirs for the city, in play most dramatically on the more open back nine.

Patrik Sjöland

final results

The Lakes Golf Club · Sydney· Australia
February 7-10 · 2002 · Par 73 · 6904 yards · 6315 metres

Pos.	Name		Rd1	Rd2	Rd3	Rd4	Total	Par	Prize Money Euro	£
1	Richard S JOHNSON	Swe	3	16	16	11	46		195079.60	118675.99
2	Scott LAYCOCK	Aus	11	16	7	10	44		91849.98	55876.62
	Craig PARRY	Aus	10	18	9	7	44		91849.98	55876.62
4	André STOLZ	Aus	11	19	9	4	43		52021.23	31646.93
5	Stephen GALLACHER	Scot	10	12	13	4	39		43351.02	26372.44
6	Ian GARBUTT	Eng	6	6	7	19	38		39015.92	23735.20
7	Jonathan LOMAS	Eng	20	1	9	7	37		34680.82	21097.96
8	Greg TURNER	NZ	10	8	12	6	36		29261.94	17801.40
	Trevor IMMELMAN	SA	10	19	3	4	36		29261.94	17801.40
	Thomas LEVET	Fr	8	4	10	14	36		29261.94	17801.40
11	Nick O'HERN	Aus	4	13	15	3	35		21675.51	13186.22
	Geoff OGILVY	Aus	7	16	1	11	35		21675.51	13186.22
	Niclas FASTH	Swe	3	11	10	11	35		21675.51	13186.22
14	Peter SENIOR	Aus	8	6	8	12	34		15693.07	9546.82
	Jean-Francois REMESY	Fr	11	6	9	8	34		15693.07	9546.82
	Anders HANSEN	Den	9	11	7	7	34		15693.07	9546.82
	John BICKERTON	Eng	5	13	11	5	34		15693.07	9546.82
	Nick DOUGHERTY	Eng	7	8	5	14	34		15693.07	9546.82
19	David HOWELL	Eng	10	3	4	16	33		11244.17	6840.35
	Brad ANDREWS	Aus	8	8	7	10	33		11244.17	6840.35
	Mathias GRÖNBERG	Swe	9	13	1	10	33		11244.17	6840.35
	Fredrik JACOBSON	Swe	3	9	7	14	33		11244.17	6840.35
	Andrew COLTART	Scot	5	11	4	13	33		11244.17	6840.35
	Patrik SJÖLAND	Swe	11	10	0	12	33		11244.17	6840.35
25	Sven STRÜVER	Ger	7	4	12	9	32		8033.49	4887.14
	Steve ALKER	NZ	7	13	4	8	32		8033.49	4887.14
	David BRANSDON	Aus	3	13	5	11	32		8033.49	4887.14
	Anthony PAINTER	Aus	4	13	9	6	32		8033.49	4887.14
	David LYNN	Eng	12	7	11	2	32		8033.49	4887.14
	Johan SKOLD	Swe	5	11	8	8	32		8033.49	4887.14
	Markus BRIER	Aut	4	10	4	14	32		8033.49	4887.14
	Christopher HANELL	Swe	9	5	4	14	32		8033.49	4887.14
33	Mark FOSTER	Eng	2	10	14	5	31		6177.52	3758.07
	Marcus NORGREN	Swe	11	3	10	7	31		6177.52	3758.07
	Carlos RODILES	Sp	10	15	5	1	31		6177.52	3758.07
	Gregory HAVRET	Fr	5	19	1	6	31		6177.52	3758.07
37	David SMAIL	NZ	11	7	4	8	30		5310.50	3230.62
	Mark PILKINGTON	Wal	3	8	8	11	30		5310.50	3230.62
	Brendan JONES	Aus	5	6	6	13	30		5310.50	3230.62
	Carl PETTERSSON	Swe	13	6	6	5	30		5310.50	3230.62
41	Jean HUGO	SA	3	9	8	9	29		4551.86	2769.11
	Matthew CORT	Eng	7	10	10	2	29		4551.86	2769.11
	Brad KENNEDY	Aus	-2	15	8	8	29		4551.86	2769.11
44	Raphaël JACQUELIN	Fr	15	4	6	3	28		3576.46	2175.73
	Gavin COLES	Aus	7	9	2	10	28		3576.46	2175.73
	Alex CEJKA	Ger	7	9	2	10	28		3576.46	2175.73
	Peter O'MALLEY	Aus	9	9	15	-5	28		3576.46	2175.73
	Gary ORR	Scot	10	5	8	5	28		3576.46	2175.73
	Nathan GREEN	Aus	-1	12	6	11	28		3576.46	2175.73
50	Euan WALTERS	Aus	12	8	5	2	27		2763.63	1681.24
	Adam CRAWFORD	Aus	4	12	7	4	27		2763.63	1681.24
52	Wei-Tze YEH	Taiwan	10	6	3	7	26		2492.68	1516.42
53	Tim ELLIOTT	Aus	5	8	6	6	25		2411.40	1466.97
	Aaron BADDELEY	Aus	2	9	1	13	25		2411.40	1466.97
55	Grant DODD	Aus	3	8	4	9	24		2330.12	1417.52
	Daren LEE	Eng	7	5	5	7	24		2330.12	1417.52
	James MCLEAN	Aus	4	8	8	4	24		2330.12	1417.52
	Ed STEDMAN	Aus	5	6	5	8	24		2330.12	1417.52
59	David GILFORD	Eng	7	11	-3	8	23		2243.42	1364.77
	Matthew ECOB	Aus	4	10	6	3	23		2243.42	1364.77
	Roger WESSELS	SA	5	9	4	5	23		2243.42	1364.77
	Greg OWEN	Eng	9	2	2	10	23		2243.42	1364.77
63	Peter FOWLER	Aus	1	10	6	5	22		2178.39	1325.22
	Alastair FORSYTH	Scot	3	13	-5	11	22		2178.39	1325.22
65	Lucas PARSONS	Aus	3	9	10	-1	21		2145.88	1305.44
66	Richard LEE	NZ	4	7	2	7	20		2124.20	1292.25
67	Paul BROADHURST	Eng	6	11	-2	4	19		2102.53	1279.06
68	Pierre FULKE	Swe	5	6	3	4	18		2070.01	1259.28
	Ben FERGUSON	Aus	2	11	-2	7	18		2070.01	1259.28
70	John WADE	Aus	6	12	-8	7	17		2026.66	1232.91
	Scott GARDINER	Aus	8	6	-5	8	17		2026.66	1232.91
72	Andrew MARSHALL	Eng	7	4	3	2	16		1994.15	1213.13
73	Jarmo SANDELIN	Swe	-7	20	-1	3	15		1961.63	1193.35
	Simon DYSON	Eng	4	8	1	2	15		1961.63	1193.35
75	Joakim HAEGGMAN	Swe	10	5	-2	1	14		1929.12	1173.57
76	Mark WILSON	USA	7	6	-5	1	9		1907.44	1160.39
77	Jeev Milkha SINGH	Ind	6	5	-1	-2	8		1865.77	1147.20

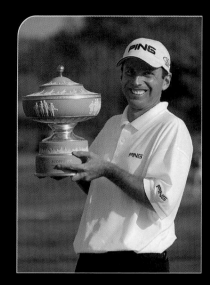

WGC-Accenture Match Play La Costa Resort and Spa · Carlsbad · California · US

sutherland's law

Champion – Kevin SUTHERLAND USA

Runner-Up – Scott McCARRON USA

Third – Brad FAXON USA

Fourth – Paul AZINGER USA

Kevin Sutherland

While stroke play golf is perceived as cold and calculating, match play golf is often reminiscent of hand to hand combat. Often the unpredictability of the contest is mirrored by the savagery of conditions at exposed locations such as Carnoustie or Pebble Beach but, occasionally, they are polarised. Such was the case at La Costa Resort and Spa in Carlsbad.

Playing conditions could not have been better for the World Golf Championships - Accenture Match Play with, most days, hardly a breath of wind disturbing the record February temperatures on the Californian coast. Yet, despite that, the cull of the fancied competitors remained as fierce as ever.

Proving the point conclusively, the top three seeds, Tiger Woods, Phil Mickelson and David Duval, were all knocked out in the first round, the former 2 and 1 by European Tour Member Peter O'Malley with the performance of the opening day. The trend continued as the week progressed and by the conclusion of the third round, only one of the top 20 seeds, US PGA Champion David Toms, remained.

Amongst those to fall by the wayside in the first couple of rounds were, unfortunately, the bulk of the 20 strong European Tour challenge, although Niclas Fasth and Sergio Garcia progressed to

Brad Faxon

Niclas Fasth

the third round while José Maria Olazábal made it to the quarter-finals.

During the week, Accenture announced their intention to sponsor the tournament for the next four years although no final decision was given on the venue. Perhaps a move to the east coast of the United States might assist the European cause given that the time change would be less demanding, but for some the event came that little bit too early in the season for eyes to be keenly focused and swings to be honed to perfection.

Padraig Harrington, playing his first tournament of the year, battled gamely in the early stages before going down on the 16th green to Steve Flesch while Colin Montgomerie's challenge was halted by eventual runner-up Scott McCarron, the American's cause helped considerably by a hole in one on the 14th.

Darren Clarke, who beat Woods in the epic 2000 final, fell to an in-form Matt Gogel, winner of the AT&T Pebble Beach Pro-Am three weeks previously, while Lee Westwood showed glimpses of the form which saw him top the Volvo Order of Merit in 2000 to ease past Shingo Katayama in round one before losing on the final green to John Cook in round two.

On the positive side, Fasth showed what an asset he will be to The European Ryder Cup Team at The De Vere Belfry in September, assured golf in his first ever professional match play tournament, seeing off Michael Campbell and Vijay Singh before he succumbed in extra holes to Paul Azinger. Garcia beat Lee Janzen and Charles Howell III before, like Montgomerie, he too fell to McCarron.

Olazábal, winner of the Buick Invitational on the US PGA Tour a fortnight earlier, continued to enjoy a renaissance, the catalyst being his straighter and truer driving. The two time Masters Champion birdied the 18th to win his first three matches against Justin Leonard, Retief Goosen and Mark Calcavecchia and repeated the

shot of the week

SCOTT McCARRON USA

Scott McCarron's hole in one on the 14th in the first round against Colin Montgomerie. In a tight match where the Scot was coming back into the picture, the American's crisply struck seven-iron used the contours of the green to perfection, rolling from the right hand edge into the hole. Montgomerie nearly repeated the feat for an outrageous half but the perfect shot gave McCarron the impetus for victory and a foundation from which to build his route to the final.

feat against Brad Faxon in the quarter-finals. Unfortunately for the Spaniard, it was only enough on that occasion to square the match, Faxon's 18 foot birdie putt at the 20th hole eventually bringing home the spoils.

From the way the seeds were scattered, it looked odds-on the final would be between two lower-ranked players and so it proved. Kevin Sutherland, the 62nd seed and McCarron, the 45th seed, had both grown up in nearby Sacramento and played junior golf together. They met in a High School Championship Match in 1982 and on that occasion Sutherland's audacious back nine saw him come from behind to win.

He mounted another rearguard action to win the rematch 20 years later, too. McCarron, who bogeyed the last to lose the chance of a play-off in the Nissan Open in Los Angeles the week before, scored better, was more accurate statistically and was not behind until the 33rd hole. However the most telling statistic was that Sutherland was ahead on the final green.

Sutherland had, a week earlier, taken to using the claw putting style, favoured by Chris DiMarco and Calcavecchia, in which the

the course

Laid out in the base of a canyon, the South Course at La Costa Resort and Spa is known primarily for its length. The last four holes measure nearly one mile and when played into the wind feel more like two.

left hand is placed on top of the shaft and the first three fingers of the right hand are placed on the side. It looked ungainly but it worked. The method saved Sutherland time and time again as he recovered from his wayward driving with a wondrous short game. One hole perfectly summed up the final, the 27th. Sutherland was in the rough from the tee, still in the rough after his second shot, played his third from beneath the branch of a tree before holing an eight foot putt for a birdie that McCarron could not match.

For 37 year old Sutherland it was his first important win after seven seasons on the US PGA Tour and, at US $1 million, far and away his biggest ever cheque. Given the success of his putting method, he had, literally, clawed his way to victory.

John Hopkins

José Maria Olazábal

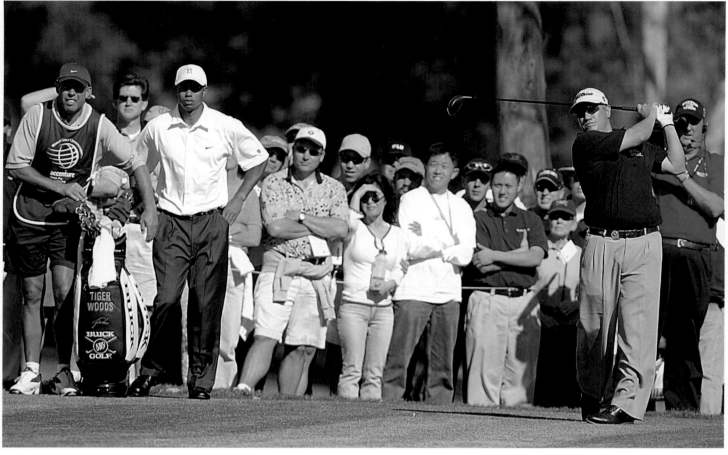

Tiger Woods and Peter O'Malley

final results

La Costa Resort and Spa · Carlsbad · California · USA
February 20 - 24 · 2002 · Par 72 · 7022 yards · 6423 metres

WINNER
KEVIN SUTHERLAND

RUNNER-UP
SCOTT McCARRON

CONSOLATION MATCH
BRAD FAXON beat
PAUL AZINGER
at 19th hole

McCarron 1 hole   Sutherland 1 hole

Sutherland 1 hole

PRIZE MONEY
Champion €1,145,476
Runner-Up €630,012
Third Place €515,464
Fourth Place €412,317
Quarter Finalists €200,458
Third Round €97,365
Second Round €63,001
First Round €31,500

Left half of draw

- 1 Tiger Woods
- **64 Peter O'Malley** — O'Malley 2 & 1
- 32 Nick Price
- **33 Angel Cabrera** — Price 2 & 1
  - Price 2 & 1
- 16 Scott Verplank
- 49 Frank Lickliter — Verplank 3 & 2
- 17 Bob Estes
- 48 Stuart Appleby — Estes 1 hole
  - Estes 20th hole
  - Estes 1 hole
- 8 Davis Love III
- **57 Phillip Price** — Love III 2 & 1
- 25 Paul Azinger
- 40 Jesper Parnevik — Azinger 1 hole
  - Azinger 1 hole
- **9 Vijay Singh**
- 56 Toru Taniguchi — Singh 3 & 2
- **24 Michael Campbell**
- **41 Niclas Fasth** — Fasth 2 & 1
  - Fasth 3 & 2
- **4 Sergio Garcia**
- 61 Lee Janzen — Garcia 3 & 2
- 29 Stewart Cink
- 36 Charles Howell III — Howell III 4 & 3
  - Garcia 1 hole
- 13 Mike Weir
- **52 Paul Lawrie** — Weir 3 & 2
- **20 Colin Montgomerie**
- 45 Scott McCarron — McCarron 2 & 1
  - McCarron 1 hole
- **5 Ernie Els**
- 60 Jeff Sluman — Els 4 & 3
- 28 Tom Lehman
- 37 Hal Sutton — Lehman 2 &1
  - Lehman 19th hole
- **12 Darren Clarke**
- 53 Matt Gogel — Gogel 2 & 1
- 21 Scott Hoch
- 44 Steve Lowery — Lowery 5 & 4
  - Gogel 20th hole

Later rounds (left):
- Estes 1 hole
- Azinger 20th hole
- Fasth 3 & 2
- McCarron 1 hole
- Lehman 4 &3
- Azinger 2 &1
- McCarron 4 & 3

Right half of draw

- Phil Mickelson 2
- John Cook 63 — Cook 3 & 2
- Shingo Katayama 31
- **Lee Westwood 34** — Westwood 3 & 2
  - Cook 1 hole
- Bernhard Langer 15
- **Adam Scott 50** — Scott 2 & 1
- Kenny Perry 18
- Brad Faxon 47 — Faxon 7 & 6
  - Faxon 3 & 2
- **Retief Goosen 7**
- Bill Mayfair 58 — Goosen 4 & 3
- **José Maria Olazábal 26**
- Justin Leonard 39 — Olazábal 1 hole
  - Olazábal 1 hole
- Chris DiMarco 10
- Steve Stricker 55 — DiMarco 3 & 2
- Mark Calcavecchia 23
- Jerry Kelly 42 — Calcavecchia 3 & 2
  - Calcavecchia 2 & 1
- David Duval 3
- Kevin Sutherland 52 — Sutherland 20th hole
- **Paul McGinley 30**
- Joe Durant 35 — McGinley 5 & 4
  - Sutherland 2 & 1
- Jim Furyk 14
- Billy Andrade 51 — Furyk 20th hole
- Toshimitsu Izawa 19
- **Pierre Fulke 46** — Izawa 4 & 3
  - Furyk 3 & 1
- David Toms 6
- Rory Sabbatini 59 — Toms 1 hole
- Rocco Mediate 27
- **John Daly 38** — Mediate 5 & 4
  - Toms 1 hole
- **Padraig Harrington 11**
- Steve Flesch 54 — Flesch 3 & 2
- Robert Allenby 22
- Kirk Triplett 43 — Triplett 3 & 2
  - Flesch 3 & 2

Later rounds (right):
- Faxon 20th hole
- Olazábal 2 holes
- Faxon 3 & 2
- Sutherland 4 & 3
- Sutherland 3 & 2
- Toms 1 hole

NB: Players in bold denote European Tour Members

MILLENNIUM
HOTELS AND RESORTS

MILLENNIUM HOTELS
COPTHORNE HOTELS

Late Escapes
Start your holiday before you fly.

The Copthorne Hotels in Gatwick are located in the heart of the Sussex countryside. They are only minutes away from Gatwick Airport, yet set in such tranquil and picturesque surroundings it's hard to imagine. These two hotels, just minutes from one another, offer the perfect facilities and accommodation, for the start of a holiday or a relaxing break.

The Copthorne Hotel London Gatwick is built around a 16th century farmhouse and has maintained all of its traditional charm. In the winter, enjoy the blazing fires and in the summer enjoy a stroll around the lake and the 100 acres of woodland and landscape Garden.

The Copthorne Hotel Effingham Park Gatwick is a fine modern building with its own nine-hole golf course. If you enjoy the golf club feel with its tranquil atmosphere and refined taste, you'll appreciate this hotel for either a quick stopover or a more relaxed weekend break.

Both hotels have superb leisure facilities including indoor swimming pools to help you get into the holiday mood or to aid relaxation after a stressful meeting, and with an airport shuttle bus service available, you can still be at the airport in minutes.

Why stay on the runway when you can escape to a little piece of luxury?

PARK AND FLY
Rates from £79.00
Reservations 0870 8900 237

Caltex Singapore Masters
flying high

Arjun Atwal

Situated under the flightpath to Changi Airport, Laguna National Golf and Country Club could hardly have provided a more appropriate setting for Arjun Atwal's first victory on The European Tour International Schedule. For, as the latest in a seemingly endless series of planes briefly disturbed the tranquil surroundings as they came in to land, Atwal could contemplate on a career that had suddenly taken off.

What is more, the manner of his triumph suggested that the 28 year old from Calcutta will not face being grounded. Indeed he is now poised to join the ranks of the established high-flyers on The European Tour.

If that sounds like a flight of fancy, it is worthwhile recalling his assured performance over the final two days, and Sunday in particular, and a confidence and self-belief which never wavered, yet equally never veered into arrogance. It was, after all, only Atwal's 18th European Tour event, but he made no secret of his confidence about becoming the first Indian golfer to win on The European Tour International Schedule.

"I expected to win the way I was playing," he said. "I was in contention in the dunhill championship after three rounds and up there after two rounds in the Bell's South African Open in Durban.

"I also led with nine to play in the London Myanmar Open on the Asian PGA Tour two weeks before Singapore and with three to play in the Hero Honda Masters the week before. I expected to win on The European Tour but not so quickly, but I'll definitely take it. It feels great and it's quite an achievement to be the first Indian golfer to win on The European Tour International Schedule."

Quite an achievement, indeed, and one which could do wonders for the game in India, where Atwal learned his craft at Royal Calcutta after being encouraged, at the age of 14, to take up the game by his father Bindi, whom he cites as the most important influence in his career.

Perhaps the main significance of Atwal's five stroke victory will be to persuade young players in India that it is possible to make it at the highest level, even if it takes the years of dedication and single-mindedness that saw Atwal quit college in Orlando in his final year when he felt the coach who had recruited him was not giving him the support he needed.

"Hopefully my win will do wonders for Indian golf," he added. "We have had a bunch of guys winning on the Asian PGA Tour but to do so on The European Tour is a whole different ball game. It will show all the young kids, who have started playing seriously in

Richard Green

the course

A typical Pete Dye layout, the Masters course at Laguna National Golf and Country Club features water on 12 holes and long expanses of sand, demanding a thoughtful approach and unrelenting accuracy. The par threes are particularly testing, with both the eighth and 17th requiring long irons into greens surrounded by water on three sides. Elsewhere, it is essential to find the right part of the fairway for the best approach to small greens, where leaving an uphill putt is the preferred option.

Anders Hansen

round leader Nick O'Hern, who had established a new course record with his eight under par 64 on Thursday, hours after Christophe Pottier had set a seemingly unbeatable target of 65.

One stroke clear of O'Hern at the start of the final day, Atwal's victory was never in doubt after he birdied the fifth and seventh to move three shots clear. A further birdie on the ninth, followed almost instantly by a bogey up ahead from nearest challenger Richard Green, left Atwal five clear and coasting to the title.

India, and are thinking of turning professional, that there is a future in golf for them."

Atwal's immediate future is secure, with a two year exemption giving him the luxury of picking and choosing his events, and forgetting all about making another visit to The European Tour Qualifying School from where he graduated 15th in November 2001.

The pressures endured at the San Roque Club and at Real Club de Golf, Sotogrande, no doubt prepared Atwal, who speaks with an American accent after studying in New York and Orlando, for the rigours of the final round at Laguna National Golf and Country Club.

Going into the sixth round at The European Tour Qualifying School Finals, Atwal was by no means certain of earning his card but fired a closing 68, a score he matched in the equally nerve-wracking denouement in Singapore.

By then all eyes were on the young Indian, who had gone unobtrusively about his business with rounds of 70 and 69, before a best of the day 67 on Saturday saw him overhaul first and second

shot of the week

ARJUN ATWAL India

A shot of Arjun Atwal's own choosing, his approach to the ninth on Sunday that set up a birdie which took him five shots clear. "I think the second shot to the ninth was the key," said the Champion. "I had 185 yards to the flag into a right-to-left head wind. With the pin where it was, (tucked close to the edge of the green which is surrounded by a bunker and then water) it was tough to get to but I hit a five iron to 18 inches. It was the perfect shot. After that I knew it would be okay."

Nick O'Hern

Another birdie on the 11th stretched the cushion still further, and even a run of four birdies in a row from the 11th by Nick Faldo could not put a serious dent in the deficit. Faldo bogeyed the treacherous par three 17th, with its green almost completely surrounded by water, to drop back to third place behind the left-handed Green, leaving Atwal to indulge in some plane-spotting as he parred the last seven holes on his way to victory.

Fittingly, for a joint-sanctioned event between The European Tour and the Davidoff Tour, Atwal has a foot in both camps, having won three events on the Asian circuit, including the Wills Indian Open in 1999 at his home course Royal Calcutta.

But his future looks like being in Europe, with a London base on the agenda to cut down on those transatlantic journeys, leaving his career as the only thing taking off.

Phil Casey

final results

Laguna National Golf and Country Club · Singapore
February 21 - 24 · 2002 · Par 72 · 7112 yards · 6504 metres

Pos.	Name		Rd1	Rd2	Rd3	Rd4	Total	Par	Prize Money Euro	£
1	Arjun ATWAL	Ind	70	69	67	68	274	-14	171855.90	104806.16
2	Richard GREEN	Aus	69	72	68	70	279	-9	114536.20	69849.79
3	Nick FALDO	Eng	68	69	73	70	280	-8	64536.16	39357.32
4	Thavorn WIRATCHANT	Thai	73	69	72	67	281	-7	47628.93	29046.46
	Ted PURDY	USA	69	69	73	70	281	-7	47628.93	29046.46
6	Chris WILLIAMS	Eng	67	71	73	71	282	-6	28969.11	17666.78
	Richard S JOHNSON	Swe	72	70	69	71	282	-6	28969.11	17666.78
	James KINGSTON	SA	70	70	72	70	282	-6	28969.11	17666.78
	Jim JOHNSON	USA	69	67	72	74	282	-6	28969.11	17666.78
10	Eduardo ROMERO	Arg	69	71	75	68	283	-5	17054.51	10400.68
	Andrew PITTS	USA	73	69	73	68	283	-5	17054.51	10400.68
	Stephen LEANEY	Aus	70	71	74	68	283	-5	17054.51	10400.68
	Gaurav GHEI	Ind	69	70	74	70	283	-5	17054.51	10400.68
	Nick O'HERN	Aus	64	71	72	76	283	-5	17054.51	10400.68
	Anthony KANG	R.Kor	69	73	71	70	283	-5	17054.51	10400.68
	Unho PARK	Aus	67	73	74	69	283	-5	17054.51	10400.68
17	Charlie WI	R.Kor	70	67	72	75	284	-4	13917.54	8487.60
18	Anders HANSEN	Den	71	72	72	70	285	-3	11894.34	7253.75
	Chris GANE	Eng	71	69	74	71	285	-3	11894.34	7253.75
	Patrik SJÖLAND	Swe	73	70	70	72	285	-3	11894.34	7253.75
	Henrik NYSTROM	Swe	71	72	71	71	285	-3	11894.34	7253.75
	Christopher HANELL	Swe	69	69	75	72	285	-3	11894.34	7253.75
	Brett RUMFORD	Aus	67	74	72	72	285	-3	11894.34	7253.75
	Sushi ISHIGAKI	Jpn	72	68	69	76	285	-3	11894.34	7253.75
	Terry PILKADARIS	Aus	70	72	70	73	285	-3	11894.34	7253.75
26	Stephen DODD	Wal	71	70	73	72	286	-2	9948.47	6067.06
	Ricardo GONZALEZ	Arg	71	71	75	69	286	-2	9948.47	6067.06
	Prayad MARKSAENG	Thai	68	71	73	74	286	-2	9948.47	6067.06
	Brad KENNEDY	Aus	70	73	70	73	286	-2	9948.47	6067.06
30	Mark MOULAND	Wal	73	70	73	71	287	-1	8170.11	4982.54
	Maarten LAFEBER	Hol	67	76	70	74	287	-1	8170.11	4982.54
	Mardan MAMAT	Sing	67	75	74	71	287	-1	8170.11	4982.54
	Jean VAN DE VELDE	Fr	67	75	71	74	287	-1	8170.11	4982.54
	Jyoti RANDHAWA	Ind	67	75	74	71	287	-1	8170.11	4982.54
	Grant HAMERTON	Eng	70	70	74	70	287	-1	8170.11	4982.54
	Bradley DREDGE	Wal	69	72	73	73	287	-1	8170.11	4982.54
	Thongchai JAIDEE	Thai	67	74	71	75	287	-1	8170.11	4982.54
38	Lian-Wei ZHANG	PRC	69	74	69	76	288	0	6804.13	4149.49
	Mike CUNNING	USA	67	70	77	74	288	0	6804.13	4149.49
	Ignacio GARRIDO	Sp	72	70	74	72	288	0	6804.13	4149.49
	Ter-Chang WANG	C.Tai	67	71	82	68	288	0	6804.13	4149.49
42	Peter SENIOR	Aus	72	69	74	74	289	1	5773.20	3520.78
	Raphaël JACQUELIN	Fr	73	70	73	73	289	1	5773.20	3520.78
	Carlos RODILES	Sp	66	72	72	79	289	1	5773.20	3520.78
	Steen TINNING	Den	68	72	76	73	289	1	5773.20	3520.78
	Gary CLARK	Eng	72	66	77	74	289	1	5773.20	3520.78
	Daniel CHOPRA	Swe	71	71	74	73	289	1	5773.20	3520.78
48	Peter HANSON	Swe	71	69	79	71	290	2	4536.09	2766.33
	Andrew MARSHALL	Eng	72	70	73	75	290	2	4536.09	2766.33
	Yu-Shu HSIEH	C.Tai	71	71	74	74	290	2	4536.09	2766.33
	Søren HANSEN	Den	71	69	78	72	290	2	4536.09	2766.33
	Des TERBLANCHE	SA	72	70	76	72	290	2	4536.09	2766.33
	David DRYSDALE	Scot	71	72	72	75	290	2	4536.09	2766.33
54	Chia-Yuh HONG	C.Tai	72	73	77	69	291	3	3505.16	2137.62
	Paul BROADHURST	Eng	70	72	75	74	291	3	3505.16	2137.62
	Mikael LUNDBERG	Swe	69	74	73	75	291	3	3505.16	2137.62
	Simon DYSON	Eng	70	73	70	78	291	3	3505.16	2137.62
58	Christophe POTTIER	Fr	65	74	74	79	292	4	2835.05	1728.96
	Stephen SCAHILL	NZ	73	70	75	74	292	4	2835.05	1728.96
	Keng-Chi LIN	Taiwan	69	71	76	76	292	4	2835.05	1728.96
	Danny ZARATE	Phil	72	71	73	76	292	4	2835.05	1728.96
	Wen-Chong LIANG	PRC	74	69	74	75	292	4	2835.05	1728.96
	Harmeet KAHLON	Ind	69	71	77	75	292	4	2835.05	1728.96
64	Robert-Jan DERKSEN	Hol	71	72	76	74	293	5	2422.68	1477.47
	Madasaamy MURUGIAH	Sing	69	74	76	74	293	5	2422.68	1477.47
66	Ross BAIN	Scot	71	72	76	75	294	6	2061.86	1257.42
	Chawalit PLAPHOL	Thai	70	72	78	74	294	6	2061.86	1257.42
	David PARK	Wal	70	72	78	74	294	6	2061.86	1257.42
	Lucas PARSONS	Aus	73	70	70	81	294	6	2061.86	1257.42
	Ted OH	R.Kor	68	74	75	77	294	6	2061.86	1257.42
	Shigimasa HIGAKI	Jpn	67	74	75	78	294	6	2061.86	1257.42

Carlsberg Malaysian Open Royal Selangor Golf Club · Kuala Lumpur · Malays

seventh heaven

the course

Royal Selangor Golf Club was built in 1893 and lies in the heart of Kuala Lumpur. The course is laid with cow grass, a broad leafed type of grass new to many European Tour players. The tree-lined fairways ensured players had to plot their way round the course, shaping shots both left and right to give themselves the best angle for their approaches.

Alastair Forsyth

Carlsberg Malaysian Open

In the shadow of the world's highest building, Alastair Forsyth stood tall to win the Carlsberg Malaysian Open and put his career firmly back in the ascendancy.

Royal Selangor Golf Club is dwarfed by the imposing twin Petronas Towers in Kuala Lumpur, which stand a mighty 452 metres high and taller than any other man-made structure in the world, but after four glorious days all eyes were focused on the towering performance of Forsyth.

It is said the toughest way to win a tournament is from the front but that is exactly what Forsyth achieved in his wire-to-wire victory. The Carlsberg Malaysian Open, however, was merely the conclusion to a saga that had seen the Scot's promising career falter before roaring back into life.

Miguel Angel Martin

After winning the 1999 European Tour Qualifying School Finals, Forsyth had the world at his feet as he set out on The European Tour International Schedule. His rookie season in 2000 started superbly as he finished third in the Heineken Classic and led at the halfway stage of the Brazil Rio de Janeiro 500 Years Open after rounds of 65 and 62. Those performances and top ten finishes in the Dubai Desert Classic and the Scottish PGA Championship kept him at the forefront of the race for the Sir Henry Cotton Rookie of the Year Award until Ian Poulter pipped him at the post by winning the Atlanet Italian Open. Nevertheless, he finished a highly creditable 46th on the Volvo Order of Merit.

The following season however, he had a string of disappointing performances and found himself in 116th position, one place outside the top 115 who gained access to the majority of the tournaments in 2002. Though he lost his card by the narrowest of margins, Forsyth received an invitation to the Carlsberg Malaysian Open and took full advantage.

Ian Woosnam

Forsyth always knew he possessed the skill to take such a chance, and he did so with style in the soaring temperatures and 95 per cent humidity of Malaysia. His career was not only back on track after four stirring rounds, but with his win he also left with a cheque for 184,366 euro (£112,894) in addition to something he valued all the more - a two year exemption for The European Tour.

From the outset he was the man to beat as he posted a course record 63, eight under par, in the opening round to share the lead with England's Barry Lane. He was equally impressive on the second day, carding a 65 to lead by a shot from Spain's Miguel Angel Martin. A third round of 69 helped him extend that lead to two shots over another Spaniard, Ignacio Garrido, with Australian Stephen Leaney and Martin three behind.

When Forsyth three putted the first green on the final day his lead was down to one stroke, but he steadied the ship and after the ninth, where he hit a magnificent eight iron to a foot, he was three strokes clear of the field. A maiden triumph was within his grasp, but just when it looked as if he would cruise to victory, the tide seemingly turned against him. Bogeys on the tenth, 11th and 14th holes, as Leaney birdied the tenth and 15th, cost Forsyth the lead for the first time.

With three holes to play the Scot was two strokes behind but just as all seemed lost, he found something from deep within to claw

Stephen Leaney

himself back. A birdie on the 16th, where he hit a wedge to three feet, closed the gap to one and when he holed a testing ten foot birdie putt on the 17th he was back on level terms with the Australian. With both players unable to convert 20 foot birdie

Ignacio Garrido

shot of the week

ALASTAIR FORSYTH Scotland

The penultimate shot of the week and one which set up Alastair Forsyth's maiden victory. Never before had Forsyth hit a nine iron 160 yards but after a perfect drive on the second hole of the sudden-death play-off that was exactly what he faced. He executed the shot perfectly, his ball nestling 15 feet from the pin from where he holed for a winning birdie three.

Whatever his thoughts were, he controlled them admirably to concentrate and stroke home the birdie putt to secure the title. The facts showed that Forsyth had become the sixth first time winner on The 2002 European Tour International Schedule and climbed to sixth on the Volvo Order of Merit. But really he was in seventh heaven.

Roddy Williams

chances on the final green, the contest moved into a sudden-death play-off.

Both players made regulation par fours at the first extra hole – the 462 yard 18th – and when they returned to the same hole moments later Forsyth hit the perfect drive down the middle before striking an outstanding nine iron to 15 feet.

What was going through his head as he stood over that putt one can only imagine. Four months earlier his career was at a crossroads. He was given a second chance in Malaysia but in the hours before that final putt he had the tournament almost won, then lost and now had the chance to win again.

Alex Cejka

Ricardo Gonzalez

final results

Royal Selangor Golf Club • Kuala Lumpur • Malaysia
February 28 - March 3 • 2002 • Par 71 • 6935 yards • 6341 metres

Pos.	Name		Rd1	Rd2	Rd3	Rd4	Total	Par	Prize Money Euro	£
1	Alastair FORSYTH	Scot	63	65	69	70	267	-17	184366.40	112894.21
2	Stephen LEANEY	Aus	67	67	66	67	267	-17	127041.00	77791.79
3	Alex CEJKA	Ger	68	65	70	65	268	-16	70743.26	43318.65
4	Miguel Angel MARTIN	Sp	66	63	71	70	270	-14	51333.11	31433.12
	Ignacio GARRIDO	Sp	65	67	67	71	270	-14	51333.11	31433.12
6	Ian WOOSNAM	Wal	68	69	66	68	271	-13	30167.80	18472.83
	Ricardo GONZALEZ	Arg	65	69	68	69	271	-13	30167.80	18472.83
	Des TERBLANCHE	SA	70	67	68	66	271	-13	30167.80	18472.83
	Prayad MARKSAENG	Thai	69	67	67	68	271	-13	30167.80	18472.83
	John BICKERTON	Eng	70	67	68	66	271	-13	30167.80	18472.83
11	Padraig HARRINGTON	Ire	70	67	66	69	272	-12	19050.72	11665.44
	Maarten LAFEBER	Hol	66	67	72	67	272	-12	19050.72	11665.44
	Arjun SINGH	Ind	67	67	70	68	272	-12	19050.72	11665.44
	Anthony KANG	R Kor	66	65	71	70	272	-12	19050.72	11665.44
15	Jyoti RANDHAWA	Ind	66	70	70	67	273	-11	16738.57	10249.63
16	Richard S JOHNSON	Swe	68	67	66	73	274	-10	15710.83	9620.31
	Brad KENNEDY	Aus	68	67	69	70	274	-10	15710.83	9620.31
18	Barry LANE	Eng	63	71	71	70	275	-9	14150.17	8664.66
	Christian PENA	USA	70	71	71	63	275	-9	14150.17	8664.66
	Joakim HAEGGMAN	Swe	72	65	68	70	275	-9	14150.17	8664.66
21	Andrew PITTS	USA	69	66	71	70	276	-8	12456.29	7627.44
	Carlos RODILES	Sp	67	69	69	71	276	-8	12456.29	7627.44
	Steen TINNING	Den	69	68	72	67	276	-8	12456.29	7627.44
	Henrik NYSTROM	Swe	71	69	68	68	276	-8	12456.29	7627.44
	Michael CAMPBELL	NZ	69	66	69	72	276	-8	12456.29	7627.44
	Ted PURDY	USA	71	68	68	69	276	-8	12456.29	7627.44
27	Eduardo ROMERO	Arg	68	70	66	73	277	-7	10400.80	6368.79
	Desvonde BOTES	SA	68	70	72	67	277	-7	10400.80	6368.79
	Jorge BERENDT	Arg	70	70	65	72	277	-7	10400.80	6368.79
	Andrew COLTART	Scot	69	68	71	69	277	-7	10400.80	6368.79
	Thongchai JAIDEE	Thai	73	68	69	67	277	-7	10400.80	6368.79
	Harmeet KAHLON	Ind	65	72	68	72	277	-7	10400.80	6368.79
33	Thomas LEVET	Fr	68	69	71	70	278	-6	8859.18	5424.80
	Philip GOLDING	Eng	66	67	73	72	278	-6	8859.18	5424.80
	Kim FELTON	Aus	69	70	68	71	278	-6	8859.18	5424.80
	Wei-Tze YEH	C.Tai	68	72	69	69	278	-6	8859.18	5424.80
	Daisuke MARUYAMA	Jpn	69	69	70	70	278	-6	8859.18	5424.80
38	Mike CUNNING	USA	69	65	69	76	279	-5	7603.04	4655.62
	Søren KJELDSEN	Den	71	69	69	70	279	-5	7603.04	4655.62
	Thavorn WIRATCHANT	Thai	66	72	67	74	279	-5	7603.04	4655.62
	Brett RUMFORD	Aus	69	72	70	68	279	-5	7603.04	4655.62
	Gary RUSNAK	USA	69	70	70	70	279	-5	7603.04	4655.62
	Wen-Chong LIANG	PRC	72	68	69	70	279	-5	7603.04	4655.62
44	Warren BENNETT	Eng	68	71	71	70	280	-4	5661.74	3466.89
	Lian-Wei ZHANG	PRC	68	69	71	72	280	-4	5661.74	3466.89
	Thammanoon SRIROJ	Thai	71	69	71	69	280	-4	5661.74	3466.89
	Nick O'HERN	Aus	67	71	72	70	280	-4	5661.74	3466.89
	Olle NORDBERG	Swe	73	67	71	69	280	-4	5661.74	3466.89
	Charlie WI	R Kor	72	69	68	71	280	-4	5661.74	3466.89
	Patrik SJÖLAND	Swe	68	70	70	72	280	-4	5661.74	3466.89
	Danny ZARATE	Phil	70	71	69	70	280	-4	5661.74	3466.89
	Christopher HANELL	Swe	69	70	67	74	280	-4	5661.74	3466.89
	Simon DYSON	Eng	69	70	70	71	280	-4	5661.74	3466.89
	Sushi ISHIGAKI	Jpn	68	69	73	70	280	-4	5661.74	3466.89
55	Robert-Jan DERKSEN	Hol	72	67	71	71	281	-3	4063.03	2487.94
	Kenny DRUCE	Aus	69	71	70	71	281	-3	4063.03	2487.94
	Chris WILLIAMS	Eng	70	71	72	68	281	-3	4063.03	2487.94
53	Chawalit PLAPHOL	Thai	68	73	68	73	282	-2	3434.96	2103.35
	Anders HANSEN	Den	69	71	71	71	282	-2	3434.96	2103.35
	Keng-Chi LIN	Taiwan	69	70	71	72	282	-2	3434.96	2103.35
	Periasamy GUNASAGARAN	Mal	70	68	73	71	282	-2	3434.96	2103.35
62	Mark MOULAND	Wal	72	69	69	73	283	-1	3092.38	1893.57
	Jarrod MOSELEY	Aus	66	73	72	72	283	-1	3092.38	1893.57
64	Olle KARLSSON	Swe	70	71	71	72	284	0	2806.89	1718.76
	Roger WESSELS	SA	70	69	72	73	284	0	2806.89	1718.76
	Jarmo SANDELIN	Swe	69	69	70	76	284	0	2806.89	1718.76
67	Wook-Soon KANG	R Kor	70	69	73	73	285	1	2516.84	1541.15
	Mark PILKINGTON	Wal	69	69	72	75	285	1	2516.84	1541.15
69	Chris GANE	Eng	69	72	69	76	286	2	2093.59	1281.98
	Craig KAMPS	SA	71	70	71	74	286	2	2093.59	1281.98
	Gerald ROSALES	Phil	71	70	72	73	286	2	2093.59	1281.98
72	Andrew MARSHALL	Eng	70	69	74	74	287	3	1708.50	1046.18
	Gregory HAVRET	Fr	69	70	76	72	287	3	1708.50	1046.18
74	Ahmad Dan BATEMAN	Can	71	69	70	78	288	4	1704.00	1043.42
75	Raphaël JACQUELIN	Fr	68	73	74	74	289	5	1701.00	1041.58
76	Peter SENIOR	Aus	71	70	73	76	290	6	1698.00	1039.75
	Scott KAMMANN	USA	71	70	72	77	290	6	1698.00	1039.75

Dubai Desert Classic Emirates Golf Club · Dubai

home and dry

The huge posters adorning the environs of the Emirates Golf Club suggested that Ernie Els was the man to beat in the Dubai Desert Classic. They were right, and it turned out that no one could.

Ernie Els

Dubai Desert Classic

After a frustrating 2001 season during which he found it difficult to win, the popular South African found that golf was suddenly fun again. In Dubai, although pushed by Sweden's Niclas Fasth, Els became the first golfer to win a second Desert Classic over the classic Karl Litton-designed Majlis course.

In the end the 'Big Easy' won by four shots and moved smoothly to the top of the Volvo Order of Merit. It was his fourth win in eight starts and earned him his tenth European Tour victory to go alongside the nine he has won in America. The victory also gave him back-to-back successes, for seven days earlier he had held off the last round challenge of Tiger Woods in the Genuity Classic at Doral Golf Resort & Spa on the US PGA Tour.

In just over two months Els had won in South Africa, in Australia, where at Royal Melbourne he triumphed in the Heineken Classic, a joint venture between The European Tour and the PGA Tour of Australasia, in America and now in The Gulf. Little wonder he was so enthusiastic about his golf.

Back in 1994 when he fired a brilliant record 61 at the Emirates to win the Dubai Desert Classic by six shots, his winning total was 20 under par. This time he was 16 under the card but that may well have represented better golf on the toughened-up course. Els was the only player to fire four rounds in the 60s and took particular delight in finally ending a jinx which had seen him fail to break 70 in the last round on five previous visits.

He jetted in with wife Liezel in their newly-leased private plane and looked the winner from the moment he stepped onto the course. His victory was a hugely popular one.

Four players have won the title leading from wire-to-wire but Els did not manage to do that. His opening 68 was one shot behind two Scandinavians - defending Champion Thomas Björn, who admitted his game was still rusty after a lengthy lay-off through injury, and Sweden's Robert Karlsson. Neither Björn nor Karlsson would maintain a challenge but Els did, remaining a shot behind Korean Charlie Wi, who snatched the lead at halfway.

Wi, who lives in California, is a rising star. He won three times on the Davidoff Tour in 2001 and finished second behind Thongchai Jaidee on the Tour's 2001 Order of Merit. Although he grew up in America and earned a degree in child psychology at the University of California at Berkeley, his hope is that before long he will have the chance to represent South Korea in the World Golf Championships - EMC^2 World Cup.

Niclas Fasth

The former first team All-American - whose team mates included Tiger Woods - had his own supporters club in Dubai . They were thrilled to see him fire a second round 67 for a nine under par 135 but with two rounds to go, he was only too well aware of the threat posed by Els.

The two-time US Open Champion retained his second place ahead of England's John Bickerton, who played despite nearly pulling out because of a wrist injury, and Fasth, who had dropped just one shot in two days. Els did so by hitting a candidate for Shot of the Year - a brilliant 213 yard four iron second from the sand through the trees and over the water at the 18th from where he holed from 35 feet for an outrageous eagle three. Caddie Ricci Roberts said: "I tried to dissuade him from going for the green but he was happy with the lie and decided that it was worth the gamble. Even if it had gone wrong and cost him shots he reckoned he had two more days to recover from it. I never fail to be amazed by what Ernie can do."

As Wi faltered with a 77 on day three, Els moved smoothly into a three shot lead over Fasth, who again dropped his only shot of the round at the 17th, with the self coached Swede Carl Pettersson, who lives in North Carolina where he attended the State

Charlie Wi

University, two shots further adrift. Pettersson, whose best finish during his rookie season in 2001 was runner-up in the Open de Argentina, fired a third round 65 which turned out to be the best round of the week.

the course

At 7185 yards, the lengthened Emirates course, designed by Karl Litton, has always been a tough test which, since 1989, has produced, a series of top class winners. There is the wind to contend with, too, either off the Gulf or from the desert, and this year the rough was graded. The grass was not longer but it was thicker, especially around the greens. It put an added premium on a player's ability to get up and down - a point illustrated by the fact that Ernie Els, although one of the game's longest hitters, also happens to have a razor-sharp short game.

shot of the week

ERNIE ELS South Africa

Norwegian Henrik Bjornstad hit the most lucrative shot of the week - a six iron into the hole with one bounce at the short seventh in the final round to win a £40,000 bonus from Emirates. But the shot that takes the prize, and the one that will long be remembered, is Ernie Els's 213 yard second at the 18th on the second day. He was fortunate with the lie in the sand that enabled him to get a four iron to the ball, but he had to bend it left through a narrow gap with little or no margin for error. "I had just a 30 per cent chance of making the green but having done that and holed the 35 footer for an eagle I rate the shot one of the best I have ever played," he said.

He ended by taking seven and Els, with a brilliant birdie at the testing ninth, went into the easier back stretch with a comfortable four shot advantage. Although Fasth kept Els on his toes by making birdies at the 12th and 13th, the end came for the Swede when he pushed another drive into the sand at the 16th. Although he made a hard-worked bogey five, Els made birdie three and that was that. In the end Fasth deservedly took second place but only by one shot from Pettersson, whose 65-69 was the best of the weekend scoring. Pettersson said: "This was a positive weekend for me. I really enjoyed getting into contention; playing with the leading groups. It is something I want to do more often. I feel my game gets better the closer I get to the top."

Ryder Cup Captain Sam Torrance, starting his 32nd year on The European Tour only weeks after keyhole surgery for a knee cartilege problem, finished joint 12th with, among others, 22 year old Amateur Champion and Walker Cup player Michael Hoey, a former winner of the Emirates Amateur title. Hoey would move on to play in the Masters Tournament, missing the cut by only one shot, and after Augusta he turned professional.

Sam Torrance

Fasth enjoys the big occasion. He proved that when finishing second to David Duval in the 2001 Open Golf Championship at Royal Lytham & St Annes and on the final day in Dubai he came out determined to upset the pre-tournament predictions that Els would stroll to success. After just seven holes, played surprisingly in rain showers, he had caught the South African, only to see his challenge falter after a pushed drive into the desert scrub at the eighth, one of the most difficult holes all week.

But the week belonged to Els. Playing his part undoubtedly was psychologist Jos Vanstiphout, who was involved, too, in Retief Goosen's 2001 US Open Championship win. "Retief introduced me to Jos who has made me more positive," said Els. "You have to believe you can do it and trust yourself. Above all you must never let yourself forget that despite all the extra prize money on offer these days, making it all so much more competitive, golf is a game for gentlemen."

Wise words from one of the true gentleman of golf who could not help but poke gentle fun at Tournament Director Mike Stewart at the official prize giving after receiving the huge coffee pot trophy from Sheikh Ahmed bin Saeed Al Maktoum, President of Dubai Civil Aviation and Chairman of Emirates. "I've played many events with Mike as Tournament Director and it has usually rained," said Els. "They don't normally have rain in Dubai in March so I thought I would have a dry week, but I was wrong!"

Rain might have fallen on the desert that final day, but Els, the man with the sunny disposition, was home...and dry.

Renton Laidlaw

John Bickerton

final results

Emirates Golf Club • Dubai
March 7-10 • 2002 • Par 72 • 7185 yards • 6572 metres

Pos.	Name		Rd1	Rd2	Rd3	Rd4	Total	Par	Prize Money Euro	£
1	Ernie ELS	SA	68	68	67	69	272	-16	273335.70	166660.00
2	Niclas FASTH	Swe	68	69	69	70	276	-12	182229.30	111110.00
3	Carl PETTERSSON	Swe	70	73	65	69	277	-11	102669.00	62600.00
4	Brian DAVIS	Eng	71	70	71	67	279	-9	82004.00	50000.00
5	Charlie WI	Rep.Kor	68	67	77	69	281	-7	63471.09	38700.00
	Gary EVANS	Eng	70	71	72	68	281	-7	63471.09	38700.00
7	Andrew OLDCORN	Scot	75	66	69	72	282	-6	37984.25	23160.00
	Mathias GRÖNBERG	Swe	72	70	71	69	282	-6	37984.25	23160.00
	Darren CLARKE	N.Ire	72	73	68	69	282	-6	37984.25	23160.00
	Bradley DREDGE	Wal	74	70	69	69	282	-6	37984.25	23160.00
	Simon DYSON	Eng	71	68	73	70	282	-6	37984.25	23160.00
12	Anders FORSBRAND	Swe	74	66	75	68	283	-5	24320.04	14828.57
	Sam TORRANCE	Scot	68	71	75	69	283	-5	24320.04	14828.57
	Klas ERIKSSON	Swe	72	74	66	71	283	-5	24320.04	14828.57
	Søren KJELDSEN	Den	74	70	69	70	283	-5	24320.04	14828.57
	Paul BROADHURST	Eng	69	70	71	73	283	-5	24320.04	14828.57
	Rolf MUNTZ	Hol	70	75	67	71	283	-5	24320.04	14828.57
	Greg OWEN	Eng	71	70	70	72	283	-5	24320.04	14828.57
	Michael HOEY (AM)	N.Ire	74	68	70	71	283	-5		
20	Padraig HARRINGTON	Ire	70	75	68	71	284	-4	18603.19	11342.86
	Raphaël JACQUELIN	Fr	71	71	68	74	284	-4	18603.19	11342.86
	Gregory HAVRET	Fr	69	71	74	70	284	-4	18603.19	11342.86
	Olle KARLSSON	Swe	68	73	73	70	284	-4	18603.19	11342.86
	Pierre FULKE	Swe	69	73	74	68	284	-4	18603.19	11342.86
	Ricardo GONZALEZ	Arg	71	67	74	72	284	-4	18603.19	11342.86
	Thomas BJÖRN	Den	67	73	71	73	284	-4	18603.19	11342.86
27	Richard GREEN	Aus	70	72	72	71	285	-3	15580.76	9500.00
	Richard BLAND	Eng	70	72	74	69	285	-3	15580.76	9500.00
	Fredrik JACOBSON	Swe	75	70	71	69	285	-3	15580.76	9500.00
	John BICKERTON	Eng	69	68	73	75	285	-3	15580.76	9500.00
	Thongchai JAIDEE	Thai	74	70	71	70	285	-3	15580.76	9500.00
32	Mark FOSTER	Eng	72	72	72	70	286	-2	12587.61	7675.00
	José Manuel LARA	Sp	71	70	74	71	286	-2	12587.61	7675.00
	Anders HANSEN	Den	72	72	74	68	286	-2	12587.61	7675.00
	Steve WEBSTER	Eng	74	70	73	69	286	-2	12587.61	7675.00
	Trevor IMMELMAN	SA	74	72	74	66	286	-2	12587.61	7675.00
	Søren HANSEN	Den	71	72	73	70	286	-2	12587.61	7675.00
	Robert KARLSSON	Swe	67	76	72	71	286	-2	12587.61	7675.00
	Lucas PARSONS	Aus	72	71	73	70	286	-2	12587.61	7675.00
40	Roger CHAPMAN	Eng	73	73	70	71	287	-1	10168.50	6200.00
	Nick FALDO	Eng	72	73	72	70	287	-1	10168.50	6200.00
	Barry LANE	Eng	73	73	71	70	287	-1	10168.50	6200.00
	Tom GILLIS	USA	75	71	72	69	287	-1	10168.50	6200.00
	Desvonde BOTES	SA	71	73	73	70	287	-1	10168.50	6200.00
	David CARTER	Eng	73	70	74	70	287	-1	10168.50	6200.00
46	Eduardo ROMERO	Arg	70	74	71	73	288	0	7544.37	4600.00
	Ian WOOSNAM	Wal	73	68	74	73	288	0	7544.37	4600.00
	Anthony WALL	Eng	70	70	74	74	288	0	7544.37	4600.00
	Jean HUGO	SA	73	71	72	72	288	0	7544.37	4600.00
	Phillip PRICE	Wal	73	71	72	72	288	0	7544.37	4600.00
	Roger WESSELS	SA	75	69	71	73	288	0	7544.37	4600.00
	Tobias DIER	Ger	72	68	75	73	288	0	7544.37	4600.00
	Nick DOUGHERTY	Eng	71	71	72	74	288	0	7544.37	4600.00
	Adam SCOTT	Aus	73	72	71	72	288	0	7544.37	4600.00
	Scott GARDINER	Aus	72	73	72	71	288	0	7544.37	4600.00
56	Sven STRÜVER	Ger	69	72	70	78	289	1	4899.74	2987.50
	Justin ROSE	Eng	72	71	72	74	289	1	4899.74	2987.50
	Carlos RODILES	Sp	72	70	70	77	289	1	4899.74	2987.50
	Gary EMERSON	Eng	74	71	71	73	289	1	4899.74	2987.50
	Ignacio GARRIDO	Sp	73	72	69	75	289	1	4899.74	2987.50
	David PARK	Wal	70	70	76	73	289	1	4899.74	2987.50
	Raymond RUSSELL	Scot	74	72	70	73	289	1	4899.74	2987.50
	Christopher HANELL	Swe	72	71	77	69	289	1	4899.74	2987.50
64	David HOWELL	Eng	74	69	72	75	290	2	3772.18	2300.00
	Ian POULTER	Eng	71	69	75	75	290	2	3772.18	2300.00
	Stephen DODD	Wal	70	76	73	71	290	2	3772.18	2300.00
	Stephen SCAHILL	NZ	70	74	73	73	290	2	3772.18	2300.00
	Johan SKOLD	Swe	72	74	70	74	290	2	3772.18	2300.00
69	Paul EALES	Eng	72	74	73	72	291	3	3198.16	1950.00
	Christophe POTTIER	Fr	73	73	77	68	291	3	3198.16	1950.00
71	Mårten OLANDER	Swe	70	72	77	73	292	4	3001.35	1830.00
72	Peter BAKER	Eng	74	71	73	75	293	5	2460.00	1499.93
73	Andrew PITTS	USA	73	71	77	73	294	6	2452.50	1495.35
	Jamie SPENCE	Eng	72	72	78	72	294	6	2452.50	1495.35
	Jarmo SANDELIN	Swe	71	73	80	70	294	6	2452.50	1495.35
	Markus BRIER	Aut	72	74	76	72	294	6	2452.50	1495.35
77	Marc FARRY	Fr	73	73	76	73	295	7	2442.00	1488.95
	Henrik BJORNSTAD	Nor	72	72	76	75	295	7	2442.00	1488.95
	Andrew BUTTERFIELD	Eng	70	76	72	77	295	7	2442.00	1488.95
80	Andrew COLTART	Scot	73	73	75	75	296	8	2436.00	1485.29
81	Ian HUTCHINGS	SA	73	71	76	77	297	9	2433.00	1483.46

pearl of wisdom

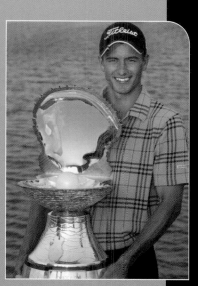

1	**Adam SCOTT** Aus		269	-19
2	**Nick DOUGHERTY** Eng		275	-13
	Jean-Francois REMESY Fr		275	-13
4	**John BICKERTON** Eng		277	-11
	Stephen GALLACHER Scot		277	-11
	Joakim HAEGGMAN Swe		277	-11
	Henrik NYSTRÖM Swe		277	-11
	Mark PILKINGTON Wal		277	-11
	Eduardo ROMERO Arg		277	-11
10	**Anders HANSEN** Den		278	-10
	David HOWELL Eng		278	-10

For Australian Adam Scott, victory in the fifth and most lucrative Qatar Masters to date was particularly rewarding. He not only took the first prize of 285,650 euro (£175,722) - more than double what Zimbabwe's Tony Johnstone had won the previous year - but also moved to 50th place in the Official World Golf Ranking to earn an eleventh hour place in The Players Championship at Sawgrass.

Adam Scott

There were other reasons, too, why the 21 year old, coached by Butch Harmon in America and his son Claude in Europe, was well pleased with his showing against the strongest field assembled in the history of the tournament at Doha Golf Club.

Although he had claimed his maiden European Tour success in the 2001 Alfred Dunhill Championship, he had failed to take advantage when afforded other winning opportunities during that season. In Qatar, however, there were, as most Australians would observe, "no worries." Leading by three shots going into the final day, a controlled and mature performance saw Scott win in the end by six, his 19 under par total of 269 just one short of the record low score for the tournament, established by Paul Lawrie in 1999.

In The 2001 Compass Group English Open he had entered the final round two shots clear of the field but shed three strokes in the first six holes, mistakes from which he never recovered. In Qatar there were no such errors. Seven straight pars in the final round steadied any nerves before sensational golf around the turn ended the tournament as a contest. At the short eighth, his pinpoint tee shot led to a birdie two before he spectacularly eagled the 634 yard ninth, holing a wedge shot from fully 132 yards out. Another birdie at the tenth and the destination of the first prize was a foregone conclusion.

Nick Dougherty

the course

By common consent, the course at Doha Golf Club had never been in better condition. It was a tribute to the hard work of the greenkeeping staff, led by golf course manager Ranald McNeil, who stayed behind to oversee the development of the course after having helped architect Peter Harradine with the construction. New grasses continue to improve the appearance aesthetically and its maintenance was helped by the arrival of state-of-the-art machinery.

The battle for second place, however, remained an intriguing sub-plot right to the end before English teenager Nick Dougherty and Frenchman Jean-Francois Remesy shared the runners-up spoils on 13 under par 275. They each earned 148,858 euro (£91,572), enough to guarantee them both their playing privileges for The 2003 European Tour International Schedule.

In a week when the younger players held the whip hand, the Qatar golf fans, mostly expatriates but with an ever increasing number of locals in the galleries, had a rare chance to see a golfing legend in action. Almost 45 years older than Scott but still fit as a fiddle, nine time Major winner Gary Player graced the scene on his first visit to the Gulf State.

On a course slightly longer than those he is used to on a weekly basis on the US Seniors Tour, the Black Knight missed the cut, which came at one under par, but stayed around for the weekend and spoke graciously at the prize giving about the new Champion and the tournament as a whole. Golf's ultimate global traveller – he has completed more than 12 million miles in his career – Player is hoping to be asked to design one of the two new courses in Qatar to cope with the expected expansion of tourism. His participation in the event will have its own rewards.

shot of the week

ADAM SCOTT Australia

Although Adam Scott's holed wedge for an eagle three at the ninth in the final round was a contender, the winner was the Champion's eagle two at the 15th, the toughest hole on the course, in round two. In the semi-rough from the tee, Scott produced a majestically struck five iron from 199 yards out which landed perfectly in the centre of the green before rolling 30 feet into the cup. It gave Scott the lead for the first time and he was never to relinquish it.

Formerly reliant on pearl-fishing, Qatar, about half the size of Wales and so flat that its highest point is just 130 feet above sea level, has few economic worries. The country, whose population has increased from 62,000 in 1965 to 750,000 in 2002, has not only oil but also owns the world's third largest natural gas field. Yet, with the move into the 21st Century, the importance of sport, and tourism, is not being missed. No doubt they have watched what has happened over the past 15 years in nearby Dubai.

The Qatar Masters is now well established on The European Tour International Schedule. The men's and women's professional tennis circuits make annual stops. There is sailing, cycling, motor cycling and soccer. In 2006 the Asian Games, with more than 40 sports including golf, will centre on Doha, a massive undertaking which the locals are looking forward to handling with considerable enthusiasm. Sport has assumed a new importance in the everyday life of Qatar with golf benefitting from a new Golf Academy at Doha Golf Club incorporating every modern teaching aid.

In the past, Andrew Coltart, Tony Johnstone, Paul Lawrie and Rolf Muntz have all picked up the unique trophy, an oyster shell with a golden pearl inside it. In Adam Scott, the tournament had unearthed another gem. During the week the Australian dropped only four shots and even if the predicted fierce Shamal winds did not materialise, the course, in its best ever condition, still provided a stiff test for a galaxy of international stars from more than 30 countries including Bahrain, who were represented by Hamad Mubarak, the recently crowned Dubai Amateur Champion.

Thongchai Jaidee and Charlie Wi, Number One and Two on the 2001 Davidoff Tour Order of Merit, were in the field, the South African and Australasian Tours were well represented and there were four Americans present one of whom, Charlie Hoffman from the Buy.com Tour, finished tied 12th. With prizemoney doubled, The European Tour's top players responded, too, including Colin Montgomerie, who made his first visit to Qatar and finished tied for 18th, and there were players from Argentina, Australia, Denmark, England, France, Holland, Scotland, South Africa, Spain, Sweden, the United States and Wales in that top 18 with Montgomerie on a superb international leader board.

Such a wonderful finish was in direct contrast to the start of the tournament which was delayed by fog for almost two hours on Thursday morning. When the mists did clear, Swedes Klas Eriksson and Joakim Haeggman and England's Mark Roe all shot 66. Scott was just one behind but moved in front by the end of the second day, helped by a fabulous eagle two at the 15th where he holed his five iron from 199 yards.

By Saturday night Scott was still three shots clear with Remesy, playing well despite a niggling back injury in second place. Stephen Gallacher, Miguel Angel Martin, Dougherty and Montgomerie shared third place one shot further adrift. Although several players carded sub-70 final rounds there was no stopping Scott whose new, more aggressive putting technique, did not let him down.

"What pleased me was that I remained so calm," said Scott. "In the past I was inclined to get a bit panicky but I remained more patient than I ever have when in contention and I always felt I was in complete control."

Renton Laidlaw

Anders Hansen

Jean-Francois Remesy

final results

Doha Golf Club · Qatar
March 14-17 · 2002 · Par 72 · 7110 yards · 6500 metres

Pos.	Name		Rd1	Rd2	Rd3	Rd4	Total	Par	Prize Money Euro	£
1	Adam SCOTT	Aus	67	66	69	67	269	-19	285650.50	175722.20
2	Jean-Francois REMESY	Fr	68	69	68	70	275	-13	148858.20	91572.36
	Nick DOUGHERTY	Eng	69	69	68	69	275	-13	148858.20	91572.36
4	Eduardo ROMERO	Arg	71	67	72	67	277	-11	58501.22	35987.91
	Joakim HAEGGMAN	Swe	66	73	72	66	277	-11	58501.22	35987.91
	Mark PILKINGTON	Wal	69	69	71	68	277	-11	58501.22	35987.91
	Henrik NYSTROM	Swe	69	72	67	69	277	-11	58501.22	35987.91
	John BICKERTON	Eng	69	70	68	70	277	-11	58501.22	35987.91
	Stephen GALLACHER	Scot	69	68	69	71	277	-11	58501.22	35987.91
10	David HOWELL	Eng	68	72	71	67	278	-10	32906.94	20243.20
	Anders HANSEN	Den	68	68	71	71	278	-10	32906.94	20243.20
12	Miguel Angel MARTIN	Sp	70	68	68	73	279	-9	25965.63	15973.15
	Peter FOWLER	Aus	70	69	69	71	279	-9	25965.63	15973.15
	José Manuel LARA	Sp	67	69	73	70	279	-9	25965.63	15973.15
	Søren HANSEN	Den	67	71	72	69	279	-9	25965.63	15973.15
	Benoit TEILLERIA	Fr	72	71	68	68	279	-9	25965.63	15973.15
	Charlie HOFFMAN	USA	70	73	69	67	279	-9	25965.63	15973.15
18	Ian WOOSNAM	Wal	69	69	70	72	280	-8	20338.32	12511.42
	Warren BENNETT	Eng	70	69	69	72	280	-8	20338.32	12511.42
	Trevor IMMELMAN	SA	70	72	67	71	280	-8	20338.32	12511.42
	Colin MONTGOMERIE	Scot	68	69	69	74	280	-8	20338.32	12511.42
	Ricardo GONZALEZ	Arg	69	72	70	69	280	-8	20338.32	12511.42
	Rolf MUNTZ	Hol	74	68	70	68	280	-8	20338.32	12511.42
24	Mark ROE	Eng	66	75	71	69	281	-7	17310.42	10648.77
	Charlie WI	R.Kor	69	70	72	70	281	-7	17310.42	10648.77
	Darren CLARKE	N.Ire	70	70	70	71	281	-7	17310.42	10648.77
	Bradley DREDGE	Wal	68	74	69	70	281	-7	17310.42	10648.77
	Christopher HANELL	Swe	75	67	69	70	281	-7	17310.42	10648.77
29	Tony JOHNSTONE	Zim	68	70	69	75	282	-6	14739.57	9067.27
	Ian GARBUTT	Eng	67	71	74	70	282	-6	14739.57	9067.27
	Diego BORREGO	Sp	73	69	68	72	282	-6	14739.57	9067.27
	Fredrik JACOBSON	Swe	70	73	73	66	282	-6	14739.57	9067.27
	Thongchai JAIDEE	Thai	69	70	72	71	282	-6	14739.57	9067.27
34	Santiago LUNA	Sp	68	71	72	72	283	-5	11997.32	7380.33
	Søren KJELDSEN	Den	70	71	69	73	283	-5	11997.32	7380.33

Pos.	Name		Rd1	Rd2	Rd3	Rd4	Total	Par	Prize Money Euro	£
	Stuart LITTLE	Eng	71	69	71	72	283	-5	11997.32	7380.33
	Carl SUNESON	Sp	73	70	68	72	283	-5	11997.32	7380.33
	Phillip PRICE	Wal	72	69	69	73	283	-5	11997.32	7380.33
	Gary ORR	Scot	69	69	73	72	283	-5	11997.32	7380.33
	Paul LAWRIE	Scot	71	72	68	72	283	-5	11997.32	7380.33
	Martin MARITZ	SA	69	71	71	72	283	-5	11997.32	7380.33
42	Des SMYTH	Ire	69	70	74	71	284	-4	9426.47	5798.83
	Christophe POTTIER	Fr	72	69	71	72	284	-4	9426.47	5798.83
	Stephen DODD	Wal	70	72	72	70	284	-4	9426.47	5798.83
	Robert COLES	Eng	69	73	73	69	284	-4	9426.47	5798.83
	Markus BRIER	Aut	70	73	67	74	284	-4	9426.47	5798.83
	Mikael LUNDBERG	Swe	72	70	70	72	284	-4	9426.47	5798.83
	Sam WALKER	Eng	68	72	73	71	284	-4	9426.47	5798.83
49	Klas ERIKSSON	Swe	66	70	74	75	285	-3	7198.39	4428.20
	Brian DAVIS	Eng	68	73	74	70	285	-3	7198.39	4428.20
	Raphaël JACQUELIN	Fr	71	72	70	72	285	-3	7198.39	4428.20
	Andrew COLTART	Scot	73	69	72	71	285	-3	7198.39	4428.20
	David CARTER	Eng	70	71	71	73	285	-3	7198.39	4428.20
	Matthew CORT	Eng	68	73	72	72	285	-3	7198.39	4428.20
55	Malcolm MACKENZIE	Eng	74	67	72	73	286	-2	5655.88	3479.30
	Richard BLAND	Eng	71	72	69	74	286	-2	5655.88	3479.30
	Carl PETTERSSON	Swe	74	68	73	71	286	-2	5655.88	3479.30
58	Mathias GRÖNBERG	Swe	70	70	74	73	287	-1	4884.62	3004.85
	Brett RUMFORD	Aus	70	73	75	69	287	-1	4884.62	3004.85
	Scott GARDINER	Aus	70	72	73	72	287	-1	4884.62	3004.85
	Kyle THOMPSON	USA	71	71	74	71	287	-1	4884.62	3004.85
62	Thomas LEVET	Fr	73	68	73	74	288	0	4284.76	2635.83
	Russell CLAYDON	Eng	70	68	76	74	288	0	4284.76	2635.83
	Iain PYMAN	Eng	73	69	71	75	288	0	4284.76	2635.83
65	Steve WEBSTER	Eng	70	72	74	74	290	2	3770.59	2319.53
	Erol SIMSEK	Ger	69	70	78	73	290	2	3770.59	2319.53
	Lucas PARSONS	Aus	72	70	71	77	290	2	3770.59	2319.53
68	Ian HUTCHINGS	SA	76	65	75	77	293	5	3342.11	2055.95
	Gustavo ROJAS	Arg	69	73	76	75	293	5	3342.11	2055.95
70	Gary EVANS	Eng	72	71	73	78	294	6	3130.73	1925.92

Madeira Island Open Santo da Serra · Madeira
high point

Diego Borrego

Compared with what had gone before, his moment of triumph now was a much more matter of fact affair. But then, it would have had to have been pretty spectacular to have surpassed his only other European Tour success, which had come - and a deep breath is needed here - in the Turespaña Masters Open Comunitat Valenciana Paradores de Turismo six years earlier. No, really.

There would have been time for Diego Borrego to have gone on a short holiday while waiting for his name to be announced back then, but it did not take José Maria Zamora, the Tournament Director, nearly as long to get to the point this time. Not that it mattered to Borrego. He would have been quite happy to wait as long as Zamora needed as long as he ended up with that precious trophy in his grasp.

Maarten Lafeber

His reward for a closing round of 69 and a total of 281, seven under par, was an exemption that would take him through the rest of the season and the whole of the following two. As a man who, for a while, had been in danger of losing his playing rights in 2001, it was at least arguable that freedom of The European Tour fairways until the last blow was struck in 2004 would mean even more to him in the long run than the 91,660 euro (£56,800) he won.

There was a neat confluence between past and present in the fact that Zamora was the man in the green blazer. The pair had partnered each other to the Spanish Doubles Championship 13 years before and the selfsame Official had been the Referee when Borrego won the charming mouthful in the first paragraph. No wonder Borrego suggested that he wouldn't mind taking Zamora round with him every week!

Borrego's victory was the culmination of another memorable week up the mountain at Santo da Serra. It might not be the easiest venue to reach on The European Tour International Schedule, requiring as it does a 20 mile journey on the wondrous Via Rapida that weaves its way through tunnels and over spidery-legged bridges from Funchal, the island's capital, and then a climb through countless hairpin bends to its lofty destination. But is it worth it when you get there? Oh yes, a thousand times yes.

David Drysdale

shot of the week

DIEGO BORREGO Spain

Not only the shot of the week but also the shot that effectively won the tournament for Diego Borrego. A five iron on the 15th it was, followed by an 18 foot putt for birdie. "I knew I could win from there," he said, and he was as good as his word.

Santo da Serra's altitude sometimes - indeed, more often than not - makes for meteorological conditions that are, to say the very least, interesting. Whether it is fog or low cloud that is the problem is a moot point, but it can wreak havoc with a Tournament Official's peace of mind, and this year was no exception.

This time it waited through two days of glorious sunshine until the third round before making its presence felt, but when it did, it had a salutary effect on the fortunes of more than one of the leading characters in the developing drama. None of them was affected more than Andrew Oldcorn.

Oldcorn, known affectionately by his peers as Bagpuss because of his alleged facial similarity to the eponymous animated feline favourite of children's television viewers back home, went into the tournament needing a high finish to displace Steve Webster from the coveted automatic qualifying places for the Great Britain and Ireland team for The Seve Trophy the following month.

For the better part of three rounds, Oldcorn was in there slugging. He had shared the lead after 36 holes on nine under par 135, thanks largely to a beautifully constructed second round 65. He was only one stroke adrift after 14 holes when day three was brought to a premature end, then had a double-bogey, bogey, par, bogey finish the next morning to mark a disconsolate 78 on his card. As a narrowly-foiled Ryder Cup candidate the previous year, Bagpuss had already missed out on the cream once; to fall short again on the last lap, as it were, would be cruel indeed.

It appeared he had, by closing with a 76. He finished in a tie for 18th and Webster, the little bantam-cock from the Midlands, tied for 23rd to apparently steal the honour for which they had been competing.

The story, however, had a happy ending for Oldcorn, if not for David Howell. The Englishman had made the team comfortably in sixth place in the Rankings only to miss out when he broke his arm in a fall. Howell's cloud featured a silver lining for Oldcorn - the Scot would take his place in Colin Montgomerie's team at Druids Glen after all.

Borrego, meanwhile, was serenely rising above such things. He had more straightforward aims - he wanted the victory, nothing less. He went into the final round three strokes off the lead held by Ivo Giner and Maarten Lafeber and slipped further in arrears when he three-putted the first.

the course

Santo da Serra is a hard physical test, angina-fodder for players and caddies alike. But what matters more than its heart-rending ascents is its examination of the shot-making abilities of those who take it on. As such, it is a test for the best - nobody has ever won over its vertiginous acres without deserving it.

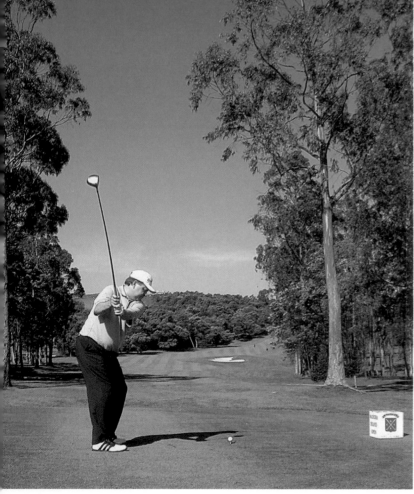

drew Oldcorn

That was the last error he was to make, however, and when Lafeber three-putted three times in four holes around the turn Borrego closed in on Giner, who was playing his first tournament of the year. The decisive moment came when Borrego birdied the 15th and, although Giner soon followed suit, it all boiled down to a four-foot par putt that would have put Giner into a play-off. He missed it.

Borrego had become only the second man to break 70 on the final day - Roger Winchester was the other, a 67 hauling him up from joint 22nd to fourth. The modest Spaniard's patience and fortitude had been tested by the strong swirling winds which made scoring desperately difficult, but he passed both examinations with honours to beat Giner and Lafeber by a shot.

A little while later, the journey back down the mountain was adorned by a rainbow and, whisper it not, even a small, infant sprinkling of something that had to be snow, so wispy and crystalline was it. Meanwhile, still up there among the peaks, was Diego Borrego. No matter what it was doing elsewhere, for him the sun was shining in all its glory.

Mel Webb

Madeira Island Open

Seve Ballesteros

final results
Santo da Serra · Madeira
March 21-24 · 2002 · Par 72 · 6664 yards · 6092 metres

Pos.	Name		Rd1	Rd2	Rd3	Rd4	Total	Par	Prize Money Euro	£
1	Diego BORREGO	Sp	72	68	72	69	281	-7	91660.00	56800.08
2	Maarten LAFEBER	Hol	74	64	71	73	282	-6	47770.00	29602.23
	Ivo GINER	Sp	73	66	70	73	282	-6	47770.00	29602.23
4	Roger WINCHESTER	Eng	73	74	69	67	283	-5	27500.00	17041.26
5	Santiago LUNA	Sp	69	70	75	70	284	-4	21285.00	13189.94
	Charley HOFFMAN	USA	70	70	73	71	284	-4	21285.00	13189.94
7	Massimo FLORIOLI	It	70	65	75	75	285	-3	15125.00	9372.70
	Paul DWYER	Eng	71	70	69	75	285	-3	15125.00	9372.70
9	Andrew SHERBORNE	Eng	71	76	66	73	286	-2	10725.00	6646.09
	Philip WALTON	Ire	70	73	68	75	286	-2	10725.00	6646.09
	Didier DE VOOGHT	Bel	71	67	73	75	286	-2	10725.00	6646.09
	David DRYSDALE	Scot	71	69	71	75	286	-2	10725.00	6646.09
13	Pehr MAGNEBRANT	Swe	73	69	72	73	287	-1	8277.50	5129.42
	Des TERBLANCHE	SA	70	74	68	75	287	-1	8277.50	5129.42
	Lee S JAMES	Eng	75	68	74	70	287	-1	8277.50	5129.42
	John BICKERTON	Eng	72	68	71	76	287	-1	8277.50	5129.42
17	Matthew BLACKEY	Eng	70	74	69	75	288	0	7425.00	4601.14
18	Andrew OLDCORN	Scot	70	65	78	76	289	1	6622.00	4103.54
	Des SMYTH	Ire	69	74	73	73	289	1	6622.00	4103.54
	Bradford VAUGHAN	SA	75	72	69	73	289	1	6622.00	4103.54
	Philip GOLDING	Eng	73	70	72	74	289	1	6622.00	4103.54
	David LYNN	Eng	73	66	74	76	289	1	6622.00	4103.54
23	Peter MALMGREN	Swe	72	76	71	71	290	2	5802.50	3595.71
	Steve WEBSTER	Eng	74	70	70	76	290	2	5802.50	3595.71
	Ilya GORONESKOUL	Fr	69	74	69	78	290	2	5802.50	3595.71
	Mikko ILONEN	Fin	76	71	70	73	290	2	5802.50	3595.71
27	Peter FOWLER	Aus	70	76	74	71	291	3	5142.50	3186.72
	Olivier DAVID	Fr	66	71	80	74	291	3	5142.50	3186.72
	Jesus Maria ARRUTI	Sp	73	74	70	74	291	3	5142.50	3186.72
	Emanuele CANONICA	It	71	73	72	75	291	3	5142.50	3186.72
31	Mark JAMES	Eng	77	68	72	75	292	4	4411.00	2733.42
	Henrik STENSON	Swe	71	73	72	76	292	4	4411.00	2733.42
	Ian HUTCHINGS	SA	74	68	78	72	292	4	4411.00	2733.42
	Massimo SCARPA	It	72	74	74	72	292	4	4411.00	2733.42
	Sion E BEBB	Wal	72	74	74	72	292	4	4411.00	2733.42
36	Mark MOULAND	Wal	74	70	76	73	293	5	3795.00	2351.69
	Peter BAKER	Eng	76	71	71	75	293	5	3795.00	2351.69
	Christophe POTTIER	Fr	70	70	78	75	293	5	3795.00	2351.69
	Benn BARHAM	Eng	70	74	71	78	293	5	3795.00	2351.69
	Benoit TEILLERIA	Fr	68	70	79	76	293	5	3795.00	2351.69
41	Euan LITTLE	Scot	74	73	73	74	294	6	3190.00	1976.79
	Chris GANE	Eng	74	74	74	72	294	6	3190.00	1976.79
	Mattias NILSSON	Swe	71	77	71	75	294	6	3190.00	1976.79
	Anthony KANG	R.Kor	75	73	72	74	294	6	3190.00	1976.79
	Simon WAKEFIELD	Eng	74	71	75	74	294	6	3190.00	1976.79
	Sam WALKER	Eng	76	71	70	77	294	6	3190.00	1976.79
47	Niels KRAAIJ	Hol	75	68	73	79	295	7	2805.00	1738.21
48	Magnus PERSSON ATLEVI	Swe	70	76	76	74	296	8	2310.00	1431.47
	Sam LITTLE	Eng	74	73	75	74	296	8	2310.00	1431.47
	Nicolas VANHOOTEGEM	Bel	73	75	75	73	296	8	2310.00	1431.47
	Robert COLES	Eng	70	78	74	74	296	8	2310.00	1431.47
	Johan SKOLD	Swe	74	73	73	76	296	8	2310.00	1431.47
	Marcus KNIGHT	Swi	75	72	74	75	296	8	2310.00	1431.47
	David HIGGINS	Ire	73	73	72	78	296	8	2310.00	1431.47
	Ben MASON	Eng	78	69	73	76	296	8	2310.00	1431.47
56	Seve BALLESTEROS	Sp	70	76	78	73	297	9	1546.11	958.10
	Yngve NILSSON	Swe	73	69	75	80	297	9	1546.11	958.10
	Shaun P WEBSTER	Eng	74	69	78	76	297	9	1546.11	958.10
	Hennie OTTO	SA	70	74	74	79	297	9	1546.11	958.10
	João Pedro CARVALHOSA	Port	75	72	71	79	297	9	1546.11	958.10
	Carl SUNESON	Sp	74	74	75	74	297	9	1546.11	958.10
	Miles TUNNICLIFF	Eng	70	74	74	79	297	9	1546.11	958.10
	Tomas Jesus MUÑOZ	Sp	74	72	75	76	297	9	1546.11	958.10
	Oskar BERGMAN	Swe	75	68	78	76	297	9	1546.11	958.10
65	Greig HUTCHEON	Scot	73	74	73	78	298	10	1182.50	732.77
	Marcello SANTI	It	74	72	74	78	298	10	1182.50	732.77
	Jorge BERENDT	Arg	73	72	72	81	298	10	1182.50	732.77
	Kariem BARAKA	Ger	74	74	73	77	298	10	1182.50	732.77
69	Marc PENDARIES	Fr	72	74	77	76	299	11	960.00	594.90
	Gary CLARK	Eng	76	71	76	76	299	11	960.00	594.90
	Scott KAMMANN	USA	74	73	71	81	299	11	960.00	594.90
72	Wolfgang HUGET	Ger	69	79	76	76	300	12	822.00	509.38
73	Neil CHEETHAM	Eng	72	74	76	79	301	13	817.50	506.59
	Van PHILLIPS	Eng	76	70	75	80	301	13	817.50	506.59
75	Jeremy ROBINSON	Eng	72	76	71	83	302	14	811.50	502.87
	Anssi KANKKONEN	Fin	74	72	81	75	302	14	811.50	502.87
77	Michele REALE	It	75	72	81	78	306	18	807.00	500.08

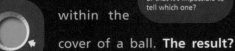

Algarve Open De Portugal · Vale do Lobo · Portugal

wind of change

Carl Pettersson

There was a certain irony that the favourite for the Martell Grand National, which took place on the Saturday of the Algarve Open de Portugal, was named 'Blowing Wind'. For on the Saturday, and for that matter throughout the tournament, a blowing wind, mixed with severe storms, contributed to the event being reduced to 36 holes.

Nevertheless there was a success story to be told to brighten the week. A Swedish golfer, who had shown considerable promise for more than a year, emerged triumphant.

Carl Pettersson received his reward for being the best performer on what was a troubled week weather-wise. The 24 year old Gothenburg-born professional, who spent much of his youth in America, realised the potential that had been clearly apparent with three top five finishes earlier in the 2002 season. Pettersson prevailed on the first hole of a sudden-death play-off against the highly experienced former Ryder Cup player David Gilford.

It was not a week for the faint-hearted, especially if you wanted to take on the 11th, Henry Cotton's formidable 224 yard par three above the tumultuous Atlantic Ocean. Exposed and vulnerable, it was the hole most susceptible to the winds ripping along the cliffs.

David Gilford

Brian Davis

shot of the week

CARL PETTERSSON Sweden

Carl Pettersson's drive at the play-off hole was his best of the week and a contender but was outdone by his approach shot to the 18th, a crisply drawn six iron which covered the flag, set tantalisingly in the back left hand portion of the green, and which held the putting surface despite the best efforts of the wind.

Nor would it have paid to be of a nervous disposition if you wanted to take a peek at the £350,000 diamond tee-peg that was on offer at the start of the week for a hole-in-one in the fourth round at the 11th, the most photographed hole in Europe. For the glittering prize was protected in its glass case inside the clubhouse, by a rattlesnake.

In the event, the sleepy rattler never got disturbed until it was time for him to go back to the zoo and the diamond to go back to the vault.

It reality it was a minor miracle that two rounds were completed. Almost as soon as the last man came in on Saturday afternoon, around 2.00pm from the composite Anniversary Course knitted together from the Royal and Ocean layouts, the gusts that had bedevilled the first two days gathered even more impetus. It seemed so prophetic. Numerous calls were made to British

bookmakers. The odds on Blowing Wind must have shortened merely on the strength of bets from the Algarve alone!

When Pettersson awoke on Sunday morning, he guessed there may have to be a play-off. His hotel room curtains were twitching ominously as the wind continued to gust around Vale do Lobo.

For himself and Gilford, co-leader after the two fractured rounds, there had to be double preparation. They knew there could be a third and final round that might stretch into Monday. Both men were armed for a filibuster. Quiet man Gilford, you felt, would only shrug if the clubhouse roof fell in. Pettersson's self-confessed laziness put him nearly on a par with the sleeping rattlesnake. Their vigil ended at 4.30pm, when the decision was made for the pair to take on the tricky uphill 18th in sudden-death.

Pettersson was nervous. Why shouldn't he be? He was only one year and a few months into his European Tour career. Gilford? The inscrutable hero of The 1995 Ryder Cup Matches at Oak Hill Country Club, Rochester, New York, typically gave no sign of how he felt at once again playing off for an Algarve Open de Portugal title. The last time had been nine years earlier when he overcame Jorge Berendt of Argentina.

Raphaël Jacquelin

A few practice swishes and putts and the protagonists were off. Two perfect drives were followed by an overhit approach by Gilford and a solid strike to the green by Pettersson. When the Englishman chipped 20 feet past and made bogey, the Swede's two putts sealed victory.

While Gilford could take consolation from producing his best performance since finishing second to Peter Mitchell in the 1998 Algarve Open de Portugal at Le Meridien Penina, Pettersson rejoiced as he became the seventh first-time winner on The 2002 European Tour International Schedule. His magnificent opening 66 that had earned him a four shot lead, the best first round advantage thus far in the season, had given him the foundation for victory.

There was to be no triumph for Blowing Wind at Aintree, but for Carl Pettersson it was a week when a dream was fulfilled as he truly lit the blue touch paper on his professional career.

Norman Dabell

the course

The combination of capricious winds and the composite of the legendary Royal and Ocean Courses, bearing the hallmark of the late Sir Henry Cotton, provided a test that many players considered one of the toughest on The European Tour.

Miguel Angel Martin

final results

Vale do Lobo · Portugal
April 4-7 · 2002 · Par 72 · 7108 yards · 6500 metres

Pos.	Name		Rd1	Rd2	Rd3	Rd4	Total	Par	Prize Money Euro	£
1	Carl PETTERSSON	Swe	66	76			142	-2	125000.00	76465.23
2	David GILFORD	Eng	70	72			142	-2	83330.00	50974.78
3	Miguel Angel MARTIN	Sp	73	70			143	-1	38750.00	23704.22
	Greg OWEN	Eng	72	71			143	-1	38750.00	23704.22
	Henrik NYSTRÖM	Swe	72	71			143	-1	38750.00	23704.22
6	Rolf MUNTZ	Hol	71	73			144	0	26250.00	16057.70
7	Diego BORREGO	Sp	77	68			145	1	20625.00	12616.76
	Bradley DREDGE	Wal	70	75			145	1	20625.00	12616.76
9	Steve WEBSTER	Eng	74	72			146	2	14115.00	8634.45
	Gary EMERSON	Eng	74	72			146	2	14115.00	8634.45
	Emanuele CANONICA	It	70	76			146	2	14115.00	8634.45
	Mikko ILONEN	Fin	70	76			146	2	14115.00	8634.45
	Alastair FORSYTH	Scot	72	74			146	2	14115.00	8634.45
14	Roger CHAPMAN	Eng	74	73			147	3	11025.00	6744.23
	Stephen DODD	Wal	71	76			147	3	11025.00	6744.23
	Mikael LUNDBERG	Swe	79	68			147	3	11025.00	6744.23
17	Andrew SHERBORNE	Eng	71	77			148	4	8212.50	5023.77
	Sam TORRANCE	Scot	75	73			148	4	8212.50	5023.77
	Brian DAVIS	Eng	73	75			148	4	8212.50	5023.77
	Mattias ELIASSON	Swe	72	76			148	4	8212.50	5023.77
	Justin ROSE	Eng	76	72			148	4	8212.50	5023.77
	Thomas LEVET	Fr	73	75			148	4	8212.50	5023.77
	Joakim HAEGGMAN	Swe	73	75			148	4	8212.50	5023.77
	Russell CLAYDON	Eng	76	72			148	4	8212.50	5023.77
	Michele REALE	It	72	76			148	4	8212.50	5023.77
	Ian GARBUTT	Eng	73	75			148	4	8212.50	5023.77
	Adam MEDNICK	Swe	74	74			148	4	8212.50	5023.77
	Ignacio GARRIDO	Sp	75	73			148	4	8212.50	5023.77
	Van PHILLIPS	Eng	72	76			148	4	8212.50	5023.77
	Sam WALKER	Eng	75	73			148	4	8212.50	5023.77
31	Des SMYTH	Ire	75	74			149	5	5756.25	3521.22
	Anders HANSEN	Den	74	75			149	5	5756.25	3521.22
	Søren KJELDSEN	Den	76	73			149	5	5756.25	3521.22
	Steen TINNING	Den	76	73			149	5	5756.25	3521.22
	Peter BAKER	Eng	77	72			149	5	5756.25	3521.22
	Marcel SIEM	Ger	75	74			149	5	5756.25	3521.22
	Jonathan LOMAS	Eng	79	70			149	5	5756.25	3521.22
	Gary ORR	Scot	76	73			149	5	5756.25	3521.22
39	Marc FARRY	Fr	80	70			150	6	4650.00	2844.51
	Raphaël JACQUELIN	Fr	76	74			150	6	4650.00	2844.51

Pos.	Name		Rd1	Rd2	Rd3	Rd4	Total	Par	Prize Money Euro	£
	Gary EVANS	Eng	70	80			150	6	4650.00	2844.51
	David PARK	Wal	77	73			150	6	4650.00	2844.51
	Jarmo SANDELIN	Swe	77	73			150	6	4650.00	2844.51
	David CARTER	Eng	75	75			150	6	4650.00	2844.51
	Zane SCOTLAND (AM)	Eng	74	76			150	6		
46	Malcolm MACKENZIE	Eng	80	71			151	7	3155.36	1930.20
	Mark MOULAND	Wal	76	75			151	7	3155.36	1930.20
	Mark FOSTER	Eng	76	75			151	7	3155.36	1930.20
	Kenneth FERRIE	Eng	75	76			151	7	3155.36	1930.20
	Trevor IMMELMAN	SA	76	75			151	7	3155.36	1930.20
	Chris GANE	Eng	73	78			151	7	3155.36	1930.20
	Dennis EDLUND	Swe	77	74			151	7	3155.36	1930.20
	Jorge BERENDT	Arg	77	74			151	7	3155.36	1930.20
	Gary CLARK	Eng	73	78			151	7	3155.36	1930.20
	David DRYSDALE	Scot	74	77			151	7	3155.36	1930.20
	Michael JONZON	Swe	75	76			151	7	3155.36	1930.20
	Daren LEE	Eng	77	74			151	7	3155.36	1930.20
	Benoit TEILLERIA	Fr	76	75			151	7	3155.36	1930.20
	Stephen GALLACHER	Scot	79	72			151	7	3155.36	1930.20
60	Costantino ROCCA	It	75	77			152	8	1800.00	1101.10
	Wayne RILEY	Aus	75	77			152	8	1800.00	1101.10
	Robert-Jan DERKSEN	Hol	78	74			152	8	1800.00	1101.10
	Warren BENNETT	Eng	76	76			152	8	1800.00	1101.10
	Maarten LAFEBER	Hol	79	73			152	8	1800.00	1101.10
	Phillip PRICE	Wal	74	78			152	8	1800.00	1101.10
	Nicolas VANHOOTEGEM	Bel	74	78			152	8	1800.00	1101.10
	Markus BRIER	Aut	75	77			152	8	1800.00	1101.10
	Nicolas KALOUGUINE	Fr	73	79			152	8	1800.00	1101.10
	Andrew COLTART	Scot	76	76			152	8	1800.00	1101.10
	Raymond RUSSELL	Scot	76	76			152	8	1800.00	1101.10
71	Gordon BRAND JNR.	Scot	80	73			153	9	1145.50	700.73
	Santiago LUNA	Sp	77	76			153	9	1145.50	700.73
	Mark ROE	Eng	80	73			153	9	1145.50	700.73
	José Manuel LARA	Sp	78	75			153	9	1145.50	700.73
	Gregory HAVRET	Fr	81	72			153	9	1145.50	700.73
	Stuart LITTLE	Eng	81	72			153	9	1145.50	700.73
	Olle KARLSSON	Swe	79	74			153	9	1145.50	700.73
	Johan SKOLD	Swe	75	78			153	9	1145.50	700.73
	Matthew CORT	Eng	78	75			153	9	1145.50	700.73
	Graham FOX	Scot	77	76			153	9	1145.50	700.73

THE PRⵔQUIP FEELING.

You can't stop the rain. But you can stop it ruining your golf. Wear ProQuip and foul weather will be like water off a duck's back.

WINNING WEATHERWEAR™

ProQuip Ltd, North Berwick, Scotland.   Sales: 01620 892219   www.proquipgolf.com

The Masters Tournament Augusta National · Augusta · Georgia · USA

true craftsmanship

Augusta National was conceived by an American who had a love for Scotland. It was designed by a Scot with a passion for golf in America.

Given the worldly views of both Bobby Jones and Alister Mackenzie, perhaps it is not surprising that their masterpiece should be a course where golfers from so many countries clearly feel comfortable.

Tiger Woods

Here is a venue that calls for true craftsmanship from tee to green, wonderful imagination around each putting surface, and the mental strength to assess whether each stroke will bring the reward that makes it worth the risk.

At the 66th Masters Tournament, Jones and Mackenzie would have felt justly proud of the leaderboard their creation produced. Filling the first eleven places were players from no less than five Continents. Seven of the eleven are global ambassadors to such an extent that they hold dual Membership of both The European Tour and the US PGA Tour.

Even Tiger Woods, who did not at the time of winning his third Masters in six years, has shown in his climb to the undisputed position of World Number One, that to make it to the top in golf you have to experience the game in all its guises. The 66th Masters Tournament, therefore, could hardly have delivered a more resounding message; namely to compete at the highest level these days means a player must broaden his horizons.

Sergio Garcia

Retief Goosen

Restricting oneself to a single market, be it Europe or the United States, Asia, Australia or South Africa, can leave players looking one dimensional in comparison to the world travellers, and that will invariably become evident at somewhere like Augusta National.

For further confirmation, take a look at the names of the last ten players to don the Green Jacket: Fred Couples, Ben Crenshaw, Nick Faldo, Bernhard Langer, Sandy Lyle, José Maria Olazábal, Mark O'Meara, Vijay Singh, Ian Woosnam and, of course, Woods. Spot anyone there who does not enjoy playing golf around the globe?

Over the years Woods has grown into his role as a roving diplomat for the game. Talk to him about the Open Golf Championship and he replies in reverential terms. He also enjoys his trip to Germany for the Deutsche Bank-SAP Open TPC of Europe so much that it has become an integral part of his schedule.

He appreciates that no-one can hope to become the complete golfer without learning the different nuances that only come through playing on each Continent. At Augusta National he showed he had.

When he first won the Masters Tournament in 1997, Woods gave an exhibition of raw talent and belligerent youth. When he claimed the Green Jacket in 2001 to make it four Major Championships in a row, he demonstrated a golden putting stroke and unimpeachable nerve.

In becoming only the third player to successfully defend the trophy after Jack Nicklaus (1965-66), who did not contend this year but still visited the scene of six of his record 18 Major Championship victories, and Faldo (1989-90), Woods showed elements of all of these things but also a maturity under pressure that was something to behold.

Time and again over the back nine during the final round the temptation arose to attack the course and extend a useful three stroke advantage into an unassailable one. On every occasion he refused the offer, showing exemplary patience, inviting his nearest challengers to gamble to see if they could close the gap.

An illustrious collection of talented shotmakers were in that grey area where they needed to make something happen but, in pressing, paid the price that Augusta National often exacts when shots stray a fraction off the money.

Ernie Els and Singh found watery graves on the 13th and 15th respectively to end their hopes while Phil Mickelson chased glory too hard with a couple of iron shots that landed in places which

the course

Augusta National was lengthened by 285 yards in 2002 and the changes met with general approval. For every player who thought it did not need changing, ten lined up to enthuse at the masterful alterations carried out under the auspices of master architect Tom Fazio.

finishing eighth; and from Adam Scott who, on his debut, shared ninth with Angel Cabrera and Miguel Angel Jiménez after 18 of the record 25 European Tour Members invited to compete were among the 45 players to survive the halfway cut mark of three over par. Indeed, 14 finished in the top 20, the best ever performance by European Tour Members in a Major Championship in the United States.

shot of the week

TIGER WOODS USA

Tiger Woods knew a birdie at the 18th hole in the third round would put him right where he wanted to be - part of the last group out on the final day. He took dead aim with his second shot, and fired the perfect seven iron approach to set up the three that gave him a psychological edge he retained for the rest of the tournament.

left him with no chance of recovery. Retief Goosen, who began the last round tied with Woods, had expressed concerns all week about his iron play and, on that final day, those fears were realised. Still, it said everything about the determined qualities of the 2001 Volvo Order of Merit winner and US Open Champion that he was still able to finish runner-up and Olazábal, too, demonstrated in finishing fourth that he would be a contender again for the Major Championships in 2002.

There were also highly creditable performances from Padraig Harrington, who in only his third Masters Tournament finished tied for fifth alongside Els despite being worried all week about his grip; Sergio Garcia, who for three rounds mastered Augusta before

Padraig Harrington

But Woods, the imperious one under pressure, duly became the youngest player ever to win seven Major Championships. That is the same number as Arnold Palmer, who made this Masters Tournament, his 48th in total, his last. Fittingly, he received the send-off due to the most loved golfer of all.

Asked what was the best piece of advice he ever received from Palmer, Woods replied: "To be the best ambassador I can be for my sport." So far he has been the perfect one – at Augusta, in America, and all around the world.

Derek Lawrenson

Vijay Singh

final results

Augusta National · Augusta · Georgia · USA
April 11-14 · 2002 · Par 72 · 7270 yards · 6648 metres

Pos.	Name		Rd1	Rd2	Rd3	Rd4	Total	Par	Prize Money Euro	£
1	Tiger WOODS	USA	70	69	66	71	276	-12	1144807.00	702439.01
2	Retief GOOSEN	SA	69	67	69	74	279	-9	686884.30	421463.47
3	Phil MICKELSON	USA	69	72	68	71	280	-8	432482.70	265365.88
4	José Maria OLAZÁBAL	Sp	70	69	71	71	281	-7	305281.90	187317.09
5	Padraig HARRINGTON	Ire	69	70	72	71	282	-6	241681.50	148292.69
	Ernie ELS	SA	70	67	72	73	282	-6	241681.50	148292.69
7	Vijay SINGH	Fiji	70	65	72	76	283	-5	213061.30	130731.70
8	Sergio GARCIA	Sp	68	71	70	75	284	-4	197161.20	120975.60
9	Miguel Angel JIMÉNEZ	Sp	70	71	74	70	285	-3	171721.10	105365.88
	Angel CABRERA	Arg	68	71	73	73	285	-3	171721.10	105365.88
	Adam SCOTT	Aus	71	72	72	70	285	-3	171721.10	105365.88
12	Brad FAXON	USA	71	75	69	71	286	-2	139920.90	85853.68
	Chris DIMARCO	USA	70	71	72	73	286	-2	139920.90	85853.68
14	Nick FALDO	Eng	75	67	73	72	287	-1	111300.70	68292.69
	Shigeki MARUYAMA	Jpn	75	72	73	67	287	-1	111300.70	68292.69
	Colin MONTGOMERIE	Scot	75	71	70	71	287	-1	111300.70	68292.69
	Davis LOVE III	USA	67	75	74	71	287	-1	111300.70	68292.69
18	Paul MCGINLEY	Ire	72	74	71	71	288	0	92220.57	56585.37
	Thomas BJÖRN	Den	74	67	70	77	288	0	92220.57	56585.37
20	Nick PRICE	Zim	70	76	70	73	289	1	74094.46	45463.42
	Justin LEONARD	USA	70	75	74	70	289	1	74094.46	45463.42
	Jerry KELLY	USA	72	74	71	72	289	1	74094.46	45463.42
	Darren CLARKE	N.Ire	70	74	73	72	289	1	74094.46	45463.42
24	Jeff SLUMAN	USA	73	72	71	74	290	2	52788.33	32390.25
	Stewart CINK	USA	74	70	72	74	290	2	52788.33	32390.25
	Mike WEIR	Can	72	71	71	76	290	2	52788.33	32390.25
	Mark BROOKS	USA	74	72	71	73	290	2	52788.33	32390.25
	Tom PERNICE	USA	74	72	71	73	290	2	52788.33	32390.25
29	Jesper PARNEVIK	Swe	70	72	77	72	291	3	43248.27	26536.59
	Robert ALLENBY	Aus	73	70	76	72	291	3	43248.27	26536.59
	Charles HOWELL III	USA	74	73	71	73	291	3	43248.27	26536.59
32	Bernhard LANGER	Ger	73	72	73	74	292	4	36808.73	22585.37
	Craig STADLER	USA	73	72	74	73	292	4	36808.73	22585.37
	Billy MAYFAIR	USA	74	71	72	75	292	4	36808.73	22585.37a
	John DALY	USA	74	73	70	75	292	4	36808.73	22585.37
36	Greg NORMAN	Aus	71	76	72	75	294	6	30607.69	18780.49
	Fred COUPLES	USA	73	73	76	72	294	6	30607.69	18780.49
	Rocco MEDIATE	USA	75	68	75	76	294	6	30607.69	18780.49
	David TOMS	USA	73	74	76	71	294	6	30607.69	18780.49
40	Tom WATSON	USA	71	76	76	72	295	7	26076.16	16000.00
	Steve LOWERY	USA	75	71	76	73	295	7	26076.16	16000.00
	Kirk TRIPLETT	USA	74	70	74	77	295	7	26076.16	16000.00
43	Scott VERPLANK	USA	70	75	76	75	296	8	23532.15	14439.03
44	Lee WESTWOOD	Eng	75	72	74	76	297	9	22260.14	13658.54

Pos.	Name		Rd1	Rd2	Rd3	Rd4	Total	Par	Prize Money Euro	£
45	Bob ESTES	USA	73	72	75	78	298	10	20988.13	12878.05
46	David DUVAL	USA	74	74			148	4	5678.61	3484.32
	Scott MCCARRON	USA	75	73			148	4	5678.61	3484.32
	Larry MIZE	USA	74	74			148	4	5678.61	3484.32
	Michael HOEY (AM)	N.Ire	75	73			148	4		
	Joe DURANT	USA	74	74			148	4	5678.61	3484.32
	Paul AZINGER	USA	75	73			148	4	5678.61	3484.32
	Tom LEHMAN	USA	76	72			148	4	5678.61	3484.32
	Michael CAMPBELL	NZ	74	74			148	4	5678.61	3484.32
	Kevin SUTHERLAND	USA	78	70			148	4	5678.61	3484.32
	Rory SABBATINI	SA	73	75			148	4	5678.61	3484.32
53	Mark O'MEARA	USA	78	71			149	5	5678.61	3484.32
	Toshimitsu IZAWA	Jpn	73	76			149	5	5678.61	3484.32
	Mark CALCAVECCHIA	USA	79	70			149	5	5678.61	3484.32
	Paul LAWRIE	Scot	75	74			149	5	5678.61	3484.32
	Lee JANZEN	USA	74	75			149	5	5678.61	3484.32
61	Tom KITE	USA	77	73			150	6	5678.61	3484.32
	Jim FURYK	USA	73	77			150	6	5678.61	3484.32
	Billy ANDRADE	USA	75	75			150	6	5678.61	3484.32
	Matt KUCHAR	USA	73	77			150	6	5678.61	3484.32
	Toru TANIGUCHI	Jpn	80	70			150	6	5678.61	3484.32
	Kenny PERRY	USA	76	74			150	6	5678.61	3484.32
	Shingo KATAYAMA	Jpn	78	72			150	6	5678.61	3484.32
	Bubba DICKERSON (AM)	USA	79	71			150	6		
69	Steve STRICKER	USA	75	76			151	7	5678.61	3484.32
	Scott HOCH	USA	76	75			151	7	5678.61	3484.32
	Niclas FASTH	Swe	76	75			151	7	5678.61	3484.32
72	Fuzzy ZOELLER	USA	75	77			152	8	5678.61	3484.32
	Craig PERKS	NZ	81	71			152	8	5678.61	3484.32
74	Raymond FLOYD	USA	79	74			153	9	5678.61	3484.32
	José COCERES	Arg	74	79			153	9	5678.61	3484.32
76	Sandy LYLE	Scot	73	81			154	10	5678.61	3484.32
	Robert HAMILTON (AM)	USA	77	77			154	10		
	Tim JACKSON (AM)	USA	76	78			154	10		
79	Ian WOOSNAM	Wal	77	78			155	11	5678.61	3484.32
80	Seve BALLESTEROS	Sp	75	81			156	12	5678.61	3484.32
81	Tommy AARON	USA	79	78			157	13	5678.61	3484.32
82	Gary PLAYER	SA	80	78			158	14	5678.61	3484.32
	Ben CRENSHAW	USA	81	77			158	14	5678.61	3484.32
84	Stuart APPLEBY	Aus	80	79			159	15	5678.61	3484.32
85	Chez REAVIE (AM)	USA	74	86			160	16		
86	Charles COODY	USA	82	84			166	22	5678.61	3484.32
87	Arnold PALMER	USA	89	85			174	30	5678.61	3484.32

herculean power

Peerages and knighthoods are pleasant baubles but surely the ultimate accolade must be to have an airport re-named to commemorate your deeds. Mostly this honour falls to presidents or statesmen, but not always. For example when you fly into Latrobe, Pennsylvania, you touch down at Arnold Palmer Airport.

It was from his hometown in the mid-fifties that Arnie first flew out to impose a whole new thrilling philosophy on professional golf. It could be summed up in three words: Go for broke.

With his axeman's swing, colossal strength and a follow-through that caused the purists to wince, he stormed his way into American hearts as powerfully as John Wayne was doing in the movies. Along the way he accumulated the biggest fan club the game has ever known. Arnie's Army dogged his heels along every fairway, never lamenting a wayward drive. Arnie could recover from anywhere.

Fortunately for British and European golf, Palmer did not confine these pyrotechnics to the United States. The late fifties were a critical period for the game this side of the Atlantic. Fewer and fewer of America's stars were prepared even to contest our Open Golf Championship. The travel was more arduous then, the prize money mere loose change by their domestic standards.

Palmer, urged on by a thrusting and percipient young business manager, Mark McCormack, arrested the trend. He came, he saw, he conquered. And how he conquered. He was a red blood transfusion to our ailing game as he smashed and flailed his progress round Royal Birkdale in 1961 and at Royal Troon in 1962 to win the Open Golf Championship in successive years.

On a tidal wave of popularity, with a private army now almost as idolatrous here as it was in America, he drew enormous galleries for his appearances at the World Match Play Championship at Wentworth Club. He won in 1964 and 1967. The event was then sponsored by the Piccadilly tobacco company and his 1967 triumph caused him some problems. He'd been a two pack a day man and was desperately striving to give up smoking. "Damn me," he said, "every time I went back to my hotel room they'd put another carton of 200 by my bedside."

If there was a single shot that validated his billing as the world's most daring player of the age, it came on the 15th hole in the final round of the Royal Birkdale Open when he was being challenged every yard of the way by the dynamic little Welshman, Dai Rees.

Arnie's drive at that par four was so atrocious that it finished so far into deep, tangled, sopping rough that it was almost out of bounds. It was still raining and blowing half a gale. His caddie found it and determined that the only conceivable way to extricate it, with enormous luck, was to wedge it out sideways on to the fairway.

Palmer thought otherwise. To concede a shot to Rees at this juncture could cost him the title. So, while sane men shook their heads, he took a six iron and with Herculean power shifted grass,

undergrowth and probably field mice and abandoned birds' nests as well. Also the ball. It landed on the green and two putts later he had overpowered Rees to the title by a single shot.

It was one of the most miraculous shots in golf history and next time you are at Royal Birkdale take time to pay homage at the nearby plaque which commemorates it. The following year at Royal Troon he successfully defended his title by six clear shots.

There is another plaque to mark a winning Palmer shot at La Manga in Spain. There in 1975 he won the Spanish Open by a single shot with an eagle at the last – slashing a huge drive then a fabulous four iron to seven feet. Not content with that he returned to the British links two months later and at Royal St George's won the PGA Championship. He did so in true Palmer style – storming from five behind in the final round. At the 508 yard 14th, the notorious Suez Canal hole, Palmer hit a three iron about as well as it is possible for even him to hit one and made eagle. His third

> " It is without doubt the greatest game " man ever invented
>
> *Arnold Palmer*

round of 71, with the wind bending the flag stick, was a masterpiece – no less than seven strokes lower than those scored by any of the players in the last five two balls that day.

Those wins also galvanised the game and The European Tour saluted Palmer. He was made an Honorary Member.

It was on his 70th birthday that Latrobe decided to name their airport after Arnold Palmer. He was never the world's greatest golfer. Jones, Hogan, Nicklaus and Woods were, or are, probably ahead of him. He was just the most exciting and remains an icon in American public life.

Ian Wooldridge

OFFICIAL SPONSOR

OFFICIAL SPONSOR

**OFFICIAL GOLF CAR
AND UTILITY VEHICLE**

OFFICIAL SUPPLIER

We build relationships that drive the game.

OFFICIAL SUPPLIER

**OFFICIAL GOLF CAR
AND UTILITY VEHICLE**

OFFICIAL SUPPLIER

play to win™

1-800-ClubCar • www.clubcar.com
(using AT&T Direct Dial Access #)

P.O. Box 2 • Chorley New Road • Horwich Bolton BL6 6JN UK

The Seve Trophy Druids Glen · Co. Wicklow · Ireland

national pride

Great Britain and Ireland   14¹⁄₂ pts

Continental Europe   11¹⁄₂ pts

Colin Montgomerie and
Seve Ballesteros

Visions of José Maria Olazábal dropping to his knees on the 17th green on Saturday to pay homage at the feet of Severiano Ballesteros, and a pair of stately swans caught in a romantic embrace on the 13th fairway on Sunday provided some light relief to the otherwise serious business of The Seve Trophy at Druids Glen.

Thomas Björn and Darren Clarke had a birds' eye view of the swans, turned a blind eye so to speak and focused on their own creative intentions. You see, Clarke was on his way to a victory, sealed two holes later, and it was one of some significance in Great Britain and Ireland's victory march.

Up ahead, Ballesteros, as in the inaugural contest at Sunningdale two years ago, was on his way to another win over rival Captain Colin Montgomerie. It gave Continental Europe understandable hope of completing an unlikely comeback from their 10-6 deficit at the start of the day, but it was not to be.

Ballesteros may have initiated the idea of the match and he was certainly the inspiration behind Continental Europe's victory in 2000, but Montgomerie's team was in no mood to be caught napping a second time. So, Seve didn't get to keep his own Trophy but the idea of a match between Continental Europe and the two islands to the west certainly appealed to the players and the public.

Darren Clarke and Lee Westwood

Seve Ballesteros and José Maria Olazábal

the course

Druids Glen improves with every year of maturity and has become one of the finest parkland courses in the country, pitched between the Wicklow mountains and The Irish Sea in the county known as the Garden of Ireland. A pretty, parkland layout, it has a par of 71 and a championship length of 7041 yards. A new hotel was opened in time to accommodate the Teams and Officials and another Championship Course, designed by Pat Ruddy, has just been opened.

The weather did not favour the event, but the Irish supporters still came out in their woollens and waterproofs and were not disappointed.

Match play is the purest form of golf. The spectators came to see the duck and dive, the nip and tuck, the unexpected, and they got plenty of that, particularly from the Continental Europe Captain who thrives on the challenge the format presents.

Ballesteros's performances in regular tournament play for the past few years have drawn sympathy from all quarters, but once again he rose to the man-to-man challenge. The agreed format between the Captains was that they should meet in the lead singles on Sunday and play in at least one other rubber on the previous two days. It was also written in the rules that every player would play a minimum of two matches over the series and the Captains obliged with their respective selections. Montgomerie, in particular, spread himself through his team, taking a different partner in each of the four sessions over the first two days.

Honours were even after the opening Greensomes on Friday morning with Raphaël Jacquelin and Thomas Levet providing the biggest talking point. French flair and Gallic grit combined to see the duo come from behind and snatch a vital 2 and 1 win over Lee Westwood and Clarke in the last match before lunch.

Paul McGinley

McGinley summed it up. "It was vintage Seve and Ollie," he admitted. "They had five putts in eight holes on the back nine. What can you do against that? They were just awesome."

Olazábal said: "It was a special day for us, just like the old days. It was amazing to watch Seve hole out from the bunker on the 17th. Padraig had hit a wonderful tee shot and we were just hoping to make three. But Seve did what he's done so often in the past and I just had to get down on my hands and knees and applaud."

Olazábal went on to partner Miguel Angel Jiménez to beat Clarke and Montgomerie by one hole in the final match of the afternoon Foursomes session to square that particular series 2-2, but overall Great Britain and Ireland were in command with a 10-6 lead going into the singles. "We would have taken that at the start," said Montgomerie while Ballesteros was disappointed. "We are further behind than I expected," he said. "We need to win seven singles to get in a play-off. That's difficult."

In the afternoon, Great Britain and Ireland won the Foursomes 3-1 to carry a 5-3 lead into the Saturday morning Fourballs. There was obvious speculation about the revival of the Ballesteros – Olazábal partnership and, given Seve's unpredictability off the tee, it was more or less guaranteed that this was the perfect stage for the greatest partnership in Ryder Cup history to be reunited. It was only right that they should come together again, perhaps for the last time. The question was, who would face them?

Montgomerie did not have to do a lot of soul-searching to join Padraig Harrington and Paul McGinley. After all, the duo had won the World Cup for Ireland at Kiawah Island in 1997. His faith would bear fruit as they emerged from the event as joint top points scorers with four out of five, and it also seemed right that they should be the ones to tackle the Swinging Señors.

It was a match made to happen and a time to savour for those lucky enough to witness it. It rekindled fond memories of the glory days as Ballesteros and Olazábal covered the last eight holes in six under par to blow away both the Irish duo 2 and 1, and Great Britain and Ireland's hopes of a clean sweep in the session. Ballesteros holing from the bunker to win the match at the 17th was simply the icing on the cake.

Raphaël Jacquelin and Thomas Levet

Continental Europe: Left to right: Top row: Thomas Björn, Niclas Fasth, Raphaël Jacquelin, Thomas Levet, Mathias Grönberg, Alex Cejka and Robert Karlsson. Front row: José Maria Olazábal, Seve Ballesteros and Miguel Angel Jiménez.

Ballesteros again gave the lead on Sunday. Montgomerie must still be smarting at the sight of the Spaniard. He beat him at Sunningdale and he did so again. Ballesteros had played an unsuccessful game of find the fairway in regular tournaments, but he didn't seem to need the closely mown areas at Druids Glen. He was seldom there but his short game was phenomenal. It is true that Montgomerie was not at his best but it was fascinating to watch the Spaniard recover from all kinds of unlikely spots to forge a one hole victory. However, not even his magic could save Continental Europe. They did win the last battle (5½ – 4½) but lost the war 14½ – 11½.

Ian Woosnam and Steve Webster

Home heroes Harrington and McGinley were the standouts for Great Britain and Ireland while Jiménez and Olazábal were the leading scorers for Continental Europe, but this was not about the Irish or the Spaniards. This was about the fusion of nine nationalities in a common cause. Team pride, national pride, and pride in playing golf as it should be, were the main issues. Team against team, player against player, in a highly competitive but fair and friendly spirit. It is, after all, only a game. Long may it continue.

Colm Smith

shot of the week

SEVE BALLESTEROS Spain

Seve Ballesteros produced a bountiful selection but the one that stands out is the bunker shot he holed for a winning birdie two at the island green on the 17th in the Saturday morning Fourballs. It put an end to the hopes of Padraig Harrington and Paul McGinley who were two down, but who looked like bringing the match up the last with Harrington just two feet from the pin. As always with Seve, you never know.

Great Britain and Ireland: Left to right: Top row: Lee Westwood, Andrew Oldcorn, Colin Montgomerie, Darren Clarke, Padraig Harrington and Paul Lawrie.
Front row: Ian Woosnam, Steve Webster, Paul Casey and Paul McGinley.

final results

Druids Glen • Co. Wicklow • Ireland
April 19-21 • 2002 • Par 71 • 7041 yards • 6439 metres

CONTINENTAL EUROPE

Captain: Seve Ballesteros

Friday April 19
Greensomes: Morning

R Karlsson & T Björn (2&1)	1	P Lawrie & C Montgomerie	0
J M Olazábal & M A Jiménez	0	I Woosnam & S Webster (3&2)	1
M Grönberg & A Cejka	0	P Harrington & P McGinley (1 hole)	1
R Jacquelin & T Levet (2&1)	1	L Westwood & D Clarke	0
	2		**2**

Foursomes: Afternoon

N Fasth & R Karlsson	0	C Montgomerie & A Oldcorn (2&1)	1
M A Jiménez & J M Olazábal (1 hole)	1	S Webster & P Casey	0
R Jacquelin & T Levet	0	P Harrington & P McGinley (1 hole)	1
A Cejka & T Björn	0	D Clarke & L Westwood (3&2)	1
	3		**5**

Saturday April 20
Fourballs: Morning

T Björn & N Fasth	0	P Lawrie & P Casey (2&1)	1
R Karlsson & M Grönberg	0	I Woosnam & C Montgomerie (4&3)	1
S Ballesteros & J M Olazábal (2&1)	1	P Harrington & P McGinley	0
M A Jiménez & R Jacquelin	0	D Clarke & L Westwood (1 hole)	1
	4		**8**

Foursomes: Afternoon

T Björn & R Karlsson (halved)	½	I Woosnam & S Webster (halved)	½
T Levet & R Jacquelin (halved)	½	P Lawrie & A Oldcorn (halved)	½
A Cejka & N Fasth	0	P Harrington & P McGinley (1 hole)	1
J M Olazábal & M A Jiménez (1 hole)	1	D Clarke & C Montgomerie	0
	6		**10**

Sunday April 21
Singles

S Ballesteros (1 hole)	1	C Montgomerie	0
T Björn	0	D Clarke (4&3)	1
M A Jiménez (4&3)	1	P Casey	0
R Karlsson (1 hole)	1	P Lawrie	0
N Fasth (halved)	½	A Oldcorn (halved)	½
R Jacquelin	0	L Westwood (3&2)	1
J M Olazábal	0	P Harrington (3&2)	1
M Grönberg	0	P McGinley (4&3)	1
T Levet (2&1)	1	S Webster	0
A Cejka (5&4)	1	I Woosnam	0
Total	**11½**	**Total**	**14½**

GREAT BRITAIN AND IRELAND

Captain: Colin Montgomerie

2002 Seve Trophy Points Record

	P	W	H	L	Pts
Continental Europe					
Ballesteros	2	2	-	-	2
Björn	5	1	1	3	1½
Cejka	4	1	-	3	1
Fasth	4	-	1	3	½
Grönberg	3	-	-	3	0
Jacquelin	5	1	1	3	1½
Jiménez	5	3	-	2	3
Karlsson	5	2	1	2	2½
Levet	4	2	1	1	2½
Olazábal	5	3	-	2	3
Great Britain and Ireland					
Montgomerie	5	2	-	3	2
Casey	3	1	-	2	1
Clarke	5	3	-	2	3
Harrington	5	4	-	1	4
Lawrie	4	1	1	2	1½
McGinley	5	4	-	1	4
Oldcorn	3	1	2	-	2
Webster	4	1	1	2	1½
Westwood	4	3	-	1	3
Woosnam	4	2	1	1	2½

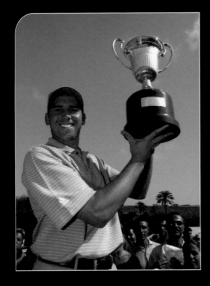

Canarias Open de España El Cortijo Club de Campo · Gran Canaria · Spain

smart hombre

Sergio Garcia

On the evidence provided by 'Los Ninos' at the Canarias Open de España at El Cortijo Club de Campo, the future of Spanish golf is indeed in good hands.

Following his eighth place in the Masters Tournament a fortnight earlier, 22 year old Sergio Garcia confirmed his stature as one of the top players in global golf with a four stroke win, his first professional victory on Spanish soil and eighth worldwide.

And 17 year old Rafael Cabrera, still at school in nearby Las Palmas and with an amateur record better than that of Garcia at the same age, confirmed with his share of fourth place that he could be another 'Sergio' in the making.

"It is a great honour but I can't really be compared to Sergio because he is a professional and I am an amateur and still at school, but he is definitely an idol of mine," said Cabrera, exhibiting a degree of humility that will stand him in good stead should he be thrust into the limelight again in future years.

Garcia's advice to his young compatriot, whom he partnered in the final round to the delight of the large gallery, was simple: "Work

Steen Tinning

hard, try hard, don't get ahead of yourself, but most importantly, have fun." It was council Garcia himself adhered to perfectly in Gran Canaria.

At the start of the week another target for the autograph hunters was Severiano Ballesteros whose first Spanish Open triumph in 1981 came when Garcia was just one year old and Cabrera was not even a twinkle in his father's eye.

However, after his heroics in The Seve Trophy at Druids Glen, Co. Wicklow, Ireland, the week before, the maestro, whose third victory in the Championship in 1995 was the last by a Spaniard, bowed out at the halfway stage.

With José Maria Olazábal, the last winner in Gran Canaria in the 1997 Turespaña Masters, taking a breather before defending his Novotel Perrier Open de France title, home hopes were pinned on Garcia. He would let no one down.

Emanuele Canonica

Before the off Garcia, already a winner on the 2002 US PGA Tour, reckoned his fourth European Tour International Schedule victory would not be long arriving. An opening 67, which left him a stroke behind co-leaders David Gilford and Søren Hansen, hinted it could come very swiftly indeed.

Crucial on day two was a gutsy five foot putt for a bogey five at the 329 yard 12th, his third hole of the day, with its precipitous plunge to the left and out of bounds right, which Garcia found. He admitted: "It was one of those holes where making bogey

Kenneth Ferrie

shot of the week

SERGIO GARCIA Spain

After his double-bogey, bogey slip-up at the 12th and 13th in the final round, and with a seven stroke advantage reduced to one, Sergio Garcia's bold drive to within inches of the green at the 298 yard 14th to set up a birdie three and launch a fighting five hole finish, was the key to victory.

actually gets you going. If I'd made double bogey that would have really got me down but making that putt really helped and it helped me make some good birdies after that." At the end of the day, a 68 left him one stroke ahead of England's Greg Owen at halfway.

It looked all over bar the shouting when Garcia repeated his opening 67 on Saturday to leap five strokes clear. When he began his final round birdie-eagle, heads nodded sagely in the galleries and in the press centre, Monday morning's articles were all but written.

However, the strong winds which had buffeted the course all week returned on the Sunday and even Garcia found it far from plain sailing, the dreaded 12th again catching him out - this time he did record a double bogey six after another drive drifted out of bounds.

When he then bogeyed the short 13th he was, astonishingly, just one stroke clear of the field led by the tenacious Swede Carl Pettersson, the man who won his maiden European Tour title in the Algarve Open de Portugal a fortnight earlier, and who had been nine shots adrift of Garcia after the first two holes that day.

The Spaniard's reaction, though, was instantaneous, and telling. A birdie at the 14th to match that of Pettersson launched a home straight flourish of majestic proportions. In the whistling wind, the finish at El Cortijo Club de Campo, with lakes left and right at the 15th, 16th and 17th, is daunting. Garcia's one under par sprint over the last five holes left his rivals, who let shots fritter away, gasping in admiration.

A 73 for a 13 under par 275 left him four clear of Emanuele Canonica, who closed with a 72, five ahead of Owen, who bravely birdied two of the last three holes for a 72, and six clear of Cabrera (73) and Pettersson (72).

The new Champion admitted: "I made a couple of bad swings and did a couple of silly things but I realised my ambition to win my own National title and it's a great feeling. I never thought I would lose it. I knew I was in control, although it looked like I wasn't for a while. I knew if I kept hitting good shots, stayed patient and played smart, everything was going to be fine."

Cabrera's was the best finish by an amateur on The European Tour International schedule since Justin Rose tied fourth in the 1998

the course

Sited between the airport and the capital Las Palmas, El Cortijo Club de Campo, designed by Blake Stirling and Marco Martin, undulates through three valleys, around six lakes (one boasting an island bunker) and 600 palm trees. At 6898 yards, with fast, sloping and windswept greens, it presented a stiff test.

Canarias Open de España

David Lynn

Open Golf Championship at Royal Birkdale. Had he not bogeyed the 17th and 18th in each of the final two rounds, he would have been second.

But to make such an assertion about the teenager's performance is unfair. The winner of the Spanish Under Ten, Under 12, Under 14, Under 16 and Under 17 titles, twice European Young Masters Champion and British Boys' finalist in 2001, can be proud of a week that left him ahead of the majority of the field including the reigning US Open Champion and 2001 Volvo Order of Merit winner Retief Goosen.

Gordon Richardson

final results

El Cortijo Club de Campo · Gran Canaria · Spain
April 25 - 28 · 2002 · Par 72 · 6898 yards · 6308 metres

Pos.	Name		Rd1	Rd2	Rd3	Rd4	Total	Par	Prize Money Euro	£
1	Sergio GARCIA	Sp	67	68	67	73	275	-13	287000.00	176360.34
2	Emanuele CANONICA	It	68	69	70	72	279	-9	191330.00	117571.51
3	Greg OWEN	Eng	67	69	72	72	280	-8	107797.20	66240.94
4	Carl PETTERSSON	Swe	68	72	69	72	281	-7	86100.00	52908.10
	Rafael CABRERA (AM)	Sp	69	72	67	73	281	-7		
6	Anders FORSBRAND	Swe	70	74	68	71	283	-5	66641.40	40950.87
	Ricardo GONZALEZ	Arg	68	75	70	70	283	-5	66641.40	40950.87
8	David GILFORD	Eng	66	77	71	70	284	-4	47355.00	29099.46
	Retief GOOSEN	SA	73	73	71	67	284	-4	47355.00	29099.46
10	Kenneth FERRIE	Eng	69	71	72	73	285	-3	29747.55	18279.75
	Ian POULTER	Eng	70	72	71	72	285	-3	29747.55	18279.75
	Steen TINNING	Den	71	73	68	73	285	-3	29747.55	18279.75
	Stuart LITTLE	Eng	68	72	70	75	285	-3	29747.55	18279.75
	Marcel SIEM	Ger	67	71	72	75	285	-3	29747.55	18279.75
	Ian HUTCHINGS	SA	70	71	69	75	285	-3	29747.55	18279.75
	David DRYSDALE	Scot	72	72	69	72	285	-3	29747.55	18279.75
	Didier De VOOGHT	Bel	70	69	71	75	285	-3	29747.55	18279.75
18	Gordon BRAND JNR.	Scot	70	72	70	74	286	-2	22271.20	13685.56
	José Manuel CARRILES	Sp	69	73	72	72	286	-2	22271.20	13685.56
	Miguel Angel JIMÉNEZ	Sp	71	72	72	71	286	-2	22271.20	13685.56
21	Mark ROE	Eng	68	73	69	77	287	-1	19493.04	11978.39
	Warren BENNETT	Eng	69	69	72	77	287	-1	19493.04	11978.39
	Carl SUNESON	Sp	68	70	73	76	287	-1	19493.04	11978.39
	Des TERBLANCHE	SA	69	72	69	77	287	-1	19493.04	11978.39
	Fredrik JACOBSON	Swe	71	73	70	73	287	-1	19493.04	11978.39
26	Søren KJELDSEN	Den	69	71	73	75	288	0	16875.60	10369.99
	Ian GARBUTT	Eng	68	75	73	72	288	0	16875.60	10369.99
	Stephen SCAHILL	NZ	72	69	76	71	288	0	16875.60	10369.99
	David LYNN	Eng	73	73	72	70	288	0	16875.60	10369.99
	Jarmo SANDELIN	Swe	68	77	69	74	288	0	16875.60	10369.99
31	Tony JOHNSTONE	Zim	73	70	71	75	289	1	13849.80	8510.65
	Klas ERIKSSON	Swe	72	72	74	71	289	1	13849.80	8510.65
	Carlos RODILES	Sp	68	75	72	74	289	1	13849.80	8510.65
	Michele REALE	It	70	74	73	72	289	1	13849.80	8510.65
	Fernando ROCA	Sp	71	75	70	73	289	1	13849.80	8510.65
	Bradley DREDGE	Wal	72	74	71	72	289	1	13849.80	8510.65
	Mark PILKINGTON	Wal	69	75	74	71	289	1	13849.80	8510.65
38	Roger CHAPMAN	Eng	73	72	72	73	290	2	10848.60	6666.42
	Mark FOSTER	Eng	71	72	77	70	290	2	10848.60	6666.42
	Marc FARRY	Fr	70	69	75	76	290	2	10848.60	6666.42
	Anders HANSEN	Den	71	71	72	76	290	2	10848.60	6666.42
	Søren HANSEN	Den	66	78	72	74	290	2	10848.60	6666.42
	Jarrod MOSELEY	Aus	71	71	75	73	290	2	10848.60	6666.42
	Ignacio GARRIDO	Sp	73	73	71	73	290	2	10848.60	6666.42
	Daren LEE	Eng	75	69	73	73	290	2	10848.60	6666.42
	Jamie DONALDSON	Wal	72	74	71	73	290	2	10848.60	6666.42
47	Andrew OLDCORN	Scot	69	71	75	76	291	3	8437.80	5184.99
	Peter BAKER	Eng	72	67	76	76	291	3	8437.80	5184.99
	Iain PYMAN	Eng	72	74	73	72	291	3	8437.80	5184.99
	Sam WALKER	Eng	69	72	69	81	291	3	8437.80	5184.99
	Nick DOUGHERTY	Eng	71	74	72	74	291	3	8437.80	5184.99
52	Jamie SPENCE	Eng	67	73	74	78	292	4	7232.40	4444.28
	Henrik BJORNSTAD	Nor	74	72	74	72	292	4	7232.40	4444.28
54	Henrik STENSON	Swe	72	73	73	75	293	5	6371.40	3915.20
	Christophe POTTIER	Fr	69	73	75	76	293	5	6371.40	3915.20
	Eduardo DE LA RIVA	Sp	73	73	74	73	293	5	6371.40	3915.20
57	Shaun P WEBSTER	Eng	68	77	73	76	294	6	5510.40	3386.12
	Adam MEDNICK	Swe	70	74	75	75	294	6	5510.40	3386.12
59	Peter FOWLER	Aus	71	74	78	72	295	7	4735.50	2909.95
	Robert-Jan DERKSEN	Hol	73	71	76	75	295	7	4735.50	2909.95
	Massimo SCARPA	It	71	74	72	78	295	7	4735.50	2909.95
	Gary ORR	Scot	68	72	76	79	295	7	4735.50	2909.95
	Markus BRIER	Aut	71	72	74	78	295	7	4735.50	2909.95
	Andrew COLTART	Scot	72	73	71	79	295	7	4735.50	2909.95
65	Chris GANE	Eng	72	72	73	79	296	8	3788.40	2327.96
	Grant HAMERTON	Eng	71	74	73	78	296	8	3788.40	2327.96
	Raymond RUSSELL	Scot	74	67	75	80	296	8	3788.40	2327.96
	Benoit TEILLERIA	Fr	69	75	72	80	296	8	3788.40	2327.96
	Mikko ILONEN	Fin	70	76	74	76	296	8	3788.40	2327.96
70	Mårten OLANDER	Swe	72	71	82	72	297	9	2998.67	1842.67
	Andrew MARSHALL	Eng	74	72	72	79	297	9	2998.67	1842.67
	Gary EVANS	Eng	71	72	75	79	297	9	2998.67	1842.67
73	Sam TORRANCE	Scot	71	75	75	77	298	10	2577.00	1583.56
	Nicolas VANHOOTEGEM	Bel	72	73	76	77	298	10	2577.00	1583.56
	Roger WESSELS	SA	72	72	78	76	298	10	2577.00	1583.56
76	José RIVERO	Sp	75	69	76	79	299	11	2569.50	1578.95
	Jean HUGO	SA	70	74	76	79	299	11	2569.50	1578.95
78	Van PHILLIPS	Eng	71	73	74	82	300	12	2563.50	1575.26
	Matthew CORT	Eng	70	75	75	80	300	12	2563.50	1575.26
80	Santiago LUNA	Sp	76	70	78	77	301	13	2557.50	1571.57
	Roger WINCHESTER	Eng	73	73	79	76	301	13	2557.50	1571.57
82	Gregory HAVRET	Fr	71	72	80	80	303	15	2553.00	1568.81
	Richard BLAND	Eng	71	73	80	79	303	15	2553.00	1568.81
84	Alfredo GARCIA (AM)	Sp	73	73	81	81	308	20		

CRIME FILE 25,259 - MARQUES DE RISCAL RIOJA RESERVA 1998.
We received a call to the incident room at 00.15 advising of
a tragic accident - a bottle of Marques de Riscal 1998 dropped
unintentionally, had suffered damage beyond repair. A deep
red stain on the carpet and a raisin fruit aroma were the
only evidence remaining of a once vibrant, juicy wine. Four
years of meticulous care in making a sublime Reserva had been
wasted. Verdict - a particularly heinous crime.

HEREDEROS DEL
MARQUES DE RISCAL

www.marquesderiscal.com

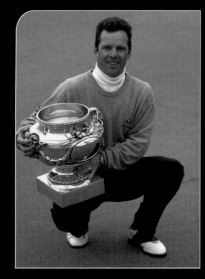

Novotel Perrier Open de France · Le Golf National · Paris · France

heart warming

1	Malcolm MACKENZIE	Eng	274	-14
2	Trevor IMMELMAN	SA	275	-13
3	Kenneth FERRIE	Eng	276	-12
	Anders HANSEN	Den	276	-12
	Ian WOOSNAM	Wal	276	-12
6	Andrew COLTART	Scot	277	-11
	José Maria OLAZÁBAL	Sp	277	-11
	Eduardo ROMERO	Arg	277	-11
9	Gary EVANS	Eng	280	- 8
	Jean-Francois REMESY	Fr	280	- 8

Malcolm Mackenzie

Only English Public School boys in April's Halford Hewitt or Oxbridge graduates in their January President's Putter will have competed in conditions as cold and windswept as the four days that greeted competitors in the Novotel Perrier Open de France at Le Golf National.

Waterproofs and woollens might have been the order of the week but one man who did not feel the cold at all come Sunday night was Malcolm Mackenzie. In fact, the victory by one of the most well-liked professionals on The European Tour was truly heart warming.

The amiable Englishman, who had turned 40 the previous September, had never won a tournament in 20 seasons on the road, and had spent the previous five years struggling just to keep his card. All that was forgotten, however, at the end of a memorable week in Paris as Mackenzie experienced true *joie de vivre*.

The rawness of conditions explained why there were no exceptional scores on day one. The best were three five under par 67s; Scotland's Colin Montgomerie, looking to be more competitive this side of the Atlantic than he had been in America in March and April, Sweden's Mårten Olander, and Frenchman Jean-Francois Remesy, who carried home hopes.

Of the three, Olander's round was the most extraordinary. Having started at the tenth, he proceeded to drop four shots in his opening three holes, before finding ten birdies in the next 15, including eight in a row from the 18th, a run which equalled The European Tour record for most birdies in succession in a round.

Andrew Coltart

Trevor Immelman

Montgomerie had appeared with one of the new mid-length putters in an attempt to take the wrist-break out of his putting stroke. The 2000 Novotel Perrier Open de France Champion briefly shared the lead early in the second round, but then three sixes came at par fives. By the time he handed in a level par 72, he was seven shots off the pace and would not trouble the leaderboards over the weekend.

The runaway leader on day two was South Africa's Trevor Immelman. He made the most of the one glorious morning of the week, and broke clear with four birdies in his last five holes to card a 64. It moved him four shots clear of the field and, as the weather closed in, gave him a lead he would take into the weekend.

One of the few who came through the weather-battered side of the draw was defending Champion José Maria Olazábal. An opening 69 was compiled in rain and wind and in many ways was more meritorious than his 67 on day two.

The two time Masters Champion began round three in spectacular style, holing in one at the second, a hole that on previous days had

shot of the week

MALCOLM MACKENZIE England

Under normal circumstances José Maria Olazábal's hole in one at the second with a four iron in round three would be the choice, but that was completely put in the shade when Malcolm Mackenzie put aside the difficulties of his previous few holes in the final round and, from an awkward spot in the 18th fairway, hit a career two iron into the wind and across the water to secure his maiden victory.

Then, enter Mackenzie. His trials and tribulations over the past five years had largely been on the greens and at the start of the week, he had turned to Sam Torrance for a lesson in the use of the broomstick. It produced immediate success.

Two rounds under 70 were, by some way, his best start of the year and, confidence renewed, he holed everything in round three for a 65 and the tournament lead by a shot from Immelman and Olazábal.

The Spaniard was his partner in the last round and by then favourite to defend the title, a mantle enhanced when Mackenzie opened with successive bogeys. Olazábal, though, did not take advantage. Rather like the previous day, he drove well, but the rest of his game was not of a similar standard and he slowly played himself out of the Championship.

By the turn Mackenzie had steadied his ship and, having covered the 12 holes from the third to the 14th in four under par, found himself three shots clear with four to play. Then he, too, wobbled. He scattered shots at the 15th, 16th, and 17th, leaving him level with Immelman with just the par five 18th to play.

cost him a four and a five. Thereafter, however, not a great deal happened for the Spaniard and another 67 was about as many as he could have taken on a day when he hit the ball well.

Immelman, despite a glittering amateur career, very much in tandem with that of Sergio Garcia, had taken some time to find his feet amongst the professionals. This was an opportunity for him to discover how he would cope. The answer was pretty well. It is always hard to follow one good round with another, but his blade kept his score respectable, 25 putts being the foundation of a third round 71.

From a perfect drive, Immelman could do no better than par, so Mackenzie had one last chance; a birdie for victory. His drive was good, if a little short. Modest lie, modest stance, should he go for it or not? His caddie was in no doubt. 'Go on, have a go,' he said. The result was a two iron, in Mackenzie's own words, "the best I have ever hit," which never left the pin and which finished 15 feet from the hole.

Two putts gave him the birdie, victory, and the satisfying knowledge that, in the end, he had won well. He knew what he had to do and he had done it. It was always going to be difficult, for 20 years and 509 tournaments is a lot of water under many bridges. After such a journey, no wonder the taste of victory was sweet indeed.

Bruce Critchley

Gary Evans

the course

Le Golf National has now matured into one of Europe's finest Championship courses. Links-like in character, it had been marginally altered since the Novotel Perrier Open de France was played there two years previously, most noticeably where sand has made way for grass, making life harder for the professional, but less daunting for the amateur.

Roger Chapman and Mark Mouland

final results

Le Golf National · Paris · France
May 2-5 · 2002 · Par 72 · 7098 yards · 6490 metres

Pos.	Name		Rd1	Rd2	Rd3	Rd4	Total	Par	Prize Money Euro	£
1	Malcolm MACKENZIE	Eng	68	69	65	72	274	-14	333330.00	205794.83
2	Trevor IMMELMAN	SA	68	64	71	72	275	-13	222220.00	137196.55
3	Ian WOOSNAM	Wal	69	71	66	70	276	-12	103333.30	63797.01
	Anders HANSEN	Den	69	70	65	72	276	-12	103333.30	63797.01
	Kenneth FERRIE	Eng	68	72	67	69	276	-12	103333.30	63797.01
6	Eduardo ROMERO	Arg	70	66	71	70	277	-11	60000.00	37043.44
	José Maria OLAZÁBAL	Sp	69	67	67	74	277	-11	60000.00	37043.44
	Andrew COLTART	Scot	71	66	71	69	277	-11	60000.00	37043.44
9	Jean-Francois REMESY	Fr	67	69	69	75	280	-8	42400.00	26177.36
	Gary EVANS	Eng	71	67	67	75	280	-8	42400.00	26177.36
11	Klas ERIKSSON	Swe	76	66	69	70	281	-7	33500.00	20682.59
	Mark DAVIS	Eng	69	70	72	70	281	-7	33500.00	20682.59
	Nick O'HERN	Aus	71	71	67	72	281	-7	33500.00	20682.59
	Ricardo GONZALEZ	Arg	71	68	69	73	281	-7	33500.00	20682.59
15	Mårten OLANDER	Swe	67	71	72	72	282	-6	27040.00	16694.24
	Søren KJELDSEN	Den	72	69	70	71	282	-6	27040.00	16694.24
	Thomas LEVET	Fr	72	70	70	70	282	-6	27040.00	16694.24
	Søren HANSEN	Den	69	72	70	71	282	-6	27040.00	16694.24
	Robert KARLSSON	Swe	69	71	70	72	282	-6	27040.00	16694.24
20	Stuart LITTLE	Eng	74	69	72	68	283	-5	23266.67	14364.62
	Gary ORR	Scot	72	69	68	74	283	-5	23266.67	14364.62
	Christopher HANELL	Swe	75	69	71	68	283	-5	23266.67	14364.62
23	Mark JAMES	Eng	72	68	73	71	284	-4	20800.00	12841.73
	Colin MONTGOMERIE	Scot	67	72	71	74	284	-4	20800.00	12841.73
	David DRYSDALE	Scot	77	64	70	73	284	-4	20800.00	12841.73
	Stephen GALLACHER	Scot	68	75	70	71	284	-4	20800.00	12841.73
	Nick DOUGHERTY	Eng	71	70	69	74	284	-4	20800.00	12841.73
28	Emanuele CANONICA	It	75	65	73	72	285	-3	18100.00	11174.77
	Markus BRIER	Aut	70	72	71	72	285	-3	18100.00	11174.77
	Daren LEE	Eng	73	69	69	74	285	-3	18100.00	11174.77
	Carl PETTERSSON	Swe	70	68	70	77	285	-3	18100.00	11174.77
32	Roger CHAPMAN	Eng	72	68	71	75	286	-2	14875.00	9183.69
	Santiago LUNA	Sp	69	71	71	75	286	-2	14875.00	9183.69
	Mark MOULAND	Wal	72	68	71	75	286	-2	14875.00	9183.69
	Alexandre BALICKI	Fr	77	65	70	74	286	-2	14875.00	9183.69
	Henrik BJORNSTAD	Nor	70	72	75	69	286	-2	14875.00	9183.69
	Erol SIMSEK	Ger	75	66	71	74	286	-2	14875.00	9183.69
	Mikael LUNDBERG	Swe	70	70	74	72	286	-2	14875.00	9183.69
	Jamie DONALDSON	Wal	69	70	74	73	286	-2	14875.00	9183.69
40	Barry LANE	Eng	69	74	70	74	287	-1	11800.00	7285.21
	Raphaël JACQUELIN	Fr	71	73	70	73	287	-1	11800.00	7285.21
	Richard GREEN	Aus	68	73	72	74	287	-1	11800.00	7285.21
	Paul EALES	Eng	70	72	68	77	287	-1	11800.00	7285.21
	Jonathan LOMAS	Eng	71	69	71	76	287	-1	11800.00	7285.21
	Christophe POTTIER	Fr	74	70	71	72	287	-1	11800.00	7285.21
	David CARTER	Eng	72	71	69	75	287	-1	11800.00	7285.21
47	David GILFORD	Eng	72	71	72	73	288	0	9600.00	5926.95
	David LYNN	Eng	71	70	72	75	288	0	9600.00	5926.95
	Patrik SJÖLAND	Swe	70	73	76	69	288	0	9600.00	5926.95
	Simon DYSON	Eng	73	69	74	72	288	0	9600.00	5926.95
51	Richard S JOHNSON	Swe	73	69	72	75	289	1	8000.00	4939.13
	Stephen SCAHILL	NZ	72	65	70	82	289	1	8000.00	4939.13
	Mark PILKINGTON	Wal	69	71	73	76	289	1	8000.00	4939.13
	John BICKERTON	Eng	69	71	70	79	289	1	8000.00	4939.13
55	Ian POULTER	Eng	71	73	68	78	290	2	5975.00	3688.91
	Gary EMERSON	Eng	72	71	74	73	290	2	5975.00	3688.91
	Thomas BJÖRN	Den	70	71	75	74	290	2	5975.00	3688.91
	Bertrand CORNUT	Fr	74	70	71	75	290	2	5975.00	3688.91
	Sebastien DELAGRANGE	Fr	70	73	73	74	290	2	5975.00	3688.91
	Henrik NYSTROM	Swe	73	68	76	73	290	2	5975.00	3688.91
	Benoit TEILLERIA	Fr	74	70	73	73	290	2	5975.00	3688.91
	Alastair FORSYTH	Scot	69	74	72	75	290	2	5975.00	3688.91
63	Costantino ROCCA	It	73	69	73	76	291	3	4900.00	3025.21
	Raymond RUSSELL	Scot	71	72	75	73	291	3	4900.00	3025.21
65	Matthew CORT	Eng	72	69	74	77	292	4	4600.00	2840.00
66	Philip GOLDING	Eng	72	72	73	76	293	5	4100.00	2531.30
	Stephen DODD	Wal	71	72	77	73	293	5	4100.00	2531.30
	Didier DE VOOGHT	Bel	73	68	76	76	293	5	4100.00	2531.30
	Gary CLARK	Eng	72	69	75	77	293	5	4100.00	2531.30
70	Magnus PERSSON ATLEVI	Swe	70	74	73	77	294	6	3650.00	2253.48
71	Tom GILLIS	USA	71	71	74	79	295	7	2997.00	1850.32
	Peter O'MALLEY	Aus	72	71	75	77	295	7	2997.00	1850.32
	Fredrik JACOBSON	Swe	70	70	76	79	295	7	2997.00	1850.32
74	Desvonde BOTES	SA	73	71	76	79	297	9	2989.50	1845.69
	Jeremy ROBINSON	Eng	74	70	77	76	297	9	2989.50	1845.69
76	Anthony WALL	Eng	72	72	77	79	300	12	2985.00	1842.91
77	Ignacio GARRIDO	Sp	70	72	77	83	302	14	2982.00	1841.06
78	Marcel Siem	Ger	75	69	DISQ		144	0		

Fit for Golf?

These days it is no longer sufficient to rely on talent and the desire to win. The right training and the right skills are important factors in performance. However, a balanced diet is also very much part of the package. Nestlé Nutrition will provide golf professionals and enthusiasts with information and up-to-date advice on sports nutrition, innovative foods and beverage products, giving them the winning edge.

Please come and ask for your free copy of the "Fit for golf" booklet at the upcoming Tour Event.

OFFICIAL PARTNER OF THE PGA EUROPEAN TOUR

Benson and Hedges International Open
The De Vere Belfry · Sutton Coldfield · England

angel delight

Angel Cabrera

It was at the back of the 16th green at The De Vere Belfry that a small boy, who had clearly been getting mixed messages from his parents, asked his father: "Who do I want to win, dad?" The father said there was no easy answer and he was right.

For almost everyone at the Benson and Hedges International Open, the matter of whom they preferred to make off with the 294,356 euro (£183,330) first prize was no less of a close run thing than the event itself.

Angel Cabrera, who ended up winning by a shot from Barry Lane, was a particular favourite, however, with the Midlands crowd. Not only had this amiable 32 year old Argentine held his own with John Daly over the first two days on the long-hitting front, but he had finished tied for second in the tournament in both 1999 and 2001.

As for Lane, everyone wanted to see this enduring enthusiast back in the winner's circle for the first time since he won the Accenture World Championship of Golf in 1995.

In the first half of 2001, when he picked up no more than £1,500, Lane had considered quitting the game. However, when his wife, Stephanie, asked what else could he do, he had had to concede that the answer was not very much.

Eduardo Romero

Peter Baker

"I'm as thick as two short planks," he explained, cheerfully, after his opening 69. Then, though, he came up with a series of perceptive remarks as to why he could not break away from life on The European Tour. He liked the camaraderie and he liked the feeling of playing golf in front of an audience. In fact, he was hooked on the general buzz of a tournament.

There was, also, the not inconsequential matter of his loyal fans. He thought the world of them. That very morning, a handful had been at the club at the crack of dawn in order to watch him practice. "There are some young guys who don't realise how privileged they are to be out here," he maintained.

Jos Vanstiphout, Lane's golf psychologist, had also played a part in helping to turn the player's career around. He told Lane that if he loved playing golf as much as he said he did, he should go out and enjoy the tournaments. Which is what he did. In the second half of 2001, he collected close to £300,000.

Colin Montgomerie and Greg Owen would have been no less popular winners. In Montgomerie's case, it would have been a great result for the tournament to have a player of his calibre coming out on top. As for Owen, he was seen as a local as he drove back and forth from his home in Mansfield. Inevitably, the crowd felt particularly proprietorial after his opening 66.

Meanwhile, Birmingham's Irish contingent had a soft spot for Padraig Harrington. Two years before, Harrington had gone into the last round with a five shot lead, only for officialdom to discover that he had failed to sign his first round scorecard. He was disqualified and the shock and disappointment of it all stayed with him until he won the Volvo Masters Andalucia in 2001.

Cabrera, who started the last round three shots behind Lane and one behind Owen, took the outright lead at the tenth, a hole which invited this huge hitter to go for the green. He narrowly missed the putting surface but was down in a pitch and putt to move to ten under par.

A bunkered drive saw him dragged back into the pack at the next hole, but he went out in front again after catching the green of the

Greg Owen

the course

The pride of the greenkeepers was mirrored in the faces of the locals - The De Vere Belfry was in glorious shape and everyone knew it. There are plenty of people who can remember when the holes on the Brabazon Course were separated by scrawny saplings but, today, the trees are mature and generations of ducks have made the lakes their home. Seldom can a course have matured better and done more to win over its critics. One player after another heaped praise on the venue for The 34th Ryder Cup Matches. "Brilliant," said Colin Montgomerie, summing up the general feeling.

564 yard 17th in two. It took him to ten under par again and one ahead of Michael Campbell, whose birdies at the 15th and 17th had helped erase the memory of a bogey five at the 13th where he drove out of bounds, Harrington, Lane and Montgomerie.

At the 18th, where Campbell, Harrington and Montgomerie all dropped shots, Cabrera hauled his second shot left, the ball coming to rest on a spectator's plastic carrier bag. He was given a free drop and, in a short game display which told everything of how confident he had been in that department all week, got down in a chip and a putt for what was his first win on European soil, following his maiden European Tour success in his native Open de Argentina in April 2001.

Lane, who had been two shots ahead of the field going into the last round, needed a birdie at the last if he were to tie. Instead, he drove into the fairway bunker and, despite the bravest of three woods to the front of the green, wound up with a par four for a nine under par total of 279 against Cabrera's 278.

The Argentine, who knows his way round British courses rather better than he does the English language, was ecstatic nevertheless

shot of the week

IAN WOOSNAM Wales

Ian Woosnam did not look like a man who was going to finish tied for 24th in the tournament when he set off from The De Vere Belfry's first tee on Thursday. Following a perfectly-placed tee shot, he opted for a punched seven iron for his second and holed it. Playing companions Aaron Baddeley and Nick Faldo applauded, with Faldo calling down the fairway that it reminded him of the 1988 Million Dollar Challenge in Sun City in which Woosnam had holed from much the same distance at the 17th to edge ahead of him. "Same club, too," replied the Welshman, giving his seven iron a congratulatory pat on the head.

at his success. "I hope this can be the start of big things for me," said this most engaging of men.

On most Sundays, one tournament ends and things move on to the next venue, the next week. In this instance, however, there was some unfinished business. Among those who had been watching the television coverage of the final round, there were some who picked up what Peter Alliss had indicated in his BBC commentary about how Cabrera's drop from the carrier bag was not, as per the textbook.

As Alliss noted, he had dropped the ball from too great a height. Shoulder-height is meant to be the level at which the ball should be released but Cabrera had been holding the ball a good six inches higher.

When John Paramor, The European Tour Chief Referee, studied the incident on television, he said there was no question of any action being taken against the player, though he would be having a quiet word with him to explain that shoulder height should be shoulder height. Since a referee had overseen the drop anyway, he said the player was in the clear.

Lane's explanation for Cabrera's actions was as good as any. "Angel was probably so anxious not to be seen to be holding it below shoulder level that he went to the other extreme. He was a worthy winner."

Lewine Mair

Phillip Price

final results

The De Vere Belfry · Sutton Coldfield · England
May 9-12 · 2002 · Par 72 · 7118 yards · 6509 metres

Pos.	Name		Rd1	Rd2	Rd3	Rd4	Total	Par	Prize Money Euro	£
1	Angel CABRERA	Arg	68	73	68	69	278	-10	294356.50	183330.00
2	Barry LANE	Eng	69	72	65	73	279	-9	196237.70	122220.00
3	Padraig HARRINGTON	Ire	71	70	70	69	280	-8	91252.17	56833.33
	Colin MONTGOMERIE	Scot	71	67	73	69	280	-8	91252.17	56833.33
	Michael CAMPBELL	NZ	70	69	71	70	280	-8	91252.17	56833.33
6	Peter BAKER	Eng	71	68	70	72	281	-7	61815.98	38500.00
7	Peter FOWLER	Aus	71	69	73	69	282	-6	48569.70	30250.00
	Steve WEBSTER	Eng	73	68	74	67	282	-6	48569.70	30250.00
9	Greg OWEN	Eng	66	72	70	75	283	-5	37442.82	23320.00
	John DALY	USA	70	69	74	70	283	-5	37442.82	23320.00
11	Nick FALDO	Eng	72	72	69	71	284	-4	28199.86	17563.33
	Tom GILLIS	USA	72	72	73	67	284	-4	28199.86	17563.33
	Olle KARLSSON	Swe	78	68	70	68	284	-4	28199.86	17563.33
	Phillip PRICE	Wal	71	70	70	73	284	-4	28199.86	17563.33
	Roger WESSELS	SA	69	69	73	73	284	-4	28199.86	17563.33
	David LYNN	Eng	73	70	68	73	284	-4	28199.86	17563.33
17	Raphaël JACQUELIN	Fr	71	70	72	72	285	-3	23313.46	14520.00
	David DRYSDALE	Scot	71	69	77	68	285	-3	23313.46	14520.00
19	Peter SENIOR	Aus	71	72	71	72	286	-2	20593.55	12826.00
	Richard GREEN	Aus	73	69	77	67	286	-2	20593.55	12826.00
	David CARTER	Eng	68	78	69	71	286	-2	20593.55	12826.00
	Retief GOOSEN	SA	73	72	73	68	286	-2	20593.55	12826.00
	Adam SCOTT	Aus	74	71	76	65	286	-2	20593.55	12826.00
24	Bernhard LANGER	Ger	72	70	73	72	287	-1	17043.55	10615.00
	Malcolm MACKENZIE	Eng	70	72	72	73	287	-1	17043.55	10615.00
	Ian WOOSNAM	Wal	67	72	78	70	287	-1	17043.55	10615.00
	Jeev Milkha SINGH	Ind	70	74	72	71	287	-1	17043.55	10615.00
	Ian POULTER	Eng	70	75	71	72	287	-1	17043.55	10615.00
	Charlie WI	R.Kor	70	74	76	67	287	-1	17043.55	10615.00
	Rolf MUNTZ	Hol	71	71	75	70	287	-1	17043.55	10615.00
	Paul LAWRIE	Scot	73	70	73	71	287	-1	17043.55	10615.00
32	Eduardo ROMERO	Arg	71	72	72	73	288	0	12951.92	8066.67
	Sam TORRANCE	Scot	72	72	71	73	288	0	12951.92	8066.67
	Jean-Francois REMESY	Fr	72	73	70	73	288	0	12951.92	8066.67
	Stuart LITTLE	Eng	71	73	77	67	288	0	12951.92	8066.67
	Michael HOEY	N.Ire	73	73	70	72	288	0	12951.92	8066.67
	Stephen SCAHILL	NZ	72	71	74	71	288	0	12951.92	8066.67
	Raymond RUSSELL	Scot	73	71	74	70	288	0	12951.92	8066.67
	Alastair FORSYTH	Scot	71	72	72	73	288	0	12951.92	8066.67

Pos.	Name		Rd1	Rd2	Rd3	Rd4	Total	Par	Prize Money Euro	£
41	Carl PETTERSSON	Swe	73	71	71	73	288	0	12951.92	8066.67
	Richard S JOHNSON	Swe	73	70	77	69	289	1	10420.41	6490.00
	Peter O'MALLEY	Aus	70	70	73	76	289	1	10420.41	6490.00
	Gary ORR	Scot	74	71	74	70	289	1	10420.41	6490.00
	Bradley DREDGE	Wal	74	70	73	72	289	1	10420.41	6490.00
	Daren LEE	Eng	70	71	74	74	289	1	10420.41	6490.00
46	David GILFORD	Eng	73	73	72	72	290	2	8654.24	5390.00
	Søren KJELDSEN	Den	75	70	71	74	290	2	8654.24	5390.00
	Richard BLAND	Eng	75	69	74	72	290	2	8654.24	5390.00
	Russell CLAYDON	Eng	71	74	74	71	290	2	8654.24	5390.00
	John BICKERTON	Eng	72	68	80	70	290	2	8654.24	5390.00
51	Santiago LUNA	Sp	72	70	75	74	291	3	6711.45	4180.00
	Anthony WALL	Eng	68	71	75	77	291	3	6711.45	4180.00
	Nick O'HERN	Aus	71	68	71	75	291	3	6711.45	4180.00
	Trevor IMMELMAN	SA	72	71	75	73	291	3	6711.45	4180.00
	Emanuele CANONICA	It	75	71	70	75	291	3	6711.45	4180.00
	Thomas BJÖRN	Den	71	70	80	70	291	3	6711.45	4180.00
57	José Maria OLAZÁBAL	Sp	74	72	77	69	292	4	5298.51	3300.00
	Brian DAVIS	Eng	73	73	73	73	292	4	5298.51	3300.00
	Henrik STENSON	Swe	73	73	71	75	292	4	5298.51	3300.00
60	Mark FOSTER	Eng	71	72	74	77	294	6	4768.66	2970.00
	Paul EALES	Eng	72	72	76	74	294	6	4768.66	2970.00
	Lucas PARSONS	Aus	72	73	76	73	294	6	4768.66	2970.00
63	Sandy LYLE	Scot	69	74	74	78	295	7	4327.12	2695.00
	Mark PILKINGTON	Wal	75	70	81	69	295	7	4327.12	2695.00
65	Des SMYTH	Ire	73	70	77	76	296	8	3973.88	2475.00
	Jarmo SANDELIN	Swe	69	77	76	74	296	8	3973.88	2475.00
67	Andrew MARSHALL	Eng	74	72	77	74	297	9	3532.34	2200.00
	Ian GARBUTT	Eng	70	76	75	76	297	9	3532.34	2200.00
	Mads VIBE-HASTRUP	Den	72	73	74	78	297	9	3532.34	2200.00
70	Benoit TEILLERIA	Fr	75	71	73	79	298	10	3227.28	2010.00
71	Eamonn DARCY	Ire	75	71	80	74	300	12	2647.50	1648.91
	Carlos RODILES	Sp	73	72	76	79	300	12	2647.50	1648.91
73	José Manuel LARA	Sp	73	73	79	77	302	14	2643.00	1646.10
74	Mark ROE	Eng	73	71	76	84	304	16	2640.00	1644.23
75	Gary EVANS	Eng	71	74	73	DISQ	218	2		

See what you can do.

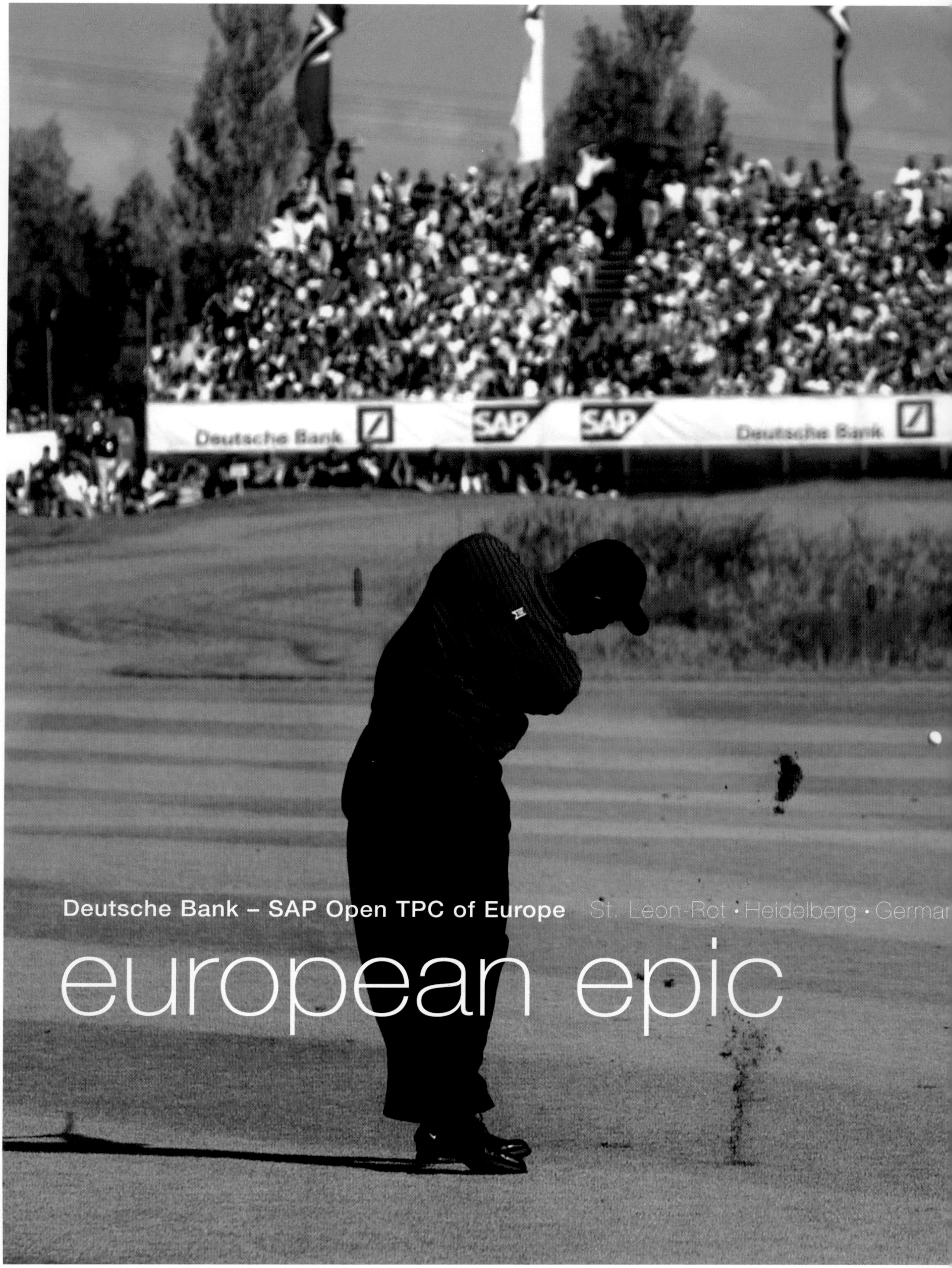

Deutsche Bank – SAP Open TPC of Europe St. Leon-Rot · Heidelberg · German

european epic

t happens only occasionally. Maybe once or twice a year if we are really lucky. But every so often there is a week that, through the sheer brilliance of the play on display from the main protagonists, transcends mere golf and becomes an epic. The 2002 Deutsche Bank - SAP Open TPC of Europe was just such an occasion. It was truly special.

Tiger Woods

All the pieces were in place by the end of the third round. Tiger Woods, the World Number One and perhaps the greatest golfer of all time, was at the revamped St. Leon-Rot course outside Heidelberg to defend his title and lay only one shot off the lead. Colin Montgomerie, Europe's most consistent performer over the last 15 years, held that lead. And close behind was Justin Rose, one of the most exciting young talents on The European Tour, poised to make a move. Just for once, the reality lived up to the anticipation.

shot of the week

TIGER WOODS USA

On the last hole of regulation play, Tiger Woods missed the green and chipped to eight feet above the hole. With Colin Montgomerie safely in for a par four and under immense pressure, he had to make his testing putt to stay alive and force a play-off. He did, dead centre.

Unlike the Masters Tournament a month earlier where Woods played a final round of great poise but his closest challengers did not, this time Montgomerie and Rose had the strength of character to metaphorically look the American in the eye with a title on the line, and perform.

Ironically, all of this did not look that likely three days earlier. Arriving in Germany, Montgomerie's form had been encouraging without quite displaying the consistency that had taken him to the top of the European game. Of more concern, however, was the seven-time Volvo Order of Merit winner's increasingly fragile back. Four months previously he had been forced to withdraw from the Johnnie Walker Classic in Perth, and since then he had been popping pain-killing pills on a regular basis.

Rose, too, arrived in Germany on the back of a missed cut in the Benson and Hedges International Open at The De Vere Belfry, a blip in an already outstanding year that had already seen him win twice in South Africa and once in Japan. However, both are battlers and proved that beyond question.

Right from the first round Montgomerie played himself into contention, even as he fought increasing pain from his lumbar region. An opening 66 was three better than Woods's 69 and had him handily placed only two shots behind the leader, Germany's Alex Cejka.

As for Woods, he professed himself happy enough with his opening effort. "I hit the ball well and could have gone lower if the putts had dropped," he said. One day later, Montgomerie had joined Cejka at the top of the leaderboard after a 68, with the ominous spectre of the World Number One only two shots back and alongside Rose, who shot through the field with a 65. Montgomerie, never a winner with Woods in the field, could feel his presence, too.

"You're not going to beat Tiger mentally," he said. "You are not going to beat him physically. You are not going to beat him by out-driving him. You are not going to beat him with putting, chipping or iron play. The only way to beat Tiger is by shooting a lower score than he does."

Which is no easy task, especially with Woods improving fast. His 67 could, and should, have been at least four shots better. "I controlled the ball well and I am very pleased with the way I am striking the ball. I'm certainly not angry or disappointed with where I'm at, especially with 36 holes to go," he said.

the course

The venue was the same as 2001, the course was not. Only the first and last holes survived as the professionals got their first taste of the new 7,255 yard St. Leon-Rot layout, redesigned by Dave Thomas. Longer and tighter than before, it played to enthusiastic reviews.

Day three, 'moving day' in professional-speak, ended with Montgomerie 17 under par and one shot clear of Woods after they had carded rounds of 65 and 64 respectively. Rose shot 66 and was next on 14 under the card. But such bare statistics concealed what was, until it was overshadowed by the even more stirring events of the final round, one of the great days on The European Tour.

All three men played wonderful golf; Woods at one time looking as if he might shoot the Tour's first ever sub-60 round. The only potential blackspot was Montgomerie's increasing struggles with his back. Both during and after his round he required attention from physiotherapist and fitness trainer Dale Richardson.

After a restless night, Montgomerie arrived on the range a full two hours before his tee-time. At first, he could not hit the ball more than 50 yards. Withdrawal looked likely. But, after more help from Richardson, his back loosened and he resolved to 'give it a go.'

Did he ever. Birdies at the opening three holes signalled his intent, but Woods stayed with him. By the time the seven-time Major Champion holed a ten foot putt for a birdie on the 455 yard tenth, they were level at 20 under par. The tournament had become, in all but name, a final afternoon, last-match-with-the-trophy-on-the-line, Ryder Cup single between the pair. It was that intense.

Both men played the final eight holes in level par - Woods made eight pars; Montgomerie had one birdie and one bogey - to finish one shot ahead of a fast-finishing Rose. After a disappointing 5-5-5 beginning to his round, the young Englishman made six birdies over the next 15 holes to close with a 67 and miss the play-off by a whisker.

Needing a birdie at the last to have any chance of catching the leaders, Rose missed the fairway and had to pitch back into play. He still made par though, after a brave eight iron approach pulled up only eight feet from the pin. "I'm happy," he said with a disarming smile. "I proved to myself that I can perform at the highest level and against the very best players."

Three holes into the play-off, after two halves in par four, it was all over and Woods had won his third Deutsche Bank - SAP Open TPC of Europe title in four years, all at St. Leon-Rot, and in the process preserved his perfect play-off record on The European Tour International Schedule, having won all five.

A par four settled matters as the pair played the closing hole for the fourth time in just over an hour. Montgomerie, whose back by that time was 'very sore', found sand from the tee and the lake with his attempted recovery, and took six.

"Monty played so well," said the magnanimous Champion, who missed only five greens all week and played his final 55 holes without a bogey. "He's a true champion, whether he has won a Major or not, and he fought all the way. It was a lot of fun and a great battle."

That it was.

John Huggan

Colin Montgomerie and Tiger Woods

final results
St. Leon-Rot · Heidelberg · Germany
May 17-20 · 2002 · Par 72 · 7255 yards · 6634 metres

Pos.	Name		Rd1	Rd2	Rd3	Rd4	Total	Par	Prize Money Euro	£
1	Tiger WOODS	USA	69	67	64	68	268	-20	450000.00	280858.55
2	Colin MONTGOMERIE	Scot	66	68	65	69	268	-20	300000.00	187239.04
3	Justin ROSE	Eng	71	65	66	67	269	-19	169020.00	105490.47
4	Greg OWEN	Eng	68	68	68	67	271	-17	135000.00	84257.57
5	Ricardo GONZALEZ	Arg	71	67	67	68	273	-15	114480.00	71450.42
6	Ian WOOSNAM	Wal	68	67	73	67	275	-13	81000.00	50554.54
	Mårten OLANDER	Swe	69	69	69	68	275	-13	81000.00	50554.54
	Thomas BJÖRN	Den	73	65	71	66	275	-13	81000.00	50554.54
9	Anders HANSEN	Den	72	68	71	65	276	-12	54720.00	34152.40
	Richard GREEN	Aus	68	67	70	71	276	-12	54720.00	34152.40
	Angel CABRERA	Arg	69	69	70	68	276	-12	54720.00	34152.40
12	Santiago LUNA	Sp	72	70	65	70	277	-11	42727.50	26667.52
	Padraig HARRINGTON	Ire	71	70	66	70	277	-11	42727.50	26667.52
	Pierre FULKE	Swe	69	70	66	72	277	-11	42727.50	26667.52
	Bradley DREDGE	Wal	70	69	70	68	277	-11	42727.50	26667.52
16	Robert KARLSSON	Swe	71	69	67	71	278	-10	35707.50	22286.13
	Alex CEJKA	Ger	64	70	71	73	278	-10	35707.50	22286.13
	Darren CLARKE	N.Ire	67	68	73	70	278	-10	35707.50	22286.13
	Michael CAMPBELL	NZ	71	72	69	66	278	-10	35707.50	22286.13
20	Søren KJELDSEN	Den	72	68	70	69	279	-9	30982.50	19337.11
	Carlos RODILES	Sp	71	69	68	71	279	-9	30982.50	19337.11
	Rolf MUNTZ	Hol	70	73	71	65	279	-9	30982.50	19337.11
	Adam SCOTT	Aus	70	73	68	68	279	-9	30982.50	19337.11
24	Eduardo ROMERO	Arg	67	70	69	74	280	-8	27270.00	17020.03
	Steve WEBSTER	Eng	73	67	70	70	280	-8	27270.00	17020.03
	Henrik BJORNSTAD	Nor	67	70	73	70	280	-8	27270.00	17020.03
	Mark PILKINGTON	Wal	71	64	72	73	280	-8	27270.00	17020.03
	David CARTER	Eng	71	67	72	70	280	-8	27270.00	17020.03
29	Greg TURNER	NZ	65	TPC	71	71	281	-7	23625.00	14745.07
	Paul LAWRIE	Scot	72	71	68	70	281	-7	23625.00	14745.07
	Fredrik JACOBSON	Swe	73	68	69	71	281	-7	23625.00	14745.07
	Niclas FASTH	Swe	71	72	72	66	281	-7	23625.00	14745.07
33	Trevor IMMELMAN	SA	67	74	70	71	282	-6	19748.57	12325.68
	Steen TINNING	Den	70	73	70	69	282	-6	19748.57	12325.68
	Søren HANSEN	Den	73	71	70	68	282	-6	19748.57	12325.68
	Joakim HAEGGMAN	Swe	71	70	68	73	282	-6	19748.57	12325.68
	Gary ORR	Scot	71	67	71	73	282	-6	19748.57	12325.68
	Gary CLARK	Eng	68	72	72	70	282	-6	19748.57	12325.68
	John BICKERTON	Eng	70	71	71	70	282	-6	19748.57	12325.68
40	Gordon BRAND JNR.	Scot	72	70	70	71	283	-5	17280.00	10784.97
	Jean VAN DE VELDE	Fr	69	70	69	75	283	-5	17280.00	10784.97
42	Sven STRÜVER	Ger	72	71	70	71	284	-4	15120.00	9436.85
	Richard S JOHNSON	Swe	68	76	70	70	284	-4	15120.00	9436.85
	Olle KARLSSON	Swe	72	70	72	70	284	-4	15120.00	9436.85
	Markus BRIER	Aut	72	71	69	72	284	-4	15120.00	9436.85
	Andrew COLTART	Scot	72	71	72	69	284	-4	15120.00	9436.85
	Patrik SJÖLAND	Swe	72	68	72	72	284	-4	15120.00	9436.85
48	Mark FOSTER	Eng	71	71	70	73	285	-3	12690.00	7920.21
	Maarten LAFEBER	Hol	73	69	71	72	285	-3	12690.00	7920.21
	Jean HUGO	SA	71	70	72	72	285	-3	12690.00	7920.21
51	Marc FARRY	Fr	71	73	69	73	286	-2	10530.00	6572.09
	Stephen SCAHILL	NZ	74	68	73	71	286	-2	10530.00	6572.09
	Sebastien DELAGRANGE	Fr	71	73	68	74	286	-2	10530.00	6572.09
	Alastair FORSYTH	Scot	69	70	69	78	286	-2	10530.00	6572.09
	Nick DOUGHERTY	Eng	74	69	74	69	286	-2	10530.00	6572.09
56	Darren FICHARDT	SA	67	75	74	71	287	-1	8302.50	5181.84
	Nick O'HERN	Aus	73	70	71	73	287	-1	8302.50	5181.84
	Gary EMERSON	Eng	70	72	74	71	287	-1	8302.50	5181.84
	Raymond RUSSELL	Scot	67	74	72	74	287	-1	8302.50	5181.84
60	Bernhard LANGER	Ger	73	71	71	73	288	0	6885.00	4297.14
	Emanuele CANONICA	It	70	73	72	73	288	0	6885.00	4297.14
	Ian GARBUTT	Eng	71	69	74	74	288	0	6885.00	4297.14
	David LYNN	Eng	71	71	71	73	288	0	6885.00	4297.14
	Daren LEE	Eng	72	72	73	71	288	0	6885.00	4297.14
	Retief GOOSEN	SA	72	69	74	73	288	0	6885.00	4297.14
66	Carl PETTERSSON	Swe	74	70	72	73	289	1	5940.00	3707.33
67	Andrew OLDCORN	Scot	72	70	72	76	290	2	5400.00	3370.30
	Jamie SPENCE	Eng	71	73	72	74	290	2	5400.00	3370.30
	Stephen GALLACHER	Scot	75	69	75	71	290	2	5400.00	3370.30
70	David DRYSDALE	Scot	71	73	76	71	291	3	4265.25	2662.07
	Mads VIBE-HASTRUP	Den	70	74	74	73	291	3	4265.25	2662.07
	Jamie DONALDSON	Wal	71	71	72	77	291	3	4265.25	2662.07
	Nick CASSINI	USA	74	70	71	76	291	3	4265.25	2662.07
74	Stephen LEANEY	Aus	75	69	75	74	293	5	4039.50	2521.17
	Diego BORREGO	Sp	70	74	77	72	293	5	4039.50	2521.17
76	Philip GOLDING	Eng	70	72	76	77	295	7	4035.00	2518.37
77	Anthony WALL	Eng	72	72	76	77	297	9	4032.00	2516.49

The Best of Golf

Deutsche Bank
SAP **Open**

TOURNAMENT PLAYERS' CHAMPIONSHIP OF EUROPE

Winner 2002

Deutsche Bank

A long standing partnership and commitment
to the Tournament Players' Championship of Europe
since 1995.

Deutsche Bank

Volvo PGA Championship Wentworth Club · Surrey · England

wildest fantasy

There are, apparently, just over five million people living on the pretty islands that make up the complex kingdom of Denmark. Of these, the last census showed that around 750,000 carry the surname Hansen. And of these, two, Anders and Søren, play on The European Tour.

Anders Hansen

Until the 2002 Volvo PGA Championship the only real reason anyone knew about either of these amiable men was that the surname thing meant they were constantly being confused with one another. At times this was mildly amusing but mostly it was irritating.

Something clearly had to be done and on a typical May English Sunday – sunshine, deluge, grey sky, sunshine, more deluge and then nightfall – Anders Hansen did what was required when he stood on the 18th green of Wentworth Club's wonderful West Course and lifted high into a leaden sky the huge, glittering trophy that is the most coveted piece of silverware on the circuit.

Beside the green the leader of the Danish pack, Thomas Björn, stood and joined in the applause. Denmark's most successful golfer could have been on his way home some hours earlier but to his credit he remained behind to greet and to congratulate his fellow countryman, as enthralled as any of the many thousands lining the fairways at the dramatic emergence of a player who had seemed destined to ply his trade somewhere towards the front of the chorus line.

Anders Hansen

Eduardo Romero

Carlos Rodiles

Indeed, in some ways this entire competition had been a classic back-to-front Championship. After day one the leader was Colin Montgomerie, a sublime eight under par 64 giving the big man a three stroke lead just three days after he had taken Tiger Woods to a play-off in Germany before conceding the Deutsche Bank - SAP Open TPC of Europe. Then on the outset of day two, in what is practically his own backyard and on a course he adores, he began to ease away from a class field. It was not to last however. Montgomerie was suffering from every professional golfer's nightmare, a painful back that necessitated repeated trips to a chiropractor and that on occasions had him wincing.

Not wincing as much, however, as the spectator whose head briefly cradled his pushed drive off the 16th tee. Thankfully John Edom, who had slipped down from nearby Ascot for some R&R rather than A&E during the second round, soon recovered consciousness and was instantly alert enough to ask for an autographed ball even if he probably thought it was Tiger he was asking. While Mr Edom was soon back on his feet, Montgomerie was equally swiftly almost on his knees thanks to a flurry of bogeys as a result of a suddenly shredded focus.

While all this was going on Hansen was making what turned out to be the biggest stride forward of a seven year professional career

Colin Montgomerie

that has been peppered with four trips to the Qualifying School. His second round 65 took him into the halfway lead on 133 – two ahead of Eduardo Romero and Montgomerie – and began at last to distinguish him properly from his Danish travelling companion of the same ilk.

shot of the week

DAVID J. RUSSELL England

David J. Russell lit up the beginning of the tournament with a spectacular eagle two on the 354 yard sixth hole in the first round. The Kedleston Park professional was 139 yards from the pin and found the bottom of the cup with a perfectly struck eight iron. "You are always surprised to see shots like that go in but it was a very good one and covered the flag all the way – it really kick started my week," he said. The shot helped Russell to an opening 68 and he eventually finished tied for 28th place, earning him an Asprey Salver as leading club professional for the week.

José Maria Olazábal

London, New York, Beverly Hills **Asprey** Since 1781

LONDON

www.asprey.com

It was a process he continued in style during Saturday's third round. By then the smart money suggested that while Hansen deserved the applause that had greeted his efforts so far he would now retreat into the background in the manner of a blind squirrel fortunate enough to have found a nut. Instead this 31 year old former Danish amateur champion decided he might as well go for the full smorgasbord and his third round 66 not only established his progress as a player but also handed him a five stroke lead ahead of young Spaniard Carlos Rodiles. Two shots further back was the comfortable and ever-smiling face of experienced Argentine Romero, and then a trio made up of Nick Faldo, Mark McNulty and Montgomerie. In an impressive aside, Hansen's 17 under par total of 199 was the lowest 54 hole total since the Volvo PGA Championship moved back to Wentworth Club in 1984.

Before leaving the course that Saturday evening, Hansen said he was retiring to his hotel where he intended to order room service, soak in a hot bath and then watch the Eurovision Song Contest on television before trying to sleep, as opposed to the rest of us who planned to try to stay awake while watching this annual celebration of massive European cultural differences.

Ken Schofield, Executive Director, The European Tour, presented Retief Goosen with his Membership Card as the newest Honorary Life Member of The European Tour.

Andrew Oldcorn

Left to right: Mel Pyatt, President and CEO, Volvo Event Management, Gerry Keaney, Managing Director, Volvo Car UK Limited, Ken Schofield, Executive Director, The European Tour, and George O'Grady, Deputy Executive Director, The European Tour, announced an extension to the partnership between The European Tour and Volvo through to and including the 2004 season.

As it turned out he enjoyed only a fretful night's rest. This may have been because the Danish Eurovision entry finished stone last and thus injected a sour note into his evening, but more probably because he was tossing and turning as he played and replayed the upcoming 18 holes that added up to the most significant event of his professional life.

One more good round would, he knew, change everything. Apart from a cheque for 528,708 euro (£333,330) there would be an invitation to the 131st Open Golf Championship at Muirfield and a five year European Tour exemption plus assorted other goodies. Most crucially, however, he would have won something as a professional at his 106th attempt. In the event, he need not have worried too much. Inevitably, one or two nibbled at his heels, first Montgomerie then Faldo and, closest of all, Romero, but they needed not only to play well, they needed Hansen to perform poorly.

That never looked likely and his solid closing 70 meant he ended the day as he had begun, five shots clear. It also meant his four round total of 269, a stunning 19 under par, was the lowest winning score in the history of the flagship event at Wentworth Club,

Andrew Coltart

Des Smyth

the course

The West Course again lived up to its reputation as one of the finest tests of golf on The European Tour International Schedule. Indeed Retief Goosen rates it in his top five in Europe and top ten in the world, praise indeed from the 2001 US Open Champion and 2001 European Number One. New bunkering on the 13th and 15th holes, plus an expanded first tee, added fine and fresh detail to the Surrey course's eternal challenge. Chris Kennedy's greenkeeping team maintained top class condition, as ever.

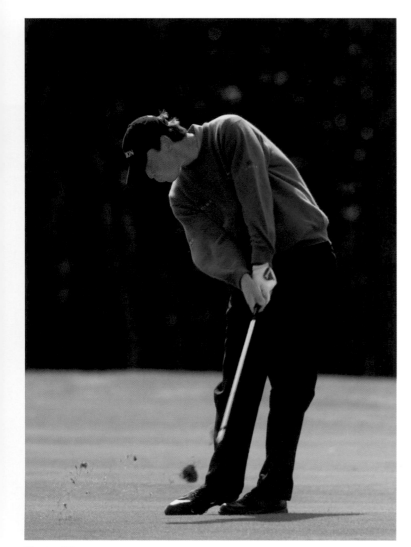

Thomas Björn

eclipsing by one stroke the previous best held by Bernhard Langer (1987) and Montgomerie (1999). "I thought it would take a lot longer to see that record bettered. Anders has played awfully well here this week and deserves huge credit, especially given the tough weather we've all had to endure," was Montgomerie's summation of a quite brilliant achievement.

A few minutes after the Scot spoke, the new great Dane struggled to fit his huge smile through the entrance to the splendid Media Centre. "To sit here as the winner of the Volvo PGA Championship is my wildest fantasy come true," he beamed. "That was the hardest 18 holes of my life. In fact I had stomach cramps I felt so nervous. This win changes everything. I love The European Tour."

Pity about the Eurovision Song Contest though.........

Bill Elliott

Volvo PGA Championship

final results

Wentworth Club · Surrey · England
May 23-26 · 2002 · Par 72 · 7072 yards · 6468 metres

Pos.	Name		Rd1	Rd2	Rd3	Rd4	Total	Par	Prize Money Euro	£
1	Anders HANSEN	Den	68	65	66	70	269	-19	528708.10	333330.00
2	Eduardo ROMERO	Arg	67	68	71	68	274	-14	275528.40	173710.00
	Colin MONTGOMERIE	Scot	64	71	72	67	274	-14	275528.40	173710.00
4	Nick FALDO	Eng	71	68	68	69	276	-12	134716.20	84933.36
	Carlos RODILES	Sp	69	67	68	72	276	-12	134716.20	84933.36
	Michael CAMPBELL	NZ	68	70	71	67	276	-12	134716.20	84933.36
7	Jarrod MOSELEY	Aus	71	73	70	63	277	-11	87237.70	55000.00
	Darren CLARKE	N.Ire	70	71	69	67	277	-11	87237.70	55000.00
9	David GILFORD	Eng	68	71	70	70	279	-9	67252.34	42400.00
	Peter O'MALLEY	Aus	69	71	69	70	279	-9	67252.34	42400.00
11	Maarten LAFEBER	Hol	71	70	67	72	280	-8	53135.69	33500.00
	Stephen LEANEY	Aus	68	71	73	68	280	-8	53135.69	33500.00
	Peter BAKER	Eng	70	70	68	72	280	-8	53135.69	33500.00
	Niclas FASTH	Swe	71	71	71	67	280	-8	53135.69	33500.00
15	Sam TORRANCE	Scot	71	68	72	70	281	-7	43777.46	27600.00
	Greg TURNER	NZ	68	71	69	73	281	-7	43777.46	27600.00
	Gregory HAVRET	Fr	73	69	70	69	281	-7	43777.46	27600.00
	Gary EVANS	Eng	68	75	67	71	281	-7	43777.46	27600.00
19	Barry LANE	Eng	71	71	69	71	282	-6	35000.82	22066.66
	Mark MCNULTY	Zim	67	69	71	75	282	-6	35000.82	22066.66
	Steen TINNING	Den	67	76	70	69	282	-6	35000.82	22066.66
	Phillip PRICE	Wal	72	72	68	70	282	-6	35000.82	22066.66
	Ricardo GONZALEZ	Arg	73	70	69	70	282	-6	35000.82	22066.66
	Ignacio GARRIDO	Sp	69	71	69	73	282	-6	35000.82	22066.66
	Thomas BJÖRN	Den	71	69	73	69	282	-6	35000.82	22066.66
	John BICKERTON	Eng	71	68	73	70	282	-6	35000.82	22066.66
	Nick DOUGHERTY	Eng	72	70	71	69	282	-6	35000.82	22066.66
28	David J RUSSELL	Eng	68	76	73	66	283	-5	29184.98	18400.00
	Søren HANSEN	Den	75	69	71	68	283	-5	29184.98	18400.00
	Alastair FORSYTH	Scot	71	68	73	71	283	-5	29184.98	18400.00
31	Robert KARLSSON	Swe	68	75	70	71	284	-4	26329.92	16600.00
	Gary CLARK	Eng	69	72	73	70	284	-4	26329.92	16600.00
	Greg OWEN	Eng	71	72	75	66	284	-4	26329.92	16600.00
34	Andrew OLDCORN	Scot	68	75	72	70	285	-3	22840.42	14400.00
	Marc FARRY	Fr	71	72	73	69	285	-3	22840.42	14400.00
	Tom GILLIS	USA	68	74	71	72	285	-3	22840.42	14400.00
	Andrew MARSHALL	Eng	72	70	72	71	285	-3	22840.42	14400.00
	Paul LAWRIE	Scot	73	70	68	74	285	-3	22840.42	14400.00
	Patrik SJÖLAND	Swe	71	71	71	72	285	-3	22840.42	14400.00
40	Jean VAN DE VELDE	Fr	71	69	74	72	286	-2	18716.45	11800.00
	Henrik BJORNSTAD	Nor	72	71	72	71	286	-2	18716.45	11800.00
	Angel CABRERA	Arg	70	71	70	75	286	-2	18716.45	11800.00
	Roger WESSELS	SA	72	71	71	72	286	-2	18716.45	11800.00
	Sebastien DELAGRANGE	Fr	70	73	71	72	286	-2	18716.45	11800.00
	David CARTER	Eng	71	72	72	71	286	-2	18716.45	11800.00
	Brett RUMFORD	Aus	72	70	74	70	286	-2	18716.45	11800.00
47	Darren FICHARDT	SA	72	72	69	74	287	-1	15544.17	9800.00
	Jorge BERENDT	Arg	73	71	74	69	287	-1	15544.17	9800.00
	Stephen GALLACHER	Scot	71	71	72	73	287	-1	15544.17	9800.00
50	Miguel Angel MARTIN	Sp	70	73	75	70	288	0	12689.12	8000.00
	José RIVERO	Sp	71	72	71	74	288	0	12689.12	8000.00
	Mark DAVIS	Eng	69	75	72	72	288	0	12689.12	8000.00
	Sion E BEBB	Wal	71	71	75	71	288	0	12689.12	8000.00
	Lucas PARSONS	Aus	68	74	72	74	288	0	12689.12	8000.00
	Mikael LUNDBERG	Swe	71	71	73	73	288	0	12689.12	8000.00
56	Gordon BRAND JNR.	Scot	70	73	77	69	289	1	9580.29	6040.00
	Robert-Jan DERKSEN	Hol	74	70	71	74	289	1	9580.29	6040.00
	Diego BORREGO	Sp	68	74	76	71	289	1	9580.29	6040.00
	Jarmo SANDELIN	Swe	69	71	73	76	289	1	9580.29	6040.00
	Andrew COLTART	Scot	67	73	77	72	289	1	9580.29	6040.00
61	Richard GREEN	Aus	71	73	75	71	290	2	8089.31	5100.00
	Jamie SPENCE	Eng	72	72	76	70	290	2	8089.31	5100.00
	Gary EMERSON	Eng	73	69	73	75	290	2	8089.31	5100.00
	Christopher HANELL	Swe	72	72	72	74	290	2	8089.31	5100.00
65	Trevor IMMELMAN	SA	69	74	73	75	291	3	7137.63	4500.00
	Wei-Tze YEH	C.Tai	73	71	73	74	291	3	7137.63	4500.00
67	Mark FOSTER	Eng	69	75	74	74	292	4	6503.17	4100.00
	Brian DAVIS	Eng	72	70	76	74	292	4	6503.17	4100.00
69	Desvonde BOTES	SA	70	74	73	76	293	5	5908.37	3725.00
	Gary MARKS	Eng	71	70	77	75	293	5	5908.37	3725.00
71	José Maria OLAZÁBAL	Sp	68	73	75	78	294	6	4756.50	2998.79
	Rolf MUNTZ	Hol	69	75	77	73	294	6	4756.50	2998.79
73	Ronan RAFFERTY	N.Ire	68	72	79	76	295	7	4750.50	2995.01
	Markus BRIER	Aut	71	72	78	74	295	7	4750.50	2995.01
75	Paul CASEY	Eng	71	72	74	79	296	8	4746.00	2992.17
76	Murray URQUHART	Scot	73	71	82	75	301	13	4743.00	2990.28

Celebrating history.
Building for the future.

VOLVO 1927–2002

Victor Chandler British Masters

Woburn Golf and Country Club · Milton Keynes · England

young lions

Justin Rose

If ever there was a natural superstar, it has to be Justin Rose. Many 21 year olds are brash and charmless, but here is a young man with time and a word for everyone, a great feeling for family, and the gift of saying the right thing at the right time, whether it be to the world's media or in a winner's acceptance speech.

Ever since holing that memorable pitch at the final hole of the 1998 Open Golf Championship at Royal Birkdale, which put a 17 year old amateur into a phenomenal share of fourth place in the world's premier golf tournament, Rose has been the centre of attention. But, in triumph or adversity, the cap size has stayed the same.

As he said after collecting the biggest cheque of his career, 329,373 euro (£208,330), his reward for becoming the youngest winner of the Victor Chandler British Masters at wonderful Woburn: "I may be only 21, but I'm old in terms of experience."

Above all, having catapulted himself at that time to the position of new English Number One, Rose is a winner, and how British sport needs all it can get of them. When he captured his first professional title on British soil after a fascinating last round shoot-out with his regular room-mate on Tour, Ian Poulter, he became at that time the most prolific title winner worldwide in 2002.

It was a second European Tour triumph to set alongside the dunhill championship in Johannesburg in January, and sandwiched between were a Sunshine Tour victory in the Nashua Masters and Japan Tour glory at The Crowns tournament.

Everybody loves a winner and to spot a great new talent coming through - though you could well understand if the applause of the sponsors was a little muted as there was huge support for rampant Rose as he powered his way to a 19 under par total of 269 on the dramatically beautiful Marquess Course.

Even his grandmother visited the state-of-the-art Victor Chandler betting unit on site to have £2 on 'her boy.' But it was more the £1500 each-way at 25-1 and £500 each-way at 28-1 from the bigger punters that hit the sponsor where it hurts. "Rose probably cost us £60,000," confirmed the firm's golf expert Don Stewart. "We were rooting for Poulter. He would have done us nicely even though there were a few bets for him after he shot the lights out in our Pro-Am."

Ian Poulter

It was an exciting betting week all round with one speciality bet giving one lucky punter a grand total of £32,000 on an investment of £180 on singles, doubles and a treble on any golfer eagling the 343 yard par four 12th on each of the last three days. Amazingly, three twos were recorded!

But if it was a busy week on the pay-out front for gentleman bookmaker Victor, who was backing the event for the fourth year running, the compensation was an immaculately staged tournament and a finish to die for.

If ever The European Tour needs an advert for the game, they should look no further than the video of the Sunday duel between young lions Poulter and Rose. The good friends never stopped smiling and joking and it was sporting spirit at its best as the pair knocked knuckles in appreciation of their half in birdie twos at the short 14th, where Poulter holed out of the bunker, only for Rose to reply with a curling ten footer.

Poulter said later: "Going head to head with a friend like Justin was just brilliant. I have never understood why some players look so miserable when they are in contention. We both felt the same as if we were playing a friendly game for a fiver - and I do believe you

Phillip Price

the course

The picture-book Marquess Course, used for only the second year, enhanced its already massive reputation. Because of the pre-tournament rain, placing was permitted on the fairways which led to masses of birdies with 75 of the 88 players who made the cut beating par on the week. The combination of a course to die for and generally amiable weather led to a record attendance of 48,525 for the four tournament days and Pro-Am, more than 7,000 up on the first year of Victor Chandler's sponsorship in 1999.

will see more tournaments now where players smile and look as if they are enjoying themselves over the finishing holes."

Rose, bogey free on the Sunday as he posted his second straight 65 for a remarkable weekend's work, leapfrogged from the pack to see off firstly third round leader Phillip Price, then Poulter in one of the most watchable finales of the year.

Price, odds-on with the sponsors going into the final round having taken over the lead at halfway from first-day pacesetters Robert-Jan Derksen and Santiago Luna, could not match strides with Poulter and Rose, but a level par 72 clinched third place ahead of the ultra-consistent Colin Montgomerie, who was rounding off a great four-week spell. "Fourth is my worst finish in a month, which can't be bad," said the Scot, while admitting that the new belly putter had not answered all his problems. "I didn't really putt well enough to challenge this week," he added.

For Rose, it was a poignant moment as he gave all his family a terrific hug behind the final green. "My other three wins were in far-off places, so it was a great feeling to have them here supporting me," he said movingly. "This week has been the greatest fun I have ever had on a golf course."

shot of the week

JUSTIN ROSE England

Justin Rose's tricky ten foot birdie response to Ian Poulter's bolt-from-the-blue bunker shot at the 14th. "Following Ian in there for a two was huge," conceded the Champion. "I did show a bit of emotion. There was a foot and a half of break, the ball stayed high for a long time, then went in via the side door. It was a very fast putt that could have gone eight feet past but it went in and kept my momentum going."

The sponsors, who were relieved to enjoy some great weather in lieu of the forecast, certainly have a Champion to be proud of. Long may Rose bloom.

Jeremy Chapman

Ken Rose, who was in the gallery to see Justin win the Victor Chandler British Masters, died three months later following a long and courageous battle with cancer. He was 57. Besides teaching Justin, Ken was his son's mentor and staunchest friend. Ken Schofield, Executive Director of The European Tour, said "Everyone at The European Tour was devasted to learn of Ken's untimely and premature death after his fight against leukaemia. Justin, of course, remains a very special talent and his father will always be closely associated with his son's success." The family picture shows: Margie Rose, Annie Rose, Justin and Ken.

final results

Woburn Golf and Country Club · Milton Keynes · England
May 30 - June 2 · 2002 · Par 72 · 7214 yards · 6597 metres

Pos.	Name		Rd1	Rd2	Rd3	Rd4	Total	Par	Prize Money Euro	£
1	Justin ROSE	Eng	70	69	65	65	269	-19	329373.90	208330.00
2	Ian POULTER	Eng	68	67	67	68	270	-18	219572.10	138880.00
3	Phillip PRICE	Wal	68	65	68	72	273	-15	123714.80	78250.00
4	Colin MONTGOMERIE	Scot	70	69	68	67	274	-14	98813.75	62500.00
5	Gary EVANS	Eng	69	69	66	71	275	-13	83794.06	53000.00
6	Mark ROE	Eng	71	68	70	68	277	-11	52331.76	33100.00
	Søren HANSEN	Den	68	69	67	73	277	-11	52331.76	33100.00
	Greg OWEN	Eng	73	67	68	69	277	-11	52331.76	33100.00
	Fredrik ANDERSSON	Swe	70	70	69	68	277	-11	52331.76	33100.00
	David CARTER	Eng	72	70	67	68	277	-11	52331.76	33100.00
11	Roger CHAPMAN	Eng	75	68	71	64	278	-10	30187.60	19093.75
	Padraig HARRINGTON	Ire	73	70	65	70	278	-10	30187.60	19093.75
	Peter HANSON	Swe	72	67	69	70	278	-10	30187.60	19093.75
	Trevor IMMELMAN	SA	72	67	68	71	278	-10	30187.60	19093.75
	Jamie SPENCE	Eng	72	68	67	71	278	-10	30187.60	19093.75
	Carlos RODILES	Sp	71	69	72	66	278	-10	30187.60	19093.75
	Roger WESSELS	SA	72	68	70	68	278	-10	30187.60	19093.75
	Paul LAWRIE	Scot	70	71	68	69	278	-10	30187.60	19093.75
19	Sandy LYLE	Scot	72	65	70	72	279	-9	23715.30	15000.00
	Barry LANE	Eng	69	74	68	68	279	-9	23715.30	15000.00
	John BICKERTON	Eng	69	71	70	69	279	-9	23715.30	15000.00
22	Nick O'HERN	Aus	71	71	66	72	280	-8	20256.82	12812.50
	Philip GOLDING	Eng	69	67	71	73	280	-8	20256.82	12812.50
	Stuart LITTLE	Eng	72	72	65	71	280	-8	20256.82	12812.50
	Jarrod MOSELEY	Aus	74	70	71	65	280	-8	20256.82	12812.50
	Paul MCGINLEY	Ire	72	72	65	71	280	-8	20256.82	12812.50
	Jorge BERENDT	Arg	70	73	68	69	280	-8	20256.82	12812.50
	Rolf MUNTZ	Hol	70	74	69	67	280	-8	20256.82	12812.50
	Gary ORR	Scot	71	71	70	68	280	-8	20256.82	12812.50
30	Santiago LUNA	Sp	67	71	72	71	281	-7	15001.72	9488.63
	Malcolm MACKENZIE	Eng	73	70	69	69	281	-7	15001.72	9488.63
	Mark FOSTER	Eng	70	70	73	68	281	-7	15001.72	9488.63
	José Manuel LARA	Sp	74	70	68	69	281	-7	15001.72	9488.63
	Thomas LEVET	Fr	68	70	73	70	281	-7	15001.72	9488.63
	Chris GANE	Eng	69	75	69	68	281	-7	15001.72	9488.63
	Bradley DREDGE	Wal	71	73	69	68	281	-7	15001.72	9488.63
	Simon KHAN	Eng	72	65	72	72	281	-7	15001.72	9488.63
	Robert COLES	Eng	69	72	67	73	281	-7	15001.72	9488.63
	Benoit TEILLERIA	Fr	71	71	68	71	281	-7	15001.72	9488.63
	Simon DYSON	Eng	70	72	72	67	281	-7	15001.72	9488.63
41	Steve WEBSTER	Eng	70	71	71	70	282	-6	11857.65	7500.00
	Paul BROADHURST	Eng	72	68	74	68	282	-6	11857.65	7500.00
	Paul EALES	Eng	70	69	71	72	282	-6	11857.65	7500.00
	Olle KARLSSON	Swe	69	71	69	73	282	-6	11857.65	7500.00
45	Costantino ROCCA	It	71	70	72	70	283	-5	10079.00	6375.00

Pos.	Name		Rd1	Rd2	Rd3	Rd4	Total	Par	Prize Money Euro	£
	Raphaël JACQUELIN	Fr	71	72	69	71	283	-5	10079.00	6375.00
	Robert KARLSSON	Swe	69	69	75	70	283	-5	10079.00	6375.00
	Lee WESTWOOD	Eng	71	70	71	71	283	-5	10079.00	6375.00
	Nick DOUGHERTY	Eng	72	72	70	69	283	-5	10079.00	6375.00
50	Andrew OLDCORN	Scot	74	70	73	67	284	-4	7905.10	5000.00
	Sam TORRANCE	Scot	71	68	69	76	284	-4	7905.10	5000.00
	Marc FARRY	Fr	69	73	75	67	284	-4	7905.10	5000.00
	Sven STRÜVER	Ger	69	72	72	71	284	-4	7905.10	5000.00
	Jean HUGO	SA	69	72	73	70	284	-4	7905.10	5000.00
	Joakim HAEGGMAN	Swe	73	70	72	69	284	-4	7905.10	5000.00
56	Jean-Francois REMESY	Fr	72	71	71	71	285	-3	6077.05	3843.75
	Henrik STENSON	Swe	72	72	74	67	285	-3	6077.05	3843.75
	Ian GARBUTT	Eng	75	67	71	72	285	-3	6077.05	3843.75
	Patrik SJÖLAND	Swe	72	70	70	73	285	-3	6077.05	3843.75
60	Des SMYTH	Ire	69	74	72	71	286	-2	4940.69	3125.00
	Brian DAVIS	Eng	70	74	71	71	286	-2	4940.69	3125.00
	Jean VAN DE VELDE	Fr	71	68	76	71	286	-2	4940.69	3125.00
	Steen TINNING	Den	71	72	71	72	286	-2	4940.69	3125.00
	Charlie WI	R.Kor	70	72	71	73	286	-2	4940.69	3125.00
	Peter HEDBLOM	Swe	69	71	72	74	286	-2	4940.69	3125.00
	Jamie DONALDSON	Wal	70	74	68	74	286	-2	4940.69	3125.00
67	Darren FICHARDT	SA	75	68	71	73	287	-1	3363.13	2127.19
	Shaun Paul WEBSTER	Eng	76	68	69	74	287	-1	3363.13	2127.19
	Ignacio GARRIDO	Sp	76	68	71	72	287	-1	3363.13	2127.19
	Gary CLARK	Eng	72	72	72	71	287	-1	3363.13	2127.19
	Raymond RUSSELL	Scot	68	70	73	76	287	-1	3363.13	2127.19
	Stephen GALLACHER	Scot	73	69	70	75	287	-1	3363.13	2127.19
	Mikael LUNDBERG	Swe	75	69	72	71	287	-1	3363.13	2127.19
	Tobias DIER	Ger	72	67	79	69	287	-1	3363.13	2127.19
	Wei-Tze YEH	C.Tai	71	71	73	72	287	-1	3363.13	2127.19
76	Gordon BRAND JNR.	Scot	70	74	74	70	288	0	2943.00	1861.46
	Ian WOOSNAM	Wal	72	71	74	71	288	0	2943.00	1861.46
	Elliot BOULT	NZ	74	70	72	72	288	0	2943.00	1861.46
	Kenneth A FERRIE	Eng	71	72	70	75	288	0	2943.00	1861.46
	Darren CLARKE	N.Ire	73	70	70	75	288	0	2943.00	1861.46
81	Adam MEDNICK	Swe	72	71	72	74	289	1	2934.00	1855.76
	Barry HUME (AM)	Scot	69	74	71	75	289	1		
83	Gustavo ROJAS	Arg	71	73	74	72	290	2	2928.00	1851.97
	Henrik NYSTROM	Swe	74	68	76	72	290	2	2928.00	1851.97
	Carl PETTERSSON	Swe	72	70	73	75	290	2	2928.00	1851.97
86	Robert-Jan DERKSEN	Hol	67	74	75	75	291	3	2920.50	1847.23
	Arjun ATWAL	Ind	70	72	76	73	291	3	2920.50	1847.23
88	Carl SUNESON	Sp	75	69	72	76	292	4	2916.00	1844.38

The Compass Group English Open
Marriott Forest of Arden · Warwickshire · England

rude health

Darren Clarke

It was difficult to determine in the build-up to The Compass Group English Open whether the latest instalment of The European Tour season was about to unfold or the next episode of Casualty.

The Media Centre at the Marriott Forest of Arden resembled more of an Accident and Emergency Unit as one by one the walking wounded returned with their stories of illness, hard luck and heartbreak. None had a sadder or more uplifting tale to tell than Salisbury 36 year old Andy Beal, courageously returning to the Tour after losing an eye to cancer just a few months earlier.

Beal explained how a little brown segment in his left eye, first spotted two years earlier, had turned into a malignant tumour. He was offered the option of Proton Beam Therapy or removal and opted for the latter, which left him without one orb, but with fewer long-term risks.

Specialists took away the offending organ, but not Beal's sense of humour as he regaled the world's Press about how he had difficulty seeing anything coming at him from the left. "I'd probably get flattened if I ever played scrum-half," he quipped.

Enter David Howell, whose own problems started when he hit the deck himself just two months earlier. It may have been mighty

Mark Roe

painful when it happened, but even the 26 year old had difficulty suppressing a laugh when he recalled the day he felt guilty about not having exercised for a week... and promptly broke his arm when he decided to do something about it.

Howell was just 300 yards short of a planned three-mile run when one of his shoelaces came undone and undid the Swindon supporter himself as he trod on the offending article and launched himself into the local hospital.

At least Howell followed this event by taking his place in the US Open Championship - a situation that International Sports Management stablemate Lee Westwood, uncharacteristically, did not find himself in after slipping out of the top 50 in the Official World Golf Ranking.

It was the least of Westwood's worries at the Warwickshire course, however, as the former European Number One joined the casualty list just a handful of holes into a first round that had started with plenty of promise. Shoulder, upper arm and elbow problems affected his ability to hold the club and he was reluctantly forced to withdraw.

Enter Darren Clarke, fit of body, but vulnerable to his own expectation levels that have occasionally prompted an attack of Loss-Of-Head Syndrome. The Marriott Forest of Arden, however,

Sandy Lyle

is a little piece of England that will remain forever Irish, or at least Ulster, and this would be another week when the Ryder Cup star's cranium would remain well and truly fixed to his neck.

Any St John's Ambulance person would have had no problem getting a part-time job as a caddie for the week but not with Clarke - the only physical concerns the Ulsterman has encountered in a glittering career have centred on preventing a waistline increasing its circumference.

Whatever its size, Clarke has always had a stomach for the fight and he was in no mood to let anybody overpower him in his bid to become the first player to win The Compass Group English Open for a third time - his first victory having come at Marriott Hanbury Manor Hotel in 1999, followed by his initial success at the Marriott Forest of Arden the following year.

shot of the week

DARREN CLARKE Northern Ireland

Champion Darren Clarke gave his army of followers plenty of outstanding shots to admire throughout one of the best ball-striking weeks of his career. But few compared to the five iron he hit to the sixth on the last day especially considering the ball had mud on it. From 197 yards out, the only thing left when it stopped rolling was a tap in.

Clarke, whose experiment with the belly putter had gone belly-up before his arrival, showed why he had returned to his trusted Scotty Cameron model with an opening 65 - a round which would have had most doing cartwheels in celebration. Not Clarke. "I played very well today," he said matter of factly and with glorious understatement. In reality, rarely had he driven with greater accuracy or hit his irons with such crispness.

It was a round with a warning to all. 'I am here to win, now come and stop me,' it seemed to say. Many tried and all failed. Once Clarke has his nose in front everybody else had theirs put out of joint and so it proved on a final day more suited to Michael Fish and his weather charts than golf.

The course took a terrific pounding from the heavens and how only one hour's play was lost all week was a testimony to its condition and high standard of greenkeeping. The most patient of souls would have been tested as downpour after downpour descended, but Clarke was unperturbed and finally hailed by all as a worthy and true Champion. The first with congratulations was his stunning wife Heather, thankfully back walking behind the ropes after a winter spent fighting, and recovering from, illness.

"I just wish I could roll this course up and take it with me," he said afterwards. No wonder after rounds of 65-70-68-68 for a 17 under par aggregate gave him a three shot win over Søren Hansen,

Jarrod Moseley

the latest in a line of Danes who are proving their country is capable of exporting far more than simply bacon and pastries.

There were other notable achievements. Not least Sandy Lyle's first top ten finish in seven years which came after discovering that he had been playing for the last decade with the wrong loft on his clubs. Asked where he had made the discovery, the Scot revealed it

was at a golf academy in Palm Springs - ironically owned by his long-time rival Nick Faldo. "I don't think he knows I was there," he said mischievously.

Sam Torrance also showed glimpses of his title-winning past, especially with a third round 65 that helped him into the top ten, while the future expressed itself again in the shape of Justin Rose, bidding for back-to-back wins but who had to settle for a share of sixth, and fellow Englishman Nick Dougherty, who completed another top 20 finish.

Nobody compared to Clarke, however. He emerged from the week with a unique treble and his ninth European Tour International Schedule victory. The performance suggested it would not be far down the line before he got into double figures - good health and fitness prevailing.

Martin Hardy

the course

It was a testimony to the skill and efficiency of the Marriott Forest of Arden greenkeepers that only a small amount of time was lost due to bad weather. There were more squeegees than hours of sunlight throughout a soggy week, but the course stood up to the battering it took from the heavens and once again proved itself to be a first class European Tour venue. No wonder Champion Darren Clarke wanted to roll it up and take it with him to the US Open Championship.

Greg Owen

final results

Marriott Forest of Arden • Warwickshire • England
June 6-9 • 2002 • Par 72 • 7213 yards • 6595 metres

Pos.	Name		Rd1	Rd2	Rd3	Rd4	Total	Par	Prize Money Euro	£
1	Darren CLARKE	N.Ire	65	70	68	68	271	-17	208797.50	133330.00
2	Søren HANSEN	Den	72	68	64	70	274	-14	139187.90	88880.00
3	Raphaël JACQUELIN	Fr	70	68	65	73	276	-12	70533.54	45040.00
	Phillip PRICE	Wal	68	68	70	70	276	-12	70533.54	45040.00
5	Wei-Tze YEH	C.Tai	68	72	69	68	277	-11	53119.40	33920.00
6	Sandy LYLE	Scot	71	70	66	71	278	-10	37584.48	24000.00
	Justin ROSE	Eng	68	69	68	73	278	-10	37584.48	24000.00
	Sam WALKER	Eng	68	71	66	73	278	-10	37584.48	24000.00
9	Bradley DREDGE	Wal	69	72	69	69	279	-9	28063.08	17920.00
10	Mark ROE	Eng	67	70	70	73	280	-8	21235.23	13560.00
	Sam TORRANCE	Scot	70	72	65	73	280	-8	21235.23	13560.00
	Steve WEBSTER	Eng	72	67	65	76	280	-8	21235.23	13560.00
	Gregory HAVRET	Fr	71	69	70	70	280	-8	21235.23	13560.00
	Dennis EDLUND	Swe	68	70	69	73	280	-8	21235.23	13560.00
	David DRYSDALE	Scot	68	67	73	72	280	-8	21235.23	13560.00
16	Robert-Jan DERKSEN	Hol	69	73	65	74	281	-7	16261.55	10384.00
	Ian POULTER	Eng	68	72	69	72	281	-7	16261.55	10384.00
	Carl SUNESON	Sp	69	72	69	71	281	-7	16261.55	10384.00
	Didier DE VOOGHT	Bel	67	71	72	71	281	-7	16261.55	10384.00
	Nick DOUGHERTY	Eng	70	73	68	70	281	-7	16261.55	10384.00
21	Barry LANE	Eng	71	70	67	74	282	-6	13593.05	8680.00
	Chris GANE	Eng	73	69	70	70	282	-6	13593.05	8680.00
	Christophe POTTIER	Fr	75	66	73	68	282	-6	13593.05	8680.00
	Niclas FASTH	Swe	70	72	68	72	282	-6	13593.05	8680.00
	Simon DYSON	Eng	69	74	67	72	282	-6	13593.05	8680.00
	Jamie DONALDSON	Wal	68	71	70	73	282	-6	13593.05	8680.00
27	Brian DAVIS	Eng	72	71	73	67	283	-5	10962.14	7000.00
	Nick O'HERN	Aus	73	68	68	74	283	-5	10962.14	7000.00
	Shaun Paul WEBSTER	Eng	69	74	69	71	283	-5	10962.14	7000.00
	Alberto BINAGHI	It	67	74	73	69	283	-5	10962.14	7000.00
	Charlie WI	R.Kor	70	70	70	73	283	-5	10962.14	7000.00
	Grant HAMERTON	Eng	67	72	71	73	283	-5	10962.14	7000.00
	Graeme STORM	Eng	67	73	72	71	283	-5	10962.14	7000.00
	Paul CASEY	Eng	69	71	70	73	283	-5	10962.14	7000.00
35	Gordon BRAND JNR.	Scot	74	68	72	70	284	-4	9020.27	5760.00
	David GILFORD	Eng	71	71	72	70	284	-4	9020.27	5760.00
	Hennie OTTO	SA	71	71	72	70	284	-4	9020.27	5760.00
	Jarrod MOSELEY	Aus	65	73	74	72	284	-4	9020.27	5760.00
39	Peter FOWLER	Aus	68	74	68	75	285	-3	7767.46	4960.00
	Mårten OLANDER	Swe	70	73	69	73	285	-3	7767.46	4960.00
	Joakim HAEGGMAN	Swe	70	73	71	71	285	-3	7767.46	4960.00
	Pierre FULKE	Swe	74	68	70	73	285	-3	7767.46	4960.00
	Adam MEDNICK	Swe	71	72	69	73	285	-3	7767.46	4960.00
	Johan SKOLD	Swe	71	68	70	76	285	-3	7767.46	4960.00
45	Santiago LUNA	Sp	70	72	70	74	286	-2	5637.67	3600.00
	David HOWELL	Eng	69	73	71	73	286	-2	5637.67	3600.00
	Paul BROADHURST	Eng	71	71	69	75	286	-2	5637.67	3600.00
	Russell CLAYDON	Eng	70	71	72	73	286	-2	5637.67	3600.00
	Emanuele CANONICA	It	69	71	69	77	286	-2	5637.67	3600.00
	Ian GARBUTT	Eng	71	71	70	74	286	-2	5637.67	3600.00
	Gary EVANS	Eng	71	68	73	74	286	-2	5637.67	3600.00
	Roger WESSELS	SA	70	72	73	71	286	-2	5637.67	3600.00
	Robert COLES	Eng	71	69	70	76	286	-2	5637.67	3600.00
	Benn BARHAM	Eng	72	68	71	75	286	-2	5637.67	3600.00
	David CARTER	Eng	71	70	69	76	286	-2	5637.67	3600.00
56	Wayne RILEY	Aus	71	70	67	79	287	-1	3783.50	2416.00
	David J RUSSELL	Eng	70	71	71	75	287	-1	3783.50	2416.00
	Marc PENDARIES	Fr	72	68	72	75	287	-1	3783.50	2416.00
	Michael ARCHER	Eng	70	73	74	70	287	-1	3783.50	2416.00
	Stephen DODD	Wal	71	70	68	78	287	-1	3783.50	2416.00
61	Philip WALTON	Ire	71	72	72	73	288	0	3132.04	2000.00
	Peter BAKER	Eng	69	72	75	72	288	0	3132.04	2000.00
	Jeremy ROBINSON	Eng	71	72	73	72	288	0	3132.04	2000.00
	Darren PROSSER	Eng	69	68	75	76	288	0	3132.04	2000.00
	Gary ORR	Scot	67	73	73	75	288	0	3132.04	2000.00
66	Peter HANSON	Swe	71	71	70	77	289	1	2568.27	1640.00
	Paul MCGINLEY	Ire	72	71	72	74	289	1	2568.27	1640.00
	Fredrik ANDERSSON	Swe	69	72	74	74	289	1	2568.27	1640.00
	Lucas PARSONS	Aus	74	68	74	73	289	1	2568.27	1640.00
70	Malcolm MACKENZIE	Eng	72	69	73	76	290	2	2090.53	1334.93
	Hennie WALTERS	SA	69	73	73	75	290	2	2090.53	1334.93
72	Andrew OLDCORN	Scot	72	70	74	75	291	3	1871.50	1195.07
	Andrew MARSHALL	Eng	72	71	72	76	291	3	1871.50	1195.07
	David LYNN	Eng	72	71	75	73	291	3	1871.50	1195.07
	Mark PILKINGTON	Wal	68	75	74	74	291	3	1871.50	1195.07
76	Roger CHAPMAN	Eng	69	71	72	80	292	4	1861.00	1188.36
	Simon KHAN	Eng	71	72	77	72	292	4	1861.00	1188.36
	Greg OWEN	Eng	70	71	71	80	292	4	1861.00	1188.36
79	Eamonn DARCY	Ire	74	68	73	78	293	5	1853.50	1183.57
	Sebastien DELAGRANGE	Fr	71	71	76	75	293	5	1853.50	1183.57
81	Van PHILLIPS	Eng	70	71	72	84	297	9	1849.00	1180.70

US Open Championship Bethpage State Park · Farmingdale · New York · USA

people's champion

1	**Tiger WOODS** USA	277	- 3
2	Phil MICKELSON USA	280	0
3	Jeff MAGGERT USA	282	2
4	Sergio GARCIA Sp	283	3
5	Nick FALDO Eng	285	5
	Scott HOCH USA	285	5
	Billy MAYFAIR USA	285	5
8	Tom BYRUM USA	286	6
	Padraig HARRINGTON Ire	286	6
	Nick PRICE Zim	286	6

Tiger Woods

Beyond a forecast that Tiger Woods would be a good bet to win, there was very little that was predictable about the 102nd US Open Championship.

For almost everyone it was a step into the unknown as America's national championship was played at a municipal course for the first time. Only Woods knew where he was heading and that was even further into the history books. For everyone else, the Black Course at Bethpage State Park and the daily 45,000 strong New York gallery made for an extraordinary week.

It is not often that the runner-up at a Major Championship walks off the course and says: "That was really neat. It was an incredible atmosphere and made for a wonderful experience." That runner-up, for the second time at a US Open Championship, was Phil Mickelson, who finished three strokes behind Woods.

"It is always awesome to win your national title," said Woods, who repeated his wire-to-wire victory at Pebble Beach in 2000. "But it was especially nice to win at a public facility and in front of this crowd. I grew up playing at public courses. I used to sleep in my car all night to get a tee-time."

Padraig Harrington

shot of the week

TIGER WOODS USA

Phil Mickelson had just got within two strokes of Tiger Woods with a birdie at the par five 13th in the final round when Woods stepped onto the tee at the same hole. At 554 yards, finding the green in two was no simple matter. Mickelson took a three wood and found the front of the green, from where he two putted. Woods, from a similar position, was left with 265 yards to the green. He smashed a two iron and was immediately walking after the shot knowing the execution was perfect. His eagle putt from 30 feet came up an inch short but he had re-established his three shot cushion. He would win by that margin.

If Bethpage is the 'People's Country Club' and this US Open was the 'People's Open' then Woods became the 'People's Champion' by winning his eighth Major Championship, moving him level with Tom Watson in joint fifth place on the all-time winners list. He also became only the fifth player to win the Masters Tournament and the US Open Championship in the same year. Whether the 26 year old would go on to claim a Grand Slam - a calendar-year version rather than his own 2000-01 rollover - would be seen in time.

Nick Price

A flurry of flash bulbs accompanied the moment when Woods secured victory in near-darkness - after a late-afternoon thunderstorm had caused a 45 minute delay - and raised his arms above his head. "This was a hard-fought victory," he said. "It was so tough out there." He was not just referring to the course. Woods blocks out distractions better than anyone and there was a lot to block out.

"The excitement level is the highest I've ever seen this early in the week," Woods said on the Tuesday. It got higher, louder, and more interactive as the week went on. The emotion of the crowd brought out emotions in the players.

Woods was sullen of face as he struggled with parts of his game at the weekend. Mickelson basked in the adulation as his 32nd birthday was serenaded on the Sunday, when his level par 70 was the best any of the leading four contenders could do, but was not quite enough to catch the Tiger.

Sergio Garcia went through every emotion humanly possible. He was at his tetchiest in the rain on Friday. The continual waggling and re-gripping of his pre-shot routine was too long for some of the vocal locals to stay silent. In a harassed moment, Garcia made a

the course

The Black Course is one of five - the others are the Green, Red, Blue and Yellow - at Bethpage State Park, the first genuine public facility to host the US Open Championship. Formerly a private estate which had its own course (now the Green), the club was formed by the parks department of New York in the 1930s, with the noted designer AW Tillinghast helping with the layout of three more 18s, including the Black. In 1997 Rees Jones renovated the course - "finishing what Tillinghast had started," said Jones - after the USGA provided $4 million worth of funding. The result was a magnificently conditioned course with two of the longest par fours in the history of the US Open Championship, the 492 yard tenth and the 499 yard 12th.

Tiger Woods and Sergio Garcia

provocative gesture with his fist. He later complained about the conditions and the following day he was heckled constantly.

But this time Garcia fed off the atmosphere and provoked deafening cheers when he holed a putt on the 16th just moments after Mickelson had done so on the nearby 17th. The 22 year old Spaniard got himself into the final pairing with Woods on Sunday, the first such occasion but surely not the last, though he was unable to mount a challenge in that final round. "This week has helped me to mature," he said. "I have learned a lot. I got myself into contention and hopefully I will do better next time."

The sign behind the first tee of the Black Course states: 'The Black Course Is An Extremely Difficult Course Which We Recommend Only For Highly Skilled Golfers.' How skilled do you have to be? Woods, at three under, was the only player to break par for the Championship. The regular clientele of Long Islanders who pay $31 during the week and $39 at weekends at least have four other courses at which to have a crack.

There were some competitors, especially those who could not make the carry off the tee at the tenth, who might have liked the same option. At 7,214 yards, this was the longest course in US Open Championship history yet the traditional principals of narrow fairways and thick rough remained. "This course tests every facet of your game," said David Duval, the 2001 Open Champion. "You can't play it from the rough."

Duval, like the defending Champion Retief Goosen, proved that statement by missing the cut. The three-ball of David Toms, Duval and Goosen, all Major Champions in 2001, had an eclectic score of 70 on Thursday, when Woods birdied his last hole (the ninth as a two-tee start was in operation) for a 67 to lead Garcia by a stroke.

Woods also birdied his last hole on Friday when his 68 was an even better round given the wet conditions. His five under par score for two days was eight strokes better than anyone else in his half of the draw, but Padraig Harrington closed within three with his own impressive 68.

Harrington, who was fifth at the Masters Tournament, has made a point of preparing carefully for such occasions and it is working. Though slightly disappointed with his performance over the weekend, the Irishman still finished in a share of eighth place.

Perhaps the most unexpected feature of the week was the identity of the player who posted the lowest score. It came on Saturday and from a man who described the course as "a gem, but a monster of a gem. I can't believe it has lain undiscovered for 60 years." It was Nick Faldo, 44 years old and in his 60th successive Major and more than justifying his special invitation from the United States Golf Association. In finishing tied for fifth, Faldo already has an exemption for next year.

Tiger Woods in the Majors			
	Masters Tournament	US Open Championship	Open Golf Championship	US PGA Championship
1997	1	19T	24T	29T
1998	8T	18T	3	10T
1999	18T	3T	7T	1
2000	5	1	1	1
2001	1	12T	25T	29T
2002	1	1	28T	2

"I never thought I could finish in the top ten on this course," he said. "When the rain came on Friday it was way out of my league. But on Saturday I was swinging really nicely on the range and went out and hit perfect shot after perfect shot. That was the best I can do, the best I've done since probably my last win at the Masters in 1996.

"I had a really good mental attitude this week. I didn't let anything rattle me. You had to be patient, accept that you were going to make mistakes and move on."

Woods was hardly mistake-free. On Saturday he did not make a birdie until the 15th but then added another at the short 17th to give himself a four stroke cushion overnight. But on the first two holes on Sunday he three putted, missing from inside two feet at the second. Yet, with the greens incredibly fast and the wind getting up as the storm approached, no one could take advantage.

Twice Mickelson got within two strokes, but no nearer. Woods covered any move and could afford two late bogeys, including three putting the last. "He is the one who controls the race," said Faldo. "He has such inner strength." But there was no doubting who was the star of the show. "This Open rocked," said David Fay, the Executive Director of the USGA. "It is not a question of if we return to Bethpage, but when."

Andy Farrell

Bernhard Langer

Nick Faldo and caddie Fanny Sunesson

final results
Bethpage State Park · Farmingdale · New York · USA
June 13-16 · 2002 · Par 70 · 7214 yards · 6596 metres

Pos.	Name		Rd1	Rd2	Rd3	Rd4	Total	Par	Prize Money Euro	£
1	Tiger WOODS	USA	67	68	70	72	277	-3	1058313.00	684744.04
2	Phil MICKELSON	USA	70	73	67	70	280	0	619113.00	400575.20
3	Jeff MAGGERT	USA	69	73	68	72	282	2	383486.00	248121.07
4	Sergio GARCIA	Sp	68	74	67	74	283	3	267272.70	172929.36
5	Nick FALDO	Eng	70	76	66	73	285	5	193546.40	125227.36
	Billy MAYFAIR	USA	69	74	68	74	285	5	193546.40	125227.36
	Scott HOCH	USA	71	75	70	69	285	5	193546.40	125227.36
8	Padraig HARRINGTON	Ire	70	68	73	75	286	6	146755.20	94952.77
	Nick PRICE	Zim	72	75	69	70	286	6	146755.20	94952.77
	Tom BYRUM	USA	72	72	70	72	286	6	146755.20	94952.77
11	Peter LONARD	Aus	73	74	73	67	287	7	126317.00	81728.95
12	Justin LEONARD	USA	73	71	68	76	288	8	108305.60	70075.31
	Dudley HART	USA	69	76	70	73	288	8	108305.60	70075.31
	Jay HAAS	USA	73	73	70	72	288	8	108305.60	70075.31
	Robert ALLENBY	Aus	74	70	67	77	288	8	108305.60	70075.31
16	Steve STRICKER	USA	72	77	69	71	289	9	91408.59	59142.70
	Shigeki MARUYAMA	Jpn	76	67	73	73	289	9	91408.59	59142.70
18	Steve FLESCH	USA	72	72	75	71	290	10	73018.29	47243.91
	Mark O'MEARA	USA	76	70	69	75	290	10	73018.29	47243.91
	Craig STADLER	USA	74	72	70	74	290	10	73018.29	47243.91
	Thomas LEVET	Fr	71	77	70	72	290	10	73018.29	47243.91
	Luke DONALD	Eng	76	72	70	72	290	10	73018.29	47243.91
	Charles HOWELL III	USA	71	74	70	75	290	10	73018.29	47243.91
24	Jeff SLUMAN	USA	73	73	72	73	291	11	50205.30	32483.57
	Davis LOVE III	USA	71	71	72	77	291	11	50205.30	32483.57
	Jim CARTER	USA	77	73	70	71	291	11	50205.30	32483.57
	Ernie ELS	SA	73	74	70	74	291	11	50205.30	32483.57
	Darren CLARKE	N.Ire	74	74	72	71	291	11	50205.30	32483.57
	Chris DIMARCO	USA	74	74	72	71	291	11	50205.30	32483.57
30	Scott MCCARRON	USA	72	72	70	78	292	12	37717.21	24403.59
	Kyoung-Ju CHOI	R.Kor	69	73	73	77	292	12	37717.21	24403.59
	Vijay SINGH	Fiji	75	75	67	75	292	12	37717.21	24403.59
	Paul LAWRIE	Scot	73	73	73	73	292	12	37717.21	24403.59
	Jason CARON	USA	75	72	72	73	292	12	37717.21	24403.59
35	Bernhard LANGER	Ger	72	76	70	75	293	13	33807.80	21874.14
	Shingo KATAYAMA	Jpn	74	72	74	73	293	13	33807.80	21874.14
37	Hidemichi TANAKA	Jpn	73	73	72	76	294	14	28344.79	18339.50
	Stuart APPLEBY	Aus	77	73	75	69	294	14	28344.79	18339.50
	Donnie HAMMOND	USA	73	77	71	73	294	14	28344.79	18339.50
	Thomas BJÖRN	Den	71	79	73	71	294	14	28344.79	18339.50
	Rocco MEDIATE	USA	72	72	74	76	294	14	28344.79	18339.50
	Niclas FASTH	Swe	72	72	74	76	294	14	28344.79	18339.50
	Kevin SUTHERLAND	USA	74	75	70	75	294	14	28344.79	18339.50
	Franklin LANGHAM	USA	70	76	74	74	294	14	28344.79	18339.50
45	Jean VAN DE VELDE	Fr	71	75	74	75	295	15	21242.46	13744.18
	Kenny PERRY	USA	74	76	71	74	295	15	21242.46	13744.18
	Tom LEHMAN	USA	71	76	72	76	295	15	21242.46	13744.18
	David TOMS	USA	74	74	70	77	295	15	21242.46	13744.18
	Frank LICKLITER	USA	74	76	68	77	295	15	21242.46	13744.18
50	José María OLAZÁBAL	Sp	71	77	75	73	296	16	17244.15	11157.22
	Tim HERRON	USA	75	74	73	74	296	16	17244.15	11157.22
	Robert KARLSSON	Swe	71	77	72	76	296	16	17244.15	11157.22
	Craig BOWDEN	USA	71	77	74	74	296	16	17244.15	11157.22
54	Corey PAVIN	USA	74	75	70	78	297	17	15624.93	10109.56
	Ian LEGGATT	Can	72	77	72	76	297	17	15624.93	10109.56
	Jesper PARNEVIK	Swe	72	76	69	80	297	17	15624.93	10109.56
	Harrison FRAZAR	USA	74	73	75	75	297	17	15624.93	10109.56
58	Brad LARDON	USA	73	73	74	78	298	18	14803.68	9578.20
59	Greg NORMAN	Aus	75	73	74	77	299	19	14279.81	9239.25
	Bob TWAY	USA	72	78	73	76	299	19	14279.81	9239.25
	John MAGINNES	USA	79	69	73	78	299	19	14279.81	9239.25
62	Jeev Milkha SINGH	Ind	75	75	75	75	300	20	13540.05	8760.61
	Paul STANKOWSKI	USA	72	77	77	74	300	20	13540.05	8760.61
	Andy MILLER (USA)	USA	76	74	75	75	300	20	13540.05	8760.61
65	Spike MCROY	USA	75	75	74	77	301	21	13059.58	8449.74
66	Brad FAXON	USA	75	74	73	80	302	22	12699.75	8216.92
	Angel CABRERA	Arg	73	73	79	77	302	22	12699.75	8216.92
68	Len MATTIACE	USA	72	73	80	78	303	23	12219.28	7906.05
	Kent JONES	USA	76	74	74	79	303	23	12219.28	7906.05
70	Tom GILLIS	USA	71	76	78	79	304	24	11729.28	7589.02
	John DALY	USA	74	76	81	73	304	24	11729.28	7589.02
72	Kevin WARRICK (Am)	USA	73	76	84	74	307	27		

The Great North Open De Vere Slaley Hall · Northumberland · England

a promise kept

1	**Miles TUNNICLIFF** Eng	279	-9
2	Sven STRÜVER Ger	283	-5
3	Bradley DREDGE Wal	284	-4
	Malcolm MACKENZIE Eng	284	-4
5	Diego BORREGO Sp	286	-2
	Brian DAVIS Eng	286	-2
	Jean HUGO SA	286	-2
	Nicolas VANHOOTEGEM Bel	286	-2
9	Rolf MUNTZ Hol	287	-1
10	David GILFORD Eng	288	0
	David LYNN Eng	288	0
	Roger WESSELS SA	288	0

Miles Tunnicliff

The truth, they say, is often stranger than fiction, and never was that old idiom better illustrated than by Miles Tunnicliff's emotionally-charged victory in The Great North Open. Not only did events at the De Vere Slaley Hall produce an enthralling golf tournament, they also restored faith in humanity itself.

Prior to the off, the 33 year old Englishman did not merit a mention in preview material or on bookmakers' listings, hardly surprising for a player who had never finished in the top five of a European Tour event and who had trod The European Tour Qualifying School path a dozen times since 1987, completing the full journey only once.

Added to that, the Marbella-based golfer had not only taken time out over the winter to recover from a wrist operation but had also undergone a recent month away from the course due to "problems at home." Hardly championship winning material, most believed.

Not Tunnicliff.

His time at home, he patiently explained, had been spent with his beloved mother Pam, nursing her through an ultimately unsuccessful battle with cancer and in those precious final few weeks, one conversation, two days before she passed away, remained uppermost in his mind. 'Go out and win,' she had told her son. He told her he would.

Had an author dropped such a script onto a publisher's desk it would have been rejected as too fanciful. Even Hollywood did not let Kevin Costner win the US Open Championship in Tin Cup. This time, however, the fairytale did come true.

Rolf Muntz

Bradley Dredge

Not that it appeared that way when Tunnicliff opened with an unspectacular level par 72 to lie six shots adrift of leader Diego Borrego. A second round 70 was an improvement but left him still six shots off the pace, held at the halfway stage by the experienced German Sven Strüver.

If he was to succeed, Tunnicliff had to make something happen quickly, and the blue touch paper was ignited on Saturday morning. The outward nine on the Hunting Course proved to be the harder of the two halves over the four days, but the Englishman made a mockery of that statistic.

Six birdies in seven holes saw him to the turn in 30, a new record for the front nine, a flawless stretch of golf which also saw him move to the top of the leaderboard as the later starters struggled to match such fireworks in the testing winds. By the end of the day, a 68 was good enough for a share of the lead with David Gilford, whom Tunnicliff would partner in the final group on the final day, and Strüver.

shot of the week

ANDREW BEAL England

There were numerous candidates, including winner Miles Tunnicliff's chip-in at the eighth in the final round. But it was the hole in one at the 179 yard 14th in the second round by Andrew Beal that took the award, a perfectly struck six iron winning the 36 year old a Renault Megane Coupe. Having recently returned to tournament golf after losing his left eye to cancer, it was another heart-warming moment and sat well alongside Tunnicliff's victory.

Perceived wisdom proclaimed the Champion would most likely be proven Tour winner Strüver or the rejuvenated Gilford, enjoying one of his best seasons of late. Even Paul Casey, the 2001 Sir Henry Cotton Rookie of the Year, who started the final round three shots off the lead, attracted a good deal of attention from tipsters. Everyone, in fact, apart from Tunnicliff. He would fall away under the glare of the spotlight. Wouldn't he?

Anyone witnessing Tunnicliff's preparation would have been convinced they were right to think that way. A largely sleepless night was followed by an equally restless morning. "I actually cried twice before I went out to play," he admitted. "I just couldn't get my mother out of my mind and I thought I might struggle because of that."

A bogey five at the opening hole confirmed such fears but, looking back, the Englishman realised that the release of pent-up emotion actually helped. It enabled him to focus, regain his composure, stay calm, and concentrate on the task in hand. What was in no doubt was Tunnicliff's form after that. Quite simply, for the remaining 17 holes, he was superb.

Highlights came at the fifth and eighth where, from tough positions off the green and with bogey fives looking likely, Tunnicliff chipped in for birdie threes on both occasions. "I think someone was looking down on me," he said. We all knew whom he meant.

Birdies at the 11th and 15th emphasised his superiority, audacious par saving efforts on both the 16th and 18th merely the icing on the cake. Tunnicliff, who in the end won by four shots from Strüver, with Bradley Dredge and Malcolm Mackenzie a further shot adrift in third, had the additional honour of being the only player to break 70 on the final day.

Sven Strüver

"What happened to my mother made me dig in a little bit more and try that little bit harder, she gave me quite a bit of positive strength," he said. "She was positive right to the end so I just took as much from that as I could out onto the golf course."

Some argued the cheque for 155,960 euro (£100,000) would mean most while others figured the two year exemption for The European Tour was the bigger reward. Not Tunnicliff. He knew the biggest prize of all was the fact he had kept his promise.

Scott Crockett

the course

There were few significant changes to the 7,088 yard Hunting Course after major alterations made a couple of years ago to improve drainage and improve the greens at the third and seventh as well as removing the out of bounds to the left of the second. Some trees were removed to the right of the first to improve air flow and aid growth and most players agreed the course was in the best condition they had seen it.

Roger Wessels

final results

De Vere Slaley Hall • Northumberland • England
June 20-23 • 2002 • Par 72 • 7088 yards • 6480 metres

Pos.	Name		Rd1	Rd2	Rd3	Rd4	Total	Par	Prize Money Euro	£
1	Miles TUNNICLIFF	Eng	72	70	68	69	279	-9	155960.00	100000.00
2	Sven STRÜVER	Ger	71	65	74	73	283	-5	103962.90	66660.00
3	Malcolm MACKENZIE	Eng	72	72	69	71	284	-4	52683.29	33780.00
	Bradley DREDGE	Wal	68	71	75	70	284	-4	52683.29	33780.00
5	Brian DAVIS	Eng	75	68	68	75	286	-2	30973.66	19860.00
	Jean HUGO	SA	72	73	69	72	286	-2	30973.66	19860.00
	Diego BORREGO	Sp	66	71	78	71	286	-2	30973.66	19860.00
	Nicolas VANHOOTEGEM	Bel	68	73	71	74	286	-2	30973.66	19860.00
9	Rolf MUNTZ	Hol	72	69	71	75	287	-1	20961.02	13440.00
10	David GILFORD	Eng	73	70	67	78	288	0	17342.75	11120.00
	Roger WESSELS	SA	69	69	74	76	288	0	17342.75	11120.00
	David LYNN	Eng	74	68	69	77	288	0	17342.75	11120.00
13	Garry HOUSTON	Wal	73	70	72	74	289	1	13793.10	8844.00
	Ian GARBUTT	Eng	73	72	73	71	289	1	13793.10	8844.00
	Jon BEVAN	Eng	72	67	78	72	289	1	13793.10	8844.00
	Simon DYSON	Eng	71	75	71	72	289	1	13793.10	8844.00
	Paul CASEY	Eng	70	69	74	76	289	1	13793.10	8844.00
18	Gordon BRAND JNR.	Scot	70	75	71	74	290	2	11266.55	7224.00
	Gary MURPHY	Ire	72	69	71	78	290	2	11266.55	7224.00
	Gary EMERSON	Eng	71	73	72	74	290	2	11266.55	7224.00
	Stephen GALLACHER	Scot	74	72	73	71	290	2	11266.55	7224.00
	Brett RUMFORD	Aus	70	70	73	77	290	2	11266.55	7224.00
23	Darren FICHARDT	SA	75	72	72	72	291	3	10293.36	6600.00
24	Santiago LUNA	Sp	73	73	73	73	292	4	9451.18	6060.00
	Mark MCNULTY	Zim	75	72	74	71	292	4	9451.18	6060.00
	Yngve NILSSON	Swe	74	73	71	74	292	4	9451.18	6060.00
	Paul BROADHURST	Eng	72	75	73	72	292	4	9451.18	6060.00
	Jesus Maria ARRUTI	Sp	73	74	69	76	292	4	9451.18	6060.00
29	Peter FOWLER	Aus	70	74	74	75	293	5	7907.17	5070.00
	Dennis EDLUND	Swe	72	71	73	77	293	5	7907.17	5070.00
	Gianluca BARUFFALDI	It	71	70	76	76	293	5	7907.17	5070.00
	Johan SKOLD	Swe	76	71	74	72	293	5	7907.17	5070.00
	Andrew COLTART	Scot	73	72	70	78	293	5	7907.17	5070.00
	Martin MARITZ	SA	73	74	72	74	293	5	7907.17	5070.00
35	Des SMYTH	Ire	69	76	73	76	294	6	6550.32	4200.00
	Richard GREEN	Aus	70	75	72	77	294	6	6550.32	4200.00
	Elliot BOULT	NZ	71	69	81	73	294	6	6550.32	4200.00
	Peter BAKER	Eng	72	73	74	75	294	6	6550.32	4200.00
	Gregory HAVRET	Fr	69	78	71	76	294	6	6550.32	4200.00
	Adam MEDNICK	Swe	71	73	76	74	294	6	6550.32	4200.00
41	Greig HUTCHEON	Scot	74	68	75	78	295	7	5240.26	3360.00
	Nick O'HERN	Aus	73	74	71	77	295	7	5240.26	3360.00
	Hennie OTTO	SA	70	73	73	79	295	7	5240.26	3360.00
	Alberto BINAGHI	It	74	73	73	75	295	7	5240.26	3360.00
	Jonathan LOMAS	Eng	75	70	70	80	295	7	5240.26	3360.00
	Paul DWYER	Eng	71	73	76	75	295	7	5240.26	3360.00
	Sion E BEBB	Wal	77	70	72	76	295	7	5240.26	3360.00
	Gary CLARK	Eng	74	71	78	72	295	7	5240.26	3360.00
49	Roger CHAPMAN	Eng	72	74	76	74	296	8	4304.50	2760.00
	Benn BARHAM	Eng	74	67	78	77	296	8	4304.50	2760.00
51	Shaun Paul WEBSTER	Eng	73	73	77	74	297	9	3743.04	2400.00
	Gustavo ROJAS	Arg	73	72	75	77	297	9	3743.04	2400.00
	Fredrik ANDERSSON	Swe	73	72	77	75	297	9	3743.04	2400.00
	Matthew BLACKEY	Eng	72	75	76	74	297	9	3743.04	2400.00
55	Peter LAWRIE	Ire	71	73	79	75	298	10	3181.58	2040.00
	Graeme STORM	Eng	73	72	76	77	298	10	3181.58	2040.00
57	Magnus PERSSON ATLEVI	Swe	70	75	78	76	299	11	2760.49	1770.00
	Ilya GORONESKOUL	Fr	72	72	75	80	299	11	2760.49	1770.00
	Stuart LITTLE	Eng	71	70	77	81	299	11	2760.49	1770.00
	Marc CAYEUX	Zim	72	73	75	79	299	11	2760.49	1770.00
61	Mark DAVIS	Eng	73	71	79	77	300	12	2479.76	1590.00
	Neil CHEETHAM	Eng	73	74	77	76	300	12	2479.76	1590.00
63	Kenneth A FERRIE	Eng	72	74	76	79	301	13	2245.82	1440.00
	Stephen SCAHILL	NZ	73	73	75	80	301	13	2245.82	1440.00
	David DRYSDALE	Scot	74	73	72	82	301	13	2245.82	1440.00
66	Andrew BEAL	Eng	74	72	75	81	302	14	2058.67	1320.00
67	Barry LANE	Eng	71	76	80	76	303	15	1965.10	1260.00
68	Raphaël JACQUELIN	Fr	75	72	76	83	306	18	1871.52	1200.00
69	Joakim RASK	Swe	73	74	77	83	307	19	1777.94	1140.00
70	Andrew OLDCORN	Scot	69	70	W/D		139	-5	857.78	550.00
	Andrew RAITT	Eng	68	73	W/D		141	-3	857.78	550.00

Pro-Golf 2003

Pro-Golf, The European Tour Media Guide respected throughout the golfing world as an essential work of reference, has chronicled the achievements of The European Tour for 32 years and the 2003 edition is packed full of records and revealing statistics.

The 2002 season was an outstanding year for European Tour Members, capped by victory for The European Team, led by Sam Torrance, in The 34th Ryder Cup Matches at The De Vere Belfry. All the facts and figures behind that memorable week can be found in Pro-Golf 2003.

In an arena full of great Champions find out how The European Tour's leading players contested the race for the Volvo Order of Merit title. Retief Goosen finally edged ahead of Padraig Harrington and Ernie Els. Pro-Golf 2003 charts the season from start to finish and shows how the race to finish Number One was won and lost.

European Tour Members excelled on the world stage throughout the 2002 season. In the Major Championships, starting with the Masters Tournament where Goosen finished second and nine European Tour Members finished in the top ten, European Tour Members rose to the top. Els went a step further at Muirfield, winning the 131st Open Golf Championship after a four-man play-off that included Frenchman Thomas Levet.

The World Golf Championships were another opportunity for European Tour Members to shine and in the WGC – American Express Championship

at Mount Juliet Goosen again pushed Tiger Woods all the way in what was the strongest field ever assembled in Ireland.

The facts and figures behind the winning of all the Major Championships, The 34th Ryder Cup Matches, the World Golf Championships plus all the events that make up The European Tour International Schedule can be found in Pro-Golf 2003.

The tremendous progress of The European Tour over the past 32 years, detailed biographies of all the international stars who make The European Tour unique, notable achievements, records and statistics are all meticulously chronicled in more than 600 pages in the illustrated Pro-Golf 2003.

Quite simply, it is a must for all students of the game.

Ordering a copy of Pro-Golf 2003 is simple: send a cheque for £15 UK and Europe (which includes postage and packaging) and £20 overseas (which includes postage and packaging), made payable to the PGA European Tour to:

Pro-Golf 2003, The European Tour, Emily Doughty, Communications Division, The European Tour, Wentworth Drive, Virginia Water, Surrey GU25 4LX or call +44 1344 840442 with credit card details.

EUROPEAN TOUR

Murphy's Irish Open Fota Island · Cork · Ireland

fond farewell

1	Søren HANSEN Den	270	-14
2	Richard BLAND Eng	270	-14
	Niclas FASTH Swe	270	-14
	Darren FICHARDT SA	270	-14
5	Thomas BJÖRN Den	272	-12
6	Alex CEJKA Ger	274	-10
	Eamonn DARCY Ire	274	-10
	Joakim HAEGGMAN Swe	274	-10
	Padraig HARRINGTON Ire	274	-10
	Søren KJELDSEN Den	274	-10
	Stuart LITTLE Eng	274	-10
	Eduardo ROMERO Arg	274	-10

Søren Hansen

Even in death, the Irish are known to throw a party. It is called a wake, and the reasoning behind such convention is that the newly departed deserve to be best remembered for all their good traits. If the final round at Fota Island on the last Sunday in June began with dark clouds dispensing tears, almost as if to lament Murphy's ending a near decade-long association with the Irish Open, it ended wreathed in smiles.

When the final putt of the last Irish Open to be sponsored by the brewing company did finally come, the atmosphere was not unlike that to be found at a carnival as, for the second time in six weeks, a Dane by the name of Hansen had won his first tournament on The European Tour International Schedule.

This time, it was Søren Hansen not Anders Hansen who tasted success. "I've been congratulated about ten times at least since Anders won the Volvo PGA Championship," remarked Søren, who is no relation to his compatriot. "I have even tried to copy his autograph - but, after this win, I expect to be recognised in my own right."

Richard Bland

Darren Fichardt

He would deserve to be, not least for the mental courage he displayed in a four-man play-off for the title. From the time that the final putt of the first round dropped, a logjam had developed at the top of the leaderboard, and the bottleneck remained right the way through the tournament until Hansen's ten foot birdie putt on the fourth hole of sudden-death ended it all.

In taking the top prize of 266,660 euro (£172,678) and becoming the 11th first-time winner on The European Tour in 2002, Hansen was fulfilling a part of his destiny. Fittingly, he had some family support on hand. In an emotional aftermath, he revealed his brother had travelled halfway round the world to watch him win.

"He has been living in Australia and I hadn't seen him in two years but he came over to this tournament. When I saw him standing by the green, I just burst into tears," said Hansen. "It has taken a lot of hard work for me to get here and suddenly it has paid off in one of the great traditional tournaments on The European Tour International Schedule."

the course

When Jeff Howes was asked to re-design Fota Island, located in the Lee estuary nine miles east of Cork City, the course owner Dr Tim Mahony handed him a simple brief. "Produce a course up to European Tour standards," he was told. "And one which would be a joy to play for golfers of all handicaps." The Canadian-born designer, now domiciled in Ireland, re-routed eight holes and rebuilt all 18 sets of greens and tees. For a second successive year, the course, measuring 6,927 yards with a par of 71, was not only immaculately presented, but also provided a great test for players with good shots rewarded and bad ones punished; how golf should be played.

Stuart Little

It was only after Ballesteros left the course that he realised his mistake. Upset and apologetic, he contacted European Tour Chief Referee John Paramor and informed him of his mistake. "I just wish my tournament had not ended like this," Ballesteros told him. The following morning, the Spaniard made a visit to the course to collect his clubs and bid farewell to some friends . . . . and he had long departed before the second day's play finished with Peter O'Malley assuming the halfway lead.

By Sunday morning, there was yet more change, and a very Scandinavian feel to events. Danes Thomas Björn and Hansen along with Sweden's Niclas Fasth started the day sharing the lead; by the conclusion of the final round, Fasth and Hansen were still locked together but were joined by England's Richard Bland and South Africa's Darren Fichardt, the quartet finishing their respective 72 holes on 14 under par 270.

Indeed, Hansen was following in the footsteps of many famous players. Since 1975, the previous 16 winners had between them won 20 Major Championships and 261 official European Tour events - but his route to the winner's enclosure was one of the most dramatic.

From Thursday's opening round, the leaderboard had a congested look about it: Nick Dougherty, Fred Funk, Joakim Haeggman, Peter O'Malley and Eduardo Romero all shot 66s to share the lead. However, it was a man far removed from such heights who commanded all the attention in 19th Hole inquests later that night.

Of all the holes on the course, the 18th was far from the hardest. In fact, it played the 14th easiest overall but it inflicted a mortal blow on Severiano Ballesteros. The five time Major Champion dunked his ball four times into the water that surrounds the final green and in the circumstances, and with everyone's heart reaching out to him, it was hardly surprising that Ballesteros lost count of what was going on. Ultimately he signed for a wrong score, pencilling in a ten that should have been a 12 and consequently a round of 87 that should have been 89, and he was subsequently disqualified.

shot of the week

SØREN HANSEN Denmark

A contender was Søren Hansen's approach to the 72nd hole, the Dane so pumped up with adrenaline that he used a wedge to hit an approach shot of 160 yards to six feet from where he holed for eagle three to get into the play-off. But the winner was his tee shot at the fourth extra hole, a superb four iron from 222 yards which finished ten feet from the pin, setting up his title winning birdie. The new Champion summed it up: "It was the best shot I hit all week," he said.

Søren Kjeldsen

On the first play-off hole, the 18th, a 507 yard par five and described by Padraig Harrington as "one of the most intimidating drives on The European Tour," Hansen's bid for glory seemed to have expired before it had got a chance to start.

Appropriately enough for a man with the logo 'H_2O' on his clothing, the Dane put his second shot from the trees into the water by the green. A penalty drop later, he chipped and putted for a par but believed his tournament was over as both Bland and Fichardt had short birdie putts. However, both missed, and the tournament that seemingly did not want to end was extended.

Back down the 18th again, and Bland was the only one of the four not to make a birdie and was eliminated. The third play-off hole was the 409 yard first and, again, the surviving three players could not be separated. So, on they went to the 17th, a 222 yard par three, for the fourth hole of sudden-death that had the huge galleries enthralled. It was here that Hansen produced a four iron tee shot to ten feet for the birdie that brought the victory and the tears.

Philip Reid

Darren Clarke

Søren Hansen and Padraic Liston, Managing Director, Heineken Ireland

final results

Fota Island · Cork · Ireland
June 27-30 · 2002 · Par 71 · 6927 yards · 6334 metres

Pos.	Name		Rd1	Rd2	Rd3	Rd4	Total	Par	Prize Money Euro	£
1	Søren HANSEN	Den	69	69	64	68	270	-14	266660.00	172678.18
2	Darren FICHARDT	SA	71	68	64	67	270	-14	119310.00	77260.31
	Richard BLAND	Eng	69	71	63	67	270	-14	119310.00	77260.31
	Niclas FASTH	Swe	72	67	63	68	270	-14	119310.00	77260.31
5	Thomas BJÖRN	Den	71	68	63	70	272	-12	67840.00	43930.43
6	Eamonn DARCY	Ire	69	68	68	69	274	-10	38400.00	24866.28
	Eduardo ROMERO	Arg	66	71	66	71	274	-10	38400.00	24866.28
	Padraig HARRINGTON	Ire	71	68	69	66	274	-10	38400.00	24866.28
	Søren KJELDSEN	Den	69	70	65	70	274	-10	38400.00	24866.28
	Stuart LITTLE	Eng	68	71	66	69	274	-10	38400.00	24866.28
	Joakim HAEGGMAN	Swe	66	69	69	70	274	-10	38400.00	24866.28
	Alex CEJKA	Ger	69	65	69	71	274	-10	38400.00	24866.28
13	Peter O'MALLEY	Aus	66	67	73	69	275	-9	24586.67	15921.33
	Gary EVANS	Eng	69	70	66	70	275	-9	24586.67	15921.33
	Paul CASEY	Eng	69	69	68	69	275	-9	24586.67	15921.33
16	Des SMYTH	Ire	67	68	72	69	276	-8	21600.00	13987.28
	Phillip PRICE	Wal	71	70	66	69	276	-8	21600.00	13987.28
	Paul LAWRIE	Scot	72	69	68	67	276	-8	21600.00	13987.28
19	Sandy LYLE	Scot	73	66	66	72	277	-7	18920.00	12251.82
	Peter FOWLER	Aus	69	70	68	70	277	-7	18920.00	12251.82
	Klas ERIKSSON	Swe	71	70	71	65	277	-7	18920.00	12251.82
	Lee WESTWOOD	Eng	67	68	72	70	277	-7	18920.00	12251.82
23	Malcolm MACKENZIE	Eng	68	73	66	71	278	-6	16880.00	10930.80
	Fred FUNK	USA	66	70	69	73	278	-6	16880.00	10930.80
	Peter HANSON	Swe	70	70	67	71	278	-6	16880.00	10930.80
	Colin MONTGOMERIE	Scot	67	67	74	70	278	-6	16880.00	10930.80
27	David GILFORD	Eng	68	70	71	70	279	-5	14000.00	9065.83
	Mark MCNULTY	Zim	68	69	75	67	279	-5	14000.00	9065.83
	Nick O'HERN	Aus	72	69	69	69	279	-5	14000.00	9065.83
	Henrik BJORNSTAD	Nor	71	68	67	73	279	-5	14000.00	9065.83
	Darren CLARKE	N.Ire	71	70	65	73	279	-5	14000.00	9065.83
	Nick DOUGHERTY	Eng	66	74	64	75	279	-5	14000.00	9065.83
	Adam SCOTT	Aus	70	66	74	69	279	-5	14000.00	9065.83
	Graeme MCDOWELL	N.Ire	70	71	65	73	279	-5	14000.00	9065.83
35	Miguel Angel MARTIN	Sp	68	70	72	70	280	-4	10720.00	6941.84
	Anders HANSEN	Den	71	70	69	70	280	-4	10720.00	6941.84
	Steen TINNING	Den	68	71	67	74	280	-4	10720.00	6941.84
	Richard S JOHNSON	Swe	68	67	71	74	280	-4	10720.00	6941.84
	Jarrod MOSELEY	Aus	72	69	69	70	280	-4	10720.00	6941.84
	Mark PILKINGTON	Wal	69	66	72	73	280	-4	10720.00	6941.84
	Raymond RUSSELL	Scot	70	67	74	69	280	-4	10720.00	6941.84
	Patrik SJÖLAND	Swe	69	68	69	74	280	-4	10720.00	6941.84
	Carl PETTERSSON	Swe	67	67	72	74	280	-4	10720.00	6941.84
44	Tony JOHNSTONE	Zim	71	68	72	70	281	-3	7840.00	5076.87
	Ian WOOSNAM	Wal	71	66	73	71	281	-3	7840.00	5076.87
	Barry LANE	Eng	69	70	71	71	281	-3	7840.00	5076.87
	Kenneth A FERRIE	Eng	70	68	73	70	281	-3	7840.00	5076.87
	Jamie SPENCE	Eng	70	69	71	71	281	-3	7840.00	5076.87
	Gary EMERSON	Eng	70	67	68	76	281	-3	7840.00	5076.87
	Andrew MARSHALL	Eng	68	69	70	74	281	-3	7840.00	5076.87
	Chris GANE	Eng	70	69	67	75	281	-3	7840.00	5076.87
	Tobias DIER	Ger	71	69	70	71	281	-3	7840.00	5076.87
53	Philip WALTON	Ire	71	69	70	72	282	-2	5600.00	3626.33
	Arjun ATWAL	Ind	71	68	70	73	282	-2	5600.00	3626.33
	Justin ROSE	Eng	72	69	69	72	282	-2	5600.00	3626.33
	Jonathan LOMAS	Eng	68	72	72	70	282	-2	5600.00	3626.33
	Stephen DODD	Wal	69	72	68	73	282	-2	5600.00	3626.33
58	Gordon BRAND JNR.	Scot	67	73	72	71	283	-1	4320.00	2797.46
	Mark JAMES	Eng	69	70	67	77	283	-1	4320.00	2797.46
	Peter BAKER	Eng	70	68	75	70	283	-1	4320.00	2797.46
	Jeremy ROBINSON	Eng	70	71	70	72	283	-1	4320.00	2797.46
	Carl SUNESON	Sp	68	72	70	73	283	-1	4320.00	2797.46
	Russell CLAYDON	Eng	69	72	76	66	283	-1	4320.00	2797.46
	Diego BORREGO	Sp	69	71	70	73	283	-1	4320.00	2797.46
65	Costantino ROCCA	It	71	70	70	73	284	0	3520.00	2279.41
	Henrik NYSTROM	Swe	71	68	72	73	284	0	3520.00	2279.41
	Christopher HANELL	Swe	72	68	70	74	284	0	3520.00	2279.41
68	Andrew COLTART	Scot	70	71	73	71	285	1	3200.00	2072.19
69	Roger CHAPMAN	Eng	71	66	76	73	286	2	2790.00	1806.69
	Didier DE VOOGHT	Bel	69	69	76	72	286	2	2790.00	1806.69
	Andrew BUTTERFIELD	Eng	69	71	72	74	286	2	2790.00	1806.69
72	Paul EALES	Eng	72	67	78	72	289	5	2397.00	1552.20
73	Johan SKOLD	Swe	71	69	79	77	296	12	2394.00	1550.26

Smurfit European Open The K Club · Dublin · Ireland

fear factor

1	Michael CAMPBELL NZ	282	-6
2	Bradley DREDGE Wal	283	-5
	Retief GOOSEN SA	283	-5
	Padraig HARRINGTON Ire	283	-5
	Paul LAWRIE Scot	283	-5
6	Angel CABRERA Arg	284	-4
	Niclas FASTH Swe	284	-4
	Colin MONTGOMERIE Scot	284	-4
9	Paul CASEY Eng	285	-3
	Darren FICHARDT SA	285	-3
	Joakim HAEGGMAN Swe	285	-3
	Barry LANE Eng	285	-3
	Jarrod MOSELEY Aus	285	-3
	Carl PETTERSSON Swe	285	-3
	Patrik SJÖLAND Swe	285	-3

Michael Campbell

The first thing that strikes you each year when you return to The K Club is how quickly the Arnold Palmer design has matured since the Championship was first played there in 1995. Even in the three years since Darren Clarke shot 60, the course has been toughened to such a degree that such a score will remain a milestone in the history of the place.

Clarke, of course, confirmed his liking for the course when in 2001 he closed with a 66 to finish first, and several more alterations were in place when he returned to defend the title. New bunkers had been added, some new tees and, significantly, an increase in length to 7,337 yards in what is only the first phase of development leading up to The 36th Ryder Cup Matches in 2006. One can only imagine the degree of difficulty that will face the Teams then, although for us mere mortals the course is already as intimidating as it is challenging.

Professional golfers are not supposed to feel the fear factor. Some do. Like David Feherty when he won the BMW International Open in Munich in 1989. He carried an eight shot lead into the final round and won by six but reflected afterwards: "Anyone who enjoys what I had to go through out there today must be a pervert. I'm serious. I was always looking over my shoulder and got afflicted by the 'what ifs.' What if I lost from eight shots in front? No, I only enjoy the game when it's over and I can look back."

Michael Campbell stood on the 15th tee of The K Club on the final day poised to win the biggest Championship of his career. The 33 year old New Zealander was five shots ahead of his nearest rival and playing partner Padraig Harrington.

Only he could lose. His destiny was in his own hands. What happened next bordered on the bizarre. One was reminded of Jean Van de Velde, who led the Open Golf Championship at Carnoustie in 1999 by three with one hole left, and of Greg Norman taking a six shot lead into the final day of the 1996 Masters Tournament. Neither man won then, but Campbell bucked the trend.

Four consecutive bogeys opened the door for Campbell's rivals but none of them came through and for that he can be forever grateful. Maybe the popular Kiwi was not as negative of mind as Feherty but he had an abject lesson on what this course can do if you take your eye off the ball.

This time the leader won but only after he suffered the slings and arrows of outrageous fortune. He said: "I hit quality shots at the 12th and 13th and was in cruise mode. I felt I would win when I holed the putt for par on the 14th. I said to myself 'this is it.'"

Paul Casey

It was then that he made the mistake of losing focus. "I began preparing my acceptance speech," he admitted. "I got too far ahead of myself and began doing the stupid things I had been trained not to do by Jos (Vanstiphout, his sports psychologist). But it was just human. I hadn't been in that position for a long time.

"As a result I had mixed feelings about winning. I was professionally disappointed with the way I performed over the last four holes but personally I was absolutely elated. The way I played the last four holes was pretty disgusting but, hey, I've got the trophy in my hands. I will learn from today and, hopefully, turn it into a more positive thing."

Let us, however, get one thing straight. There is not the slightest doubt that Campbell was the most consistent player in the field. He was at, or near the top of the leaderboard, from the outset and led the field on his own into Saturday and Sunday.

That was achieved by staying focused and playing golf of the highest calibre. Moreover he remained in the same mode on the final day. Many among the record crowd of 28,000 had, of course, come to watch one particular member of the chasing pack. Harrington had started sharing second place with Paul Lawrie - one behind Campbell - and he appeared more than likely to be inspired by the vocal support that would be accorded to him.

There were others hoping to snap at Campbell's heels, and these were to include the charging Bradley Dredge and Retief Goosen, but they, too, seemed to be playing for second place as Campbell birdied the 12th and 13th en route to walking onto that 15th tee with a five shot lead. The New Zealander had one hand on the trophy.

Then came one of those swings which tell you that in golf you can never be sure of anything and, as Lee Trevino once said: "It's not over, 'til the fat lady sings."

First Harrington made birdie at the 15th and Campbell bogeyed. The gap between the two was reduced to three. Campbell made another bogey at the 16th, and Harrington, despite a visit to the water, grabbed another shot back albeit only with a par. The gap would have been down to one after the 17th but there Harrington missed from three feet after Campbell had dropped another shot.

Campbell still held a two shot lead playing the last, but he hit his approach into the water. Now was the chance for Harrington and all his supporters. Yet, if Campbell was surprised that Harrington went for the flag at the 18th, tucked hard to the waterside, the spectators were dumbstruck. Their hearts and hopes drowned with the ball. Why did he not go for the fat part of the green to the right, secure the birdie and possibly, at worst, a play-off?

shot of the week

PADRAIG HARRINGTON Ireland

Padraig Harrington knew he needed a big finish to the third round. The 18th measures 537 yards with a 280 yard carry over the bunkers at the dog leg. He needed only a seven iron for his second. He hit it sweetly to six feet and made eagle to be just one shot behind Campbell going into the last day.

The man himself had no regrets. "Sure I was gutted," he said. "Of course I feel sorry for myself. But my thinking was that if I hit the middle of the green, Michael would probably get up and down from there 50 per cent of the time. I had it in my head that if I wanted to win it there and then I had to get the eagle. I didn't want to hit it to the middle or the right of the green.

"I hit a bad shot and it went into the water but I'll tell you this, it would have killed me if I had hit it to the right or middle of the green and three putted and Michael had got up and down. I went for eagle and I feel better that I did."

Colm Smith

David Lynn

the course

The K Club was opened in 1993 and has hosted the Smurfit European Open since 1995. It will also be the home of The 36th Ryder Cup Matches in 2006. The course has matured and toughened with each passing year. There are several more phases to the plan to present a fitting test for the best golfers from Europe and America.

Joakim Haeggman

final results

The K Club · Dublin · Ireland
July 4-7 · 2002 · Par 72 · 7337 yards · 6706 metres

Pos.	Name		Rd1	Rd2	Rd3	Rd4	Total	Par	Prize Money Euro	£
1	Michael CAMPBELL	NZ	68	71	70	73	282	-6	515584.80	333330.00
2	Padraig HARRINGTON	Ire	72	69	69	73	283	-5	205805.50	133055.00
	Paul LAWRIE	Scot	70	71	69	73	283	-5	205805.50	133055.00
	Bradley DREDGE	Wal	71	71	73	68	283	-5	205805.50	133055.00
	Retief GOOSEN	SA	71	72	72	68	283	-5	205805.50	133055.00
6	Colin MONTGOMERIE	Scot	69	75	68	72	284	-4	92806.20	60000.00
	Angel CABRERA	Arg	72	71	71	70	284	-4	92806.20	60000.00
	Niclas FASTH	Swe	69	77	68	70	284	-4	92806.20	60000.00
9	Barry LANE	Eng	69	71	71	74	285	-3	54844.04	35457.14
	Darren FICHARDT	SA	67	74	76	68	285	-3	54844.04	35457.14
	Jarrod MOSELEY	Aus	67	75	73	70	285	-3	54844.04	35457.14
	Joakim HAEGGMAN	Swe	68	73	71	73	285	-3	54844.04	35457.14
	Patrik SJÖLAND	Swe	71	70	73	71	285	-3	54844.04	35457.14
	Paul CASEY	Eng	71	73	69	72	285	-3	54844.04	35457.14
	Carl PETTERSSON	Swe	71	71	74	69	285	-3	54844.04	35457.14
16	Søren KJELDSEN	Den	75	72	72	67	286	-2	40912.07	26450.00
	Nick O'HERN	Aus	77	69	71	69	286	-2	40912.07	26450.00
	Peter O'MALLEY	Aus	74	72	69	71	286	-2	40912.07	26450.00
	Lee WESTWOOD	Eng	72	71	72	71	286	-2	40912.07	26450.00
20	Mark MOULAND	Wal	70	76	71	70	287	-1	34073.13	22028.57
	Ian WOOSNAM	Wal	73	74	67	73	287	-1	34073.13	22028.57
	Fred FUNK	USA	72	75	67	73	287	-1	34073.13	22028.57
	Robert KARLSSON	Swe	70	72	72	73	287	-1	34073.13	22028.57
	Darren CLARKE	N.Ire	74	70	76	67	287	-1	34073.13	22028.57
	Rolf MUNTZ	Hol	72	73	72	70	287	-1	34073.13	22028.57
	Mark PILKINGTON	Wal	71	69	75	72	287	-1	34073.13	22028.57
27	Mark JAMES	Eng	73	72	71	72	288	0	29388.63	19000.00
	Richard S JOHNSON	Swe	71	72	73	72	288	0	29388.63	19000.00
	Sebastien DELAGRANGE	Fr	69	73	74	72	288	0	29388.63	19000.00
30	Roger CHAPMAN	Eng	73	73	71	72	289	1	24163.98	15622.22
	Eamonn DARCY	Ire	75	72	73	69	289	1	24163.98	15622.22
	Santiago LUNA	Sp	71	73	73	72	289	1	24163.98	15622.22
	Eduardo ROMERO	Arg	74	69	71	75	289	1	24163.98	15622.22
	Gary MURPHY	Ire	72	73	74	70	289	1	24163.98	15622.22
	Richard GREEN	Aus	74	70	75	70	289	1	24163.98	15622.22
	Paul BROADHURST	Eng	73	73	70	73	289	1	24163.98	15622.22
	Steen TINNING	Den	70	74	74	71	289	1	24163.98	15622.22
	Ignacio GARRIDO	Sp	73	72	71	73	289	1	24163.98	15622.22
39	Markus BRIER	Aut	75	71	74	70	290	2	20417.36	13200.00
	Henrik NYSTROM	Swe	70	77	72	71	290	2	20417.36	13200.00
41	Jean-Francois REMESY	Fr	71	76	70	74	291	3	17633.18	11400.00
	Sven STRÜVER	Ger	70	73	76	72	291	3	17633.18	11400.00
	Maarten LAFEBER	Hol	73	72	75	71	291	3	17633.18	11400.00
	Peter HANSON	Swe	73	72	74	70	291	3	17633.18	11400.00
	Andrew MARSHALL	Eng	74	72	74	71	291	3	17633.18	11400.00
	Jorge BERENDT	Arg	68	73	76	74	291	3	17633.18	11400.00
	David CARTER	Eng	73	74	70	74	291	3	17633.18	11400.00
48	Marc FARRY	Fr	74	72	73	73	292	4	13302.22	8600.00
	Brian DAVIS	Eng	73	72	76	71	292	4	13302.22	8600.00
	Mårten OLANDER	Swe	73	72	75	72	292	4	13302.22	8600.00
	Anders HANSEN	Den	71	73	75	73	292	4	13302.22	8600.00
	Richard BLAND	Eng	75	72	76	69	292	4	13302.22	8600.00
	Roger WESSELS	SA	72	73	73	74	292	4	13302.22	8600.00
	Jarmo SANDELIN	Swe	74	71	70	77	292	4	13302.22	8600.00
55	Warren BENNETT	Eng	75	70	75	73	293	5	10518.04	6800.00
	Paul EALES	Eng	77	70	76	70	293	5	10518.04	6800.00
57	Greg NORMAN	Aus	69	76	72	77	294	6	8971.27	5800.00
	Sam TORRANCE	Scot	74	74	75	71	294	6	8971.27	5800.00
	Mark MCNULTY	Zim	70	74	73	77	294	6	8971.27	5800.00
	Emanuele CANONICA	It	71	75	74	74	294	6	8971.27	5800.00
	Ian GARBUTT	Eng	72	71	80	71	294	6	8971.27	5800.00
62	Peter FOWLER	Aus	76	71	76	72	295	7	7733.85	5000.00
	Ricardo GONZALEZ	Arg	73	71	75	76	295	7	7733.85	5000.00
	Gary CLARK	Eng	73	74	80	68	295	7	7733.85	5000.00
65	Lucas PARSONS	Aus	70	75	76	75	296	8	6960.47	4500.00
	Jamie DONALDSON	Wal	70	71	77	78	296	8	6960.47	4500.00
67	Chris GANE	Eng	69	78	77	73	297	9	6341.76	4100.00
	Raymond RUSSELL	Scot	75	70	75	77	297	9	6341.76	4100.00
69	David HOWELL	Eng	72	72	79	75	298	10	5877.73	3800.00
70	Andrew COLTART	Scot	72	70	77	80	299	11	5142.85	3324.90
	John DWYER	Ire	69	75	77	78	299	11	5142.85	3324.90
72	Gregory HAVRET	Fr	77	70	78	75	300	12	4637.00	2997.86

Innobook
The first worldwide database for packaging creation.

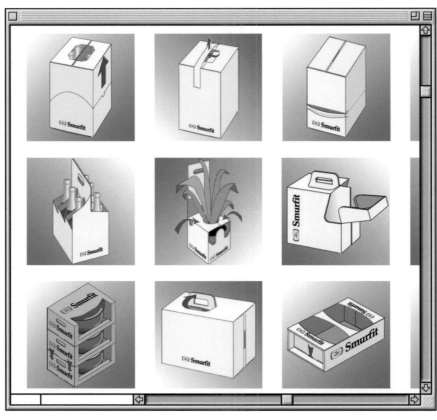

More .... http//www.innobook.com

Innobook allows instant access to the imagination of all the design centres in the Jefferson Smurfit Group.

If you have a packaging problem, we have no doubt addressed your problem before in one of our design centres. And the foundation of your next packaging solution is already in Innobook, the global Smurfit packaging solutions database. Using a clear definition of your packaging constraints (pack types, functions, mechanisation), Innobook provides Smurfit solutions that come closest to satisfying your needs. Simpler to mechanise, easier to transport, lighter, more practical, more resistant, more compact, more appealing, more promotional are just some of the features of the packaging solutions in Innobook. Today, with Innobook and Smurfit, you don't have packaging problems because we have the solutions.

 **Smurfit**
Corrugated Cases

Dublin	Phone 01 4090000	Fax 01 4564509
Cork	Phone 021 4962033	Fax 021 4962051
Lurgan	Phone 048 38323611	Fax 048 38324422
Tamworth	Phone 01827 306300	Fax 01827 306301
Nelson	Phone 01282 616321	Fax 01282 601855
West Auckland	Phone 01388 832531	Fax 01388 833766

The Barclays Scottish Open Loch Lomond Golf Club · Glasgow · Scotland

age of experience

Eduardo Romero

Three days after winning at Loch Lomond, Eduardo Romero and his wife Adriana were walking through the tented village at Muirfield in East Lothian. There isn't an exact Spanish translation for the Scottish phrase, 'Go on yersel, big man,' but the popular Argentine, who had just turned 48, appreciated he could hardly have encountered more well-wishers if he had been transported back to his home town of Cordoba.

Romero's success in landing the most lucrative cheque of his career - a whopping 573,016 euro (£366,660) - was that rare event in sport, a celebration. A regular on The European Tour International Schedule for 15 years, there is hardly a player his peers like more than this genial golfer. Always smiling and polite, Romero's strength of personality, not to mention the quality of his golf, won the hearts of the knowledgeable Scottish galleries.

Once he had defeated Sweden's Fredrik Jacobson on the first hole of a play-off, after the pair had tied on 11 under par 273, Romero made his feelings about the Home of Golf plain. He'd been competing in this part of the world since the 1980s and always saw resemblances between the landscapes of Scotland and Argentina. "When I look at the lochs and the mountains, I think of home and it meant a lot to me to win here," he observed. "The Scottish people are fantastic."

Romero's fair-mindedness, as much as his power off the tee and the knack of finding greens in regulation, was the quality which most

impressed the Scots. Coming down the stretch, it was clear Jacobson's nerves were starting to get the better of him as he battled to secure the first professional victory of his career.

On the 16th, a testing 490 yard par four, the Swede had already enjoyed one stroke of good fortune from the tee when his wayward drive flew into the rough but from where he received a free drop for landing in tyre tracks. Jacobson's next blow was equally unconvincing and his ball was only located when Romero found it plugged in a bank just a couple of feet short of the stream which runs in front of the green.

Jacobson was given another free drop, chipped to ten feet and holed the putt for a four which even rivalled Gary Evans's five on the penultimate hole at Muirfield the following week as one of the most remarkable pars of the season. "Freddy made an unbelievable par on that hole but then dropped a shot at the 17th," Romero recalled. "His hands were shaking and I could see he was nervous."

The 27 year old was a promising ice hockey player in his youth but his decision to make golf his profession had been vindicated with a number of outstanding performances. Indeed he had finished runner-up in no fewer than five events on The European Tour International Schedule including, most recently, the 2000 Murphy's Irish Open and the 2001 Linde German Masters. He launched his challenge to go one better in the first round when he took advantage of the benign weather conditions to trail the leader,

Sandy Lyle

Justin Rose, by a shot, with Miles Tunnicliff, fresh from his win in The Great North Open, alongside him at five under.

On Friday, Jacobson kept up the good work. His 65 followed on from the 66 posted in the sepulchral hush of Thursday evening. "There weren't too many people around by the time I finished my first round - even the scoreboard people had gone home by the time I was done," he smiled. "But the second round was a bit different and after my run on the front nine there were quite a few following me after the turn."

Jacobson's 'run' was a breathtaking sequence of five consecutive birdies between the fifth and ninth holes. He carded 2-4-3-2-3 against the card of 3-5-4-3-4, inspiring memories of a similar

shot of the week

EDUARDO ROMERO Argentina

Playing well under pressure is the hallmark of any Champion. When Eduardo Romero walked onto Loch Lomond's 18th tee for the second time on Sunday and took out his driver, the Argentine knew the shot would make the difference between winning and losing the shoot-out with Fredrik Jacobson. A tricky prospect with water on the left and bunkers to the right, Romero unleashed a perfect drive - long, straight and exhilarating. It set him up for a tidy approach to the green and the nine foot uphill birdie putt which gave him the title.

onslaught on the Thursday when he made four birdies over the last six holes.

With much attention also focusing on Sandy Lyle's welcome return to form - on Saturday the Scot, alongside Jacobson, played in the last group of a Tour event for the first time in ten years - Romero, seven shots back at the halfway stage, made stealthy progress.

After opening up with 72, he carded 66 in the company of Gary Orr and Sam Torrance, which moved him back into contention. Even better was to follow in the third round when Romero posted a superb 65 and narrowed the gap on Jacobson to one shot. Always a prodigious striker of a golf ball, it was the South American's short game which served him well in a round that included seven birdies.

Come the final showdown, many wondered if Jacobson would be able to utilise the advantage of youth. Certainly Romero, with more than 80 successes in South America to his credit as well as seven previous European Tour wins, gave a convincing impression of a man looking forward to the Seniors Tour. "There are too many young players on this Tour and it's become too difficult for me," he suggested.

Romero's tongue must have been firmly in his cheek, however, as experience proved more than a match for youth. In carding a birdie three on the first extra hole of the play-off, Romero, at the age of

the course

Scotland's soggiest summer in living memory produced a challenge eagerly accepted and superbly executed by Ken Siems, the course superintendent, and his excellent team. The beautifully manicured course, with outstanding greens, set a wonderful examination and the players responded in great style with no fewer than 52 finishing with sub-par totals.

47 years and 362 days, followed Des Smyth (48 and 34 days when winning the 2001 Madeira Island Open) and Neil Coles (48 and 14 days when winning the 1982 Sanyo Open) as the third oldest golfer ever to win a European Tour event. It was a measure of Romero's affability that even the disappointed Jacobson gave him a hug after he had holed a nine foot, uphill putt at the first extra hole, the 430 yard 18th, into which he had struck a pitching wedge following a perfect drive.

Romero, a devotee of yoga to assist his concentration, had beaten an impressive field which included Ernie Els, who would move on the next week to win the 131st Open Golf Championship, Retief Goosen, the defending Champion, and the American Tom Lehman.

Roger Chapman and the South African Tim Clark tied for third, ahead of Rose, but it was entirely fitting that Romero should resemble the cat who got the cream. He is after all, known as El Gato because of his knack of stalking opponents.

Mike Aitken

Fredrik Jacobson

The European Tour Sport Relief Challenge raised in total £35,692 for Sport Relief, launched by Comic Relief and BBC Sport, who were fundraising in 2002 to help children and young people at home in the UK and around the world who are leading unimaginably tough lives. Birdies and eagles made by competitors at the Volvo PGA Championship, The Compass Group English Open and The Barclays Scottish Open earned £1 and £2 respectively from each of the companies pledging their support. Darren Clarke handed his cheque to Steve Rider of the BBC as Sport Relief culminated in a blockbusting night on BBC 1 of Sport, entertainment and fundraising.

final results

Loch Lomond Golf Club · Glasgow · Scotland
July 11-14 · 2002 · Par 71 · 7083 yards · 6475 metres

Pos.	Name		Rd1	Rd2	Rd3	Rd4	Total	Par	Prize Money Euro	£
1	Eduardo ROMERO	Arg	72	66	65	70	273	-11	573016.30	366660.00
2	Fredrik JACOBSON	Swe	66	65	71	71	273	-11	382010.80	244440.00
3	Roger CHAPMAN	Eng	70	70	66	68	274	-10	193568.40	123860.00
	Tim CLARK	SA	71	68	67	68	274	-10	193568.40	123860.00
5	Justin ROSE	Eng	65	71	68	71	275	-9	145778.00	93280.00
6	Jean-Francois REMESY	Fr	70	72	67	67	276	-8	91042.48	58256.00
	Stephen LEANEY	Aus	72	65	67	72	276	-8	91042.48	58256.00
	Ricardo GONZALEZ	Arg	72	70	69	65	276	-8	91042.48	58256.00
	Tom LEHMAN	USA	69	69	71	67	276	-8	91042.48	58256.00
	Michael CAMPBELL	NZ	72	67	66	71	276	-8	91042.48	58256.00
11	Warren BENNETT	Eng	67	70	68	72	277	-7	59250.96	37913.34
	John BICKERTON	Eng	67	73	67	70	277	-7	59250.96	37913.34
	Paul CASEY	Eng	72	69	65	71	277	-7	59250.96	37913.34
14	Barry LANE	Eng	74	66	69	69	278	-6	46611.63	29825.72
	Marc FARRY	Fr	71	69	70	68	278	-6	46611.63	29825.72
	Jamie SPENCE	Eng	70	69	67	72	278	-6	46611.63	29825.72
	Colin MONTGOMERIE	Scot	72	71	69	66	278	-6	46611.63	29825.72
	Paul MCGINLEY	Ire	69	73	68	68	278	-6	46611.63	29825.72
	Retief GOOSEN	SA	72	69	69	68	278	-6	46611.63	29825.72
	Carl PETTERSSON	Swe	70	66	73	69	278	-6	46611.63	29825.72
21	Maarten LAFEBER	Hol	74	68	69	68	279	-5	38851.21	24860.00
	Nick O'HERN	Aus	72	69	69	69	279	-5	38851.21	24860.00
	Richard BLAND	Eng	68	71	71	69	279	-5	38851.21	24860.00
	Barry HUME (AM)	Scot	67	70	72	70	279	-5		
25	Ian WOOSNAM	Wal	72	67	70	71	280	-4	33693.97	21560.00
	Rodney PAMPLING	Aus	74	67	68	71	280	-4	33693.97	21560.00
	Peter HANSON	Swe	76	65	68	71	280	-4	33693.97	21560.00
	Søren HANSEN	Den	72	68	70	70	280	-4	33693.97	21560.00
	Jonathan LOMAS	Eng	69	70	70	71	280	-4	33693.97	21560.00
	Darren CLARKE	N.Ire	70	73	66	71	280	-4	33693.97	21560.00
	Nick DOUGHERTY	Eng	72	69	70	69	280	-4	33693.97	21560.00
32	David HOWELL	Eng	68	71	67	75	281	-3	26015.41	16646.67
	Michael HOEY	N.Ire	68	72	72	69	281	-3	26015.41	16646.67
	Dean WILSON	USA	68	73	70	70	281	-3	26015.41	16646.67
	Gary EVANS	Eng	73	66	71	71	281	-3	26015.41	16646.67
	José COCERES	Arg	70	66	74	71	281	-3	26015.41	16646.67
	Bradley DREDGE	Wal	72	70	70	69	281	-3	26015.41	16646.67
	Jeff MAGGERT	USA	71	72	68	70	281	-3	26015.41	16646.67

Pos.	Name		Rd1	Rd2	Rd3	Rd4	Total	Par	Prize Money Euro	£
	Alastair FORSYTH	Scot	72	70	69	70	281	-3	26015.41	16646.67
	Rory SABBATINI	SA	69	71	68	73	281	-3	26015.41	16646.67
41	Sandy LYLE	Scot	67	68	75	72	282	-2	19597.51	12540.00
	Klas ERIKSSON	Swe	74	68	71	69	282	-2	19597.51	12540.00
	Cameron BECKMAN	USA	71	68	72	71	282	-2	19597.51	12540.00
	Raphaël JACQUELIN	Fr	73	70	70	69	282	-2	19597.51	12540.00
	Søren KJELDSEN	Den	69	74	68	71	282	-2	19597.51	12540.00
	Fred FUNK	USA	71	71	69	282		-2	19597.51	12540.00
	Stephen DODD	Wal	69	71	74	68	282	-2	19597.51	12540.00
	Phillip PRICE	Wal	73	69	69	71	282	-2	19597.51	12540.00
	Niclas FASTH	Swe	70	68	79	65	282	-2	19597.51	12540.00
50	Richard S JOHNSON	Swe	71	65	75	72	283	-1	15471.72	9900.00
	Ernie ELS	SA	68	74	69	72	283	-1	15471.72	9900.00
	Gary ORR	Scot	73	67	72	71	283	-1	15471.72	9900.00
53	Gordon BRAND JNR.	Scot	68	74	74	68	284	0	11345.93	7260.00
	Miguel Angel MARTIN	Sp	72	70	74	68	284	0	11345.93	7260.00
	Sam TORRANCE	Scot	68	73	74	69	284	0	11345.93	7260.00
	Robert-Jan DERKSEN	Hol	69	72	72	71	284	0	11345.93	7260.00
	Brad FAXON	USA	68	72	70	74	284	0	11345.93	7260.00
	Henrik BJORNSTAD	Nor	72	71	68	73	284	0	11345.93	7260.00
	Peter O'MALLEY	Aus	69	71	74	70	284	0	11345.93	7260.00
	Mathias GRÖNBERG	Swe	73	69	69	73	284	0	11345.93	7260.00
	Paul LAWRIE	Scot	69	73	72	70	284	0	11345.93	7260.00
	Simon DYSON	Eng	68	74	75	67	284	0	11345.93	7260.00
63	Arjun ATWAL	Ind	74	69	72	70	285	1	8251.58	5280.00
	Thomas LEVET	Fr	73	70	73	69	285	1	8251.58	5280.00
	Miguel Angel JIMÉNEZ	Sp	74	69	69	73	285	1	8251.58	5280.00
	Per-Ulrik JOHANSSON	Swe	69	73	71	72	285	1	8251.58	5280.00
	Joakim HAEGGMAN	Swe	71	71	71	72	285	1	8251.58	5280.00
68	Jorge BERENDT	Arg	72	68	72	74	286	2	7220.14	4620.00
69	Diego BORREGO	Sp	75	68	74	70	287	3	6704.41	4290.00
	Matt GOGEL	USA	69	68	76	74	287	3	6704.41	4290.00
71	Philip GOLDING	Eng	72	70	74	72	288	4	6282.46	4020.00
72	Miles TUNNICLIFF	Eng	66	70	76	77	289	5	5155.50	3298.89
	Mark PILKINGTON	Wal	71	67	79	72	289	5	5155.50	3298.89
74	Tony JOHNSTONE	Zim	68	71	76	75	290	6	5151.00	3296.00
	Costantino ROCCA	It	71	72	76	71	290	6	5151.00	3296.00

Caddies aren't the only ones
with good advice.

Barclays sponsors the Scottish Open.

BARCLAYS

FLUENT IN FINANCE

131st Open Golf Championship Muirfield · East Lothian · Scotland

survive and prosper

Sport, like life itself, needs an injection of genuine, unremitting drama now and again if we are to truly realise and appreciate what sheer fun it all is. One such occasion came to pass on the third day of the 131st Open Golf Championship at Muirfield.

Ernie Els

On that particular Saturday afternoon, the wind and rain rose from the Firth of Forth and smacked the world's best golfers right between the eyes. The rest of us either cowered before the elements or, if fortunate enough to be in front of a television set, merely sat all afternoon until our mouths ached from gaping so much at what was happening.

There has been wind and rain before on the Saturday of an Open Golf Championship. In recent times the unpredictable British summer struck most notably at Muirfield in 1987, Royal Lytham & St Annes in 1988 and Royal Birkdale in 1998. This time, however, the Gods decided to have a lie-in so that the tempest struck as the third round leaders were either making their way to the first tee or meandering down the opening fairways.

As mid-July echoed mid-January, no-one was struck harder than Tiger Woods. The American, in search of the grandest of Grand Slams, had played sedately up to this point, his 70-68 start placing him handily at four under par and within two strokes of the lead. Now his game plan was to switch off the cruise control and accelerate through the field so that his name thumped onto the top of the leaderboards, giving his main rivals a familiar sense of *déjà vu*.

It was a good plan, too. Except that Woods had not quite revealed his A-game over those first two rounds and when the weather broke spectacularly it seemed to affect him, adversely, more than most.

Here was a man used to creating his own electrical storm suddenly enveloped by a force more powerful than even he could muster. It has to be said, he looked rather panic-stricken and he was not alone. If you listened carefully, the sound of grown men yelping with pain could be heard from every point on the course.

Thomas Levet

It was not, however, the only sound in East Lothian. Listen even more intently and you could just about make out two players squealing with ill-disguised delight; namely the two Justins, Leonard of the United States and Rose of England. Each had just scraped inside the halfway cut at one over par and, at the time, lamented that their chance of victory had gone.

Instead it turned out that they, unwittingly, had come up with not a game plan but a master plan, a cunning scheme that consisted of

Gary Evans

Colin Montgomerie

simply playing early and enjoying pleasant, calm conditions. Paired together, each shot 68 which, at the time, was good enough to move them into a share of 35th place. Then, while doing nothing more strenuous than sipping a clubhouse coffee, each was able to watch as their efforts lifted them so high that they ended the day tied for third, their astonishment matched only by their great, good fortune.

Everything, it appeared had been turned upside down. Everything, that is, except Ernie Els, whose one over par 72 was a tribute to his determination as well as to his talent. Ironically, the storm was probably the best thing to happen to the South African for two reasons; firstly it effectively removed Woods from the equation, and secondly it meant the big man stopped fretting about what Woods was doing in a Major Championship for once. "Usually I'm looking up at the leaderboards and waiting for his charge but this time I hardly thought about Tiger at all," said Els. "I was too busy just trying to survive."

Of course, he did much more than survive. He prospered, ending the day five under par for the Championship, two strokes ahead of Denmark's Søren Hansen and three ahead of a seven strong group that included some of Europe's finest in Thomas Björn, Sergio Garcia and Rose, and, glory be, good old Des Smyth. Not that old actually, but at 49 an Irishman who was supposed to be along for the ride and not up there in the lead coach. "Unbelievable," he grinned. "When the storm broke I just thought, 'Well, I can't do anything about this so I might as well just try to enjoy myself'."

shot of the week

ERNIE ELS South Africa

The short 13th at Muirfield was as easy a hole as could be found on the last day. At 191 yards long it required no more than a six iron and, at an average score of 3.16, it was alongside the short 16th as a 'no real problem' challenge. Unless you hit the pot bunker to the front left of the green that is. On the last day, Ernie Els did just that and very few experts believed he could get anywhere close to the hole which was at least ten feet above his head and some 25 feet distant. Indeed some feared he would not get out at all unless he took the sideways route. Els, however, had other ideas, splashing his ball vertically as well as forwards - a motion that would have confounded even Albert Einstein - to send it trundling to within a few inches of the hole. It was, he admitted later, the shot that made eventual victory possible.

Which is exactly what he did, his head swathed in an enormous tea-cosy hat, his battling 74 a reflection both of a younger life spent trawling the great links of his homeland and of the skill and determination he showed in becoming the oldest winner in the history of The European Tour International Schedule when he triumphed in the 2001 Madeira Island Open.

Perhaps, understandably, it did not last, Smyth slipping back gracefully with a final day 73 that meant he shared 28th place alongside, amongst others, Woods, whose own closing 65 suggested he may pay Muirfield back with interest in future visits.

Els, meanwhile, seemed determined to win by the hardest means possible, almost as though he did not wish to allow the great drama of the final day, played out in idyllic sunkissed conditions, to dry up. Indeed, the 131st Open Golf Championship enjoyed the longest climax of any in recent memory, an escalating excitement that was ignited early by England's Gary Evans.

Des Smyth

The best way
to go round the world
in 365 days.

The European Tour. From Taiwan to Mexico via England, Rolex follows The European Tour International Schedule every step of the way – with 48 tournaments across 21 countries through 5 continents.

Rolex Day-Date.
Officially Certified Swiss Chronometer.

ROLEX

The 33 year old, who has yet to taste victory on The European Tour International Schedule, returned a scintillating 65 almost before Els was properly awake, to set a target of five under par. During a round crammed with improbably long putts in addition to some seriously fine play, Evans's most memorable moment came at the long 17th where, having lost a ball, he saved par with a putt of some 50 feet.

Later he revealed that his main thought all day had been to play as "strong as a bull" which is what a friend had advised. This he did, although his ecstatic reaction on the 17th, a hopping, jumping, fist-pumping celebration that ended with him screaming "that one's for you mum" into a television lens, appeared more mad cow than bullish.

Several hours later Els had the Claret Jug in his hands. Apparently. When he stood on the 16th tee with a seven iron in his hands, all he had to do was to par the last three holes to clinch the deal. Instead he hooked his tee shot down a steep, grassy bank from where he chipped back off the front of the green before taking three more to get down. From being in the lead at seven under par he was suddenly a stroke behind and only a birdie at the 17th saved his embarrassment, sending him into a four man, four hole play-off against Australians Stuart Appleby and Steve Elkington and Frenchman Thomas Levet.

An hour later it was down to two, the Frenchman and the South African, and into the sudden-death phase over the minefield that is the 18th. Levet, all French flamboyance, selected his driver and paid for his bravado by watching his ball plunge into a bunker from where a bogey five was a good effort.

Els, meanwhile, used a long iron to find the fairway before tugging another iron into a greenside bunker. But he adores sand and, although it required a stroke of sublime delicacy, he knocked his ball out to three feet and holed the winning putt before the admirable Levet, six inches shorter and several stone lighter, hoisted the Champion in his arms up into the evening air.

Nick Price

Levet, who the previous season had enthralled the crowds by "high-fiving" the galleries following victory in another four man play-off for the Victor Chandler British Masters, was this time a hero in defeat. He said: "Je ne regret rien. I had a four to win the Open first time around but hit a bad drive and took five. Ernie is a great Champion."

The 33 year old from Paris had played a leading role in a thrilling production. For the 131st Open Golf Championship had been absolutely brilliant and Ernie Els had, without doubt, moved centre stage. Storming stuff, indeed, from beginning to end.

Bill Elliott

Carl Pettersson

the course

At just 7,034 yards, Muirfield is not an obvious monster but its curling fairways and punishing rough on top of occasional wind made it a real test for the very best players on the planet. Presented in immaculate condition, the harshest examination questions were, as ever, the first and the 18th. The latter was the longer, by one yard at 449 yards, but between them they provided early and late obstacles to anyone with ambitions of a decent score. Even in the benign conditions that greeted Thursday, Friday and Sunday, they took their toll. On Saturday when the tempest raged they were all but impossible. It was at Muirfield in 1744 that the game's first 13 laws were written down. Several wags finishing play on the Saturday cheekily suggested that the 14th unwritten one could suggest more fun would be had by starting at the second tee and finishing on the 17th green.

235

Thomas Levet, Steve Elkington and Stuart Appleby

final results

Muirfield · East Lothian · Scotland
July 18-21 · 2002 · Par 71 · 7034 yards · 6433 metres

Pos.	Name		Rd1	Rd2	Rd3	Rd4	Total	Par	Prize Money Euro	£
1	Ernie ELS	SA	70	66	72	70	278	-6	1095514.00	700000.00
2	Steve ELKINGTON	Aus	71	73	68	66	278	-6	448639.10	286666.69
	Stuart APPLEBY	Aus	73	70	70	65	278	-6	448639.10	286666.69
	Thomas LEVET	Fr	72	66	74	66	278	-6	448639.10	286666.69
5	Padraig HARRINGTON	Ire	69	67	76	67	279	-5	219102.80	140000.00
	Shigeki MARUYAMA	Jpn	68	68	75	68	279	-5	219102.80	140000.00
	Gary EVANS	Eng	72	68	74	65	279	-5	219102.80	140000.00
8	Sergio GARCIA	Sp	71	69	71	69	280	-4	121289.00	77499.97
	Søren HANSEN	Den	68	69	73	70	280	-4	121289.00	77499.97
	Peter O'MALLEY	Aus	72	68	75	65	280	-4	121289.00	77499.97
	Scott HOCH	USA	74	69	71	66	280	-4	121289.00	77499.97
	Thomas BJÖRN	Den	68	70	73	69	280	-4	121289.00	77499.97
	Retief GOOSEN	SA	71	68	74	67	280	-4	121289.00	77499.97
14	Nick PRICE	Zim	68	70	75	68	281	-3	77859.74	49750.00
	Justin LEONARD	USA	71	72	68	70	281	-3	77859.74	49750.00
	Davis LOVE III	USA	71	72	71	67	281	-3	77859.74	49750.00
	Peter LONARD	Aus	72	72	68	69	281	-3	77859.74	49750.00
18	Greg NORMAN	Aus	71	72	71	68	282	-2	64165.82	41000.00
	Scott MCCARRON	USA	71	68	72	71	282	-2	64165.82	41000.00
	Bob ESTES	USA	71	70	73	68	282	-2	64165.82	41000.00
	Duffy WALDORF	USA	67	69	77	69	282	-2	64165.82	41000.00
22	Corey PAVIN	USA	69	70	75	69	283	-1	50080.64	32000.00
	Mark O'MEARA	USA	69	69	77	68	283	-1	50080.64	32000.00
	David DUVAL	USA	72	71	70	70	283	-1	50080.64	32000.00
	Toshimitsu IZAWA	Jpn	76	68	72	67	283	-1	50080.64	32000.00
	Justin ROSE	Eng	68	75	68	72	283	-1	50080.64	32000.00
	Chris RILEY	USA	70	71	76	66	283	-1	50080.64	32000.00
28	Bernhard LANGER	Ger	72	72	71	69	284	0	37560.48	24000.00
	Des SMYTH	Ire	68	69	74	73	284	0	37560.48	24000.00
	Tiger WOODS	USA	70	68	81	65	284	0	37560.48	24000.00
	Loren ROBERTS	USA	74	69	70	71	284	0	37560.48	24000.00
	Jesper PARNEVIK	Swe	72	72	70	70	284	0	37560.48	24000.00
	Jerry KELLY	USA	73	71	70	70	284	0	37560.48	24000.00
	Pierre FULKE	Swe	72	69	78	65	284	0	37560.48	24000.00
	Bradley DREDGE	Wal	70	72	74	68	284	0	37560.48	24000.00
	Niclas FASTH	Swe	70	73	71	70	284	0	37560.48	24000.00
37	Ian WOOSNAM	Wal	72	72	73	68	285	1	26474.92	16916.67
	Stephen LEANEY	Aus	71	70	75	69	285	1	26474.92	16916.67
	Scott VERPLANK	USA	72	68	74	71	285	1	26474.92	16916.67
	Darren CLARKE	N.Ire	72	67	77	69	285	1	26474.92	16916.67
	Andrew COLTART	Scot	71	69	74	71	285	1	26474.92	16916.67
	Neal LANCASTER	USA	71	71	76	67	285	1	26474.92	16916.67
43	Trevor IMMELMAN	SA	72	72	71	71	286	2	21519.03	13750.00
	Steve JONES	USA	68	75	73	70	286	2	21519.03	13750.00
	Esteban TOLEDO	Mex	73	70	75	68	286	2	21519.03	13750.00
	Carl PETTERSSON	Swe	67	70	76	73	286	2	21519.03	13750.00
47	Paul EALES	Eng	73	71	76	67	287	3	18780.24	12000.00
	Rocco MEDIATE	USA	71	72	74	70	287	3	18780.24	12000.00
	Jeff MAGGERT	USA	71	68	80	68	287	3	18780.24	12000.00
50	Warren BENNETT	Eng	71	68	82	67	288	4	16067.54	10266.67
	Barry LANE	Eng	74	68	72	74	288	4	16067.54	10266.67
	Ian POULTER	Eng	69	69	78	72	288	4	16067.54	10266.67
	Bob TWAY	USA	70	66	78	74	288	4	16067.54	10266.67
	Ian GARBUTT	Eng	69	70	74	75	288	4	16067.54	10266.67
	Fredrik ANDERSSON	Swe	74	70	74	70	288	4	16067.54	10266.67
	Mikko ILONEN	Fin	71	70	77	70	288	4	16067.54	10266.67
	Shingo KATAYAMA	Jpn	72	68	74	74	288	4	16067.54	10266.67
	Craig PERKS	NZ	72	70	71	75	288	4	16067.54	10266.67
59	Nick FALDO	Eng	73	69	76	71	289	5	14554.69	9300.00
	Steve STRICKER	USA	69	70	81	69	289	5	14554.69	9300.00
	Richard GREEN	Aus	72	72	75	70	289	5	14554.69	9300.00
	Stewart CINK	USA	71	69	80	69	289	5	14554.69	9300.00
	Joe DURANT	USA	72	71	73	73	289	5	14554.69	9300.00
	Paul LAWRIE	Scot	70	70	78	71	289	5	14554.69	9300.00
	Kuboya KENICHI	Jpn	70	73	73	73	289	5	14554.69	9300.00
66	Jarrod MOSELEY	Aus	70	73	75	72	290	6	13772.18	8800.00
	Phil MICKELSON	USA	68	76	76	70	290	6	13772.18	8800.00
	Chris DIMARCO	USA	72	69	75	74	290	6	13772.18	8800.00
69	Mike WEIR	Can	73	69	74	75	291	7	13328.76	8516.67
	Toru TANIGUCHI	Jpn	71	73	76	71	291	7	13328.76	8516.67
	Jim CARTER	USA	74	70	73	74	291	7	13328.76	8516.67
	Stephen AMES	T&T	68	70	81	72	291	7	13328.76	8516.67
	Matthew CORT	Eng	73	71	78	69	291	7	13328.76	8516.67
	Len MATTIACE	USA	68	73	77	73	291	7	13328.76	8516.67
75	Sandy LYLE	Scot	68	76	73	75	292	8	13302.67	8500.00
	Chris SMITH	USA	74	69	71	78	292	8	13302.67	8500.00
77	Anders HANSEN	Den	71	72	79	71	293	9	13302.67	8500.00
	Roger WESSELS	SA	72	71	73	77	293	9	13302.67	8500.00
79	David PARK	Wal	73	67	74	80	294	10	13302.67	8500.00
80	Mark CALCAVECCHIA	USA	74	66	81	74	295	11	13302.67	8500.00
	Lee JANZEN	USA	70	69	84	72	295	11	13302.67	8500.00
82	Colin MONTGOMERIE	Scot	74	64	84	75	297	13	13302.67	8500.00
83	David TOMS	USA	67	75	81	75	298	14	13302.67	8500.00

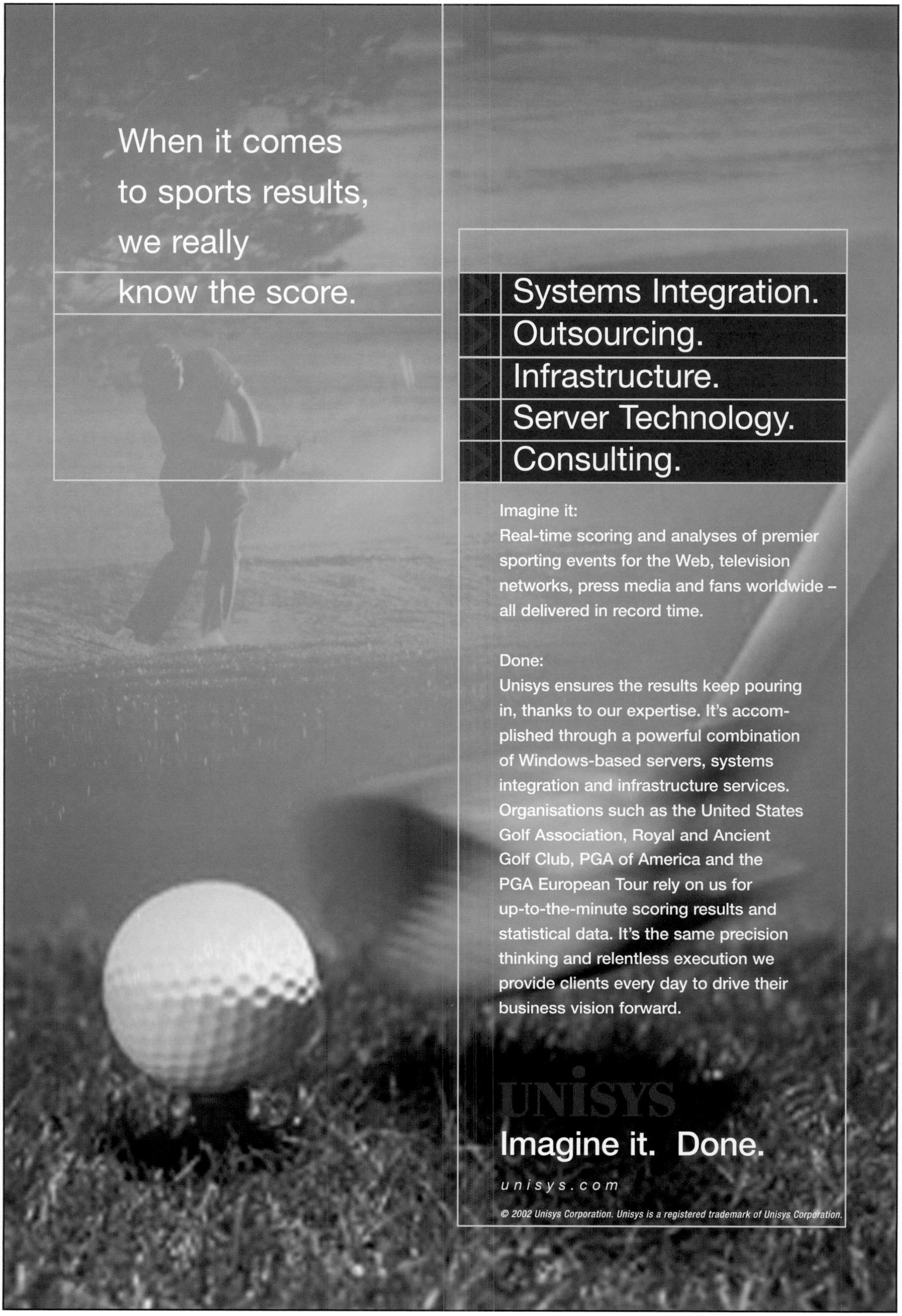

When it comes
to sports results,
we really
know the score.
Systems Integration.
Outsourcing.
Infrastructure.
Server Technology.
Consulting.
Imagine it:
Real-time scoring and analyses of premier sporting events for the Web, television networks, press media and fans worldwide – all delivered in record time.
Done:
Unisys ensures the results keep pouring in, thanks to our expertise. It's accomplished through a powerful combination of Windows-based servers, systems integration and infrastructure services. Organisations such as the United States Golf Association, Royal and Ancient Golf Club, PGA of America and the PGA European Tour rely on us for up-to-the-minute scoring results and statistical data. It's the same precision thinking and relentless execution we provide clients every day to drive their business vision forward.
UNISYS
Imagine it. Done.
unisys.com
© 2002 Unisys Corporation. Unisys is a registered trademark of Unisys Corporation.

The TNT Open Hilversumsche Golf Club · Hilversum · Netherlands

dream on

When Germany's Tobias Dier teed off in The TNT Open at the delightful Hilversumsche Golf Club he had but one thought in his mind – survival. After missing a dozen cuts on his previous 15 European Tour outings to slip to 182nd on the Volvo Order of Merit, making the weekend was, understandably, top of his list of priorities.

Twenty-four hours later, however, his target was the title itself.

Tobias Dier

What turned the unlikely into the eminently attainable was a remarkable Thursday afternoon during which he became only the ninth player in the history of The European Tour International Schedule to post a score of 60. At the same time, he sent shock waves through the statistics for the season.

The flawless ten birdie effort was the lowest start by a winner in 2002 as well as being the lowest first 18 hole score. His five stroke lead at the end of the day was also the largest of the season, beating the previous best of four held by Carl Pettersson in the Algarve Open de Portugal.

It did not stop there for the 1998 German Amateur Champion. Further rounds of 67-67 saw him set the lowest 36 hole total of the season, 127, and the lowest 54 hole total of 194. It left Dier with a three shot lead going into the last round and he held his nerve admirably to become the sixth wire-to-wire winner of the season. He claimed the 300,000 euro (£193,019) first prize and a priceless two year exemption.

Peter Lonard

Dier had proved that fairytales can, and do, come true on The European Tour although closer inspection of his credentials might have yielded some clues as to his capabilities.

A year earlier, he had led from the second round to win his maiden title in the North West of Ireland Open and had dropped a hint as to his fondness for Hilversumsche in the curtain-raising Pro-Am when he holed out for an albatross two on the 18th. Had he performed the feat a day later he would have fired a 58, but nothing could detract the 25 year old biochemistry graduate from what he had achieved overall.

"My victory in Ireland, where I'd shot a course record in 2000, was fantastic but it was a double badge event with the Challenge Tour in the week of the US PGA Championship and I'd been competing on a day to day basis with most of the guys who were playing at Slieve Russell," he said.

the course

Co-designed by Colt and Burrows in 1910, the tightly wooded layout, although no monster at 6,617 yards, presented a tough test with a par reduced from 72 to 70. After a punishing opening 11 holes, the closing seven offered scoring chances, as illustrated perfectly by Tobias Dier's homeward 29 in his opening 60 and Jamie Spence's closing 29 in his opening 66.

Lucas Parsons

"The field at Hilversumsche was much stronger and if anyone had told me at the start of the week that I'd walk away with the title I'd have told them 'dream on.' I was wondering where the money was going to come from. Now I've got a regular job for the next two years."

Dier was right about the quality of the opposition which included compatriot and defending Champion Bernhard Langer along with the likes of John Daly, Nick Faldo, Retief Goosen, Padraig Harrington and Lee Westwood. Also teeing up were the in-form Gary Evans and Justin Rose alongside visiting US PGA Tour players Matt Kuchar and Jerry Pate.

But all had to defer to Dier who, after storming home in 29 for his 60, confessed: "I don't think I'm on earth at the moment - I'm still in orbit. I've had 65s three or four times, but never anything like this. It's a number everybody dreams about."

To his eternal credit, the following day's 'predictable' reaction round never occurred. Instead the young man who contemplated a football career before achilles trouble struck produced another bogey free effort, this time a 67, on what Australian Peter Lonard, who would ultimately share third place with Harrington, called, "the tightest course I've played all year."

Saturday saw Dier eventually yield a shot to the Hilversumsche course, a bogey five coming at the 465 yard fourth hole, his 40th of the week, but a 20 foot eagle three at the last secured a second 67 and preserved his three stroke advantage.

Klas Eriksson

shot of the week

TOBIAS DIER Germany

England's Mark Foster holed in one at the 125 yard fifth on day one to win a 50,000 euro Lancia Thesis, but after bogeys at the eighth and the 11th, the most crucial shot of the week was Champion Tobias Dier's five iron to seven feet for eagle at the 486 yard 12th in the final round. It gave him a two stroke cushion and reaffirmed his belief that it was to be his day.

All week the slim Bavarian with the solid swing looked cool, calm and collected and although he saw his lead twice shrunk to a single stroke in the final round he was never overawed by playing partner Harrington, fresh from tieing fifth in the 131st Open Golf Championship to move up to number eight in the Official World Golf Ranking. Indeed, after matching the Irishman's eagle three at the 486 yard 12th, he enjoyed the luxury of six par figures to finish for victory.

Like a seasoned Champion Dier eased home one ahead of Jamie Spence, another man who had shot 60 when coming from ten shots behind to win the 1992 Canon European Masters at Crans-sur-Sierre in Switzerland.

Dier was proud to follow in the footsteps of role model Langer, who finished 15 strokes behind him, but respectfully cautioned any direct comparisons. "I'm 25 and he's 45 with 70 tournaments wins, including two Majors," he said. "I haven't even played in a Major. I might have beaten him here, but it wasn't head to head and I can't begin to compare myself with him."

He felt the reason the more fancied names were unable to shoot him down had much to do with the dearth of birdie opportunities in the first 11 holes, added to the fact that he was only  once in the trees in four days. He also insisted he was not the ice man he appeared. "I'm not typically German," he said. "People who know me would say I can be temperamental, outgoing and like to talk a lot. But I'm focused on the golf course."

The stars left in his slipstream at Hilversumsche can vouch for that.

Gordon Richardson

Jamie Spence

final results

Hilversumsche Golf Club • Hilversum • Netherlands
July 25-28 • 2002 • Par 70 • 6617 yards • 6052 metres

Pos.	Name		Rd1	Rd2	Rd3	Rd4	Total	Par	Prize Money Euro	£
1	Tobias DIER	Ger	60	67	67	69	263	-17	300000.00	193019.14
2	Jamie SPENCE	Eng	66	64	69	65	264	-16	200000.00	128679.43
3	Padraig HARRINGTON	Ire	66	67	64	68	265	-15	101340.00	65201.87
	Peter LONARD	Aus	67	63	68	67	265	-15	101340.00	65201.87
5	Jarrod MOSELEY	Aus	66	67	67	67	267	-13	76320.00	49104.07
6	Justin ROSE	Eng	67	67	67	67	268	-12	50580.00	32543.03
	Ian POULTER	Eng	67	69	66	66	268	-12	50580.00	32543.03
	Pierre FULKE	Swe	68	65	65	70	268	-12	50580.00	32543.03
	Alastair FORSYTH	Scot	68	69	68	63	268	-12	50580.00	32543.03
10	Kenneth FERRIE	Eng	68	67	65	69	269	-11	33360.00	21463.73
	Gary EVANS	Eng	69	64	69	67	269	-11	33360.00	21463.73
	Raymond RUSSELL	Scot	65	70	64	70	269	-11	33360.00	21463.73
13	Nick FALDO	Eng	68	68	67	67	270	-10	27660.00	17796.36
	Andrew OLDCORN	Scot	68	69	68	65	270	-10	27660.00	17796.36
	Steen TINNING	Den	70	66	67	67	270	-10	27660.00	17796.36
16	Mark ROE	Eng	64	66	67	74	271	-9	22577.14	14526.07
	Klas ERIKSSON	Swe	69	68	67	67	271	-9	22577.14	14526.07
	Greg TURNER	NZ	70	69	68	64	271	-9	22577.14	14526.07
	Trevor IMMELMAN	SA	70	67	64	70	271	-9	22577.14	14526.07
	Russell CLAYDON	Eng	68	71	68	64	271	-9	22577.14	14526.07
	Roger WESSELS	SA	68	72	64	67	271	-9	22577.14	14526.07
	Matthew CORT	Eng	69	69	64	69	271	-9	22577.14	14526.07
23	Jean-Francois REMESY	Fr	68	71	66	67	272	-8	18720.00	12044.39
	Nick O'HERN	Aus	71	66	69	66	272	-8	18720.00	12044.39
	Peter O'MALLEY	Aus	71	65	71	65	272	-8	18720.00	12044.39
	Robert COLES	Eng	68	70	66	68	272	-8	18720.00	12044.39
	David LYNN	Eng	68	67	68	69	272	-8	18720.00	12044.39
28	David GILFORD	Eng	65	69	70	69	273	-7	16560.00	10654.66
	Peter HEDBLOM	Swe	68	66	73	66	273	-7	16560.00	10654.66
	Ignacio GARRIDO	Sp	69	70	66	68	273	-7	16560.00	10654.66
31	Maarten LAFEBER	NL	66	70	70	68	274	-6	14436.00	9288.08
	Matt KUCHAR	USA	66	66	69	70	274	-6	14436.00	9288.08
	Retief GOOSEN	SA	69	68	67	70	274	-6	14436.00	9288.08
	Scott GARDINER	Aus	69	70	65	70	274	-6	14436.00	9288.08
	Jamie DONALDSON	Wal	70	67	68	69	274	-6	14436.00	9288.08
36	Santiago LUNA	Sp	71	69	71	64	275	-5	12240.00	7875.18
	Warren BENNETT	Eng	68	69	68	70	275	-5	12240.00	7875.18
	Stuart LITTLE	Eng	72	68	68	67	275	-5	12240.00	7875.18

Pos.	Name		Rd1	Rd2	Rd3	Rd4	Total	Par	Prize Money Euro	£
	Richard S JOHNSON	Swe	70	69	69	67	275	-5	12240.00	7875.18
	Ian GARBUTT	Eng	68	69	67	71	275	-5	12240.00	7875.18
	Fredrik ANDERSSON	Swe	68	72	67	68	275	-5	12240.00	7875.18
42	Gordon BRAND JNR.	Scot	69	70	75	62	276	-4	10080.00	6485.44
	Raphaël JACQUELIN	Fr	73	66	68	69	276	-4	10080.00	6485.44
	Anders HANSEN	Den	69	68	71	68	276	-4	10080.00	6485.44
	Marcel SIEM	Ger	71	67	66	72	276	-4	10080.00	6485.44
	Markus BRIER	Aut	69	70	69	68	276	-4	10080.00	6485.44
	Wei-Tze YEH	C.Tai	69	71	66	70	276	-4	10080.00	6485.44
48	Stephen LEANEY	Aus	68	71	68	70	277	-3	8280.00	5327.33
	Philip GOLDING	Eng	69	71	68	69	277	-3	8280.00	5327.33
	Jonathan LOMAS	Eng	70	67	71	69	277	-3	8280.00	5327.33
	Andrew COLTART	Scot	69	69	67	72	277	-3	8280.00	5327.33
	Jamie ELSON (AM)	Eng	69	69	67	72	277	-3		
53	Bernhard LANGER	Ger	71	69	69	69	278	-2	6480.00	4169.21
	Marc FARRY	Fr	67	72	69	70	278	-2	6480.00	4169.21
	James KINGSTON	SA	68	71	69	70	278	-2	6480.00	4169.21
	Andrew BUTTERFIELD	Eng	68	71	70	69	278	-2	6480.00	4169.21
	John DALY	USA	70	67	70	71	278	-2	6480.00	4169.21
	Christopher HANELL	Swe	66	73	71	68	278	-2	6480.00	4169.21
59	Ronan RAFFERTY	N.Ire	65	72	74	68	279	-1	5040.00	3242.72
	David HOWELL	Eng	66	73	69	71	279	-1	5040.00	3242.72
	Chris GANE	Eng	68	71	71	69	279	-1	5040.00	3242.72
	Jerry PATE	USA	68	69	74	68	279	-1	5040.00	3242.72
	Gary ORR	Scot	71	65	66	77	279	-1	5040.00	3242.72
64	Gary EMERSON	Eng	76	64	68	72	280	0	4230.00	2721.57
	Paul EALES	Eng	69	70	70	71	280	0	4230.00	2721.57
	John BICKERTON	Eng	67	69	70	74	280	0	4230.00	2721.57
	Guido VAN DER VALK	NL	68	72	68	72	280	0	4230.00	2721.57
68	Darren RICHARDT	SA	69	71	67	74	281	1	3600.00	2316.23
	Carl SUNESON	Sp	72	68	74	67	281	1	3600.00	2316.23
	Rory SABBATINI	SA	69	70	68	74	281	1	3600.00	2316.23
71	Lee WESTWOOD	Eng	70	66	72	75	283	3	2990.00	1923.76
	Lucas PARSONS	Aus	69	69	72	73	283	3	2990.00	1923.76
73	Mattias ELIASSON	Swe	70	70	70	74	284	4	2695.50	1734.28
	Carlos RODILES	Sp	67	69	74	74	284	4	2695.50	1734.28
75	Mark MOULAND	Wal	68	72	75	70	285	5	2691.00	1731.38
76	Joakim RASK	Swe	69	71	72	75	287	7	2688.00	1729.45

Volvo Scandinavian Masters   Kungsängen · Stockholm · Sweden

true gem

Kungsängen members waited in eager anticipation for the arrival of their new touring professional, Graeme McDowell, on the Tuesday before the Volvo Scandinavian Masters, the biggest golfing event of the year in Sweden.

Graeme McDowell

the course

The heathland course north west of Stockholm, designed by Anders Forsbrand in 1994 and re-designed by European Golf Design in 1995 and 1996, is embroidered by heavy rough, rugged rocky outcrops and water. A more difficult back nine frequently claimed back the glut of birdies and eagles it had conceded on the outward half.

The young Ulsterman, who had just celebrated his 23rd birthday, kept them waiting for a few extra hours. His flight was delayed. After a few hurried greetings, McDowell was off to walk around his new attachment. It was a strange thought, an Irishman representing a Swedish golf course. However, it was a deal brokered by his managers, International Sports Management, and Denis O'Brien, the owner of the course, that would pay off in spectacular fashion.

Thus McDowell, a member of the successful Great Britain and Ireland Walker Cup team which defeated the United States 15-9 at Sea Island in Georgia in 2001, arrived with his first priority being to fashion a top ten finish.

If he could accomplish that, he would also automatically earn a place the following week in The Celtic Manor Resort Wales Open. He had missed the cut in two of his three previous tournaments, one of them on his debut at De Vere Slaley Hall in The Great North Open. Even so a second place at the Golf Challenge in Hamburg on the European Challenge Tour two weeks before the trip to Sweden was not only highly encouraging but also good for that vital ingredient - confidence.

Much was expected of the lads from the Walker Cup 'Class of 2001'. McDowell was not initially headline material in the mould of Luke Donald and Nick Dougherty, but he knew he had the

Warren Bennett

right stuff – as six collegiate victories in America from 12 starts with a better stroke average (69.6) than Tiger Woods and Donald proved. He had, after all, eclipsed both of them in the record books. Indeed at the University of Alabama, McDowell was ranked Number One collegiate golfer in the United States.

What concerned McDowell was his putting. He had mentioned this to his idol Darren Clarke when the two played together in the final round of the Murphy's Irish Open at Fota Island. Clarke gave McDowell one of his centre-shafted Odyssey putters to see if it might change his fortune – it was as if he had been handed a magic wand.

McDowell raked home a series of telling putts in the first round at Kungsängen to break the course record with a superb seven under par 64. Although he could not always find his 'A' game off the tee, as a 73 in the second round indicated when he surrendered the lead to England's Warren Bennett, Clarke's putter continued to work its magic in McDowell's hands. A third round 66 hauled him back into a share of the lead with Niclas Fasth, continuing to build confidence for his Ryder Cup debut in September, and the visiting American Jeff Sluman.

Sluman, the 1988 US PGA Champion, had been in town to attend the wedding of Jesper Parnevik's sister Jill to Per-Ulrik Johansson. Johansson celebrated his first week of marriage by breaking

shot of the week

GRAEME McDOWELL N. Ireland

After driving into a fairway bunker on the 18th in the final round, Graeme McDowell had to splash out from under the lip. "I now faced a third shot 143 yards uphill into the breeze. Normally it would be a nine iron, but I decided to go down the grip on an eight iron and play a punch shot." He could not have played it any better .... and a maiden European Tour win was his.

McDowell's course record, a third round 63 putting him briefly in contention before he fell back over the final 18 holes.

On a pulsating last day, McDowell produced 12 single putts, seven of them on the inward half, as The European Tour's newest professional refused to bow to his adopted course's lethal holes.

Fasth's hopes sank in the water with a double bogey at the short 16th. Sluman hovered, but the finale was enacted by McDowell and another youngster, his 22 year old South African playing partner Trevor Immelman, trying to go one better than his best performance to date on The European Tour International Schedule, tied second in the Novotel Perrier Open de France in May.

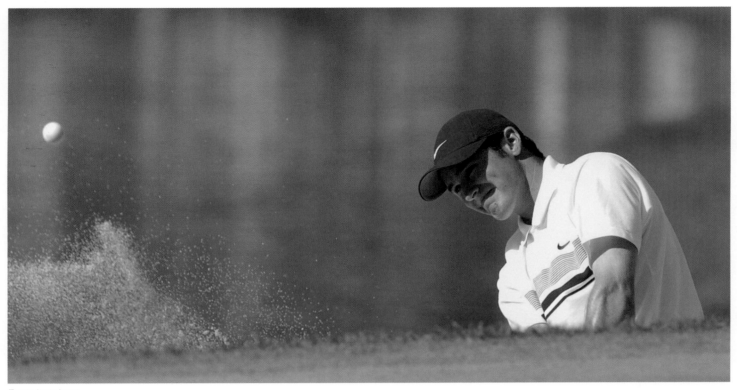

Trevor Immelman

It would have been understandable if McDowell had capitulated when a dreaded shank at the 15th saw his ball squirt from a greenside bunker into the lake, but the Ulsterman bravely made bogey five before climbing level with Immelman again at the 16th with a nerveless birdie putt from 12 feet.

McDowell was to save the best for last. Tied at 14 under par with Immelman on the 18th tee, the advantage looked to have gone to the South African when McDowell drove into the fairway bunker. Under the lip, he could only splash out but played a momentous third shot with his eight iron to two feet to not only save par, but to also win the tournament outright as Immelman overshot the green and made bogey five.

If they had not realised it after his course record opening round, the members of Kungsängen knew then they had unearthed a true gem as a touring professional. However, they were not the only ones celebrating. A quick call to Rathmore, his home club at Portrush, set up  free drinks for the members, just as his putting saviour Clarke had done nine years before for the members of Dungannon, when he claimed his maiden European Tour win in the Alfred Dunhill Open at Royal Zoute in Belgium.

Henrik Bjornstad

Norman Dabell

Jamie Donaldson

final results

Kungsängen · Stockholm · Sweden
August 1-4 • 2002 • Par 71 • 6761 yards • 6182 metres

Pos.	Name		Rd1	Rd2	Rd3	Rd4	Total	Par	Prize Money Euro	£
1	Graeme McDOWELL	N.Ire	64	73	66	67	270	-14	316660.00	200142.84
2	Trevor IMMELMAN	SA	70	67	67	67	271	-13	211110.00	133430.67
3	Jeff SLUMAN	USA	69	69	65	69	272	-12	106970.00	67609.68
	Henrik BJORNSTAD	Nor	70	69	66	67	272	-12	106970.00	67609.68
5	Carl PETTERSSON	Swe	68	69	68	68	273	-11	80560.00	50917.41
6	Gary EVANS	Eng	71	69	68	66	274	-10	53390.00	33744.79
	Niclas FASTH	Swe	67	71	65	71	274	-10	53390.00	33744.79
	Matthew CORT	Eng	66	73	68	67	274	-10	53390.00	33744.79
	Adam SCOTT	Aus	65	74	68	67	274	-10	53390.00	33744.79
10	Peter LONARD	Aus	72	69	66	68	275	-9	36480.00	23056.94
	David DRYSDALE	Scot	74	68	65	68	275	-9	36480.00	23056.94
12	Warren BENNETT	Eng	66	70	69	71	276	-8	31635.00	19994.69
	Alastair FORSYTH	Scot	74	70	66	66	276	-8	31635.00	19994.69
14	Fredrik ANDERSSON	Swe	71	66	68	72	277	-7	27930.00	17652.97
	David CARTER	Eng	71	71	67	68	277	-7	27930.00	17652.97
	Mikael LUNDBERG	Swe	72	71	68	66	277	-7	27930.00	17652.97
17	Jesper PARNEVIK	Swe	67	73	68	70	278	-6	22657.50	14320.52
	Richard GREEN	Aus	74	71	66	67	278	-6	22657.50	14320.52
	Peter HEDBLOM	Swe	71	69	67	71	278	-6	22657.50	14320.52
	Joakim HAEGGMAN	Swe	71	70	66	71	278	-6	22657.50	14320.52
	Adam MEDNICK	Swe	72	68	68	70	278	-6	22657.50	14320.52
	David LYNN	Eng	67	74	68	69	278	-6	22657.50	14320.52
	Christopher HANELL	Swe	70	68	71	69	278	-6	22657.50	14320.52
	Jamie DONALDSON	Wal	72	68	68	71	278	-6	22657.50	14320.52
25	Mark FOSTER	Eng	70	68	69	72	279	-5	18905.00	11948.78
	Colin MONTGOMERIE	Scot	70	69	74	66	279	-5	18905.00	11948.78
	Marcel SIEM	Ger	67	72	68	72	279	-5	18905.00	11948.78
	Ignacio GARRIDO	Sp	67	70	73	69	279	-5	18905.00	11948.78
29	Barry LANE	Eng	70	68	69	73	280	-4	17480.00	11048.12
30	Maarten LAFEBER	Hol	70	71	67	73	281	-3	15057.50	9516.99
	Thomas LEVET	Fr	69	73	72	67	281	-3	15057.50	9516.99
	Søren HANSEN	Den	71	71	73	66	281	-3	15057.50	9516.99
	Charlie WI	R.Kor	68	75	69	69	281	-3	15057.50	9516.99
	Thomas BJÖRN	Den	69	72	71	69	281	-3	15057.50	9516.99
	Simon KHAN	Eng	69	71	73	68	281	-3	15057.50	9516.99
	Iain PYMAN	Eng	74	70	72	65	281	-3	15057.50	9516.99
	Brett RUMFORD	Aus	71	71	71	68	281	-3	15057.50	9516.99
38	Santiago LUNA	Sp	68	70	71	73	282	-2	12350.00	7805.74
	Olle NORDBERG	Swe	74	70	65	73	282	-2	12350.00	7805.74
	Per-Ulrik JOHANSSON	Swe	70	74	63	75	282	-2	12350.00	7805.74
	Robert KARLSSON	Swe	71	74	68	69	282	-2	12350.00	7805.74
	Robert COLES	Eng	70	71	68	73	282	-2	12350.00	7805.74
43	Mattias ELIASSON	Swe	75	70	68	70	283	-1	10260.00	6484.76
	Anthony WALL	Eng	69	72	71	71	283	-1	10260.00	6484.76
	Grant HAMERTON	Eng	66	73	74	70	283	-1	10260.00	6484.76
	Markus BRIER	Aut	70	71	73	69	283	-1	10260.00	6484.76
	Michael CAMPBELL	NZ	67	74	70	72	283	-1	10260.00	6484.76
	Mads VIBE-HASTRUP	Den	71	74	68	70	283	-1	10260.00	6484.76
49	Ian POULTER	Eng	68	76	72	68	284	0	8550.00	5403.97
	David PARK	Wal	68	74	70	72	284	0	8550.00	5403.97
	Fredrik WIDMARK	Swe	75	70	68	71	284	0	8550.00	5403.97
52	Paul BROADHURST	Eng	72	71	71	71	285	1	7220.00	4563.35
	Rolf MUNTZ	Hol	73	70	70	72	285	1	7220.00	4563.35
	Mark PILKINGTON	Wal	73	72	71	69	285	1	7220.00	4563.35
	John BICKERTON	Eng	71	69	69	76	285	1	7220.00	4563.35
56	Ronan RAFFERTY	N.Ire	67	71	75	73	286	2	5537.14	3499.71
	Fredrik OREST	Swe	69	73	71	73	286	2	5537.14	3499.71
	Marc FARRY	Fr	72	73	70	71	286	2	5537.14	3499.71
	Jarrod MOSELEY	Aus	73	70	71	72	286	2	5537.14	3499.71
	Emanuele CANONICA	It	70	73	67	76	286	2	5537.14	3499.71
	Fredrik JACOBSON	Swe	71	73	73	69	286	2	5537.14	3499.71
	Raymond RUSSELL	Scot	72	69	73	72	286	2	5537.14	3499.71
63	Raimo SJÖBERG	Swe	72	71	73	71	287	3	4655.00	2942.16
	Graeme STORM	Eng	72	70	69	76	287	3	4655.00	2942.16
65	Jonathan LOMAS	Eng	68	76	73	71	288	4	4370.00	2762.03
66	Gary EMERSON	Eng	70	72	76	71	289	5	4085.00	2581.90
	Nick DOUGHERTY	Eng	71	68	75	75	289	5	4085.00	2581.90
68	Stuart LITTLE	Eng	71	73	74	72	290	6	3626.67	2292.21
	Paul EALES	Eng	71	73	69	77	290	6	3626.67	2292.21
	Benoit TEILLERIA	Fr	70	70	78	72	290	6	3626.67	2292.21
7*	Andrew OLDCORN	Scot	71	73	74	73	291	7	2848.50	1800.38
	Pierre FULKE	Swe	73	72	75	71	291	7	2848.50	1800.38
73	Mark MOULAND	Wal	71	73	74	74	292	8	2842.50	1796.58
	Jamie SPENCE	Eng	73	72	67	80	292	8	2842.50	1796.58
75	Joakim RASK	Swe	73	72	75	74	294	10	2838.00	1793.74
76	Sebastien DELAGRANGE	Fr	72	71	78	75	296	12	2835.00	1791.84
77	Andrew BUTTERFIELD	Eng	70	74	79	75	298	14	2832.00	1789.95
78	Arjun ATWAL	Ind	69	73	78	80	300	16	2829.00	1788.05
79	Robert-Jan DERKSEN	Hol	71	73	83	77	304	20	2826.00	1786.15

The Celtic Manor Resort Wales Open The Celtic Manor Resort · Newport · Wale

man for all seasons

Displaying the patience of a Saint alongside the stamina of a Sherpa, Paul Lawrie won The Celtic Manor Resort Wales Open with a score which, under the circumstances, said as much about the durability of the course as the player. In a rain-affected tournament, Lawrie rose to the surface with two rounds of 70 on a marathon final day to triumph handsomely with an aggregate of 272, 16 under par.

Paul Lawrie

shot of
the week

PAUL LAWRIE Scotland

In between completing his second round early on Saturday and starting the 36 hole marathon on Sunday, Paul Lawrie had plenty of time to plan his strategy. An unexpected bonus awaited him at the fourth hole in the third round. After his drive had left him with a shade over 100 yards to the flag at the 413 yard hole, his downhill approach shot with a sand wedge rolled unerringly towards the pin, hit the flagstick and disappeared. The eagle two enabled Lawrie not only to increase his lead but strengthened his belief that The Celtic Manor Resort Wales Open was in his hands.

A man for all seasons, the Scot is, nevertheless, regarded as a safer bet when the going gets tough as it did when Wentwood Hills was hit by a combination of rain, mist and the threat of lightning during the second round. For the second year running the schedule was disrupted but Tournament Director Mike Stewart and Jim McKenzie, Celtic Manor Resort's Director of Golf, managed to squeeze a quart into a pint pot by completing 72 holes. Not everybody was happy with the late finishes and the early starts dictated by the weather, but the long distance Lawrie, for one, was not complaining.

He was on the leaderboard after a 67 in the first round although several others improved on that score, namely Richard Green of Australia and James Kingston of South Africa with 65s and Bradley Dredge and Sam Torrance with 66s. Torrance had a flawless round despite the fact that he almost missed his tee time. He thought he was off at 1.30pm when in fact it was 20 minutes earlier and was grateful for a hasty reminder from Tournament Recorder Jennie Janes. "I did a Colin Jackson over the fence around the practice putting green and made it with ten seconds to spare," he gasped.

It was when the weather turned ugly on day two that all the best laid plans were diluted. Play was delayed for three hours in the

the course

Set in 1400 acres of panoramic parkland at the gateway to Wales, The Celtic Manor Resort, the brainchild of Welsh telecommunications entrepreneur Sir Terry Matthews, boasts three Championship Courses designed by the Trent Jones dynasty. The par 72 Wentwood Hills, which measures 7355 yards, opened in 1999. The venue for The Celtic Manor Resort Wales Open, it has been chosen to stage The 38th Ryder Cup Matches in 2010. A third of the course will be re-designed and a new clubhouse built at the base of the River Usk Valley.

morning and suspended again in mid-afternoon by which time Lawrie was at the top of the leaderboard, advancing to nine under par for the Championship. The Aberdonian went to the turn in 32, with birdies at the third, fifth, sixth and seventh. When play was suspended he had completed 11 holes of his second round and led by a stroke from Green and by two from Kingston. Green had time to play only five holes, while Kingston never left the locker room.

"With some players hanging around for more than 12 hours we felt that was enough for the day," said Stewart. When play in the second round resumed early on Saturday morning, Lawrie returned to the 12th green, the scene of his demise 12 months earlier.

On that day, after play had been decimated by bad weather, the three leaders, Englishman Daren Lee, Irishman Paul McGinley and Lawrie, went to the 211 yard par three 12th hole for a sudden death play-off. Lawrie made an early exit after three-putting before McGinley, on his fifth visit to the green, took the title.

This time around, however, the 'Glorious 12th' belonged to Lawrie as he rolled in a putt of eight feet for a birdie two and when he picked up further strokes at the 16th and 18th for a fragmented

second round of 65, he stood at 12 under par, two in front of John Bickerton, who had two rounds of 67, and Green.

Lawrie, who won the 128th Open Golf Championship at Carnoustie in 1999, coming from ten strokes behind to catch Jean Van de Velde, had the opportunity to show he could win from the front just as impressively – and how he did just that.

The leaders had to play 36 holes on the Sunday and nobody could get close to Lawrie's third and fourth round scores of 70. He increased his lead early in the morning's third round, illuminating Wentwood Hills with an eagle two at the fourth where he holed a sand wedge from 101 yards and followed it up with a birdie at the next. Although the tough, uphill finishing stretch impeded his march, he had almost an hour's break before the afternoon fourth round and when he birdied the second, third and fourth he had again put clear blue water between himself and the rest. In the end his total was a stroke lower than Steen Tinning's inaugural record of 273, set in 2000.

At the end of what might have seemed like Groundhog Day, Lawrie finished five strokes in front of Bickerton, who closed with rounds of 73 and 70, and six in front of Mikko Ilonen of Finland.

John Bickerton

Stephen Dodd

"It was nice to come back and win this time," said Lawrie. "I don't make many mistakes when I've got the chance to win. If I hadn't started a fitness campaign I probably wouldn't have got round. I'm sure I would have struggled. The course was wet and long and hard on the legs. But I'm committed to improving my fitness, working out every second day and it stood me in good stead."

It was his fifth European Tour victory, his ninth as a professional and the prize of 291,432 euro (£183,330) took him past the £3 million mark in career earnings. Bickerton, who won 194,288 euro (£122,220), said: "I was never going to catch Paul. He played some  lovely golf but it was nice to hang on at the end for second spot. It is up there with the best performances of my career." Ilonen echoed the sentiment. "It was a long day and I felt it on the back nine," said the Finn. "I didn't make many putts but I hit the ball well. It was my highest finish and I really needed this."

Tim Glover

Mikko Ilonen

final results

The Celtic Manor Resort · Newport · Wales
August 8-11 · 2002 · Par 72 · 7355 yards · 6727 metres

Pos.	Name		Rd1	Rd2	Rd3	Rd4	Total	Par	Prize Money Euro	£
1	Paul LAWRIE	Scot	67	65	70	70	272	-16	291432.40	183330.00
2	John BICKERTON	Eng	67	67	73	70	277	-11	194288.30	122220.00
3	Mikko ILONEN	Fin	70	68	70	70	278	-10	109464.00	68860.00
4	Lucas PARSONS	Aus	71	69	67	72	279	-9	80786.52	50820.00
	Martin MARITZ	SA	71	69	67	72	279	-9	80786.52	50820.00
6	Trevor IMMELMAN	SA	68	70	71	71	280	-8	52458.78	33000.00
	Ian POULTER	Eng	71	71	69	69	280	-8	52458.78	33000.00
	Paul MCGINLEY	Ire	69	71	69	71	280	-8	52458.78	33000.00
9	Jean-Francois REMESY	Fr	73	68	70	70	281	-7	32909.14	20702.00
	Richard GREEN	Aus	65	69	73	74	281	-7	32909.14	20702.00
	Jarrod MOSELEY	Aus	71	70	69	71	281	-7	32909.14	20702.00
	Robert KARLSSON	Swe	70	67	73	71	281	-7	32909.14	20702.00
	Bradley DREDGE	Wal	66	74	70	71	281	-7	32909.14	20702.00
14	Peter FOWLER	Aus	72	70	69	71	282	-6	26229.39	16500.00
	Jamie DONALDSON	Wal	70	73	66	73	282	-6	26229.39	16500.00
16	Maarten LAFEBER	Hol	71	72	71	69	283	-5	21595.53	13585.00
	Elliot BOULT	NZ	68	75	69	71	283	-5	21595.53	13585.00
	Shaun Paul WEBSTER	Eng	72	71	71	69	283	-5	21595.53	13585.00
	Jeremy ROBINSON	Eng	69	68	73	73	283	-5	21595.53	13585.00
	Adam MEDNICK	Swe	70	72	69	72	283	-5	21595.53	13585.00
	Fredrik ANDERSSON	Swe	74	68	70	71	283	-5	21595.53	13585.00
	Henrik NYSTROM	Swe	70	75	71	67	283	-5	21595.53	13585.00
	Graeme MCDOWELL	N.Ire	73	69	71	70	283	-5	21595.53	13585.00
24	Barry LANE	Eng	69	72	72	71	284	-4	16874.24	10615.00
	David GILFORD	Eng	72	73	69	70	284	-4	16874.24	10615.00
	Sven STRÜVER	Ger	69	74	71	70	284	-4	16874.24	10615.00
	Joakim HAEGGMAN	Swe	74	69	69	72	284	-4	16874.24	10615.00
	Ian GARBUTT	Eng	71	71	70	72	284	-4	16874.24	10615.00
	Roger WESSELS	SA	67	70	72	75	284	-4	16874.24	10615.00
	Fredrik JACOBSON	Swe	71	71	70	72	284	-4	16874.24	10615.00
	Christopher HANELL	Swe	71	73	70	70	284	-4	16874.24	10615.00
32	Ronan RAFFERTY	N.Ire	70	75	71	69	285	-3	12642.57	7953.00
	Des SMYTH	Ire	68	74	73	70	285	-3	12642.57	7953.00
	Greg TURNER	NZ	71	72	70	72	285	-3	12642.57	7953.00
	Steve WEBSTER	Eng	70	73	69	73	285	-3	12642.57	7953.00
	Anthony WALL	Eng	69	73	71	72	285	-3	12642.57	7953.00
	Didier DE VOOGHT	Bel	67	74	72	72	285	-3	12642.57	7953.00
	Darren CLARKE	N.Ire	68	74	72	71	285	-3	12642.57	7953.00
	David LYNN	Eng	71	73	70	71	285	-3	12642.57	7953.00
	David DRYSDALE	Scot	68	72	69	76	285	-3	12642.57	7953.00
	Ashley ROESTOFF	SA	72	71	69	73	285	-3	12642.57	7953.00
42	Henrik STENSON	Swe	73	68	71	74	286	-2	10316.89	6490.00
	Charlie WI	R.Kor	71	70	70	75	286	-2	10316.89	6490.00
	Lee WESTWOOD	Eng	72	70	71	73	286	-2	10316.89	6490.00
45	Mark ROE	Eng	70	71	72	74	287	-1	8743.13	5500.00
	Sam TORRANCE	Scot	66	73	76	72	287	-1	8743.13	5500.00
	Gary EMERSON	Eng	71	72	74	70	287	-1	8743.13	5500.00
	Stuart LITTLE	Eng	72	71	70	74	287	-1	8743.13	5500.00
	Stephen DODD	Wal	72	70	70	75	287	-1	8743.13	5500.00
	Nick DOUGHERTY	Eng	69	72	68	78	287	-1	8743.13	5500.00
51	Emanuele CANONICA	It	71	74	68	75	288	0	6819.64	4290.00
	Rolf MUNTZ	Hol	67	71	72	78	288	0	6819.64	4290.00
	Sion E BEBB	Wal	70	73	72	73	288	0	6819.64	4290.00
	James KINGSTON	SA	65	75	74	74	288	0	6819.64	4290.00
	Mark WIGGETT	Eng	71	71	72	74	288	0	6819.64	4290.00
56	Malcolm MACKENZIE	Eng	71	74	73	71	289	1	5377.02	3382.50
	Magnus PERSSON ATLEVI	Swe	70	74	70	75	289	1	5377.02	3382.50
	Ian WOOSNAM	Wal	70	74	72	73	289	1	5377.02	3382.50
	Richard BLAND	Eng	74	70	72	73	289	1	5377.02	3382.50
60	Miguel Angel MARTIN	Sp	71	73	73	73	290	2	4721.29	2970.00
	Paul EALES	Eng	73	71	71	75	290	2	4721.29	2970.00
	Nicolas VANHOOTEGEM	Bel	69	72	72	77	290	2	4721.29	2970.00
63	Robert-Jan DERKSEN	Hol	71	72	75	73	291	3	4284.13	2695.00
	Stephen SCAHILL	NZ	68	72	74	77	291	3	4284.13	2695.00
65	Phillip PRICE	Wal	73	72	75	73	293	5	3846.98	2420.00
	Barry HUME	Scot	69	74	75	75	293	5	3846.98	2420.00
	Marc WARREN	Scot	72	73	75	73	293	5	3846.98	2420.00
68	Costantino ROCCA	It	73	70	73	78	294	6	3159.47	1987.51
	Philip GOLDING	Eng	73	70	74	77	294	6	3159.47	1987.51
	Mark PILKINGTON	Wal	74	68	79	73	294	6	3159.47	1987.51
	Alastair FORSYTH	Scot	70	75	72	77	294	6	3159.47	1987.51
72	Iain FERRIE	Eng	72	73	74	76	295	7	2620.00	1648.15

rich pickings

Two days after the completion of the US PGA Championship, Andrew 'Chubby' Chandler surveyed a practice ground full of textbook swings and determined faces and gave his thoughts on the state of the game.

Rich Beem

"It is just brilliant at the moment, isn't it?" declared the boss of International Sports Management, with obvious sincerity. "Everywhere you look there are young players who are clearly going to be something special. We have the best athlete in the world in Tiger Woods. And then we have Major Championships that have you absolutely glued to the edge of your seat."

That heady Tuesday, Chandler was like everyone else involved with the game, warm with the afterglow of a US PGA Championship so mesmerising there was a case for wondering whether it was the most exciting yet staged.

To think, following hard on the heels of a wonderful Open Golf Championship at Muirfield, many had travelled to Hazeltine National Golf Club wondering whether the season's final Major would prove something of a letdown. From the moment Justin Rose opened with a 69 in his first professional round in America, that fear was eased as the Championship built to a truly thrilling crescendo.

Along the way this 72 hole joyride hallmarked a rich assortment of characters. We had Fred Funk, revelling like Thomas Levet at Muirfield in the unique atmosphere these events produce. We had

Peter Lonard

the course

Unrecognisable from the course where Tony Jacklin won the US Open Championship in 1970. Then it was described by American Dave Hill as just needing some bales of hay and a few cows. Now it has matured into one of the most complete tests in American golf.

Mark Calcavecchia, who has never travelled down the middle of a road in his life, and was not about to start. But most of all, of course, we had the eventual winner Rich Beem. Even now, that sounds a little bizarre. Let us see, the winners of the four Major Championships in 2002 were Tiger Woods, Tiger Woods, Ernie Els and .... Rich Beem?

Odd it may sound, but there is not a soul who knows anything about golf who could possibly cast doubt on the integrity of his success. 'Incredible' is one of the most overused words in a sportswriter's vocabulary but in this instance hardly any other applies.

For how else do you describe a man who goes from selling mobile phones for $7 an hour to winning back-to-back golf tournaments just seven years later with first prizes worth a combined $1.8 million?

Beem's story is one that every struggling professional probably has stuck on his wall to be used as inspiration. Some people thought Tin Cup a far-fetched Hollywood movie, but if they want something truly out on a limb they should listen to the real life saga of Rich Beem.

Vijay Singh

This Major Championship was just the fourth in which he had competed. His chronological record now reads: Charged by the police in Carnoustie for driving under the influence of drink; Missed cut; Tied 70th; Winner by one shot over a charging Woods, who birdied all of the last four holes!

Chandler made another good point that Tuesday morning. He talked about how Beem had won because he played to his own strengths rather than Woods's. He said: "Take one of my players, Darren Clarke, who is as good a driver of the ball as there is. Yet he will hit a two iron on many holes, because that is what Tiger does, and I keep asking him why. Beem never went down to a two iron off the tee. He stuck to his own game plan, stuck to being Rich Beem, and that is why he won."

It sounds easy on paper, of course, but having the courage to keep hitting a driver when Tiger is on your tail takes some gumption. When he got to the 16th still in front Beem had reached the point where he had said the previous evening that he thought he would have to find a quiet corner to throw up if he was leading. In reality he nailed a drive, put a nine iron on the right of the green, and knocked in a hail-Mary putt that rendered all of Woods's birdies null and void.

shot of the week

RICH BEEM USA

In the second round Tiger Woods played a shot from a bunker that he called one of the finest he has ever played. But the best shot came from the winner, a 271 yard three wood on the final day that finished just seven feet from the flag to set up the only eagle on the 11th hole all week. It extended Rich Beem's lead from a slender one stroke to a pivotal three.

'If I birdie the last four, I will win', Woods had told himself on the 15th tee. Not on this day. Not in this Championship.

We await to see whether Beem will go on to become a big player in the game or whether this was his 15 minutes at the top of the pile. Even if it proves the latter, it certainly beats selling mobile phones. Not that he will ever forget selling mobile phones. He still carries his ID card around with him from the store in Seattle where he was a salesman. "I don't want to ever forget where I came from," he said.

For Rose, the tournament never went on to match the heights of his opening round but he left rightly contented with his second top 25 finish in consecutive Majors. Here is a player born to play on the biggest stage.

Sergio Garcia has reached the moment in his career where a tie for tenth place felt nothing special but he can be proud of the fact that it meant he finished in the top ten in each of the season's Majors. He has acquired consistency and in 2003 he will be looking to push on and claim his first Major Championship win.

But it was the man with the wonderfully alliterative name who secured his place in history at Hazeltine National Golf Club. Rich by name and now nature. And Beeming.

Derek Lawrenson

Pierre Fulke

Bernhard Langer

final results

Hazeltine National Golf Club • Chaska • Minnesota • USA
August 15-18 • 2002 • Par 72 • 7360 yards • 6732 metres

Pos.	Name		Rd1	Rd2	Rd3	Rd4	Total	Par	Prize Money Euro	£
1	Rich BEEM	USA	72	66	72	68	278	-10	1019144.00	649819.24
2	Tiger WOODS	USA	71	69	72	67	279	-9	611486.60	389891.67
3	Chris RILEY	USA	71	70	72	70	283	-5	385010.10	245487.36
4	Justin LEONARD	USA	72	66	69	77	284	-4	241918.10	154250.07
	Fred FUNK	USA	68	70	73	73	284	-4	241918.10	154250.07
6	Rocco MEDIATE	USA	72	73	70	70	285	-3	190446.20	121430.93
7	Mark CALCAVECCHIA	USA	70	68	74	74	286	-2	177063.50	112897.95
8	Vijay SINGH	Fiji	71	74	74	68	287	-1	163680.80	104364.97
9	Jim FURYK	USA	68	73	76	71	288	0	153386.40	97801.13
10	Sergio GARCIA	Sp	75	73	73	68	289	1	113973.60	72671.02
	Steve LOWERY	USA	71	71	73	74	289	1	113973.60	72671.02
	Stewart CINK	USA	74	74	72	69	289	1	113973.60	72671.02
	Pierre FULKE	Swe	72	68	78	71	289	1	113973.60	72671.02
	Ricardo GONZALEZ	Arg	74	73	71	71	289	1	113973.60	72671.02
	José COCERES	Arg	72	71	72	74	289	1	113973.60	72671.02
	Robert ALLENBY	Aus	76	66	77	70	289	1	113973.60	72671.02
17	Steve FLESCH	USA	72	74	73	71	290	2	74119.59	47259.60
	Padraig HARRINGTON	Ire	71	73	74	72	290	2	74119.59	47259.60
	Stuart APPLEBY	Aus	73	74	74	69	290	2	74119.59	47259.60
	Peter LONARD	Aus	69	73	75	73	290	2	74119.59	47259.60
	Charles HOWELL III	USA	72	69	80	69	290	2	74119.59	47259.60
22	Heath SLOCUM	USA	73	74	75	69	291	3	58678.01	37413.85
23	Bernhard LANGER	Ger	70	72	77	73	292	4	45552.67	29044.96
	Jeff SLUMAN	USA	70	75	74	73	292	4	45552.67	29044.96
	Justin ROSE	Eng	69	73	76	74	292	4	45552.67	29044.96
	Retief GOOSEN	SA	69	69	79	75	292	4	45552.67	29044.96
	Michael CAMPBELL	NZ	73	70	77	72	292	4	45552.67	29044.96
	Adam SCOTT	Aus	71	71	76	74	292	4	45552.67	29044.96
29	Brad FAXON	USA	74	72	75	72	293	5	34486.20	21988.84
	Kenny PERRY	USA	73	68	78	74	293	5	34486.20	21988.84
	Tom LEHMAN	USA	71	72	77	73	293	5	34486.20	21988.84
	Kirk TRIPLETT	USA	75	69	79	70	293	5	34486.20	21988.84
	Craig PERKS	NZ	72	76	74	71	293	5	34486.20	21988.84
34	David DUVAL	USA	71	77	76	70	294	6	27074.24	17262.88
	Mike WEIR	Can	73	74	77	70	294	6	27074.24	17262.88
	Ernie ELS	SA	72	71	75	76	294	6	27074.24	17262.88
	Phil MICKELSON	USA	76	72	78	68	294	6	27074.24	17262.88
	Neal LANCASTER	USA	72	73	75	74	294	6	27074.24	17262.88
39	Joel EDWARDS	USA	73	74	77	71	295	7	22132.93	14112.24
	Scott McCARRON	USA	73	71	79	72	295	7	22132.93	14112.24
	John HUSTON	USA	74	74	75	72	295	7	22132.93	14112.24
	Chris DiMARCO	USA	76	69	77	73	295	7	22132.93	14112.24
43	Loren ROBERTS	USA	77	70	77	72	296	8	17500.46	11158.52
	Shigeki MARUYAMA	Jpn	76	72	75	73	296	8	17500.46	11158.52
	Søren HANSEN	Den	73	69	78	76	296	8	17500.46	11158.52
	Kevin SUTHERLAND	USA	72	75	71	78	296	8	17500.46	11158.52
	Briny BAIRD	USA	79	69	73	75	296	8	17500.46	11158.52
48	Tom WATSON	USA	76	71	83	67	297	9	13506.24	8611.75
	Steve ELKINGTON	Aus	72	75	76	74	297	9	13506.24	8611.75
	Davis LOVE III	USA	70	75	76	76	297	9	13506.24	8611.75
	Angel CABRERA	Arg	71	73	77	76	297	9	13506.24	8611.75
	Len MATTIACE	USA	74	73	76	74	297	9	13506.24	8611.75
53	Greg NORMAN	Aus	71	74	73	80	298	10	12088.55	7707.81
	Cameron BECKMAN	USA	74	71	75	78	298	10	12088.55	7707.81
	Toshimitsu IZAWA	Jpn	72	73	75	78	298	10	12088.55	7707.81
	Lee JANZEN	USA	70	76	77	75	298	10	12088.55	7707.81
	Tim CLARK	SA	74	74	76	76	298	10	12088.55	7707.81
	Brian GAY	USA	73	74	78	73	298	10	12088.55	7707.81
	Chris SMITH	USA	75	73	72	78	298	10	12088.55	7707.81
60	Nick FALDO	Eng	71	76	74	78	299	11	11529.71	7351.49
	Joe DURANT	USA	74	71	79	75	299	11	11529.71	7351.49
	Hal SUTTON	USA	73	73	75	78	299	11	11529.71	7351.49
63	J.J. HENRY	USA	78	70	77	76	301	13	11323.83	7220.22
64	Joey SINDELAR	USA	77	71	78	76	302	14	11066.47	7056.12
	J.P. HAYES	USA	73	75	78	76	302	14	11066.47	7056.12
	Matt GOGEL	USA	74	73	83	72	302	14	11066.47	7056.12
	Jon BERRY	USA	76	71	80	75	302	14	11066.47	7056.12
68	Dave TENTIS	USA	76	72	78	78	304	16	10809.11	6892.03
69	José María OLAZÁBAL	Sp	73	75	77	80	305	17	10706.16	6826.38
70	Pat PEREZ	USA	77	71	85	76	309	21	10603.22	6760.75
71	Thomas LEVET	Fr	78	70	82	80	310	22	10500.28	6695.11
72	Stephen AMES	T&T	73	74	RETD		147	3	2058.88	1312.77

swede dreams

Ballyliffin, once the best kept secret in golf, is a course talked about in whispers. Visitors are invariably blown away by the sheer beauty of the place. During the North West of Ireland Open, however, it was the high winds off the neighbouring Atlantic Ocean which threatened to do the blowing away, but for eventual winner Adam Mednick the prevailing conditions proved not only surmountable but positively hospitable!

Adam Mednick

Jean-François Lucquin

Opening day winds gusting at 35 miles an hour swept across the spectacular Glashedy Links, a seemingly infinite stretch of wild duneland and one which, despite only opening in 1995, had the appearance of a course that has been there forever.

There was talk of its ferocity rivalling that experienced during the Saturday afternoon of the Open Golf Championship at Muirfield a few weeks earlier, only this time the rain stayed away making the course difficult but not impossible.

Initially it was the oldest player in the field, Costantino Rocca, who led the way. Drawing on the imagination and experience which helped him finish runner-up in the 1995 Open Golf Championship at St Andrews, he negotiated his way round the towering dunes in one under par 71.

Rarely did the 45 year old Italian play a full shot, opting time and again to bump the ball up the tight fairways and onto the greens with a series of three quarter swings and punch shots. His was a masterclass of shot making in the most examining of conditions.

Rocca, aiming to win the 'double badge' event which counted for both the Challenge Tour Rankings and the Volvo Order of Merit for a second time in four years, was joined at the top of the leaderboard by four players – Jesus Maria Arruti, Massimo Florioli, Anders Forsbrand and Allan Hogh – all of whom started later in the day as the elements began to subside.

When play resumed for the second round the Glashedy Links was transformed, the high winds of the first day reduced to a gentle zephyr. This was reflected in the scores. Andrew Coltart muscled into contention with a course record 66, six under par, to move within two shots of the lead still held by Rocca after a second round 69.

The second round, however, was merely the calm before the storm. Overnight the winds whipped into a frenzy. The 35 miles per hour blasts of the first day were surpassed by gusts of more than 40 mph. Within 90 minutes of play starting, the third round was suspended as the golf balls could no longer hold their own and started moving on the greens. Even the main scoreboard on the 18th hole had to be dismantled as the supports began to buckle in the face of such an overhead onslaught.

By mid-morning the wind had eased sufficiently for play to be possible on the greens and the tournament resumed, but three hours later the gale force winds were back to full force and play was again suspended. Eventually, as the shadows started to lengthen, the players returned but with the wind still ferocious, and the flags bent double, this was a war of attrition.

There were casualties aplenty with more than 50 of the 88 players who made the cut failing to break 80. Many stood firm with Mednick defying the conditions to reach the turn in one under par, the only player in the field to break par on the front nine. When darkness fell he had completed 13 holes in level par, a remarkable achievement.

Happily the weather changed again for the final day. Mednick returned, picked up three birdies in the remaining five holes of his third round and completed a 69. It put him within one stroke of Florioli, who claimed the lead from compatriot Rocca by virtue of a superb 71 for a four under par total of 212.

Mednick started his fourth round, quickly drew level with birdies on the second and at the par five fourth hole, before picking up another birdie at the ninth to take the outright lead for the first time. From that moment Mednick looked composed, calmly holding his challengers at bay. Indeed he birdied the last two holes to win the title by five shots.

the course

Situated close to Malin Head on Donegal's Inishowen Peninsula, Ballyliffin Golf Club is Ireland's most northerly links. Nestled beneath towering mountains, overlooking Pollan Bay and Glashedy Rock, the new Glashedy Links makes the most of a genuinely dramatic location. The course, designed by Pat Ruddy and Tom Craddock, only opened in 1995 but is already establishing a reputation as one of the best.

There were many other performances to admire. Coltart finished in style with a 67 to share second place with Rocca. Jean-François Lucquin, experiencing links golf for the first time, showed commendable resilience as well as demonstrating his talent. His closing 71 gave him a share of fourth place with Forsbrand.

shot of the week

ANDREW COLTART Scotland

Almost every shot which hit its target during Saturday could stake a claim to being the shot of the week but Andrew Coltart's recovery from thick rough on the 18th hole during the final round outdid them all. The Scot could hardly see his ball but, having identified it, played a miraculous pitch, the ball popping out of the thick grass to within four feet of the hole. The resultant par four earned Coltart a share of second.

Anders Forsbrand

However, ten years after making his European Tour debut, Mednick had made the breakthrough he had long craved and with it had gained a one year exemption to The European Tour. He had been asked some gruelling questions over the four days, but answered them all.

Bord Fáilte
North West of Ireland Open
BALLYLIFFIN GOLF CLUB
www.europeantour.com
15-18 August 2002
CHAMPIONSHIP STAFF
ADMIT TO
COURSE & CLUBHOUSE
Nº 0002

There will be no whispering about Ballyliffin in the Mednick household from now on.

Rod Williams

Costantino Rocca

final results

Ballyliffin Golf Club • Co Donegal • Ireland
August 15-18 • 2002 • Par 72 • 7222 yards • 6601 metres

Pos.	Name		Rd1	Rd2	Rd3	Rd4	Total	Par	Prize Money Euro	£
1	Adam MEDNICK	Swe	76	68	69	68	281	-7	58330.00	37191.95
2	Costantino ROCCA	It	71	69	74	72	286	-2	30395.00	19380.24
	Andrew COLTART	Scot	76	66	77	67	286	-2	30395.00	19380.24
4	Anders FORSBRAND	Swe	71	73	75	68	287	-1	16170.00	10310.20
	Jean-François LUCQUIN	Fr	75	67	74	71	287	-1	16170.00	10310.20
6	Philip WALTON	Ire	75	70	71	72	288	0	10500.00	6694.93
	Massimo FLORIOLI	It	71	70	71	76	288	0	10500.00	6694.93
	Adam CRAWFORD	Aus	77	68	75	68	288	0	10500.00	6694.93
9	Joakim RASK	Swe	75	72	75	68	290	2	7840.00	4998.88
10	Michele REALE	It	78	68	73	73	292	4	7000.00	4463.29
11	Titch MOORE	SA	73	74	75	71	293	5	5588.33	3563.19
	Paul BROADHURST	Eng	76	72	74	71	293	5	5588.33	3563.19
	Jesus Maria ARRUTI	Sp	71	72	78	72	293	5	5588.33	3563.19
	David PARK	Wal	75	72	77	69	293	5	5588.33	3563.19
	Mark SANDERS	Eng	72	72	79	70	293	5	5588.33	3563.19
	Allan HOGH	Den	71	72	79	71	293	5	5588.33	3563.19
17	Andrew OLDCORN	Scot	77	69	75	73	294	6	4620.00	2945.77
	Per NYMAN	Swe	76	69	80	69	294	6	4620.00	2945.77
19	Nicolas COLSAERTS	Bel	75	71	78	72	296	8	4081.00	2602.10
	Pehr MAGNEBRANT	Swe	72	73	78	73	296	8	4081.00	2602.10
	Didier DE VOOGHT	Bel	78	69	80	69	296	8	4081.00	2602.10
	Iain PYMAN	Eng	76	70	78	72	296	8	4081.00	2602.10
	Ciaran MCMONAGLE	Ire	74	72	80	70	296	8	4081.00	2602.10
24	Euan LITTLE	Scot	74	73	77	73	297	9	3692.50	2354.39
	Alexander RENARD	Den	77	71	80	69	297	9	3692.50	2354.39
26	Hennie WALTERS	SA	74	74	78	69	298	10	3377.50	2153.54
	Michael ARCHER	Eng	78	71	82	67	298	10	3377.50	2153.54
	James KINGSTON	SA	77	70	76	75	298	10	3377.50	2153.54
	Regis GUSTAVE	St.L	79	71	76	72	298	10	3377.50	2153.54
30	Damien MCGRANE	Ire	72	73	80	74	299	11	2815.00	1794.88
	Mattias NILSSON	Swe	80	70	79	70	299	11	2815.00	1794.88
	Ian HUTCHINGS	SA	78	72	76	73	299	11	2815.00	1794.88
	Sion E BEBB	Wal	78	72	81	68	299	11	2815.00	1794.88
	Van PHILLIPS	Eng	83	68	78	70	299	11	2815.00	1794.88
	Marco BERNARDINI	It	76	71	78	74	299	11	2815.00	1794.88
	Oskar BERGMAN	Swe	80	70	78	71	299	11	2815.00	1794.88
37	Kristofer SVENSSON	Swe	76	73	81	70	300	12	2450.00	1562.15
	Simon KHAN	Eng	74	72	83	71	300	12	2450.00	1562.15
39	Andrew SHERBORNE	Eng	78	72	80	71	301	13	2170.00	1383.62
	Knud STORGAARD	Den	76	73	80	72	301	13	2170.00	1383.62
	Denny LUCAS	Eng	76	71	82	72	301	13	2170.00	1383.62
	Gianluca BARUFFALDI	It	81	69	78	73	301	13	2170.00	1383.62
	Andrew BUTTERFIELD	Eng	81	69	80	71	301	13	2170.00	1383.62
	Graham FOX	Scot	81	69	77	74	301	13	2170.00	1383.62
45	Tomas Jesus MUÑOZ	Sp	76	73	83	70	302	14	1715.00	1093.51
	Alan MCLEAN	Scot	78	72	76	76	302	14	1715.00	1093.51
	Francis HOWLEY	Ire	75	73	78	76	302	14	1715.00	1093.51
	James HEPWORTH	Eng	76	74	81	71	302	14	1715.00	1093.51
	Karlem BARAKA	Ger	78	71	85	68	302	14	1715.00	1093.51
	Tino SCHUSTER	Ger	79	69	81	73	302	14	1715.00	1093.51
	John DWYER	Ire	75	75	82	70	302	14	1715.00	1093.51
52	Michael HOEY	N.Ire	77	71	83	72	303	15	1295.00	825.71
	Carl SUNESON	Sp	76	72	79	76	303	15	1295.00	825.71
	David J GEALL	Eng	81	69	80	73	303	15	1295.00	825.71
	Simon HURD	Eng	79	71	79	74	303	15	1295.00	825.71
	Benn BARHAM	Eng	74	76	80	73	303	15	1295.00	825.71
57	Fredrik HENGE	Swe	75	75	83	71	304	16	1032.50	658.34
	Sam LITTLE	Eng	76	74	80	74	304	16	1032.50	658.34
	Olivier EDMOND	Fr	77	69	77	81	304	16	1032.50	658.34
	Richard DINSDALE	Wal	77	71	82	74	304	16	1032.50	658.34
61	Marc PENDARIES	Fr	79	72	81	73	305	17	875.00	557.91
	Bradford VAUGHAN	SA	77	74	80	74	305	17	875.00	557.91
	Grant HAMERTON	Eng	75	75	82	73	305	17	875.00	557.91
	Andreas LJUNGGREN	Swe	79	72	83	71	305	17	875.00	557.91
	Richard STERNE	SA	77	73	80	75	305	17	875.00	557.91
66	Michael WELCH	Eng	74	73	84	75	306	18	717.50	457.49
	Luis CLAVERIE	Sp	76	74	81	75	306	18	717.50	457.49
	Thomas NORRET	Den	79	72	82	73	306	18	717.50	457.49
	David DIXON	Eng	78	73	84	71	306	18	717.50	457.49
70	Jamie LITTLE	Eng	77	74	87	69	307	19	540.83	344.84
	Federico BISAZZA	It	76	75	82	74	307	19	540.83	344.84
	Marcus KNIGHT	Swi	77	70	80	80	307	19	540.83	344.84
	Ivo GINER	Sp	78	73	85	71	307	19	540.83	344.84
	Fredrik WIDMARK	Swe	75	76	83	73	307	19	540.83	344.84
	David PATRICK	Scot	75	76	83	73	307	19	540.83	344.84
76	Gustavo ROJAS	Arg	79	72	85	72	308	20	510.00	325.18
77	Stefano REALE	It	81	70	82	76	309	21	505.50	322.31
	Raimo SJÖBERG	Swe	79	72	87	71	309	21	505.50	322.31
79	Gary MURPHY	Ire	78	73	85	74	310	22	495.00	315.62
	Kalle BRINK	Swe	78	71	91	70	310	22	495.00	315.62
	André BOSSERT	Swi	76	72	86	76	310	22	495.00	315.62
	Guido VAN DER VALK	Hol	78	73	83	76	310	22	495.00	315.62
	Scott GARDINER	Aus	76	74	86	74	310	22	495.00	315.62
84	Francesco GUERMANI	It	80	70	85	76	311	23	486.00	309.88
85	Niels KRAAIJ	Hol	72	79	86	75	312	24	481.50	307.01
	Joakim GRÖNHAGEN	Swe	78	73	82	79	312	24	481.50	307.01
87	Thomas BESANCENEZ	Fr	77	74	87	76	314	26	477.00	304.14
88	Lee S JAMES	Eng	75	71	RETD		146	2		

NEC

	PAR	4	5	4	4	3	4		4	4
LEADERS		1	2	3	4	5	6		7	8
10 PARRY		10	11	12	13	13	13		13	13
10 ALLENBY		10	9	10	10	10	11		11	11
9 FUNK				9	10	10	9		10	10
WOODS				8	9	10	10		10	9
						9	9		9	9
						8	9		9	9
									6	6

WGC - NEC Invitational Sahalee Country Club · Redmond · Washington · USA

straight and true

Craig Parry doesn't sport a tattoo, chew on a battered wooden pipe or ingest copious quantities of tinned spinach. However, the owner of a pair of frighteningly well-developed, muscular forearms is fully deserving of the nickname 'Popeye' which he has carried around with him for all of his 17 years in professional golf.

Craig Parry

However there is a subtle difference between real life and cartoon fiction. In celluloid, Popeye dutifully ate his greens and proceeded to rebuff the evil Bluto's advances towards his beloved Olive Oyl. Without exception, Popeye's bulging biceps won the day.

Top level sport, though, has a habit of tearing up the script and delivering an altogether more stark and bleak denouement. In Parry's case, adversity presented itself on his doorstep soon after he decided to ply his trade on the US PGA Tour after enjoying a period of success on The European Tour.

Four victories in Europe persuaded the small but stocky Australian, born and raised in Victoria, that further triumphs lay across the Atlantic. The year was 1992. Little did he realise at the time that it would be a full decade and a sackful of near misses before destiny would finally come calling in the 2002 World Golf Championships - NEC Invitational at Sahalee Country Club.

As his second shot to the 72nd green, set among a cathedral canopy of Douglas Firs high in the hills above Seattle, flew straight and true towards the putting surface, a beatific smile crossed Parry's face. "You beaut...I've got it now," he muttered to himself as the ball came to rest, ensuring a four stroke triumph.

José Maria Olazábal

the course

Sahalee, Indian for 'High Heavenly Ground,' was prepared in divine condition, receiving widespread praise from the high-class field. The tight chutes of Douglas Fir trees provided a serious test of ingenuity and accuracy while at the same time being a place of beguiling beauty.

Unlike our cartoon hero, Parry didn't get the gawky girl with her hair tied in a bun, but he did satisfy a yearning which had smouldered deep inside him for ten years. A decade in which 'Popeye' had been beaten up by the bully.

It all started in the 1992 Masters Tournament at Augusta National. Parry shared the 36 hole lead with Ian Woosnam and led on his own early in the final round where he partnered eventual winner, Fred Couples.

"After two holes I was three in front," he recalled. "It was a hot afternoon, the crowd had had a few beers and they got very vocal. It was all 'Freddie, Freddie.' It was only a handful of spectators, but it was difficult to handle because I hadn't been used to that."

Parry eventually finished in the pack tied for 13th, and went away to lick his wounds. Still he continued to suffer as fate dealt a series of punishing blows to the solar plexus. He recounted other tales of woe with the spontaneity of a father reeling off the names of his children.

shot of the week

JUSTIN ROSE England

Justin Rose finished one place below Tiger Woods, but produced a stroke straight from the American's repertoire on Sunday. Blocked out by a tree at the 16th, Rose put away his eight iron, selected a six iron and from 158 yards out, cut the ball "40 or 50 yards" onto the green before sinking the ten foot putt for birdie. He said: "I stole two shots from the course there."

"Well, let's see," he continued. "I had Tom Lehman go birdie, birdie to beat me in the Colonial. Phil Mickelson chipped in at the Byron Nelson for an eagle on the 16th one year. He beat me by a shot and Nick Price got me at the Honda. I was always playing well but other guys were doing that little bit extra and beating me."

Then, of course, there was his close call in the 1999 Open Golf Championship at Carnoustie. Parry suffered a triple bogey at the 12th hole on the last day and a double bogey at the 17th, yet still finished just one stroke outside of the play-off involving eventual Champion Paul Lawrie, Justin Leonard and Jean Van de Velde. "Hmm, Carnoustie wasn't very good either," he mused, in a manner which suggested he would happily consign the entire episode to the furthest recesses of his memory bank.

At last, though, Parry had come out on top and he deserved the opportunity to savour the moment. He had, after all, prevailed in a

José Coceres

American Fred Funk, who had performed with great merit in the previous week's US PGA Championship, enjoyed another profitable week, having gained his place in the field by the margin of one two hundredths of a World Ranking point. He shared the runners-up position with Australian Robert Allenby, who birdied the last four holes.

Fifth place was occupied by a young man competing in only his second tournament in America. England's Justin Rose displayed immense composure and control to finish in the upper echelons of the leaderboard. A sterling effort which augurs well for the future.

But at the end of the day, the abiding memory was Parry's serene smile at the 72nd hole. If ever there was a cue for the Australian to break into a chorus of 'Popeye the Sailor Man,' this was it. Thank goodness the temptation was resisted.

Gordon Simpson

tournament that had become the private preserve of Tiger Woods. Attempting to become the first golfer in 72 years to win an event four successive times in America, the World Number One played well, but only well enough to take fourth place.

final results

Sahalee Country Club · Redmond · Washington · USA
August 22-25 · 2002 · Par 71 · 6949 yards · 6363 metres

Pos.	Name		Rd1	Rd2	Rd3	Rd4	Total	Par	Prize Money Euro	£
1	Craig PARRY	Aus	72	65	66	65	268	-16	1016673.00	650533.33
2	Fred FUNK	USA	68	68	68	68	272	-12	416836.00	266718.71
	Robert ALLENBY	Aus	69	63	71	69	272	-12	416836.00	266718.71
4	Tiger WOODS	USA	68	70	67	68	273	-11	218584.70	139864.67
5	Justin ROSE	Eng	67	67	72	68	274	-10	190626.20	121975.01
6	Jim FURYK	USA	70	67	68	70	275	-9	152501.00	97580.03
	Rich BEEM	USA	74	67	67	67	275	-9	152501.00	97580.03
8	Steve LOWERY	USA	67	65	73	71	276	-8	122000.80	78064.02
9	Phil MICKELSON	USA	66	69	71	71	277	-7	106750.70	68306.02
	Matt GOGEL	USA	68	69	68	72	277	-7	106750.70	68306.02
11	Davis LOVE III	USA	66	74	69	69	278	-6	80063.02	51229.51
	Vijay SINGH	Fiji	68	69	69	72	278	-6	80063.02	51229.51
	Retief GOOSEN	SA	65	68	74	71	278	-6	80063.02	51229.51
	Michael CAMPBELL	NZ	70	69	70	69	278	-6	80063.02	51229.51
15	Ernie ELS	SA	71	67	67	74	279	-5	61889.98	39601.22
	Thomas BJÖRN	Den	68	69	72	70	279	-5	61889.98	39601.22
	Lee WESTWOOD	Eng	68	69	72	70	279	-5	61889.98	39601.22
	David TOMS	USA	69	68	71	71	279	-5	61889.98	39601.22
19	Kyoung-Ju CHOI	R.Kor	73	67	73	67	280	-4	51240.33	32786.89
	Bob ESTES	USA	71	71	69	69	280	-4	51240.33	32786.89
	Darren CLARKE	N.Ire	66	74	68	72	280	-4	51240.33	32786.89
	Angel CABRERA	Arg	72	70	70	68	280	-4	51240.33	32786.89
	Peter LONARD	Aus	70	71	72	67	280	-4	51240.33	32786.89
24	Toshimitsu IZAWA	Jpn	65	73	73	71	282	-2	45750.29	29274.00
	Mike WEIR	Can	69	70	71	72	282	-2	45750.29	29274.00
	Rocco MEDIATE	USA	68	69	73	72	282	-2	45750.29	29274.00
	Kenny PERRY	USA	67	70	73	72	282	-2	45750.29	29274.00
28	Loren ROBERTS	USA	70	66	76	71	283	-1	41937.77	26834.51
	Nick PRICE	Zim	74	66	72	71	283	-1	41937.77	26834.51
	David DUVAL	USA	72	75	71	65	283	-1	41937.77	26834.51
	Justin LEONARD	USA	70	74	69	70	283	-1	41937.77	26834.51
	John COOK	USA	70	64	69	70	283	-1	41937.77	26834.51
	Ricardo GONZALEZ	Arg	71	72	68	72	283	-1	41937.77	26834.51
	Kirk TRIPLETT	USA	71	69	70	73	283	-1	41937.77	26834.51
	Chris DIMARCO	USA	68	70	74	71	283	-1	41937.77	26834.51
36	Shigeki MARUYAMA	Jpn	69	72	69	74	284	0	39396.09	25208.17
	Len MATTIACE	USA	69	72	72	71	284	0	39396.09	25208.17
38	Bernhard LANGER	Ger	70	70	75	70	285	1	37871.07	24232.37
	Matt KUCHAR	USA	71	68	71	75	285	1	37871.07	24232.37
	Paul AZINGER	USA	68	72	73	72	285	1	37871.07	24232.37
	Tom LEHMAN	USA	72	70	69	74	285	1	37871.07	24232.37
42	Stuart APPLEBY	Aus	70	72	74	70	286	2	35583.56	22768.67
	Hal SUTTON	USA	73	71	70	72	286	2	35583.56	22768.67
	Carlos Daniel FRANCO	Par	75	72	67	72	286	2	35583.56	22768.67
	Pierre FULKE	Swe	69	73	73	71	286	2	35583.56	22768.67
	Craig PERKS	NZ	68	70	73	75	286	2	35583.56	22768.67
47	Eduardo ROMERO	Arg	71	71	67	78	287	3	33092.71	21174.86
	Padraig HARRINGTON	Ire	72	70	73	72	287	3	33092.71	21174.86
	Joel EDWARDS	USA	73	73	71	70	287	3	33092.71	21174.86
	José Maria OLAZÁBAL	Sp	71	68	75	73	287	3	33092.71	21174.86
	Stewart CINK	USA	73	71	73	70	287	3	33092.71	21174.86
52	Søren HANSEN	Den	76	69	69	74	288	4	31771.04	20329.17
	Notah BEGAY III	USA	70	77	70	71	288	4	31771.04	20329.17
	Graeme MCDOWELL	N.Ire	72	69	73	74	288	4	31771.04	20329.17
55	Greg NORMAN	Aus	69	74	73	73	289	5	31008.53	19841.27
	Scott HOCH	USA	72	77	69	71	289	5	31008.53	19841.27
	Chris SMITH	USA	75	73	73	68	289	5	31008.53	19841.27
58	Sergio GARCIA	Sp	68	73	76	73	290	6	29991.86	19190.74
	Anders HANSEN	Den	71	76	74	69	290	6	29991.86	19190.74
	Scott VERPLANK	USA	71	75	76	68	290	6	29991.86	19190.74
	Niclas FASTH	Swe	73	68	79	70	290	6	29991.86	19190.74
	Kevin SUTHERLAND	USA	74	71	71	74	290	6	29991.86	19190.74
63	Brad FAXON	USA	71	72	71	77	291	7	29102.27	18621.52
	Charlie WI	R.Kor	73	73	72	73	291	7	29102.27	18621.52
65	Nobuhito SATO	Jpn	74	76	73	70	293	9	28593.93	18296.25
	Paul LAWRIE	Scot	73	69	81	70	293	9	28593.93	18296.25
67	Paul MCGINLEY	Ire	79	69	73	74	295	11	28212.68	18052.30
68	Steve ELKINGTON	Aus	76	77	74	69	296	12	27704.34	17727.03
	Tobias DIER	Ger	76	75	72	73	296	12	27704.34	17727.03
	Nicholas LAWRENCE	SA	76	72	78	70	296	12	27704.34	17727.03
71	Jesper PARNEVIK	Swe	76	74	73	74	297	13	27068.92	17320.45
	Phillip PRICE	Wal	73	73	73	78	297	13	27068.92	17320.45
73	John DALY	USA	73	78	74	73	298	14	26687.67	17076.50
74	Mark CALCAVECCHIA	USA	74	81	75	69	299	15	26433.50	16913.87
75	Scott MCCARRON	USA	74	74	77	75	300	16	26052.25	16669.92
	José COCERES	Arg	69	71	76	84	300	16	26052.25	16669.92
77	Jerry KELLY	USA	75	79	74	73	301	17	25671.00	16425.97
78	Colin MONTGOMERIE	Scot	71	RETD			71	0	25416.83	16263.34

Reuters Performance Data

As the official sponsor of Performance Data on
The European Tour, Reuters provides relevant
and insightful information on player
performance, allowing professionals everywhere
to make accurate and informed decisions.

www.reuters.com

DRIVING INFORMATION FURTHER.
Reuters and The European Tour

Diageo Scottish PGA Championship The Gleneagles Hotel
Perthshire · Scotland

ten shot rule

1	Adam SCOTT Aus	262	-26
2	Raymond RUSSELL Scot	272	-16
3	Sam TORRANCE Scot	273	-15
4	Scott GARDINER Aus	276	-12
5	Marcel SIEM Ger	277	-11
6	Ignacio GARRIDO Sp	278	-10
7	Henrik BJORNSTAD Nor	279	- 9
	Matthew CORT Eng	279	- 9
	Ian GARBUTT Eng	279	- 9
	Andrew OLDCORN Scot	279	- 9

Adam Scott

Imitation, they say, is the sincerest form of flattery. If that is the case, had Greg Norman caught any of the action from the Diageo Scottish PGA Championship at The Gleneagles Hotel, he would have been a very proud man indeed.

The friendship between the Great White Shark and Adam Scott, Australia's latest young golfing superstar, has been well documented, the younger man regularly turning to his more experienced compatriot for advice and guidance whether it be face-to-face on the range or on the end of a telephone.

Indeed, in the build-up to the tournament itself, Scott spoke of the inspiration he drew from Norman's trail-blazing performances in Europe in the 1970s and 1980s. "It seems like every clubhouse you walk into over here, Greg's name is on the Honour Boards," he enthused. "He has certainly won all the big ones and that is something I definitely want to do, too, before I'm done."

Unquestionably the most memorable Norman conquest came in Scotland in 1986, his second round 63 in atrocious weather at Turnberry still revered as one of the greatest rounds of golf ever played and one which proved the catalyst for his victory in the 115th Open Golf Championship.

Fitting, then, that his young protégé should choose the same country, the same round and similarly abysmal weather to not only lay the foundations for his eventual success, but also to reaffirm his potential as one of the most exciting talents in the game.

An indication of how bad conditions were on The PGA Centenary Course on the Friday was that of the 156 competitors, only eight broke 70. Three of those just made the statistic with 69s while three more managed only one shot better. Adam Scott shot 65.

Starting at the tenth hole, the winner of the Qatar Masters in March met the wind and rain head on and was totally flawless, his seven birdie putts ranging in length from inside a foot at the second to outside 20 at the seventh.

Afterwards, he spoke of the growing comfort he felt in tandem with new caddie Alastair McLean, for so long the bagman of Colin Montgomerie. He also paid tribute to recent work done with coach Butch Harmon both during a visit to his Las Vegas home and on the range during the US PGA Championship at Hazeltine National Golf Club.

Ian Garbutt

the course

Despite the punishing rough, the venue for The 2014 Ryder Cup Matches drew universal praise not least for the way it stood up to the inclement weather of the second day and the fact that an average year's rainfall had deposited itself in the area over the previous six months. Fittingly, in a week dominated by Adam Scott, the final view on the course should be his. "Visually it is very nice and as soon as I got here I liked it," he said.

Modesty forbade the softly-spoken 22 year old from overstating his own part in it all but other players were not slow in enunciating. "Incredible," said fellow Antipodean Scott Gardiner. Nobody disagreed.

Main talking point of the first round, when Scott opened with a 67 to trail yet another Australian, Richard Green by two, was the incredible misfortune suffered by defending Champion Paul Casey. The 25 year old Englishman, whose victory 12 months ago helped him win the Sir Henry Cotton Rookie of the Year Award on The European Tour, was going well before his second shot on the 516 yard second hole, his 11th of the day, disappeared from view.

It was assumed it had embedded in the thick rough but when the requisite five minute search found nothing, Casey turned back to play another ball, only to spot his original one down a drain in the centre of the fairway, the ball having somehow pierced the plastic cover before nestling underneath.

It was, as Casey admitted after running up a double bogey seven, "a million to one chance, but just proves it can happen." Although it was not apparent at the time, the incident was an omen for the remainder of the tournament. It would be Scott, however, not the ball, who would disappear out of sight.

If his second round heroics, which gave him a four shot lead at the halfway stage, or a third round 67 which opened up a five shot advantage on the field, were not impressive enough, Scott unquestionably saved the best for last.

Similarly, if his assault on the par fives of The PGA Centenary Course had not been brutal enough over the opening 54 holes, standing a total of 15 under par for the 15 par fives played, in the final round they were battered into submission. Birdies came once again at the 516 yard second, the 564 yard ninth and the 503 yard 12th before eagle putts of 30 and 40 feet respectively at the 543 yard 16th and the 533 yard 18th sent the crowd into raptures.

Santiago Luna

Fredrik Andersson

shot of the week

ADAM SCOTT Australia

Several of Adam Scott's during his superb 65 on day two could qualify, as could many during his closing 63. But the winner was the Champion's final stroke of the week, a 40 foot eagle putt on the 72nd hole which helped smash the season's record books and elicited the biggest cheer of the week from the packed galleries around the 18th green. It also won the Australian a £3350 Rolex watch for low round of the tournament, beating the 64 carded by Rolf Muntz in round three.

It left Scott 22 under par for the week on the par fives, a birdie two at the 17th for good measure helping him to a 26 under par total of 262 overall, a score which represented the lowest winning aggregate of the season. Not only that, his ten shot winning margin was the biggest of the year and his closing 63 the lowest final round by a winner in 2002.

When the dust had settled, Scotland's own Raymond Russell took second on 16 under par 272 with fellow countryman Sam Torrance third and Gardiner fourth. It was a shake-up of the positions the trio had held going into the final round but, as had been the case all week, they were merely part of the chorus line as Scott stood alone in the spotlight.

At the start of the week, Scott conceded he was a little disappointed to have missed out on a place in the 78 strong field for the World Golf Championships – NEC Invitational at Sahalee Country Club. It was understandable. After all, he is a burgeoning young talent eager to pit his skills against the best in the world.

But he accepted the situation and admitted he was happy to be in Scotland, eager to give of his best and determined to win. Set your target, go after it, and achieve it; Greg Norman could not have put it any better.

Scott Crockett

Gregory Havret

Matthew Cort

final results

The Gleneagles Hotel • Perthshire • Scotland
August 22-25 • 2002 • Par 72 • 7060 yards • 6456 metres

Pos.	Name		Rd1	Rd2	Rd3	Rd4	Total	Par	Prize Money Euro	£
1	Adam SCOTT	Aus	67	65	67	63	262	-26	260461.30	166660.00
2	Raymond RUSSELL	Scot	67	71	66	68	272	-16	173646.00	111110.00
3	Sam TORRANCE	Scot	69	68	69	67	273	-15	97833.16	62600.00
4	Scott GARDINER	Aus	67	72	65	72	276	-12	78141.50	50000.00
5	Marcel SIEM	Ger	70	66	73	68	277	-11	66263.99	42400.00
6	Ignacio GARRIDO	Sp	67	71	73	67	278	-10	54699.05	35000.00
7	Andrew OLDCORN	Scot	67	71	72	69	279	-9	38054.91	24350.00
	Henrik BJORNSTAD	Nor	68	72	70	69	279	-9	38054.91	24350.00
	Ian GARBUTT	Eng	67	74	71	67	279	-9	38054.91	24350.00
	Matthew CORT	Eng	67	71	70	71	279	-9	38054.91	24350.00
11	Raphaël JACQUELIN	Fr	67	75	69	69	280	-8	25536.64	16340.00
	Richard GREEN	Aus	65	71	72	72	280	-8	25536.64	16340.00
	Mathias GRÖNBERG	Swe	70	70	72	68	280	-8	25536.64	16340.00
	Paul CASEY	Eng	72	74	68	66	280	-8	25536.64	16340.00
	Marc WARREN	Scot	71	70	72	67	280	-8	25536.64	16340.00
16	David GILFORD	Eng	69	74	69	69	281	-7	20668.43	13225.00
	David LYNN	Eng	69	73	70	69	281	-7	20668.43	13225.00
	Greg OWEN	Eng	74	72	66	69	281	-7	20668.43	13225.00
	Fredrik ANDERSSON	Swe	66	72	70	73	281	-7	20668.43	13225.00
20	Santiago LUNA	Sp	69	74	69	70	282	-6	17213.46	11014.29
	Peter FOWLER	Aus	70	71	69	72	282	-6	17213.46	11014.29
	Nick O'HERN	Aus	71	76	67	68	282	-6	17213.46	11014.29
	Alex CEJKA	Ger	69	74	69	70	282	-6	17213.46	11014.29
	Stephen DODD	Wal	67	73	69	73	282	-6	17213.46	11014.29
	Rolf MUNTZ	Hol	70	75	64	73	282	-6	17213.46	11014.29
	Fredrik JACOBSON	Swe	76	69	71	66	282	-6	17213.46	11014.29
27	David HOWELL	Eng	68	74	71	70	283	-5	14378.04	9200.00
	Richard BLAND	Eng	71	73	71	68	283	-5	14378.04	9200.00
	Jeremy ROBINSON	Eng	68	70	71	74	283	-5	14378.04	9200.00
	Olivier EDMOND	Fr	73	70	71	69	283	-5	14378.04	9200.00
	Brett RUMFORD	Aus	69	73	70	71	283	-5	14378.04	9200.00
32	Stephen LEANEY	Aus	71	71	70	72	284	-4	12307.29	7875.00
	Jean HUGO	SA	72	74	67	71	284	-4	12307.29	7875.00
	David PARK	Wal	68	69	74	73	284	-4	12307.29	7875.00
	Patrik SJÖLAND	Swe	67	78	71	68	284	-4	12307.29	7875.00
36	Mark ROE	Eng	69	68	74	74	285	-3	11096.09	7100.00
	Maarten LAFEBER	Hol	68	76	68	73	285	-3	11096.09	7100.00
	Michele REALE	It	75	72	69	69	285	-3	11096.09	7100.00
39	Jamie SPENCE	Eng	67	77	69	73	286	-2	10002.11	6400.00
	Adam MEDNICK	Swe	72	73	66	75	286	-2	10002.11	6400.00
	Gary ORR	Scot	69	73	74	70	286	-2	10002.11	6400.00
	Martin MARITZ	SA	75	72	72	67	286	-2	10002.11	6400.00
43	Mark JAMES	Eng	70	73	75	69	287	-1	8283.00	5300.00
	Des SMYTH	Ire	71	72	71	73	287	-1	8283.00	5300.00
	Philip WALTON	Ire	68	70	76	73	287	-1	8283.00	5300.00
	Klas ERIKSSON	Swe	71	71	73	72	287	-1	8283.00	5300.00
	Warren BENNETT	Eng	73	70	73	71	287	-1	8283.00	5300.00
	Colin GILLIES	Scot	71	71	71	74	287	-1	8283.00	5300.00
	Miles TUNNICLIFF	Eng	72	73	69	73	287	-1	8283.00	5300.00
50	Greg TURNER	NZ	72	73	70	73	288	0	6251.32	4000.00
	Shaun P WEBSTER	Eng	73	72	73	70	288	0	6251.32	4000.00
	Stuart LITTLE	Eng	70	74	71	73	288	0	6251.32	4000.00
	Alastair FORSYTH	Scot	68	78	73	69	288	0	6251.32	4000.00
	Simon DYSON	Eng	74	73	69	72	288	0	6251.32	4000.00
	Craig LEE	Scot	68	75	71	74	288	0	6251.32	4000.00
56	Roger CHAPMAN	Eng	73	71	71	74	289	1	4805.70	3075.00
	Robert-Jan DERKSEN	Hol	74	73	70	72	289	1	4805.70	3075.00
	Van PHILLIPS	Eng	72	69	77	71	289	1	4805.70	3075.00
	Barry HUME	Scot	73	68	72	76	289	1	4805.70	3075.00
60	Jean-François REMESY	Fr	71	74	74	71	290	2	4063.36	2600.00
	Massimo SCARPA	It	70	77	72	71	290	2	4063.36	2600.00
	Didier DE VOOGHT	Bel	72	74	71	72	290	2	4063.36	2600.00
	Stephen SCAHILL	NZ	68	78	72	72	290	2	4063.36	2600.00
	John BICKERTON	Eng	68	79	73	70	290	2	4063.36	2600.00
65	Peter SENIOR	Aus	69	75	73	74	291	3	3438.23	2200.00
	Anthony WALL	Eng	72	71	75	73	291	3	3438.23	2200.00
	Stephen GALLACHER	Scot	71	75	71	74	291	3	3438.23	2200.00
68	Mattias ELIASSON	Swe	73	74	76	69	292	4	2663.00	1703.96
	Gregory HAVRET	Fr	71	75	72	74	292	4	2663.00	1703.96
	Scott HENDERSON	Scot	73	73	73	73	292	4	2663.00	1703.96
	David DRYSDALE	Scot	76	70	74	72	292	4	2663.00	1703.96
	Andrew COLTART	Scot	70	77	73	72	292	4	2663.00	1703.96
	Lucas PARSONS	Aus	74	73	72	73	292	4	2663.00	1703.96
74	Jonathan LOMAS	Eng	72	75	74	72	293	5	2333.50	1493.12
	Benoit TEILLERIA	Fr	69	74	73	77	293	5	2333.50	1493.12
76	Robert COLES	Eng	69	76	70	79	294	6	2329.00	1490.25
77	Dennis EDLUND	Swe	73	73	74	75	295	7	2326.00	1488.33
78	Gary EMERSON	Eng	70	77	76	73	296	8	2321.50	1485.45
	Gary EVANS	Eng	73	73	73	77	296	8	2321.50	1485.45
80	Iain PYMAN	Eng	74	73	75	77	299	11	2317.00	1482.57
81	Nick DOUGHERTY	Eng	72	74	78	77	301	13	2314.00	1480.65
82	Simon KHAN	Eng	71	76	80	78	305	17	2311.00	1478.73

BMW International Open   Golfclub München
Nord-Eichenried · Munich · Germany

no doubting thomas

This was an odyssey, from beginning to end, about incapacity and the various ways that men dealt with it. The four days of the BMW International Open were visited at regular intervals by the frailties of the human body. Not that the eventual winner was discommoded by any of that sort of stuff however.

Thomas Björn

The record will show that Thomas Björn, the great Dane with the sort of ramrod-straight back of which a Grenadier Guardsman would be proud, prevailed with a closing round of 66 and a total of 264, 24 under par. But the sub-plot in this week of uninterrupted sunshine in the hinterland of Bavaria was made the more intriguing not by he who succeeded but by those who narrowly failed.

Until the final denouement, two of the leading characters in this German passion-play were affected, in one way or another, by either sickness or injury. Bernhard Langer succumbed to a bout of food poisoning that struck his caddie as much as himself, and Ian Poulter was deeply concerned about his own ailing bagman almost as much as his own efforts to win his third European Tour title.

To Langer first. Over a long and distinguished career, he has been a victim of many adversities as far as physical wellbeing is concerned, so much so he would probably feel bereft if not challenged in one way or another. He was again here, and it might have made the difference between success and ultimate, glorious failure.

Gordon Brand Jnr.

the course

Golfclub München Nord-Eichenried won a universal accolade from all those who played on it throughout the week, and that was that its greens were virtually perfection. It is possible to score low on this course when it is at its best. It was precious close to it on its biggest week of the year.

When Langer signed for a 69 in the second round of the tournament, it was, he later admitted, the result of the toughest round of golf he had ever had to play. If he had not been in contention and not been seeking to win the only German title he had yet to claim, he might not have started the round, let alone finished it. But complete it he did in the typical, dogged style of which only he is capable. It kept him in the chase right to the bitter end: to do anything but his best at all times, in all places, is anathema to the gentle German.

And so to Poulter. The feisty young Englishman does not know the meaning of the word 'fear', but he was more than a little put out when his faithful caddie, Jimmy Rae, became so ill in the first round that he ended up on a drip in hospital in nearby Erding with what was eventually diagnosed as pneumonia.

Poulter, who has the utmost respect and professional affection for his often outspoken sidekick, was worried about his employee, but was also concerned about his own prospects for the rest of the event. Not one to fret about the economics of the affair, he sent for Andy Prodger, enjoying a week off in Perth while Colin Montgomerie, his regular boss, tried to fight off the effects of a back injury.

It meant all sorts of logistical nightmares for Prodger to respond to the call, but he got to Nord-Eichenried 40 minutes before Poulter was due to tee off in the second round and was delighted when his new, and temporary, master, carded a 66 to share the lead on 13 under par with Richard Bland and Jamie Spence.

Meanwhile, while all this mayhem was proceeding, Björn was going about his business with his usual quiet intensity. Just about 18 months before, he had partnered Tiger Woods in all four rounds of the Dubai Desert Classic and had gone on to win by two strokes.

This time his task was hardly less testing. He was compelled to go through the entire tournament in the company of Langer, and playing with the German hero in front of his own people is, in its own way, just as daunting as having a Tiger on your tail for 72 holes.

Having gone into an intense final day two strokes ahead of Bland and Langer, Björn put on a performance that, although three strokes short of John Daly's epic winning score in the tournament the previous year, was a small masterpiece of not only pure golf but also of strategy.

First, he said after his third round, he would have to take the course on with aggressive golf. In this he succeeded admirably, reaching the turn on Sunday in an outward half of 32.

Then came the difficult bit. He had got the rest where he wanted them, now for some sensible husbandry of a winning score. By now his two principal challengers were John Bickerton and Langer, Bickerton having come bursting through from the second last group on the course.

The pivotal moment in the whole day's play came on the par five ninth. Langer was 25 feet away in three and holed it to the tumultuous acclaim of his compatriots. Patiently, Björn waited for the hubbub to die down, not allowing his concentration to waver for a second. He was on the fringe, 15 feet from the pin, and holed the putt to lead by three strokes.

Gary Orr

With Bickerton still a presence and virtually everybody else who had started the round with fond hopes fading away, the piece resolved itself into a three-hander. Björn and Langer both bogeyed the tenth, while Bickerton birdied the 11th and 12th to become the Dane's closest challenger. He was only one behind, so what did Björn do? He birdied the 11th and 12th to restore his lead.

By now the hard part was over. He had taken the course and his rivals on and had achieved a psychological victory over both. Aggression had got him where he was - now was the time to defend what he had.

He did it to perfection, reeling off five pars after the 12th while both Bickerton and Langer suffered agonies on the greens. Langer did not pick up a shot after the 13th, Bickerton closed with six straight pars. They were the epitome of steadiness, but steadiness was not what was needed now. Steadiness, on the other hand, suited Thomas Björn very nicely indeed.

Mel Webb

shot of the week

THOMAS BJÖRN Denmark

Only a small one by comparison, but a precious one nevertheless. Thomas Björn had just watched Bernhard Langer hole from 25 feet for a birdie on the par five ninth in the last round. Nervelessly, he sank his 15 footer for a matching four. In the context of a tautly-fought final day, it was probably the moment that clinched it.

Ian Poulter

final results

Golfclub München Nord-Eichenried · Munich · Germany
August 29 - September 1 · 2002 · Par 72 · 6963 yards · 6366 metres

Pos.	Name		Rd1	Rd2	Rd3	Rd4	Total	Par	Prize Money Euro	£
1	Thomas BJÖRN	Den	68	64	66	66	264	-24	300000.00	191771.71
2	Bernhard LANGER	Ger	64	69	67	68	268	-20	156340.00	99938.63
	John BICKERTON	Eng	67	69	66	66	268	-20	156340.00	99938.63
4	Ian POULTER	Eng	65	66	70	70	271	-17	83160.00	53159.12
	David PARK	Wal	68	67	69	67	271	-17	83160.00	53159.12
6	Richard BLAND	Eng	65	66	69	72	272	-16	63000.00	40272.06
7	Philip GOLDING	Eng	69	65	69	70	273	-15	46440.00	29686.26
	David LYNN	Eng	67	67	68	71	273	-15	46440.00	29686.26
	Paul CASEY	Eng	72	63	71	67	273	-15	46440.00	29686.26
10	Trevor IMMELMAN	SA	66	72	65	71	274	-14	33360.00	21325.01
	Miguel Angel JIMÉNEZ	Sp	68	68	69	69	274	-14	33360.00	21325.01
	John DALY	USA	70	70	65	69	274	-14	33360.00	21325.01
13	Anthony WALL	Eng	70	69	65	71	275	-13	27090.00	17316.99
	Jamie SPENCE	Eng	67	64	70	74	275	-13	27090.00	17316.99
	Joakim HAEGGMAN	Swe	69	67	67	72	275	-13	27090.00	17316.99
	Robert COLES	Eng	65	73	71	66	275	-13	27090.00	17316.99
17	Peter SENIOR	Aus	70	68	67	71	276	-12	23280.00	14881.49
	Padraig HARRINGTON	Ire	70	70	68	68	276	-12	23280.00	14881.49
	Barry LANE	Eng	68	69	71	68	276	-12	23280.00	14881.49
20	Mårten OLANDER	Swe	69	67	71	70	277	-11	20655.00	13203.48
	Steen TINNING	Den	68	67	73	69	277	-11	20655.00	13203.48
	Mathias GRÖNBERG	Swe	70	67	68	72	277	-11	20655.00	13203.48
	Mikael LUNDBERG	Swe	70	69	68	70	277	-11	20655.00	13203.48
24	Mark ROE	Eng	71	69	69	69	278	-10	16830.00	10758.39
	David HOWELL	Eng	70	65	68	75	278	-10	16830.00	10758.39
	Darren FICHARDT	SA	67	71	72	68	278	-10	16830.00	10758.39
	Justin ROSE	Eng	70	67	71	70	278	-10	16830.00	10758.39
	Paul MCGINLEY	Ire	70	68	66	74	278	-10	16830.00	10758.39
	Rolf MUNTZ	Hol	70	65	70	73	278	-10	16830.00	10758.39
	Simon KHAN	Eng	68	71	66	73	278	-10	16830.00	10758.39
	Simon DYSON	Eng	70	67	71	70	278	-10	16830.00	10758.39
	Nick DOUGHERTY	Eng	70	67	70	71	278	-10	16830.00	10758.39
	Carl PETTERSSON	Swe	71	68	65	73	278	-10	16830.00	10758.39
34	Richard GREEN	Aus	71	69	66	73	279	-9	13320.00	8514.66
	Marcel SIEM	Ger	72	67	71	69	279	-9	13320.00	8514.66
	Ian GARBUTT	Eng	71	68	69	71	279	-9	13320.00	8514.66
	Alastair FORSYTH	Scot	68	67	75	69	279	-9	13320.00	8514.66
38	Santiago LUNA	Sp	71	69	65	75	280	-8	11160.00	7133.91
	Warren BENNETT	Eng	72	66	69	73	280	-8	11160.00	7133.91
	Thomas LEVET	Fr	69	71	66	74	280	-8	11160.00	7133.91
	Jean HUGO	SA	71	68	69	72	280	-8	11160.00	7133.91
	Emanuele CANONICA	It	67	67	76	70	280	-8	11160.00	7133.91
	Gary EVANS	Eng	68	72	72	68	280	-8	11160.00	7133.91
	Bradley DREDGE	Wal	70	68	71	71	280	-8	11160.00	7133.91
	Gary CLARK	Eng	70	67	72	71	280	-8	11160.00	7133.91
46	Andrew MARSHALL	Eng	69	69	69	74	281	-7	9360.00	5983.28
	Fredrik JACOBSON	Swe	69	65	73	74	281	-7	9360.00	5983.28
48	Henrik BJORNSTAD	Nor	69	66	76	71	282	-6	7920.00	5062.77
	Gary ORR	Scot	70	68	73	71	282	-6	7920.00	5062.77
	Markus BRIER	Aut	69	70	74	69	282	-6	7920.00	5062.77
	Andrew COLTART	Scot	70	68	68	76	282	-6	7920.00	5062.77
	Mikko ILONEN	Fin	70	69	67	76	282	-6	7920.00	5062.77
	Thongchai JAIDEE	Thai	69	70	70	73	282	-6	7920.00	5062.77
54	Jeev Milkha SINGH	Ind	71	69	71	72	283	-5	6300.00	4027.21
	Klas ERIKSSON	Swe	67	72	70	74	283	-5	6300.00	4027.21
	Robert KARLSSON	Swe	70	69	71	73	283	-5	6300.00	4027.21
	Christian REIMBOLD (AM)	Ger	72	68	70	73	283	-5		
58	David GILFORD	Eng	70	70	74	70	284	-4	5220.00	3336.83
	Russell CLAYDON	Eng	67	72	73	72	284	-4	5220.00	3336.83
	Jorge BERENDT	Arg	69	70	70	75	284	-4	5220.00	3336.83
	Adam MEDNICK	Swe	72	65	72	75	284	-4	5220.00	3336.83
	Scott GARDINER	Aus	71	68	69	76	284	-4	5220.00	3336.83
63	Sven STRÜVER	Ger	68	72	71	75	286	-2	4410.00	2819.04
	Gary EMERSON	Eng	69	71	74	72	286	-2	4410.00	2819.04
	Greg OWEN	Eng	69	69	73	75	286	-2	4410.00	2819.04
	Tino SCHUSTER	Ger	73	67	73	73	286	-2	4410.00	2819.04
67	Robert-Jan DERKSEN	Hol	73	67	73	74	287	-1	3780.00	2416.32
	David J GEALL	Eng	70	68	73	76	287	-1	3780.00	2416.32
	Daren LEE	Eng	68	68	78	73	287	-1	3780.00	2416.32
70	Gordon BRAND JNR.	Scot	68	72	78	72	290	2	3420.00	2186.20
71	Alex CEJKA	Ger	68	72	RETD		140	-4	3280.00	2096.70

weird and wonderful

Even in mid-summer, the slopes around Crans-sur-Sierre have to be treated with respect. They are the easiest place in the world to take a tumble and many thought that that was the fate awaiting long-time leader Robert Karlsson when he began his final round with three bogeys in the first four holes.

Robert KARLSSON

As it turned out, the 33 year old Swede handled the crisis with all the cool you would expect of one who is better trained than most in the art of survival.

Two years ago, when he was working with an off-beat psychologist by name of Dr Bengt Stern, a man who was seen as a genius in some quarters and an out-and-out eccentric in others, Karlsson put himself through a fortnight's fast. More recently, he spent an entire night on his feet hitting putts.

The idea of the putting exercise, which may or may not catch on, was that he should face a level of frustration that would go way beyond anything he could ever know in a tournament context.

Accompanied by a friend who baited him every time he missed, he hit one ten footer after another from eight o'clock until midnight before taking time out for an hour's run. Aside from another hour's running break at four in the morning, he kept relentlessly at the putting, forcing himself to soldier on when every bone in his body was telling him to stop.

"It taught me a lot about myself," he said. "I could have walked away and I didn't. Now, regardless of how bad a day I might be having on the course, I know I can stick it out."

Barry Lane

the course

As Nick Faldo said, it is the inspirational surrounds and the atmosphere which brings the players back to Crans-sur-Sierre year after year. They love the touch of St Andrews about the place, not least in the way they bump into the same people on the streets as on the fairways. The Seve Ballesteros greens provided for on-going discussion but, as the Spaniard said himself after the official ceremony which named the course, 'The Seve Ballesteros Course', he had merely done what was asked of him in making the surfaces more demanding.

In opening with rounds of 65-66, Karlsson did not have much to get upset about. There was a less than perfect chip at the 17th on the second day but he promptly holed from 12 feet to escape with par.

A bit of scrambling was involved in a third round 68 but, at the end of it, Karlsson, who had bedded down each evening with the overnight lead, was still two shots ahead. Emanuele Canonica, who scored a third round 65, was the man in second place.

On the Sunday morning, the players awoke to a boisterous mountain wind which was hardly the best of news for the six foot five inch Karlsson. He, though, was calmness personified despite the fact his lead evaporated as a result of the three shots he dropped early on.

"I did not feel too worried when I was caught," he explained afterwards. "I knew that the others still had to beat me. I also knew that I was going to start making birdies at some point."

It was hardly the easiest afternoon to be making birdies, what with horror stories reverberating round the mountain such as that relating to Marcel Siem, who was playing alongside Nick Faldo. At the short par four seventh, which offered the best chance of an

eagle besides boasting one of the finest views in the golfing world, Siem sliced three consecutive drives out of bounds in the left to right wind. He finished with a ten. No-one would have wished such a mishap on a young man playing with a winner of six Major Championships but Faldo, whose seven at the 14th on the Friday had included a shank, could not have eyed him more sympathetically.

Miguel Angel Jiménez

shot of the week

ROBERT KARLSSON Sweden

Although Stephen Dodd came up with a shot in a million which settled atop a television tower behind the 17th green, the shot of the week belonged to Robert Karlsson. Barry Lane had just made a birdie at the 176 yard eighth to draw level with the Swede and Karlsson, who was putting out on the nearby seventh green, knew all about it. His response, however, was to birdie the eighth for himself, knocking an eight iron through the mountain air to 'gimme' distance from the hole.

Ernie Els was another who felt shot to pieces by the Sunday. "I got very angry with myself," confessed the Open Champion after his 23rd place at a venue where a poster of himself or Cindy Crawford featured on every street corner. "It's a bit late in the season and I was allowing little things to get to me."

Karlsson got back on track with the eight iron he struck to within a foot of the hole at the short eighth. He had been caught by Barry Lane in the party in front but now he had moved ahead again. What is more, he rapidly turned his one shot lead into a two shot affair as Lane followed his birdie at the eighth with a bogey at the ninth.

From the turn, Karlsson had a run of par, birdie, par, birdie, par, birdie which told him the title was virtually his.

In the process, he also shook off Paul Lawrie, who had been looking a genuine threat until he blocked his six iron second into the water at the 14th. As for Lane, his last hopes, along with his ball, disappeared with a shot stuck up a tree at the 16th. Chief Referee John Paramor and others peered through their binoculars to try and identify the missile, while Joey Jones, from the caddying corps, provided something of a diversion for the crowd as he shinned up the branches. Alas, with no-one able to read the number and make a positive identification, Lane had to return to the tee from where he took seven on his way to a share of 13th place.

For Karlsson, waiting behind, it all seemed to take forever. "I was just dying to run out of holes," he said at the end of what was a closing 71 and four round aggregate of 14 under par 270.

Karlsson, who won by four shots from the fast-improving Trevor Immelman and Lawrie, had 'done a Tiger Woods' in wearing a red shirt on the last day to make himself feel powerful but, intriguingly, it was the first he had ever heard of the World Number One's theory matching his own.

You had to assume that the idea – which has its origins in the Buddhist faith – had been passed on to Karlsson by Dr Stern, whose name Karlsson would bring up again at his post-tournament press conference. Apparently, the doctor, who was in his seventies, had died on the Friday of the tournament and the Swede wanted to dedicate his victory to the man he felt had done most for his career.

Karlsson had always been the first to admit that not a few of the doctor's theories were as weird as they were wonderful and, when he was asked to name the piece of advice which had meant the most, he passed it on in the knowledge that there would be a few raised eyebrows in his audience.

Whenever Karlsson had the feeling that he was playing badly, the doctor had told him that he did not have to believe it. "I have to remember that I am not my feelings. I am Robert," he said.

What he also was, of course, was a Champion.

Lewine Mair

final results
Crans-sur-Sierre • Montana • Switzerland
September 5-8 • 2002 • Par 71 • 6857 yards • 6239 metres

Pos.	Name		Rd1	Rd2	Rd3	Rd4	Total	Par	Prize Money Euro	£
1	Robert KARLSSON	Swe	65	66	68	71	270	-14	250000.00	158407.31
2	Trevor IMMELMAN	SA	70	67	65	72	274	-10	130280.00	82549.22
	Paul LAWRIE	Scot	66	70	66	72	274	-10	130280.00	82549.22
4	Bradley DREDGE	Wal	73	66	69	67	275	-9	69300.00	43910.51
	Simon DYSON	Eng	69	70	68	68	275	-9	69300.00	43910.51
6	Stephen LEANEY	Aus	68	70	68	70	276	-8	42150.00	26707.47
	Jarrod MOSELEY	Aus	72	68	69	67	276	-8	42150.00	26707.47
	Alex CEJKA	Ger	67	69	68	72	276	-8	42150.00	26707.47
	Emanuele CANONICA	It	68	68	65	75	276	-8	42150.00	26707.47
10	Jeev Milkha SINGH	Ind	71	70	66	70	277	-7	27800.00	17614.89
	Michael CAMPBELL	NZ	71	69	67	70	277	-7	27800.00	17614.89
	Paul CASEY	Eng	68	69	76	64	277	-7	27800.00	17614.89
13	Barry LANE	Eng	70	68	64	76	278	-6	23550.00	14921.97
	Fredrik ANDERSSON	Swe	68	70	70	70	278	-6	23550.00	14921.97
15	Marc FARRY	Fr	70	71	71	67	279	-5	21150.00	13401.26
	David PARK	Wal	72	66	74	67	279	-5	21150.00	13401.26
	Sam WALKER	Eng	73	65	67	74	279	-5	21150.00	13401.26
18	Nick FALDO	Eng	66	72	69	73	280	-4	18060.00	11443.34
	Mark ROE	Eng	73	66	70	71	280	-4	18060.00	11443.34
	Carlos RODILES	Sp	70	66	73	71	280	-4	18060.00	11443.34
	Carl PETTERSSON	Swe	67	70	70	73	280	-4	18060.00	11443.34
	Jamie DONALDSON	Wal	69	71	69	71	280	-4	18060.00	11443.34
23	David HOWELL	Eng	71	70	71	69	281	-3	15600.00	9884.62
	Thomas LEVET	Fr	69	71	71	70	281	-3	15600.00	9884.62
	Jean HUGO	SA	70	71	68	72	281	-3	15600.00	9884.62
	Ernie ELS	SA	70	71	66	74	281	-3	15600.00	9884.62
	Thomas BJÖRN	Den	69	74	68	70	281	-3	15600.00	9884.62
28	Klas ERIKSSON	Swe	68	67	73	74	282	-2	12693.75	8043.13
	Andrew MARSHALL	Eng	72	68	69	73	282	-2	12693.75	8043.13
	Miles TUNNICLIFF	Eng	73	68	71	70	282	-2	12693.75	8043.13
	Ian GARBUTT	Eng	70	71	69	72	282	-2	12693.75	8043.13
	Phillip PRICE	Wal	69	68	73	72	282	-2	12693.75	8043.13
	Fredrik JACOBSON	Swe	72	68	69	73	282	-2	12693.75	8043.13
	Sebastien DELAGRANGE	Fr	72	70	70	70	282	-2	12693.75	8043.13
	Mikko ILONEN	Fin	74	68	69	71	282	-2	12693.75	8043.13
36	Henrik BJORNSTAD	Nor	69	69	72	73	283	-1	10050.00	6367.97
	Søren HANSEN	Den	72	69	68	74	283	-1	10050.00	6367.97
	Dennis EDLUND	Swe	72	71	71	69	283	-1	10050.00	6367.97
	Andrew COLTART	Scot	70	65	70	78	283	-1	10050.00	6367.97
	Mikael LUNDBERG	Swe	71	70	71	71	283	-1	10050.00	6367.97
	Matthew CORT	Eng	72	65	69	77	283	-1	10050.00	6367.97
	Brett RUMFORD	Aus	67	73	76	67	283	-1	10050.00	6367.97
43	Brian DAVIS	Eng	68	72	73	71	284	0	7650.00	4847.26
	Mathias GRÖNBERG	Swe	66	76	70	72	284	0	7650.00	4847.26
	Robert COLES	Eng	72	68	73	71	284	0	7650.00	4847.26
	Francis VALERA	Sp	72	71	73	68	284	0	7650.00	4847.26
	Patrik SJÖLAND	Swe	69	71	71	73	284	0	7650.00	4847.26
	Henrik NYSTROM	Swe	71	67	74	72	284	0	7650.00	4847.26
	Retief GOOSEN	SA	70	73	69	72	284	0	7650.00	4847.26
	Stephen GALLACHER	Scot	71	72	70	71	284	0	7650.00	4847.26
	Scott GARDINER	Aus	70	73	71	70	284	0	7650.00	4847.26
52	Mark FOSTER	Eng	68	71	74	72	285	1	5156.25	3267.15
	Raphaël JACQUELIN	Fr	70	72	65	78	285	1	5156.25	3267.15
	Chris GANE	Eng	72	70	73	70	285	1	5156.25	3267.15
	Olle KARLSSON	Swe	69	69	74	73	285	1	5156.25	3267.15
	Ignacio GARRIDO	Sp	72	70	69	74	285	1	5156.25	3267.15
	Gary ORR	Scot	68	71	72	74	285	1	5156.25	3267.15
	Stephen SCAHILL	NZ	73	70	70	72	285	1	5156.25	3267.15
	David DRYSDALE	Scot	70	73	70	72	285	1	5156.25	3267.15
60	Mårten OLANDER	Swe	72	70	72	72	286	2	4125.00	2613.72
	Marcel SIEM	Ger	71	67	69	79	286	2	4125.00	2613.72
62	Santiago LUNA	Sp	70	73	68	76	287	3	3900.00	2471.15
63	Miguel Angel JIMÉNEZ	Sp	67	73	71	77	288	4	3750.00	2376.11
64	Markus BRIER	Aut	72	71	76	70	289	5	3600.00	2281.07
65	Peter HANSON	Swe	70	72	70	78	290	6	3375.00	2138.50
	Ian POULTER	Eng	70	72	71	77	290	6	3375.00	2138.50
67	Craig STADLER	USA	71	72	67	81	291	7	3150.00	1995.93
68	Stuart LITTLE	Eng	70	71	78	73	292	8	3000.00	1900.89
	Christopher HANELL	Swe	72	68	75	77	292	8	3000.00	1900.89
70	Jarmo SANDELIN	Swe	77	66	78	W/D	221	8	2740.00	1736.14

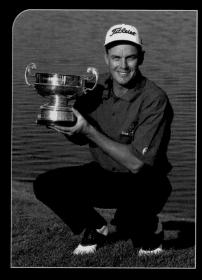

Linde German Masters Gut Lärchenhof · Cologne · Germany

brave and bright

Stephen Leaney

Stephen Leaney is the very embodiment of the old sporting adage "when the going gets tough, the tough get going," as a star-studded field discovered in the Linde German Masters.

Nine members of the European Team were flexing their muscles at the Gut Lärchenhof course near Cologne with The 34th Ryder Cup Matches only a fortnight away. Open Champion Ernie Els and US PGA Champion Rich Beem were also in a line-up alongside 22 of the leading 25 players in the Volvo Order of Merit.

Defending Champion Bernhard Langer, who co-founded the event with brother Erwin back in 1987, was the favourite of the home galleries to win for a record fifth time after having stormed home with a 22 par total of 266, 12 months ago. But it was 33 year old Leaney, the quiet Australian, who would rule the roost on 266 this time.

Not such a surprise, however, when you consider his previous three European Tour victories had come on equally demanding layouts in Royal Agadir in the Moroccan Open in 1998 and Hilversum and Noordwijk in The TNT Opens of 1998 and 2000.

Mathias Grönberg

After scooping a princely 500,000 euro (£315,541) first prize, together with a five year Tour exemption, Leaney admitted: "This is the biggest cheque of my career, but it's the winning itself that is most satisfying. I thrive on a challenge and this is a major tournament on a very difficult golf course. Shooting those scores 64-69-66-67 makes me very proud.

"It's great to put yourself in pressure situations and hit the shots you need to hit. That's what I did and no amount of money can give you that amount of pressure. That is the most enjoyable part about it. I've been playing well and had chances to win. It was very pleasing to finish it off here because it was tight on the final nine."

Leaney is not only brave but bright. He learned from his mistakes of the previous year's event when he went into action on Sunday a single stroke behind leader Langer only to stumble to a 77 and joint 32nd place.

He explained: "I didn't cope well mentally then. This time I concentrated on staying positive and keeping all thoughts of the title, the money and all the fringe benefits out of my brain and just executing the shots I needed. I seemed to wear out my two, three and four irons on the par fours and the key was all the hard work I'd done on my swing with my coach Denis Pugh the last couple of years."

Alex Cejka

Leaney, whose win saw him jump from 38th to tenth on the Volvo Order of Merit and nudge his career earnings past two million euro, also earned a starting place in the following week's World Golf Championships - American Express Championship in Ireland, causing him to cancel his Monday flight home to Perth with wife Tracey.

He had an inkling that might be the case when a brilliant opening 64 gave him a one stroke lead over Retief Goosen and Welshman Mark Pilkington, but at halfway Leaney found himself one behind a resurgent Ian Woosnam, who added a 64 to his opening 68 to move to 12 under par.

A new set of clubs and the decision to settle on the short putter were the key to the razor sharp scoring that would keep the 44 year old European Ryder Cup Vice-Captain's nose in front of his eight surviving team charges throughout the weekend.

Nevertheless Paul Casey led going into the final round after a record third round 62 for a 19 under par total of 197, two clear of Alex Cejka and Leaney. Casey had pipped Cejka at The Gleneagles Hotel the year before in the Scottish PGA Championship.

Henrik Nyström

the course

Designed by Jack Nicklaus, Gut Lärchenhof is sited 20 minutes up the autobahn from Cologne, measures 7289 yards, and boasts an abundance of water hazards, the lake coming vitally into play to the right of the ninth and the left of the 18th and, because it is basically flat, it has little protection from the wind.

Casey, a star of the 1999 Walker Cup victory by Great Britain and Ireland at Nairn, was hot after carding a 63 in the BMW International Open in Germany and a 64 in the Omega European Masters in Switzerland. However, he had to settle for a tie for third with another fast rising English star Nick Dougherty (66) and Woosnam (68), as Leaney edged out Cejka (68) by a stroke.

This was a final round of which Leaney, who took 18 months to recover from illness following an operation in 1993 after doctors diagnosed a blood clot, could be proud. For this time around there was not a wobble in sight. Indeed he put his rivals to the torch with four birdies in an outward 32 followed by another at the tenth then stood firm with eight consecutive pars to claim the title.

There was also more reason for Gary Evans, following his outstanding performance in the Open Golf Championship, to celebrate. He took sixth place with scores of 67-68-65 and 69 and by climbing into the top 20 in the 2002 Volvo Order of Merit he qualified for the WGC - American Express Championship the following week.

shot of the week

PIERRE FULKE Sweden

Jarmo Sandelin holed in one at the 11th but the award goes to fellow Swede Pierre Fulke's 55 yard pitch to eight feet to salvage a par four at the 18th in round one - played while standing up to his knees on the slippery bottom of the lake with the ball perched precariously 20 centimetres from the water.

Even so Stephen Leaney wore the biggest smile. He had collected 50 World Ranking points to boost his hopes of playing in more Major Championships and World Golf Championships events in the future and he declared: "I'm grateful to the promoters, the Tour and the sponsors for making this tournament big enough to carry a five year exemption. It's hard for Australians having to travel so much and this makes things much easier."

Gordon Richardson

Linde German Masters

Paul Casey

final results

Gut Lärchenhof · Cologne · Germany
September 12-15 · 2002 · Par 72 · 7289 yards · 6665 metres

Pos.	Name		Rd1	Rd2	Rd3	Rd4	Total	Par	Prize Money Euro	£
1	Stephen LEANEY	Aus	64	69	66	67	266	-22	500000.00	315541.03
2	Alex CEJKA	Ger	68	68	63	68	267	-21	333330.00	210358.58
3	Ian WOOSNAM	Wal	68	64	68	68	268	-20	155000.00	97817.72
	Nick DOUGHERTY	Eng	68	65	69	66	268	-20	155000.00	97817.72
	Paul CASEY	Eng	68	67	62	71	268	-20	155000.00	97817.72
6	Gary EVANS	Eng	67	68	65	69	269	-19	105000.00	66263.62
7	Mathias GRÖNBERG	Swe	67	69	66	68	270	-18	82500.00	52064.27
	Ricardo GONZALEZ	Arg	68	69	66	67	270	-18	82500.00	52064.27
9	Colin MONTGOMERIE	Scot	71	66	68	67	272	-16	67200.00	42408.71
10	Bernhard LANGER	Ger	68	70	66	69	273	-15	57600.00	36350.33
	Warren BENNETT	Eng	67	66	70	70	273	-15	57600.00	36350.33
12	Padraig HARRINGTON	Ire	69	66	71	68	274	-14	49950.00	31522.55
	Pierre FULKE	Swe	69	71	66	68	274	-14	49950.00	31522.55
14	Maarten LAFEBER	Hol	69	67	71	68	275	-13	45000.00	28398.69
	David LYNN	Eng	70	69	65	71	275	-13	45000.00	28398.69
16	Eduardo ROMERO	Arg	70	68	64	74	276	-12	37628.57	23746.72
	Peter O'MALLEY	Aus	67	72	68	69	276	-12	37628.57	23746.72
	Emanuele CANONICA	It	68	68	69	71	276	-12	37628.57	23746.72
	Thomas BJÖRN	Den	67	70	70	69	276	-12	37628.57	23746.72
	Mark PILKINGTON	Wal	65	69	70	72	276	-12	37628.57	23746.72
	Patrik SJÖLAND	Swe	71	68	66	71	276	-12	37628.57	23746.72
	Alastair FORSYTH	Scot	69	71	73	63	276	-12	37628.57	23746.72
23	Nick FALDO	Eng	71	70	69	67	277	-11	29850.00	18837.80
	Brian DAVIS	Eng	68	72	68	69	277	-11	29850.00	18837.80
	Anthony WALL	Eng	70	65	71	71	277	-11	29850.00	18837.80
	Miguel Angel JIMÉNEZ	Sp	72	69	67	69	277	-11	29850.00	18837.80
	Robert KARLSSON	Swe	68	72	69	68	277	-11	29850.00	18837.80
	Ernie ELS	SA	69	70	68	70	277	-11	29850.00	18837.80
	Bradley DREDGE	Wal	69	69	71	68	277	-11	29850.00	18837.80
	Retief GOOSEN	SA	65	70	69	73	277	-11	29850.00	18837.80
31	David HOWELL	Eng	70	69	72	67	278	-10	23700.00	14956.64
	Steve WEBSTER	Eng	70	68	68	72	278	-10	23700.00	14956.64
	Gary EMERSON	Eng	71	70	66	71	278	-10	23700.00	14956.64
	Jarrod MOSELEY	Aus	70	71	70	67	278	-10	23700.00	14956.64
	Jonathan LOMAS	Eng	67	72	71	68	278	-10	23700.00	14956.64
	Fredrik JACOBSON	Swe	74	67	70	67	278	-10	23700.00	14956.64
37	Barry LANE	Eng	72	70	67	70	279	-9	18900.00	11927.45
	Marc FARRY	Fr	74	66	68	71	279	-9	18900.00	11927.45
	Darren FICHARDT	SA	67	69	73	70	279	-9	18900.00	11927.45
	Richard BLAND	Eng	67	70	71	71	279	-9	18900.00	11927.45
	Jean HUGO	SA	72	69	67	71	279	-9	18900.00	11927.45
	Angel CABRERA	Arg	71	65	74	69	279	-9	18900.00	11927.45
	Raymond RUSSELL	Scot	71	70	71	67	279	-9	18900.00	11927.45
	David CARTER	Eng	68	67	70	74	279	-9	18900.00	11927.45
	Jamie DONALDSON	Wal	67	71	69	72	279	-9	18900.00	11927.45
46	Anders HANSEN	Den	69	71	72	68	280	-8	15000.00	9466.23
	Trevor IMMELMAN	SA	68	72	71	69	280	-8	15000.00	9466.23
	Jamie SPENCE	Eng	71	71	68	70	280	-8	15000.00	9466.23
	Søren HANSEN	Den	67	72	71	70	280	-8	15000.00	9466.23
50	Miguel Angel MARTIN	Sp	71	67	70	73	281	-7	11700.00	7383.66
	Henrik BJORNSTAD	Nor	70	69	69	73	281	-7	11700.00	7383.66
	Michele REALE	It	68	74	66	73	281	-7	11700.00	7383.66
	Ignacio GARRIDO	Sp	70	70	69	72	281	-7	11700.00	7383.66
	Niclas FASTH	Swe	70	71	75	65	281	-7	11700.00	7383.66
	Lee WESTWOOD	Eng	70	67	73	71	281	-7	11700.00	7383.66
	Tobias DIER	Ger	73	69	69	70	281	-7	11700.00	7383.66
57	Peter FOWLER	Aus	68	73	72	69	282	-6	8850.00	5585.08
	Jeev Milkha SINGH	Ind	72	70	68	72	282	-6	8850.00	5585.08
	Richard GREEN	Aus	71	67	72	72	282	-6	8850.00	5585.08
	Ian POULTER	Eng	72	68	71	71	282	-6	8850.00	5585.08
61	Mark JAMES	Eng	72	69	70	72	283	-5	7500.00	4733.12
	Costantino ROCCA	It	70	72	71	70	283	-5	7500.00	4733.12
	Richard S JOHNSON	Swe	71	71	68	73	283	-5	7500.00	4733.12
	Carl SUNESON	Sp	70	70	72	71	283	-5	7500.00	4733.12
	Henrik NYSTROM	Swe	70	70	72	71	283	-5	7500.00	4733.12
66	Raphaël JACQUELIN	Fr	72	69	69	77	285	-3	6150.00	3881.15
	Stephen DODD	Wal	71	70	68	76	285	-3	6150.00	3881.15
	Stephen SCAHILL	NZ	70	72	70	73	285	-3	6150.00	3881.15
	Graeme MCDOWELL	N.Ire	73	68	70	74	285	-3	6150.00	3881.15
70	Paul MCGINLEY	Ire	70	70	71	75	286	-2	4985.00	3145.94
	Jorge BERENDT	Arg	74	68	68	76	286	-2	4985.00	3145.94
72	Christopher HANELL	Swe	75	67	76	70	288	0	4497.00	2837.98
73	Carl PETTERSSON	Swe	71	69	75	75	290	2	4494.00	2836.08
74	Anders FORSBRAND	Swe	68	71	75	77	291	3	4491.00	2834.19

Technique for professionals.

More often than not it's the right technique that makes the difference between success and failure – in the game of golf as much as in business. In the same way that golf pro Bernhard Langer continually works at perfecting his play, we at Linde daily take up the technical challenge anew. With our aim set on innovations enabling Linde customers to do an increasingly professional and successful job.

www.linde.com

We know how.

Gas and Engineering

Material Handling

Refrigeration

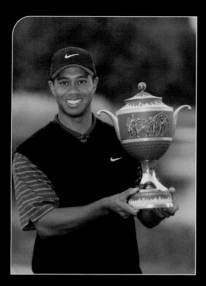

WGC - American Express Championship Mount Juliet · Thomastown · Ireland

true artist

1	**Tiger WOODS** USA	263	-25
2	Retief GOOSEN SA	264	-24
3	Vijay SINGH Fiji	267	-21
4	Jerry KELLY USA	268	-20
	David TOMS USA	268	-20
6	Scott McCARRON USA	269	-19
7	Sergio GARCIA Sp	270	-18
8	Davis LOVE III USA	271	-17
9	Michael CAMPBELL NZ	272	-16
	Bob ESTES USA	272	-16

Tiger Woods

Three topics dominated all conversation when 49 of the world's top 50 assembled at Mount Juliet in County Kilkenny for the World Golf Championships - American Express Championship. The presence of the game's top player, Tiger Woods, guaranteed the record attendances that duly materialised later in the week. The weather, calm and warm, surprised the many people who had been warned of the vagaries of the Irish climate, especially in the month of September. And then there was the course itself, manicured to perfection by course superintendent Aidan O'Hara and his staff.

Woods enjoyed the ambience from the time he pulled up on the Tuesday morning. He was accompanied by his glamorous Swedish girlfriend Elin Nordegren and settled comfortably into the elegant Mount Juliet House hotel. A leisurely nine holes that afternoon checking out what he had learned on a previous visit in July assured him that the Jack Nicklaus-designed layout remained very much to his liking. He knew immediately he could shoot seriously low numbers. The only trouble from his perception was that many of the star-studded field would do likewise and that he would need to be at his best.

From the outset, Woods was unstoppable. Remarkable opening day galleries followed his match with Padraig Harrington, who by this stage had assumed the role of 'People's Champion' where the Irish public was concerned. Much as they wanted to see the local hero match or even outscore the World Number One, they were knowledgeable enough to realise it was not going to happen and that here was a true artist at work. Harrington played nicely enough for a 69 but in such benign conditions, the 7246 yard course was at Tiger's mercy and he shot 65 without ever appearing to be off the leash.

Another scintillating 65 on the second day might well have burned off most of the opposition but as Woods himself observed, there were too many good players in the line-up for that to happen. He knew he would have to battle all the way to the wire and so it transpired. The American influence at the top of the leaderboard was profound with Jerry Kelly, Steve Lowery and David Toms comfortably within striking distance, while South African Ernie Els had given himself every chance of a first victory since the Open Golf Championship with rounds of 68 and 67.

Angel Cabrera

the course

All greenkeeping staff at Mount Juliet emerged from the tournament with praise ringing in their ears. Tiger Woods went so far as to say the greens were the best he had putted on all year and there was not a dissenting voice. A Jack Nicklaus design which opened in the late 1980s and was deemed good enough in 1992 to host the first of three Irish Opens, the Mount Juliet estate is one of the finest in Ireland and caters for several other sporting activities. Its putting course provided great fun throughout the week and was tried out with varying success by several of the players, most of whom stayed on site. At 7,246 yards, Mount Juliet is not a short course, even by modern standards, but a combination of its pristine condition, highly favourable weather and the quality of the field, made for remarkably low scoring.

Gary Evans

from there he went birdie-birdie-par-birdie-birdie-eagle-par to set the clubhouse target at a hugely impressive 24 under par 264.

Indeed, as Els was holing out on the 18th, a long and dangerous par four, a couple of errant shots left Tiger struggling on the 17th for the birdie four which would retain his, by now, two stroke advantage coming down the last. He had to conjure up a remarkable recovery shot and then hole a fifteen footer to achieve his target. That more or less clinched the title but there was still one other ambition to realise. Woods had never before played a 72 hole tournament without a single dropped shot and it looked a cast iron certainty that another record would fall to this remarkable man when he ripped a fairway-splitting tee shot down the 18th.

However, a photographer chose to click as he prepared for his approach and threw his focus on the shot. He missed the green to the right, chipped to six feet but missed the putt. He was Champion alright but admitted to being "hot" at what had happened.

Michael Campbell

More than 32,000 people turned up to see Saturday's action on the hottest day of all with Woods, inevitably, the chief source of interest. This time, the maestro rattled off a 67 that provided him with a five shot cushion entering the final round. By this stage, he was quietly suggesting that the course was playing perhaps a little too easily and that the fairways might have been narrower and the rough more penalising. But all the time he asserted that the quality of the greens was the key to the low scoring as Els gently suggested that Tiger mightn't know a whole lot about how tough the weather can be at that time of year in Ireland and that if the wind and rain had got up, it would have been a far different proposition.

The consensus was that Woods would enjoy a stroll in the park in the final round on his way to another WGC title and when he hit two glorious shots to the par five tenth and holed from ten feet, that view hardened still further. Even then, though, several others, and most notably Retief Goosen, had the Tiger in their sights. The 2001 Volvo Order of Merit winner bogeyed the short 11th but

shot of the week

TIGER WOODS USA

Tiger Woods's third shot wedge at the long 17th on the final day didn't appear to be one of earth shattering proportions but the Champion himself claimed it was the one that clinched the title. He desperately needed to birdie the par five to stay two ahead coming down the 18th but a couple of wayward shots left him with a problem. He explained: "I made a pretty miraculous recovery and that third shot was one of the best I hit all week. People think, yeah, you hit it to fifteen feet, big deal, but that lie was pretty ghastly. I knew it was going to be the crucial shot of the tournament for I was fully aware of what Retief Goosen was doing up front. So I said to myself, just suck it up there, put it on the green and put yourself in a position to make a putt. And I did that."

Paul Lawrie

Championship at Pebble Beach in 2000 remained the pinnacle. He was hugely appreciative of the support he had received from the fans who numbered more than 120,000 over the four days, pointing out "they were extremely knowledgeable, they didn't applaud just because guys got the ball airborne."

They had many other magnificent performances to cheer on that final day, like the record setting 62s shot by Sergio Garcia and Goosen. Michael Campbell and Phil Mickelson also covered their respective nines in 30 on a day, and a week's golf, few who witnessed it will ever forget.

Charlie Mulqueen

"Of all the times to do such a thing, I had a four iron of 236 yards and that's not easy with so much sand and water around," he said before cheering up and accepting that his win with a tournament record low of 25 under par 263 was "right up there" with his many previous successes, although he insisted that the US Open

Sergio Garcia

final results

Mount Juliet • Thomastown • Ireland
September 19-22 • 2002 • Par 72 • 7246 yards • 6627 metres

Pos.	Name		Rd1	Rd2	Rd3	Rd4	Total	Par	Prize Money Euro	£
1	Tiger WOODS	USA	65	65	67	66	263	-25	1026378.00	641642.65
2	Retief GOOSEN	SA	67	67	68	62	264	-24	554244.10	346487.02
3	Vijay SINGH	Fiji	67	69	66	65	267	-21	377193.90	235803.66
4	Jerry KELLY	USA	67	65	70	66	268	-20	241198.80	150786.00
	David TOMS	USA	66	67	69	66	268	-20	241198.80	150786.00
6	Scott MCCARRON	USA	71	67	64	67	269	-19	184748.00	115495.65
7	Sergio GARCIA	Sp	69	69	70	62	270	-18	159088.60	99454.62
8	Davis LOVE III	USA	69	67	68	67	271	-17	133429.10	83413.52
9	Bob ESTES	USA	68	68	69	67	272	-16	113928.00	71222.36
	Michael CAMPBELL	NZ	71	66	71	64	272	-16	113928.00	71222.36
11	Justin LEONARD	USA	68	68	69	68	273	-15	86472.34	54058.39
	Stuart APPLEBY	Aus	69	66	70	68	273	-15	86472.34	54058.39
	Niclas FASTH	Swe	68	69	72	64	273	-15	86472.34	54058.39
	Chris DIMARCO	USA	67	69	70	67	273	-15	86472.34	54058.39
15	Nick PRICE	Zim	68	71	69	66	274	-14	66714.56	41706.77
	Steve LOWERY	USA	66	67	69	72	274	-14	66714.56	41706.77
	Mike WEIR	Can	67	70	68	69	274	-14	66714.56	41706.77
	Scott VERPLANK	USA	68	72	68	66	274	-14	66714.56	41706.77
	Gary EVANS	Eng	67	68	73	66	274	-14	66714.56	41706.77
	Rocco MEDIATE	USA	69	67	67	71	274	-14	66714.56	41706.77
21	Padraig HARRINGTON	Ire	69	70	67	69	275	-13	59529.92	37215.27
22	Kenny PERRY	USA	68	71	68	69	276	-12	57477.16	35931.98
23	Stephen LEANEY	Aus	69	67	71	70	277	-11	53884.84	33686.24
	Ernie ELS	SA	68	67	72	70	277	-11	53884.84	33686.24
	Scott HOCH	USA	71	68	67	71	277	-11	53884.84	33686.24
	Phil MICKELSON	USA	70	72	71	64	277	-11	53884.84	33686.24
27	José Maria OLAZÁBAL	Sp	68	72	69	69	278	-10	49779.33	31119.67
	Trevor IMMELMAN	SA	71	71	67	69	278	-10	49779.33	31119.67
	Thomas BJÖRN	Den	72	68	66	72	278	-10	49779.33	31119.67
	Kevin SUTHERLAND	USA	69	68	70	71	278	-10	49779.33	31119.67
31	Colin MONTGOMERIE	Scot	72	70	69	68	279	-9	46700.20	29194.74
	Robert ALLENBY	Aus	72	70	67	70	279	-9	46700.20	29194.74
33	Bernhard LANGER	Ger	72	68	70	70	280	-8	44134.25	27590.63
	Jim FURYK	USA	69	69	69	73	280	-8	44134.25	27590.63
	Mark CALCAVECCHIA	USA	72	70	71	67	280	-8	44134.25	27590.63
36	Eduardo ROMERO	Arg	70	71	70	70	281	-7	41055.12	25665.71
	José COCERES	Arg	68	72	71	70	281	-7	41055.12	25665.71
	Angel CABRERA	Arg	71	66	73	71	281	-7	41055.12	25665.71
39	Søren HANSEN	Den	75	68	65	74	282	-6	38232.57	23901.18
	Tom LEHMAN	USA	73	72	67	70	282	-6	38232.57	23901.18
	Chris RILEY	USA	73	68	70	71	282	-6	38232.57	23901.18
	Adam SCOTT	Aus	70	70	69	73	282	-6	38232.57	23901.18
43	Jeff SLUMAN	USA	69	69	72	73	283	-5	36436.42	22778.31
	Paul AZINGER	USA	73	73	71	66	283	-5	36436.42	22778.31
	John ROLLINS	USA	73	72	67	71	283	-5	36436.42	22778.31
46	David DUVAL	USA	71	65	72	76	284	-4	34896.85	21815.85
	Justin ROSE	Eng	73	70	72	69	284	-4	34896.85	21815.85
	Len MATTIACE	USA	70	73	69	72	284	-4	34896.85	21815.85
49	Brad FAXON	USA	70	77	67	71	285	-3	32844.09	20532.56
	Fred FUNK	USA	69	70	72	74	285	-3	32844.09	20532.56
	John COOK	USA	75	71	71	68	285	-3	32844.09	20532.56
	Craig PARRY	Aus	68	71	74	72	285	-3	32844.09	20532.56
	Rich BEEM	USA	70	69	74	72	285	-3	32844.09	20532.56
54	Paul LAWRIE	Scot	71	70	74	71	286	-2	30791.34	19249.28
	Peter LONARD	Aus	71	69	72	74	286	-2	30791.34	19249.28
	Carl PETTERSSON	Swe	72	72	68	74	286	-2	30791.34	19249.28
57	Anders HANSEN	Den	71	72	72	74	289	1	29251.77	18286.81
	Peter O'MALLEY	Aus	75	73	71	70	289	1	29251.77	18286.81
	Thongchai JAIDEE	Thai	72	74	73	70	289	1	29251.77	18286.81
60	Scott LAYCOCK	Aus	74	72	72	72	290	2	28225.39	17645.17
61	Craig PERKS	NZ	74	74	75	68	291	3	27712.20	17324.35
62	Tim CLARK	SA	74	69	76	73	292	4	27199.02	17003.53
63	Darren CLARKE	N.Ire	75	76	70	74	295	7	26685.83	16682.71
64	Kenichi KUBOYA	Jpn	77	72	73	76	298	10	26172.64	16361.89
65	Shigeki MARUYAMA	Jpn	75	WD			75	3	25659.45	16041.07

home and hosed

It was Paul McGinley who announced on his arrival in Scotland, three days after holing the winning putt in The 34th Ryder Cup Matches at The De Vere Belfry, that he had no wish to come down from his 'high'. "I don't want a reality check," he added with a beam as wide as Dublin Bay.

Padraig Harrington

the courses

The Old Course at St Andrews and the Championship Course at Carnoustie were in immaculate condition, although much greener than many would have remembered. Rough is not one of the Old Course's many perils, but there was plenty of it this time, especially at the Road Hole 17th, where the premium on accuracy with the second shot was greater than ever. Kingsbarns, one of the finest new links courses in the world, is still very new, and a long-term grow-in of fescue grass has begun to ensure the characteristics of the course are retained for all time.

Five days later it was his Ryder Cup team-mate and 1997 winning World Golf Championships - EMC[2] World Cup partner Padraig Harrington, who remained exalted, the 31 year old's head high in the clouds after the play-off victory over Eduardo Romero had given him a cheque for 818,662 euro (£511,663). "Even if I had finished last here, these would have been the best two weeks of my life," he noted.

As it had been at The De Vere Belfry, in the end it came down to putting. Until the gloriously sunny final day on the Old Course at St Andrews, Harrington had not been rapturous about his work on the greens. Discovering their exact pace had not been easy. However when, in the closing moments of the second dunhill links championship, it virtually came down to match play, he suddenly found his touch.

For much of this 'celebration of links golf' at St Andrews, Carnoustie and Kingsbarns, Harrington and Romero had either been in the lead individually, shared it, or were only a shot behind. It remained that way throughout the last afternoon despite the best efforts of Colin Montgomerie, who blazed round the Old Course in a record-equalling 63.

It would have been 62 had he not taken three putts from the Valley of Sin on the 18th. Indeed if he had finished with a birdie he would have made it a three-way play-off on 19 under par 269 alongside the Irishman and the Argentine. That Harrington featured in a play-off at all was due to a 20 foot birdie putt on the 18th green followed by a miss from five feet by Romero, who had led after 71 holes.

Following a half in four at the first extra hole, Harrington again struck Romero lethally, holing from eight feet for a birdie three at the second. Romero could not respond, his putt from five feet sliding past the right lip of the hole. His dream of a double Scotch - The Barclays Scottish Open and the dunhill links championship - was over.

After winning at Loch Lomond he said the idyllic setting reminded him of the lakes and hills of home. Carnoustie, perhaps, had a similar effect. The tenth hole, for example, is called 'South America' in memory of an inebriated local who, at the turn of the century, proclaimed he was off to seek his fortune in the far-away land only to be found the next morning, after his going away party, fast asleep in a greenside bunker.

There was to be, however, no hangover for Romero at Carnoustie. The 48 year old stormed round in seven under par 65, one shot above the course record set by Montgomerie in the 1995 Barclays Scottish Open, to take the outright lead by a shot from South Africa's Nic Lawrence, India's Jyoti Randhawa and Harrington.

On day two Harrington leapfrogged Romero, the Irishman sweeping serenely on by repeating his Carnoustie 66 at Kingsbarns. At 12 under par he was now one in front of Romero and two ahead of Sweden's Mikael Lundberg.

DUNHILL LINKS CHAMPIONSHIP PRO-AM TOP 12

Pos	Name	Rd1	Rd2	Rd3	Rd4	Total	Par	Prize Money Euro
1	Padraig HARRINGTON/JP McMANUS	62	62	61	66	251	-37	32,158.48
2	Lucas PARSONS/Jeremy LAMBOURNE	67	65	60	65	257	-31	12,059.43
	Eduardo ROMERO/Neil CRICHTON	61	64	64	68	257	-31	12,059.43
	Steve ELKINGTON/Clay WALKER	64	65	65	63	257	-31	12,059.43
	Angel CABRERA/Steve CARR	62	68	65	62	257	-31	12,059.43
6	Thomas BJÖRN/Gary LINEKER	65	63	66	65	259	-29	3,014.86
	Mikael LUNDBERG/Mike NORRIS	65	66	63	65	259	-29	3,014.86
8	Alan MCLEAN/Mark MILLN	66	63	67	64	260	-28	3,014.86
	Sandy LYLE/Duncan LAWRIE	66	64	65	65	260	-28	3,014.86
	JEAN-FRANCOIS REMESY/Francois GOOSEN	62	69	65	64	260	-28	3,014.86
	Henrik STENSON/Barry RICHARDS	63	65	66	66	260	-28	3,014.86
	Adam SCOTT/Philip MORSE	65	67	64	64	260	-28	3,014.86

Mikael Lundberg

shot of the week

COLIN MONTGOMERIE Scotland

Only five days after leading Europe to glory in The 34th Ryder Cup Matches, Colin Montgomerie produced not only the shot of the week but also arguably the shot of the year. His four iron from 209 yards out at Kingsbarns's 516 yard third hole went straight into the cup for the first albatross of The 2002 European Tour International Schedule and the second of his career, the first coming in Switzerland in 1990. "I must be getting longer," joked Montgomerie. "I eagled the hole last year and now an albatross this time!"

Kenny Dalglish's 75 yard wedge shot for an eagle two on the tenth at St Andrews and Anders Forsbrand's eight iron hole-in-one at Carnoustie's 169 yard 13th.

Had it not been for Mongomerie's albatross, former Masters and US PGA Champion Vijay Singh's holed chip shot from 40 yards at the 18th on the Old Course in the third round would have been the shot of the week.

At the time its significance looked considerable. Harrington and Romero had put some distance between themselves and the rest of the field at 16 under par, the Irishman recovering from a double bogey six at the Road Hole 17th with a birdie three at the last for a 68, while Romero continued to defy the years with a 67 constructed with the mental aid of his thrice weekly yoga sessions. However, with his eagle two for a 64, Singh was only one behind, having put two shots between himself and the joint fourth pairing of Ignacio Garrido and Sandy Lyle.

Ernie Els's attempt to improve on his second place finish in 2001 behind Paul Lawrie was buried at the 17th, where the Road Hole bunker cost him a quadruple bogey eight. Little more than 12 hours later, however, he was gone, wife Liezl having gone into labour with their second child, leaving the stage clear for Harrington, Romero and Singh to play out Sunday's final act.

However, Singh's expected charge did not materialise and the Fijian's 70 left him in a share of third place with Lyle, who produced his most stimulating day on a golf course since he won the 1992 Volvo Masters at Valderrama, and Montgomerie, who well and truly produced his Sunday best. Up ahead though, the most telling statistic was that Harrington's win over Romero was his first play-off success on The European Tour at his fourth attempt.

To complete his two weeks of euphoria, the Dubliner also won the team event on 37 under par alongside his amateur partner, the legendary Irish racehorse owner, JP McManus. After McGinley had prevailed at The De Vere Belfry, it was another week which saw Irish eyes smile.

Jock MacVicar

There were a number of stunning second round cameo performances, too, including Montgomerie's albatross two on the third hole at Kingsbarns, former Celtic and Liverpool footballer

Padraig Harrington and JP McManus

final results

October 3-6 • 2002

St Andrews • Fife • Scotland Par 72 • 7115 yards • 6506 metres

Carnoustie • Angus • Scotland Par 72 • 7102 yards • 6504 metres

Kingsbarns • Fife • Scotland Par 72 • 7059 yards • 6456 metres

Pos.	Name		Rd1	Rd2	Rd3	Rd4	Total	Par	Prize Money Euro	£
1	Padraig HARRINGTON	Ire	66	66	68	69	269	-19	818662.20	511663.87
2	Eduardo ROMERO	Arg	65	68	67	69	269	-19	545771.40	341107.13
3	Sandy LYLE	Scot	69	67	67	68	271	-17	253785.30	158615.81
	Colin MONTGOMERIE	Scot	70	69	69	63	271	-17	253785.30	158615.81
	Vijay SINGH	Fiji	70	67	64	70	271	-17	253785.30	158615.81
6	Jyoti RANDHAWA	Ind	66	69	69	68	272	-16	171919.10	107449.44
7	Brian DAVIS	Eng	70	69	69	65	273	-15	135079.30	84424.56
	Thomas BJÖRN	Den	67	68	73	65	273	-15	135079.30	84424.56
9	Rolf MUNTZ	Hol	68	74	66	66	274	-14	104133.80	65083.63
	Adam SCOTT	Aus	68	70	68	68	274	-14	104133.80	65083.63
11	Ignacio GARRIDO	Sp	70	66	67	72	275	-13	87433.13	54645.71
	Mikael LUNDBERG	Swe	67	67	73	68	275	-13	87433.13	54645.71
13	Santiago LUNA	Sp	67	69	70	70	276	-12	77117.98	48198.74
	David GILFORD	Eng	72	69	67	68	276	-12	77117.98	48198.74
15	Mark MCNULTY	Zim	68	72	70	67	277	-11	67785.23	42365.77
	Angel CABRERA	Arg	73	70	70	64	277	-11	67785.23	42365.77
	Fredrik JACOBSON	Swe	70	73	67	67	277	-11	67785.23	42365.77
	Nic LAWRENCE	SA	66	70	72	69	277	-11	67785.23	42365.77
19	Peter FOWLER	Aus	70	73	65	70	278	-10	58084.09	36302.56
	José Maria OLAZÁBAL	Sp	71	71	69	67	278	-10	58084.09	36302.56
	Trevor IMMELMAN	SA	73	67	67	71	278	-10	58084.09	36302.56
	Carlos RODILES	Sp	70	70	67	71	278	-10	58084.09	36302.56
23	Jean-Francois REMESY	Fr	68	75	68	68	279	-9	52558.11	32848.82
	Maarten LAFEBER	Hol	71	69	72	67	279	-9	52558.11	32848.82
	Ricardo GONZALEZ	Arg	74	69	68	68	279	-9	52558.11	32848.82
26	Stephen LEANEY	Aus	75	71	66	68	280	-8	43716.56	27322.85
	Justin ROSE	Eng	70	71	70	69	280	-8	43716.56	27322.85
	Gary EMERSON	Eng	75	69	68	68	280	-8	43716.56	27322.85
	Paul EALES	Eng	72	67	68	73	280	-8	43716.56	27322.85
	Jonathan LOMAS	Eng	68	75	71	66	280	-8	43716.56	27322.85
	Phillip PRICE	Wal	69	68	73	70	280	-8	43716.56	27322.85
	Greg OWEN	Eng	76	68	70	66	280	-8	43716.56	27322.85
	Andrew COLTART	Scot	73	67	70	70	280	-8	43716.56	27322.85
	Simon DYSON	Eng	71	68	69	72	280	-8	43716.56	27322.85
35	Nick FALDO	Eng	75	68	66	72	281	-7	34875.01	21796.88
	Ian POULTER	Eng	74	73	67	67	281	-7	34875.01	21796.88
	Stephen DODD	Wal	75	71	66	69	281	-7	34875.01	21796.88
	Darren CLARKE	N.Ire	72	72	69	68	281	-7	34875.01	21796.88
	Retief GOOSEN	SA	70	67	73	71	281	-7	34875.01	21796.88
40	Gordon BRAND JNR.	Scot	71	67	72	72	282	-6	27015.85	16884.91
	Warren BENNETT	Eng	78	70	66	68	282	-6	27015.85	16884.91
	Steve ELKINGTON	Aus	73	70	70	69	282	-6	27015.85	16884.91
	Søren KJELDSEN	Den	70	72	70	70	282	-6	27015.85	16884.91
	Joakim HAEGGMAN	Swe	74	69	68	71	282	-6	27015.85	16884.91
	Paul LAWRIE	Scot	74	68	71	69	282	-6	27015.85	16884.91
	James KINGSTON	SA	76	66	72	68	282	-6	27015.85	16884.91
	Niclas FASTH	Swe	71	71	70	70	282	-6	27015.85	16884.91
	Lee WESTWOOD	Eng	76	68	70	68	282	-6	27015.85	16884.91
	Brett RUMFORD	Aus	75	69	68	70	282	-6	27015.85	16884.91
	Barry HUME	Scot	74	67	68	73	282	-6	27015.85	16884.91
51	Richard GREEN	Aus	71	70	70	72	283	-5	19156.70	11972.94
	Paul BROADHURST	Eng	72	68	71	72	283	-5	19156.70	11972.94
	Alan MCLEAN	Scot	76	65	73	69	283	-5	19156.70	11972.94
	Tobias DIER	Ger	75	71	68	69	283	-5	19156.70	11972.94
	Mikko ILONEN	Fin	74	69	71	69	283	-5	19156.70	11972.94
56	Andrew OLDCORN	Scot	73	73	68	70	284	-4	15718.31	9823.94
	Mathias GRÖNBERG	Swe	76	70	68	70	284	-4	15718.31	9823.94
58	David HOWELL	Eng	79	67	67	72	285	-3	13262.33	8288.96
	Raphaël JACQUELIN	Fr	73	71	70	71	285	-3	13262.33	8288.96
	Scott DRUMMOND	Scot	74	68	70	73	285	-3	13262.33	8288.96
	Paul MCGINLEY	Ire	73	72	69	71	285	-3	13262.33	8288.96
	David LYNN	Eng	73	71	67	74	285	-3	13262.33	8288.96
	Gary CLARK	Eng	71	73	66	75	285	-3	13262.33	8288.96
	John BICKERTON	Eng	74	68	71	72	285	-3	13262.33	8288.96
63	Richard S JOHNSON	Swe	71	71	72	72	286	-2	10806.34	6753.96
	Amandeep JOHL	Ind	70	72	72	72	286	-2	10806.34	6753.96
	Jamie DONALDSON	Wal	70	74	70	72	286	-2	10806.34	6753.96
63	Marc FARRY	Fr	71	74	68	74	287	-1	9578.35	5986.47
	Richard LEE	NZ	72	73	67	75	287	-1	9578.35	5986.47
70	Raymond RUSSELL	Scot	70	72	71	75	288	0	8954.12	5596.32
71	Henrik STENSON	Swe	70	70	74	75	289	1	7368.00	4605.00
72	Ernie ELS	SA	72	67	72	W/D	211	-5		

flying the flag

It was only a tiny thing, really, no more than something not being where it should have been. But perhaps in its very incongruity lay the portent to what was to become a momentous victory.

Alex Cejka

Trophée Lancôme

It happened on the second day of the 33rd Trophée Lancôme in the beautiful countryside that borders the gorgeous town of Versailles 20 miles or so west of Paris, and it involved a Czech who had become a German and was now living back in the nation of his birth.

His name was Alex Cejka and he had already made his mark in the tournament on the first day with a 64 that gave him the lead. Now he was part of a three ball that was the first group to leave the tenth tee on the Friday and when he and his partners, David Howell and Miguel Angel Martin, reached the 15th something very odd happened to them.

They all hit decent tee shots on the 438 yard par four but, when they sized up their approach shots, they discovered that a vital piece of furniture was missing from the green. To whit, a flagstick.

There was a hole, but nothing in it. The green was innocent of anything the slightest bit vertical. There was not the faintest glimmering of anything that might, given the right conditions, flutter. No pin meant not knowing where the hole was and not knowing where the hole was meant not knowing where to aim. Consternation reigned and confusion followed not far behind.

Carlos Rodiles

the course

The combined course that is put together for this tournament was in as good a condition as it has ever been in the long history of the event. The fairways were immaculate, the greens were pristine. No wonder people come back to Saint-Nom-la-Bretèche year after year.

It was never established precisely what had happened to the flagstick, but the likeliest explanations were that it had not been put there in the first place (Likely Guilty Party: amnesiac greenkeeper) or that it had been put there but had subsequently been purloined (LGP: kleptomaniac souvenir hunter).

Given that the efficient greenkeeping staff were unlikely to be responsible for such an elementary gaffe, the hunt was immediately launched for an individual creeping around the environs of Saint-Nom-la-Bretèche with a very long pole jammed down his trousers or sticking out of his sunroof. One had to hope that, for his sake, he was not driving a Smart car. You cannot conceal anything longer than a cricket stump in one of those.

A substitute pin having been summoned off the bench at short notice, play continued in more orthodox fashion for the rest of the round. Not one tee box missing, not a single bunker with the sand shovelled out, not the merest hint of a lake with no water. Not as interesting as an errant flagstick perhaps, but definitely a lot more like golf as we know it.

Cejka, not a jot discomfited by the slightly surreal experience, went on to complete a 68 to leave himself two strokes behind Maarten Lafeber, who had his second successive 65 to go into the weekend in pole position.

Bradley Dredge

shot of the week

ALEX CEJKA Germany

Alex Cejka faced defeat for the last time when he cast his tee shot right on the 15th in the final round into trees. With not much to aim for and even less space to hit it through, he penetrated the forest with a masterly stroke which found the back of the green and from where he went on to save his four. It kept his momentum going and, three holes later, he was the Champion.

For Lafeber, it was to be as good as it would get – five over par for the last 36 holes left him in a tie for 13th place. For Cejka, though, things were to become a whole lot better. He had a 72 on a windy third day and, with Lafeber recording a muted 74, the pair went into the final day tied at the head of affairs on nine under par 204.

Thus far Cejka had played cool, efficient golf that was slightly at odds with the devil-may-care insouciance with which he leads his colourful private life. For a man who professes a love of fast cars and even more rapid motorcyles, he was the very model of discretion, making pars when he was forced to and taking just about every birdie chance that came his way.

He had not won on The European Tour International Schedule since 1995 – his fourth year on The European Tour – when he triumphed three times, and the seven year itch was beginning to get under his skin. He wanted to prove the doubters wrong. Gloriously he did so, becoming the victor ludorum with a closing 68 and a total of 272, 12 under par.

The road that Cejka had travelled had been a perilous one, starting when, at the age of nine, he travelled with his father through Yugoslavia, Italy and Switzerland to escape the then oppressive Communist regime before eventually arriving in Munich. He had long regarded Germany as his homeland, but for all that he had moved back to Prague in 1997.

Now life was good and sweet. He had shown that he might have been coming back when he had finished second in the Linde German Masters the previous month. But he had not won for seven years. It was too long, much too long, and he had to do something about it. So he did.

At one stage during the final afternoon ten players were on ten under par. Cejka might have felt that he needed to do something about it but, in the event, he did not have to. Several of them took a short, sweet dart at him but he remained massively calm throughout.

With others faltering, Cejka birdied the tenth and even survived a scare at the 15th where he struck his drive way to starboard and into trees. A fortuitous gap and a brave shot through it enabled him to salvage his par.

Suitably encouraged, he birdied the next to take a two stroke lead into the final two holes. Immaculately and safely, he had pars on both to clinch his victory.

Suddenly, that missing pin on the second day assumed its rightful, irrelevant place in the world that Cejka now inhabited again. Right now, the drums were beating and the flag was flying. Right now, that would do very nicely.

Mel Webb

Paul Eales

final results

Saint-Nom-la-Bretèche • Paris • France
October 10-13 • 2002 • Par 71 • 6903 yards • 6311 metres

Pos.	Name		Rd1	Rd2	Rd3	Rd4	Total	Par	Prize Money Euro	£
1	Alex CEJKA	Ger	64	68	72	68	272	-12	239640.00	150000.00
2	Carlos RODILES	Sp	67	69	72	66	274	-10	159760.00	100000.00
3	Jean-François LUCQUIN	Fr	69	72	68	66	275	-9	80950.39	50670.00
	Angel CABRERA	Arg	69	68	71	67	275	-9	80950.39	50670.00
5	Gordon BRAND JNR.	Scot	68	69	70	69	276	-8	37815.19	23670.00
	Sergio GARCIA	Sp	67	70	70	69	276	-8	37815.19	23670.00
	Ian POULTER	Eng	68	71	70	67	276	-8	37815.19	23670.00
	Steen TINNING	Den	70	70	67	69	276	-8	37815.19	23670.00
	Thomas LEVET	Fr	67	69	73	67	276	-8	37815.19	23670.00
	Paul EALES	Eng	68	69	69	70	276	-8	37815.19	23670.00
	Robert KARLSSON	Swe	68	69	69	70	276	-8	37815.19	23670.00
	Bradley DREDGE	Wal	68	67	70	71	276	-8	37815.19	23670.00
13	Ian WOOSNAM	Wal	70	70	65	72	277	-7	19950.03	12487.50
	Greg TURNER	NZ	70	68	67	72	277	-7	19950.03	12487.50
	Maarten LAFEBER	Hol	65	65	74	73	277	-7	19950.03	12487.50
	Jonathan LOMAS	Eng	68	69	70	70	277	-7	19950.03	12487.50
	Ian GARBUTT	Eng	68	69	68	72	277	-7	19950.03	12487.50
	Mark PILKINGTON	Wal	70	71	74	62	277	-7	19950.03	12487.50
	Simon DYSON	Eng	68	70	67	72	277	-7	19950.03	12487.50
	Paul CASEY	Eng	68	71	67	71	277	-7	19950.03	12487.50
21	Jean-François REMESY	Fr	70	69	69	70	278	-6	16463.27	10305.00
	Joakim HAEGGMAN	Swe	69	67	73	69	278	-6	16463.27	10305.00
23	Eduardo ROMERO	Arg	70	70	70	69	279	-5	14953.54	9360.00
	Anders HANSEN	Den	71	70	71	67	279	-5	14953.54	9360.00
	Jean HUGO	SA	70	70	70	69	279	-5	14953.54	9360.00
	Mathias GRÖNBERG	Swe	66	73	68	72	279	-5	14953.54	9360.00
	Ricardo GONZALEZ	Arg	70	65	77	67	279	-5	14953.54	9360.00
28	Søren KJELDSEN	Den	70	67	72	71	280	-4	12796.78	8010.00
	Trevor IMMELMAN	SA	74	66	69	71	280	-4	12796.78	8010.00
	Chris GANE	Eng	70	68	71	71	280	-4	12796.78	8010.00
	Fredrik JACOBSON	Swe	65	77	71	67	280	-4	12796.78	8010.00
	Dean ROBERTSON	Scot	65	72	72	71	280	-4	12796.78	8010.00
33	Nick FALDO	Eng	65	74	68	74	281	-3	10812.56	6768.00
	Marc FARRY	Fr	71	69	73	68	281	-3	10812.56	6768.00
	Colin MONTGOMERIE	Scot	69	71	72	69	281	-3	10812.56	6768.00
	Gary ORR	Scot	69	69	74	69	281	-3	10812.56	6768.00
	Patrik SJÖLAND	Swe	71	70	68	72	281	-3	10812.56	6768.00
38	Des SMYTH	Ire	70	68	73	71	282	-2	9058.39	5670.00
	Steve WEBSTER	Eng	66	70	70	76	282	-2	9058.39	5670.00
	Gary EMERSON	Eng	71	70	72	69	282	-2	9058.39	5670.00
	Miles TUNNICLIFF	Eng	70	67	71	74	282	-2	9058.39	5670.00
	Paul MCGINLEY	Ire	67	69	76	70	282	-2	9058.39	5670.00
	Andrew COLTART	Scot	74	66	72	70	282	-2	9058.39	5670.00
	Lucas PARSONS	Aus	70	69	73	70	282	-2	9058.39	5670.00
45	Mark ROE	Eng	68	72	73	70	283	-1	7620.55	4770.00
	Peter HANSON	Swe	69	70	71	73	283	-1	7620.55	4770.00
	David CARTER	Eng	71	66	75	71	283	-1	7620.55	4770.00
48	Sam TORRANCE	Scot	72	68	71	73	284	0	6757.85	4230.00
	David LYNN	Eng	68	71	74	71	284	0	6757.85	4230.00
	Markus BRIER	Aut	68	73	73	70	284	0	6757.85	4230.00
51	Sandy LYLE	Scot	70	71	76	68	285	1	5751.36	3600.00
	Warren BENNETT	Eng	69	70	73	73	285	1	5751.36	3600.00
	Brian DAVIS	Eng	69	74	70	72	285	1	5751.36	3600.00
	Richard S JOHNSON	Swe	65	73	71	76	285	1	5751.36	3600.00
55	Darren RICHARDT	SA	70	69	72	75	286	2	4744.87	2970.00
	Daren LEE	Eng	67	73	75	71	286	2	4744.87	2970.00
	Christopher HANELL	Swe	73	70	71	72	286	2	4744.87	2970.00
58	David GILFORD	Eng	74	69	74	70	287	3	3954.06	2475.00
	Tom GILLIS	USA	65	74	75	73	287	3	3954.06	2475.00
	Paul BROADHURST	Eng	71	72	69	75	287	3	3954.06	2475.00
	Gregory HAVRET	Fr	68	75	73	71	287	3	3954.06	2475.00
	Gary CLARK	Eng	71	69	74	73	287	3	3954.06	2475.00
	John BICKERTON	Eng	70	71	75	71	287	3	3954.06	2475.00
64	François ILLOUZ (AM)	Fr	71	68	72	77	288	4		
	Andrew MARSHALL	Eng	68	74	75	71	288	4	3378.92	2115.00
	Roger WESSELS	SA	70	72	73	73	288	4	3378.92	2115.00
67	Graeme MCDOWELL	N.Ire	71	69	78	71	289	5	3163.25	1980.00
68	Justin ROSE	Eng	70	73	73	74	290	6	2947.57	1845.00
	Greg OWEN	Eng	67	74	72	77	290	6	2947.57	1845.00
70	Richard BLAND	Eng	70	70	75	76	291	7	2502.99	1566.72
	Stephen SCAHILL	NZ	66	77	76	72	291	7	2502.99	1566.72
	Raymond RUSSELL	Scot	70	70	75	76	291	7	2502.99	1566.72
	Philippe LIMA (AM)	Fr	70	73	70	78	291	7		
74	Nick O'HERN	Aus	76	67	75	75	293	9	2154.00	1348.27
75	Christian CÉVAÉR	Fr	74	69	76	75	294	10	2151.00	1346.39
76	Philip GOLDING	Eng	72	71	76	76	295	11	2148.00	1344.52
77	Henrik BJORNSTAD	Nor	72	69	81	76	298	14	2145.00	1342.64
78	Thomas BJÖRN	Den	69	73	81	WD	223	10		

Cisco World Match Play Championship Wentworth Club · Surrey · England

something to savour

Champion – Ernie ELS SA

Runner-Up – Sergio GARCIA Sp

Ernie Els

What do you give the man who has everything? Even before the Cisco World Match Play Championship, Ernie Els made the short trip from his Wentworth home to the first tee of the famous West Course and admitted that 2002 had been "the perfect year."

In July, he had claimed the 131st Open Golf Championship at Muirfield and the day before events began at Wentworth Club, he had celebrated his 33rd birthday with wife Liezl, daughter Samantha, and their new baby son Ben, who had been born the week before.

However, the best was about to get even better for the contented South African and there was almost an air of quiet inevitability about the outcome - despite the high quality of opposition he faced in an elite 12 man field which boasted five Major Champions and five of the current top ten in the Official World Golf Ranking.

There may have been no British winner like last year when Ian Woosnam beat Padraig Harrington, but when Els defeated Sergio Garcia, at 22 the youngest finalist in the history of the event, 2 and 1 after a fascinating duel, the crowds were still able to acclaim a 'home' Champion.

When it was all over and Els had the massive silver trophy in his hands he was able to reflect on a fourth Cisco World Match Play Championship crown to follow his hat-trick of titles from 1994 to 1996. One more victory will enable him to equal the record of five World Match Play Championship titles set by Gary Player (1965, 1966, 1968, 1971, 1973) and matched by Severiano Ballesteros (1981, 1982, 1984, 1985, 1991).

Colin Montgomerie

Els had also become the seventh player in the history of the Championship to win the Open Golf Championship and this unique prize in the same year - following in the footsteps of Gary Player (1968), Jack Nicklaus (1970), Seve Ballesteros (1984), Greg Norman (1986), Nick Faldo (1992) and Mark O'Meara (1998). He said: "I have a great family and have always been very happy here at Wentworth. It is nice to have a good club to look after you. It means even more to win this Championship now we have lived here for four years.

"It's eight years since I won this for the first time but at times out there it felt like it was yesterday. When I won three in a row it seemed easy, but after I lost to Vijay Singh in the 1997 final I found it much harder to make an impression again. It really hurt losing to Lee Westwood in the semi-final two years ago, but right from the start of this week I felt great."

Being seeded number two, Els was given the luxury of avoiding the rigours of the first round and, when he gazed at the exertions put in by some players, especially Michael Campbell and Nick Faldo, he must have been mightily relieved.

The tee shot on the 17th hole of the West Course is recognised as one of the toughest in golf in any circumstance but to face it cold at 8.15am with an entire match resting on the outcome, made it all the more examining, not to mention crucial, for Campbell and Faldo.

They had to face the dawn patrol after their epic nine-hour encounter on the opening day had to be halted at the sixth extra hole when fast fading light made it impossible to continue. By then they had already gone two holes beyond the record for the longest match of the 384 contests played in the 39 year history of the event.

Only three matches: Darren Clarke v Nick Faldo in 2000; Isao Aoki v Severiano Ballesteros in 1979, and the 1973 final between Graham Marsh and Gary Player had previously gone as far as 40 holes. The end, however, was quick with Faldo, who had been three down at lunch and two down with three to play, unable to match Campbell's birdie at what was in all their 43rd hole.

In the other matches which did finish on schedule on day one, Colin Montgomerie set up an enthralling second round encounter against Els by outgunning American Fred Funk 3 and 2. The Scot, who was never behind in the 82 holes he played against the United States in The 34th Ryder Cup Matches at The De Vere Belfry, was one down after two against the 46 year old from Florida, but superior overall play from tee to green finally settled the issue.

the course

After a tinder-dry September, with just one wet day in 30, the West Course was doused by two inches of rain in the five days preceding the Championship. Even so, new Champion Ernie Els led a chorus of approval for Chris Kennedy, Graham Matheson and the greenkeeping team, declaring: "It seems whenever the weather does its worst, Chris and the lads just keep getting it better."

Harrington, another of Europe's Ryder Cup stars, was, by his own admission, not in top form, but it was still enough to see him come from two holes down after ten to complete a convincing 4 and 3 win over Canadian left hander Mike Weir.

And Justin Rose, who most observers believe will be a Ryder Cup golfer of the future, put on a valiant show in his Cisco World Match Play Championship debut against the 1997 Champion Vijay Singh, fighting back from three down to take the match to the 36th hole much to the delight of the spectators.

After Campbell and Faldo had provided the entrée, the main course on the second day was served against a dull and damp background. The match between Els and Montgomerie was always destined to produce golf of the highest calibre. It did not stray from that course. Montgomerie was round in 65 in the morning, gathering no fewer than ten birdies, but whereas he might have been enjoying lunch with a healthy lead instead he found himself four down.

Els went round in approximately 60 shots – a record for the tournament – and had a putt for a 59. "I don't know what it is but Monty just seems to bring out the best in me," admitted Els. "I wanted to tell him that at the end, but I did not think it was the right moment. To be 12 under par against one of the best players in the world was a great feeling."

Els, who eventually won 6 and 5, was not the only player knee deep in red figures in the morning round with the eclectic score for the eight players being an almost unbelievable 51 (21 under par) as they collected no fewer than five eagles and 53 birdies.

Campbell followed his marathon with Faldo by coming out strongly to overcome the defending Champion and Number One seed Ian Woosnam 3 and 2. Campbell was two up at lunch after shooting a 66 and though the Welshman hit back to take the lead briefly with three successive birdies early in the afternoon, the New Zealander finished the stronger to end the match on the 16th green. Campbell said: "Two older statesmen in one day – that's not bad is it?"

Fourth seed Garcia showed tremendous fighting spirit to defeat Harrington, who was three up after just four holes and held a commanding four hole lead after the 16th. Garcia had cut the deficit to two by lunch, helped by an out of bounds drive from the Irishman at the 17th, and he slowly took control in the afternoon.

When Harrington again hooked out of bounds at the 17th (their 35th hole) it was all over with the Spaniard winning 2 and 1. The first round action was completed when Singh got the better of the 2001 European Number One and the Number Three seed Retief Goosen 4 and 3.

The semi-finals were played on one of those gorgeously crisp English autumn days that you wish you could bottle. For the dazzling greens and yellows of Augusta National's Magnolia Drive, read the glowing russets and golds of Surrey's Wentworth Club. Once more Garcia found himself behind, this time against the impressive Campbell, but once more he fought back to win.

Campbell, three up after six holes, remained in control until he lost holes by dropping shots at the 30th and 31st. This was a match which produced not only honest golf but also good humour with the two golfers sharing jokes and applauding each other. Indeed at the 17th (35th) Campbell could only applaud as Garcia, now with the advantage, chipped in from 30 yards with his opponent on the green. "I was just hoping to get a four," said Garcia. Campbell responded: "It was fun. We had a great time."

Els, ruthless and relentless, ground out a 3 and 2 victory over Singh to go some way to erasing the memory of that defeat by the Fijian in 1997, and to earn a place in the final.

There was much consternation that the final might not take place at all, such were the gloomy forecasts of gales and storms, but thankfully all that transpired was light rain and a raw wind. This was a match that conjured up the delicious thought of contrasting styles and personalities producing something to truly savour at the end of another memorable Championship. It did not disappoint.

shot of the week

SERGIO GARCIA Spain

Wentworth Club has witnessed some incredible shots by the Spanish maestro Severiano Ballesteros over the years, but even he would have been proud of the escape act performed by his compatriot Sergio Garcia in the semi-final. Completely blocked out by trees on the right of the 18th fairway, Garcia somehow conjured a three wood recovery that bent some 40 yards left to right on its 230 yard journey, to finish 18 feet from the pin and ensured he squared matters with Michael Campbell at lunch. "My shot at Medinah in the 1999 US PGA Championship remains my favourite, but this one has to be in my top three," he said.

Els is as laid back as they come on a golf course; Garcia is a bundle of energy. Els, at 6 feet 3 inches, not only towered over the baby-faced Garcia (5 foot 10 inches) but in a sense it did appear that he was playing his younger brother.

Els has played the West Course more than 300 times and it was inevitable that he would sweep ahead. The fact is he played 104 holes in the course of the entire event and was never behind at any stage. Garcia had come from behind against first Harrington and then Campbell, and he would need to do so again. Els, five up after an eagle at the 12th and despite a Garcia eagle at the fourth, was coasting but Garcia did lunch only three down.

Cisco World Match Play Championship

Back row: (left to right) Mike Weir, Sergio Garcia, Retief Goosen, Vijay Singh, Nick Faldo, Justin Rose, Padraig Harrington, Michael Campbell, Fred Funk.
Front row: Colin Montgomerie, Robert Lloyd, President-EMEA Operations, Senior Vice President-Cisco Systems Inc., Ian Woosnam, Mark H McCormack, Chairman and CEO of the International Management Group and Founder of the World Match Play Championship, and Ernie Els

Garcia began the afternoon with a rare birdie at the first and after another at the sixth (24th), by which time Els had remarkably gone twelve holes without winning one, the deficit was just one. Els, of course, won the next, but Garcia immediately hit back. Els, however, won the ninth and then the tenth (28th), with a long birdie putt, to go three up again. Yet Garcia contrived to reduce his deficit to one again by winning successive holes.

It was, however, all to no avail for Els eventually secured another chance to celebrate in what many now call his own backyard. "It was great fun but Ernie played the best today," said Garcia. Els just shrugged his shoulders, smiled as only he can, sipped something cold then sauntered off on his way back to Liezl, Samantha and new born Ben. "What more can you ask for in one year?" he said.

John Whitbread

Cisco World Match Play Championship
Wentworth Club • Surrey • England
October 17-20 • 2002 • Par 72 • 7072 yards • 6468 metres

		euro	£
FIRST ROUND			
(8) Michael Campbell (NZ) beat Nick Faldo (Eng)	at 43rd	79,181	50,000
(5) Padraig Harrington (Ire) beat Mike Weir (Can)	4 & 3	79,181	50,000
(6) Vijay Singh (Fiji) beat Justin Rose (Eng)	1 hole	79,181	50,000
(7) Colin Montgomerie (Scot) beat Fred Funk (USA)	3 & 2	79,181	50,000
QUARTER-FINALS			
Michael Campbell beat (1) Ian Woosnam (Wal)	3 & 2	102,935	65,000
(4) Sergio Garcia (Sp) beat Padraig Harrington	2 & 1	102,935	65,000
Vijay Singh beat (3) Retief Goosen (SA)	4 & 3	102,935	65,000
(2) Ernie Els (SA) beat Colin Montgomerie	6 & 5	102,935	65,000
SEMI-FINALS			
Sergio Garcia beat Michael Campbell	2 & 1	134,608	85,000
Ernie Els beat Vijay Singh	3 & 2	134,608	85,000
FINAL			
Ernie Els beat Sergio Garcia	2 & 1	395,907	250,000
		190,035	120,000
Figures in brackets indicate seeding	Total:	1,583,630	1,000,000

WENTWORTH, WHERE ELS?

WENTWORTH CLUB, WENTWORTH DRIVE, VIRGINIA WATER, SURREY GU25 4LS
WWW.WENTWORTHCLUB.COM

Telefonica Open de Madrid Club de Campo · Madrid · Spain

danish delight

Steen Tinning

The leaves were already falling in Spain's capital when one of the most exciting events of the year – the Telefonica Open de Madrid – showed once again that European Tour titles can be won by players in the autumn of their playing careers.

Sam Torrance and Des Smyth will be playing seniors golf in 2003, and they might well have won at Club de Campo at the ripe old age of 49, but on this occasion it was a player nine years their junior who claimed this famous title.

Steen Tinning is the elder-statesmen of Danish professional golf. With Anders Sørensen, now a respected teacher of the game nationally, Tinning paved the way for compatriots like Thomas Björn and, indeed, Anders Hansen and Søren Hansen, on The European Tour.

He had turned professional in 1985 after representing his country in the Eisenhower Trophy. For many years Sørensen and Tinning were partners in the World Cup of Golf and, after Björn had become the first Danish golfer to win on The European Tour and earn Ryder Cup honours, Tinning enjoyed his own moment of glory when he won The Celtic Manor Resort Wales Open in 2000.

Brian Davis

Jean-Francois Remesy

This was an outstanding achievement against a background of accidents which threatened on one occasion to take his life. He can still remember the time, date and place – "11pm, Friday, March 30, 1990, near Freiburg in southern Germany" – when both he and his wife, Anne, were lucky to escape with their lives after a multiple car crash in Germany. He was to be out of action for 18 months which, perhaps, was not surprising since his right arm had been left dangling by skin and muscle alone.

Then came a shock practice range accident in 1999 when an amateur's wayward shot crushed his thumb. So to the wear and tear, caused by hitting thousands of balls on the range, that left Tinning with the legacy of crippling lower-back pain. He was compelled to spend much of his time in physiotherapy, rather than honing his game on the range, and by the time he came to the BMW International Open in 2001 had confessed to his wife that he was ready to call it a day.

"I didn't say goodbye to people but in my mind I was finished," he said. "My back was giving me so many problems just to get to the first tee. I was in the physio unit two or three times a day; I was just hurting and hurting."

A three birdie finish in Munich, however, gave him new hope. So he embarked on a five months fitness routine which included repetitive and monotonous back exercises.

By his own admission he was not setting the world on fire. Nevertheless considering what he had been through he was reasonably content as he arrived in Madrid for the tournament which was starting 17 days after he had celebrated his 40th birthday. Then the hours, days, weeks, months that he had dedicated to being fit for action, were rewarded when on the Saturday afternoon he powered into contention with a quite magnificent round of 62. It lifted him alongside Adam Scott, and only one behind third round leader Padraig Harrington, and, more importantly, gave him the belief that he could win again on Tour.

This, of course, would be quite something in a year when no fewer then three of his compatriots – Thomas Björn (BMW International Open), Anders Hansen (Volvo PGA Championship) and Søren Hansen (Murphy's Irish Open) – had all won. It would also require something special for that victory to be secured because, as autumn turned to summer that Sunday afternoon in Madrid, so the lead changed an amazing 26 times under the hot sun.

the course

Club de Campo is one of Spain's most revered golfing venues. The first of its eight Spanish Opens was quite an occasion in 1957 when the 1951 Open Champion Max Faulkner won. It was here that José Maria Cañizares, Antonio Garrido and Manuel Piñero, among others, attended the country's famous caddie school - learning the 'three Rs' as well as the rudiments of the Royal and Ancient game.

Scotland's Andrew Coltart and England's Brian Davis were the first to reach 18 under par and, as they waited in the clubhouse, so their rivals sought to overhaul them. Scott was the favourite to do so until the 17th when he took three to get down from a greenside bunker whereas Tinning holed from 25 feet for a birdie two. So Tinning was ahead and he played the final hole in the manner of a true Champion.

The Telefonica Open de Madrid had provided a collection of topics throughout the week. First there was sadness at Club de Campo, when Seve Ballesteros, one of the greatest swashbucklers to grace its fairways, had to pull out of the event due to the death of his 83 year old mother Carmen Sota. She died in her sleep at her home in Pedrena, 16 years after the death of her husband Baldomero, with whom she had four golf professional sons - Baldomero, Manuel, Vicente and Severiano.

Then there was anticipation, with the Volvo Order of Merit leader and defending Champion Retief Goosen trying to hold off Harrington, no more than £33,000 adrift of top place. In the first round, Harrington finished only one stroke adrift of the leader Lee Westwood, another man in rehabilitation who carded a faultless

shot of the week

STEEN TINNING Denmark

Danes were always in the news. Søren Hansen holed in one at the 210 yard 11th with a six iron but missed out on the $10,000 'Heavenly Bed' on offer at the ninth. But Steen Tinning's 25 footer on the 17th in the final round proved a heavenly putt that won the tournament. "A perfect read, with the speed just right," said the Champion.

seven under par 64. Sharing second place was newly-married Davis, who brought his wife Julie, daughter of England goalkeeping legend Ray Clemence, to Madrid for their honeymoon. Dutchman Maarten Lafeber was also one stroke off the lead, trying to put right what went wrong for him in the Trophée Lancôme. Lafeber returned to the course on Saturday morning, because of Friday's fog delay, and found the two birdies in his remaining three holes that earned him a one shot second round lead. Smyth after a blistering 63, was in the thick of things, as was Torrance, free of Ryder Cup pressures.

Harrington took over in the third round, finding two late birdies in a four shot swing on top of the leaderboard when Scott threw in two late bogeys. With Goosen five behind, it looked like two wins in three years in Madrid for Harrington and a change in Europe's Volvo Order of Merit. This was not to be the case and Goosen eventually tied seventh with Harrington so there was no change at the top.

Then to the final chapter. Davis had narrowly failed to make a bunker shot for a birdie at the last; Coltart, however, had rammed in a birdie putt. So the pair were level and they waited. For Steen Tinning, however, the wait was over for, as he celebrated on the 18th green, so the affable Dane knew that he had proudly hoisted that famous red and white flag high into the sky for a record fourth time on The 2002 European Tour International Schedule.

Norman Dabell

Mårten Olander

final results

Club de Campo · Madrid · Spain
October 24-27 · 2002 · Par 71 · 6967 yards · 6371 metres

Pos.	Name		Rd1	Rd2	Rd3	Rd4	Total	Par	Prize Money Euro	£
1	Steen TINNING	Den	68	68	62	67	265	-19	233330.00	146507.93
2	Brian DAVIS	Eng	65	72	66	63	266	-18	104396.70	65550.70
	Andrew COLTART	Scot	66	68	68	64	266	-18	104396.70	65550.70
	Adam SCOTT	Aus	67	65	66	68	266	-18	104396.70	65550.70
5	Bradley DREDGE	Wal	71	65	67	64	267	-17	59360.00	37272.15
6	Paul LAWRIE	Scot	70	64	69	65	268	-16	49000.00	30767.11
7	Padraig HARRINGTON	Ire	65	66	66	72	269	-15	36120.00	22679.75
	Trevor IMMELMAN	SA	66	65	68	70	269	-15	36120.00	22679.75
	Retief GOOSEN	SA	66	69	67	67	269	-15	36120.00	22679.75
10	Des SMYTH	Ire	69	63	69	69	270	-14	25946.67	16291.92
	Jean-Francois REMESY	Fr	70	66	65	69	270	-14	25946.67	16291.92
	Søren KJELDSEN	Den	69	68	65	68	270	-14	25946.67	16291.92
13	Maarten LAFEBER	NL	65	65	72	69	271	-13	22540.00	14152.87
14	Santiago LUNA	Sp	69	67	68	68	272	-12	20160.00	12658.47
	Anders HANSEN	Den	68	67	69	68	272	-12	20160.00	12658.47
	Nick O'HERN	Aus	66	70	65	71	272	-12	20160.00	12658.47
	Lee WESTWOOD	Eng	64	70	66	72	272	-12	20160.00	12658.47
18	David HOWELL	Eng	72	68	68	65	273	-11	16380.00	10285.00
	Mårten OLANDER	Swe	67	66	70	70	273	-11	16380.00	10285.00
	Ian POULTER	Eng	70	69	67	67	273	-11	16380.00	10285.00
	Miguel Angel JIMÉNEZ	Sp	70	69	67	67	273	-11	16380.00	10285.00
	Miles TUNNICLIFF	Eng	70	63	70	70	273	-11	16380.00	10285.00
	Markus BRIER	Aut	66	69	69	69	273	-11	16380.00	10285.00
	Paul CASEY	Eng	70	65	67	71	273	-11	16380.00	10285.00
25	Andrew OLDCORN	Scot	69	71	66	68	274	-10	14140.00	8878.51
	Sam TORRANCE	Scot	67	66	71	70	274	-10	14140.00	8878.51
	Mark FOSTER	Eng	74	67	65	68	274	-10	14140.00	8878.51
28	David GILFORD	Eng	72	68	71	64	275	-9	12460.00	7823.64
	Darren FICHARDT	SA	70	72	65	68	275	-9	12460.00	7823.64
	Ignacio GARRIDO	Sp	71	66	69	69	275	-9	12460.00	7823.64
	John BICKERTON	Eng	71	73	68	69	275	-9	12460.00	7823.64
	Jamie DONALDSON	Wal	69	68	69	69	275	-9	12460.00	7823.64
33	Steve WEBSTER	Eng	70	68	66	72	276	-8	10675.00	6702.83
	Jorge BERENDT	Arg	68	73	70	65	276	-8	10675.00	6702.83
	Tomas Jesus MUÑOZ	Sp	68	69	70	69	276	-8	10675.00	6702.83
	Fredrik JACOBSON	Swe	68	66	69	73	276	-8	10675.00	6702.83
37	Miguel Angel MARTIN	Sp	69	66	68	74	277	-7	9240.00	5801.80
	José Manuel CARRILES	Sp	69	68	70	70	277	-7	9240.00	5801.80
	Anthony WALL	Eng	69	67	70	71	277	-7	9240.00	5801.80

Pos.	Name		Rd1	Rd2	Rd3	Rd4	Total	Par	Prize Money Euro	£
	Joakim HAEGGMAN	Swe	72	67	70	68	277	-7	9240.00	5801.80
	Rolf MUNTZ	NL	71	67	69	70	277	-7	9240.00	5801.80
	Stephen SCAHILL	NZ	66	72	69	70	277	-7	9240.00	5801.80
43	Roger CHAPMAN	Eng	67	70	67	74	278	-6	7420.00	4659.02
	Mark MOULAND	Wal	69	70	70	69	278	-6	7420.00	4659.02
	Søren HANSEN	Den	69	73	68	68	278	-6	7420.00	4659.02
	Diego BORREGO	Sp	67	70	70	71	278	-6	7420.00	4659.02
	Gary ORR	Scot	68	68	69	73	278	-6	7420.00	4659.02
	Patrik SJÖLAND	Swe	67	70	71	70	278	-6	7420.00	4659.02
	Brett RUMFORD	Aus	72	70	68	68	278	-6	7420.00	4659.02
50	Robert-Jan DERKSEN	NL	70	68	70	71	279	-5	5880.00	3692.05
	Warren BENNETT	Eng	70	68	69	72	279	-5	5880.00	3692.05
	Chris GANE	Eng	71	69	69	70	279	-5	5880.00	3692.05
	Ian GARBUTT	Eng	73	67	69	70	279	-5	5880.00	3692.05
54	Daren LEE	Eng	73	69	69	69	280	-4	4648.00	2918.48
	Henrik NYSTROM	Swe	68	72	71	69	280	-4	4648.00	2918.48
	Stephen GALLACHER	Scot	72	70	70	68	280	-4	4648.00	2918.48
	Christopher HANELL	Swe	67	71	71	71	280	-4	4648.00	2918.48
	Simon DYSON	Eng	69	70	74	67	280	-4	4648.00	2918.48
59	Grant HAMERTON	Eng	70	72	68	71	281	-3	3990.00	2505.32
	Lucas PARSONS	Aus	70	72	72	67	281	-3	3990.00	2505.32
61	Mark JAMES	Eng	71	67	73	71	282	-2	3290.00	2065.79
	Peter FOWLER	Aus	71	71	72	68	282	-2	3290.00	2065.79
	Alvaro SALTO	Sp	71	66	70	75	282	-2	3290.00	2065.79
	Paul EALES	Eng	72	70	68	72	282	-2	3290.00	2065.79
	Johan RYSTRÖM	Swe	71	69	69	73	282	-2	3290.00	2065.79
	Stephen DODD	Wal	71	69	73	69	282	-2	3290.00	2065.79
	Gary EVANS	Eng	69	72	70	71	282	-2	3290.00	2065.79
	Carlos BALMASEDA	Sp	67	72	70	73	282	-2	3290.00	2065.79
69	Raphaël JACQUELIN	Fr	70	70	73	70	283	-1	2440.00	1532.08
	Henrik STENSON	Swe	69	68	76	70	283	-1	2440.00	1532.08
	Sebastien DELAGRANGE	Fr	74	66	70	73	283	-1	2440.00	1532.08
72	Malcolm MACKENZIE	Eng	69	73	73	69	284	0	2095.50	1315.76
	José RIVERO	Sp	68	73	69	74	284	0	2095.50	1315.76
74	Carlos RODILES	Sp	76	65	77	67	285	1	2091.00	1312.94
75	Gordon BRAND JNR.	Scot	69	72	74	71	286	2	2088.00	1311.06
76	Greg OWEN	Eng	70	72	75	73	290	6	2085.00	1309.17
77	Gregory HAVRET	Fr	73	69	72	80	294	10	2082.00	1307.29
78	Olle KARLSSON	Swe	71	71	77	77	296	12	2079.00	1305.40

Bahiá Del Velerín

Location, value for money and quality, are our key requirements when selecting the best homes for our clients. **Resort Properties** offer you a complete professional service, headed by our UK qualified Surveyor to ensure your dream of owning a home in Spain becomes an enjoyable reality.

We specialize in offering fabulous new Homes direct from the Developer-Builder. Your home will be fully guaranteed and finished to the latest building specifications.

Bahiá Del Velerín... the ocean in your garden

The development is located on the seashore facing one of the finest beaches on the Costa del Sol, with spectacular views of the Mediterranean, Gibraltar and North Africa. Top quality specifications, underfloor heating in all bathrooms with Italian Travertino marble from floor to ceiling, ensuite bathrooms in master suites with separate shower and jacuzzi, double glazing with specially treated wooden window frames, electric blinds on all windows, air conditioning, fireplace, pre-installation of Bang & Olufsen audio-visual equipment and installation of LUTRON lighting system, fully fitted and equipped kitchen as well as top quality and exclusive installations and details throughout the whole apartment all combine to make *Bahía Del Velerín* leader in a supremely comfortable lifestyle.

Aloha Park... the natural place to live

Designed to enhace the relationship between environment and lifestyles, *Aloha Park* is a stunning new development of only 54 apartments and penthouses situated in the heart of Nueva Andalucia's Golf Valley. Aimed at the discerning client, all apartments and penthouses are generous in space, and garden apartments include private splash pools while others feature terrace jacuzzis. Underfloor heating, hydromassage baths and a home automation system are just some of the special features which will make *Aloha Park* the natural choice.

For more information

RESORT PROPERTIES
*Fellow of The Architecture and Surveying Institute
Membership No. G000689/6473

Head Office : Real Golf de Bendinat - Mallorca - Spain
Tel. 00 34 971 70 19 00 - Fax. 00 34 971 40 15 90
johngraham@telefonica.net

Canyamel Golf Course, Mallorca, Spain

RMP Golf Services offer you one of the most efficient, hassle free and best golf services available, for Spain and Portugal. The most popular Golf destinations in Europe. With over 10 years experience our highly trained staff provide you with a fast service designed to get you onto the golf course of your choice.

Being one of the biggest golf service company in Europe we have preferential booking times throughout the year. This is a real bonus for our golfers when you consider demand exceeds supply at certains times of the year in many areas. That is why year after year Golfers return to use our services, they have tried the rest and now always enjoy a first class professional service.

You can telephone, fax or email your requirement or go on line and visit our web site www.golfservices.org
Sit back and we will do the rest.

Our Golf Services are used by Top UK Touroperators and Corporate Events companies, they want a professional service, at no extra cost, that s easy as we do not charge you for our services. So when you book your next golf break in Spain or Portugal tee off with us .

RMP Golf Services Pre-bookable Tee Off Times at no extra cost.

GOLF SERVICES ◀

Mallorca · Ibiza · Costa Blanca · Costa del Sol · Costa Brava · Costa Dorada · Algarve · Madeira · Lisboa · Canaries

Pre-book your guaranteed tee off times
Tel: +34 971 703 070 - 402 907 - Fax: +34 971 401 590
E-mail: golfservices@telefonica.net
Internet: www.golfservices.org
Office hours: 09.30 - 19.00 Mon. to Fri. - 09.30 - 14.00 Sat.

59th Italian Open Telecom Italia · Olgiata Golf Club · Rome · Italy

eternal pleasure

Ian Poulter

Dante would have loved it. The scene came direct from the seventh circle of hell in the inferno that was the second day of the 59th Italian Open Telecom Italia, with thunder rattling the bones of Rome and lightning sending millions of volts crashing to earth.

Rome and its outer suburbs were under attack from above in more ways than one in the latter part of October. To their credit, everybody at Olgiata Golf Club, from cleaning lady to course manager to secretary to generalissimo, or whatever they call the head honcho in Italy, did The European Tour proud.

True, the tournament had to be reduced to three rounds after the second day's play was lost because of lightning and occasional heavy rain. It was, put simply, just impossible, and Miguel Vidaor, the Tournament Director, acted commendably swiftly in sending everybody back to their billets when it became obvious that the infernal thunder and lightning was just not going away.

It was a tribute to an immensely successful return to the Italian mainland after two happy years at Is Molas in Sardinia that the second day disruption was accepted with good humour by the players in this 59th Italian Open Telecom Italia. Nobody wants a

couple of squillion volts up their lob-wedge at any time and particularly not in the middle of a tournament that could have and, in some cases, did have a dramatic effect on the immediate future of some of its competitors.

For a start, Padraig Harrington had abandoned his plans to have a few days off with Caroline, his wife, in the Costa del Sol so that he could continue his campaign for what he hoped would be the first of many Volvo Order of Merit victories. Retief Goosen, at the time the only man on The European Tour to head the personable Dubliner in earnings, was away for the week, and Harrington reasoned that Goosen's absence provided him with a perfect chance to close the gap between them in the top two places in the Volvo Order of Merit. The permutations were endless: suffice to say that in finishing in a tie for sixth place, Harrington got nearer to his South African pal by a margin big enough to have made it worthwhile abandoning the sun and jousting with the meteorological nasties that came to call on the second day.

At the other end of The European Tour food-chain, the two most grateful recipients of the breaks they needed were Paul Eales and Gary Emerson, who both earned enough of the folding stuff to ensure their places on The European Tour in 2003.

Marc Farry

the course

Olgiata Golf Club, the design of the great C K Cotton, is a gently undulating lay-out that achieves the aim of any first class golf course in that it rewards good golf and punishes anything that is the slightest bit loose. In spite of the awful weather, it stood up to the challenge of The European Tour with head held high.

Important though that was to both men, however, the most meaningful action centred upon Ian Poulter, who had quite a week on the outskirts of the Eternal City. He had a round on the first day that went within two strokes of becoming the first 59 recorded on The European Tour International Schedule, failing only because he missed makeable birdie putts on the last two holes, followed it with a hole in one in the delayed second round, then survived a wobble in the last two holes of the tournament to record his third European Tour victory. Easy it was not, but then, when is anything ever worth winning if it comes easily?

The upshot, in any case, was a victory from the bright and supremely self-confident young chap from Milton Keynes via Leighton Buzzard with a total of 197, 19 under par. He finished two strokes ahead of Paul Lawrie with big-hitting local favourite Emanuele Canonica, Anders Hansen and Anthony Wall sharing third place two shots further back.

Winning any tournament by two strokes or more usually betokens a comparatively easy experience for the victor. This time, it was anything but - in fact, it was settled only by a bizarre set of circumstances on the last two holes. Lawrie, Open Golf Championship winner in 1999, moved into a one stroke lead with a 15 foot putt for a birdie on the 17th hole. Poulter, playing in the same group as the Aberdonian, compounded the situation by putting himself in trouble with his second shot to the par five's green then three putting for a bogey.

It seemed at that moment that something remarkable would have to happen if Poulter was to lay his hands once more on the trophy. It did.

Lawrie, who had hit everything with a straightness that was almost eerie throughout a tournament that had been reduced to 54 holes, suddenly and calamitously lost his accuracy on the final hole. He

Mario Pinzi (right), the co-ordinator of the Italian Open Telecom Italia since 1974 who retired this year, was presented with the Peter Dobereiner Award by Franco Chimenti (left), President of the Italian Golf Federation, during the week of the tournament. The annual award is traditionally presented by the Italian Golf Federation in recognition of a significant contribution to the Italian Open.

Gary Emerson

shot of the week

IAN POULTER England

An easy decision - Ian Poulter's hole in one with a four iron on the 16th hole, his seventh, in the second round. In the light of what happened later on, it was not so much the ace in itself that was significant, but the two strokes he gained against par. It might have been the stroke that won it for him.

Poulter's 61 on the first day was a thing of beauty and he then had a hole in one with a four iron at the 16th, his seventh, in the delayed second round.

It enabled him to go into the final round a vital shot ahead of Lawrie. In the event, Poulter had a closing 69 against Lawrie's 70 to prevail, but he will for ever be grateful for his stroke of magic on the 25th hole he played.

Like any good professional, he would claim that since getting in the hole in the least number of strokes is the prime objective, he achieved his end at that point.

He would be right, too. But even he would have to admit that a large slice of luck played its part, too. Yes, it was played for: but it was also a bit of a fluke, Ian, wasn't it now? You can tell all – you're among friends here.

Mel Webb

carved his drive out of bounds and in the fullness of time, with victory still not a lost cause, missed his bogey putt from ten feet.

Poulter, gazing down the long road of defeat just a few moments before, now had to focus his attention on a much closer target. He had been one behind, now he was one ahead. The serpentine finish had come down to this: two putts for the title. In the light of what had gone before, it came as little surprise when he holed the five footer for a momentous victory.

Without wishing any ill-will to Lawrie, victory went to the right man, if only for his deeds of derring-do earlier in the tournament.

Anthony Wall

Tony Johnstone

final results

Olgiata Golf Club · Rome · Italy
October 31 - November 3 · 2002 · Par 72 · 6966 yards · 6370 metres

Pos.	Name		Rd1	Rd2	Rd3	Rd4	Total	Par	Prize Money Euro	£
1	Ian POULTER	Eng	61	67	69		197	-19	183330.00	115275.79
2	Paul LAWRIE	Scot	66	63	70		199	-17	122220.00	76850.52
3	Anders HANSEN	Den	64	71	66		201	-15	56833.33	35736.14
	Anthony WALL	Eng	69	67	65		201	-15	56833.33	35736.14
	Emanuele CANONICA	It	66	65	70		201	-15	56833.33	35736.14
6	Padraig HARRINGTON	Ire	71	68	63		202	-14	30910.00	19435.85
	Barry LANE	Eng	69	67	66		202	-14	30910.00	19435.85
	Jarrod MOSELEY	Aus	66	66	70		202	-14	30910.00	19435.85
	Angel CABRERA	Arg	72	61	69		202	-14	30910.00	19435.85
10	Nick O'HERN	Aus	71	69	63		203	-13	20386.67	12818.90
	Henrik NYSTRÖM	Swe	67	66	70		203	-13	20386.67	12818.90
	Stephen GALLACHER	Scot	69	69	65		203	-13	20386.67	12818.90
13	Philip GOLDING	Eng	66	75	63		204	-12	17270.00	10859.18
	Andrew MARSHALL	Eng	69	67	68		204	-12	17270.00	10859.18
15	Mark MOULAND	Wal	68	68	69		205	-11	14093.75	8861.99
	Robert-Jan DERKSEN	NL	71	68	66		205	-11	14093.75	8861.99
	Brian DAVIS	Eng	69	69	67		205	-11	14093.75	8861.99
	Maarten LAFEBER	NL	68	67	70		205	-11	14093.75	8861.99
	Thomas LEVET	Fr	69	66	70		205	-11	14093.75	8861.99
	Jean HUGO	SA	70	69	66		205	-11	14093.75	8861.99
	Miles TUNNICLIFF	Eng	64	70	71		205	-11	14093.75	8861.99
	Markus BRIER	Aut	70	68	67		205	-11	14093.75	8861.99
23	Peter FOWLER	Aus	70	67	69		206	-10	11110.00	6985.84
	Jean-Francois REMESY	Fr	71	66	69		206	-10	11110.00	6985.84
	Raphaël JACQUELIN	Fr	76	62	68		206	-10	11110.00	6985.84
	Trevor IMMELMAN	SA	70	68	68		06	-10	11110.00	6985.84
	Francesco MOLINARI (AM)	It	70	66	70		206	-10		
	Robert KARLSSON	Swe	70	68	68		206	-10	11110.00	6985.84
	Gary ORR	Scot	66	69	71		206	-10	11110.00	6985.84
	Niclas FASTH	Swe	68	69	69		206	-10	11110.00	6985.84
31	Steve WEBSTER	Eng	71	68	68		207	-9	8847.14	5562.98
	Peter HANSON	Swe	68	69	70		207	-9	8847.14	5562.98
	Paul EALES	Eng	72	69	66		207	-9	8847.14	5562.98
	Søren HANSEN	Den	70	68	69		207	-9	8847.14	5562.98
	Joakim HAEGGMAN	Swe	69	69	69		207	-9	8847.14	5562.98
	Christopher HANELL	Swe	69	69	69		207	-9	8847.14	5562.98
	Alastair FORSYTH	Scot	69	68	70		207	-9	8847.14	5562.98
38	Mark ROE	Eng	69	69	70		208	-8	7260.00	4565.00
	Mårten OLANDER	Swe	70	71	67		208	-8	7260.00	4565.00
	Massimo FLORIOLI	It	72	68	68		208	-8	7260.00	4565.00
	Ignacio GARRIDO	Sp	74	67	67		208	-8	7260.00	4565.00
	Sebastien DELAGRANGE	Fr	71	68	69		208	-8	7260.00	4565.00
	Graeme MCDOWELL	N.Ire	71	70	67		208	-8	7260.00	4565.00
44	Gordon BRAND JNR.	Scot	68	71	70		209	-7	5830.00	3665.84
	Darren FICHARDT	SA	69	70	70		209	-7	5830.00	3665.84
	Jamie SPENCE	Eng	68	71	70		209	-7	5830.00	3665.84
	Gary EMERSON	Eng	74	67	68		209	-7	5830.00	3665.84
	Peter BAKER	Eng	69	71	69		209	-7	5830.00	3665.84
	Gary CLARK	Eng	72	68	69		209	-7	5830.00	3665.84
	Brett RUMFORD	Aus	67	73	69		209	-7	5830.00	3665.84
51	Anders FORSBRAND	Swe	72	67	71		210	-6	4730.00	2974.17
	Tony JOHNSTONE	Zim	71	69	70		210	-6	4730.00	2974.17
	Eduardo ROMERO	Arg	72	68	70		210	-6	4730.00	2974.17
54	David HOWELL	Eng	69	72	70		211	-5	3960.00	2490.00
	Mark MCNULTY	Zim	71	69	71		211	-5	3960.00	2490.00
	Diego BORREGO	Sp	69	72	70		211	-5	3960.00	2490.00
	Patrik SJÖLAND	Swe	66	74	71		211	-5	3960.00	2490.00
58	Roger CHAPMAN	Eng	70	68	74		212	-4	3135.00	1971.25
	Alberto BINAGHI	It	69	69	74		212	-4	3135.00	1971.25
	Jonathan LOMAS	Eng	71	70	71		212	-4	3135.00	1971.25
	Rolf MUNTZ	NL	71	70	71		212	-4	3135.00	1971.25
	Mikael LUNDBERG	Swe	70	71	71		212	-4	3135.00	1971.25
	Mikko ILONEN	Fin	71	70	71		212	-4	3135.00	1971.25
64	Stephen DODD	Wal	69	72	72		213	-3	2585.00	1625.42
	Mark PILKINGTON	Wal	71	70	72		213	-3	2585.00	1625.42
	Daren LEE	Eng	70	70	73		213	-3	2585.00	1625.42
	Mads VIBE-HASTRUP	Den	71	69	73		213	-3	2585.00	1625.42
68	Ricardo GONZALEZ	Arg	67	74	73		214	-2	2310.00	1452.50
69	Alessandro TADINI	It	71	68	77		216	0	2145.00	1348.75
	Jorge BERENDT	Arg	67	74	75		216	0	2145.00	1348.75
71	Marco BERNARDINI	It	69	72	76		217	1	2010.00	1263.86

Volvo Masters Andalucia Club de Golf · Valderrama · Spain

familiar fable

1	Bernhard LANGER	Ger	281	-3
	Colin MONTGOMERIE	Scot	281	-3
3	Bradley DREDGE	Wales	283	-1
4	Angel CABRERA	Arg	285	1
	Peter O'MALLEY	Aus	285	1
6	Jarmo SANDELIN	Swe	286	2
7	Sergio GARCIA	Sp	287	3
	Adam SCOTT	Aus	287	3
9	Darren CLARKE	N.Ire	288	4
	Robert KARLSSON	Swe	288	4

After five years at Montecastillo near Jerez the season-ending Volvo Masters Andalucia returned to Valderrama, its home from 1988 to 1996 and scene of so much drama whenever the stars of the game come to play.

Colin Montgomerie and Bernhard Langer

This was to be no different and at the end of it there were uniquely not just one, not just two, but three players holding the silverware on offer.

The first was Retief Goosen, who not without some difficulty held off Padraig Harrington to become the first non-European ever to win the Volvo Order of Merit two years in a row.

It was the same one-two as in 2001, but the difference between them had come down from over 770,000 euro to a mere 25,472 euro. One stroke separated them in the final event, but once Harrington had incurred a two-shot penalty for unwittingly repairing a pitch mark just off the green on the opening hole of the opening round the gifted Irishman was simply not able to turn things round. Both players, however, had plenty of reasons for looking back at the campaign with pride in their performance.

Darren Clarke

Their private battle over, attention turned to the championship itself. And what excitement and incident it provided.

Colin Montgomerie and Bernhard Langer had not won all year, but at The De Vere Belfry in September had linked up as Ryder Cup partners again and had used all their experience to good effect to help Europe win back the trophy. Montgomerie top-scored with 4¹/₂ points out of five and Langer was next best with 3¹/₂ out of four.

Now they were locked in battle at a setting where they both had happy memories. Montgomerie, having lost a play-off to Sandy Lyle in the 1992 Volvo Masters, returned 12 months later to capture a title which set him off on his run of seven successive Volvo Order of Merit titles, while Langer won the tournament in 1994 and his stunning second round 62 then still stands as the course record.

The 1997 Ryder Cup should not be forgotten either. Langer was the man to ensure Europe kept the trophy, Montgomerie the one to send the United States to defeat on the final hole of the final game.

Angel Cabrera

Padraig Harrington is presented with a Harold Riley Sketch for winning the Stroke Average Category in the Reuters Performance Data by Carston Thode, Co-operative Marketing & Sponsorship Director, Group Marketing of Reuters.

Neither was to the fore straightaway, however. The opening day belonged to Argentina's Angel Cabrera, who with four closing birdies finished only one outside Langer's eight year old course record.

Cabrera led by four and finished the second round still holding that advantage. But the fact that he had been seven clear and ran up a double bogey seven on the 17th gave all the chasing pack heart.

On Saturday a wind arrived and sent scores soaring. Sergio Garcia had a nine on the fourth and yet remained in the hunt, Darren Clarke had a hole in one on the 15th and then closed with two double bogeys and Cabrera managed only a 76.

It all left Welshman Bradley Dredge out in front and while he had never been in the final group on the final day before – nor won – he handled it superbly and was denied only by some remarkable golf on the back nine by The European Tour's two leading money-winners over the years, with 86 worldwide titles between them.

On a day when only six others broke par Langer eagled the 11th, birdied the 13th and 17th and saw a 12 foot attempt for another at the last hang agonisingly on the back lip. But Montgomerie was equal to the task. He birdied the 11th, 13th and 16th and when he made another on the long 17th the Scot led by one.

Retief Goosen

Fredrik Jacobson

A closing par to win then. But Montgomerie bogeyed and so they tied at three under par, two ahead of Dredge. So to a play-off - yet only after Montgomerie had been taken to the television compound to study a video of him holing out at the tenth.

The point at issue was whether he had addressed his ball before it had come to rest. But it was quickly ruled that there was no infringement and Langer was joined on the 18th tee.

Two par fours there meant they switched to the tenth. That, though, was halved in four as well when Montgomerie missed from ten feet and once they walked across to the 18th again for the third extra hole it was obvious that the light was fading far too quickly for them to continue.

Retief Goosen and Padraig Harrington

Offered the option of sharing the prestigious trophy, the two agreed. The tournament had two winners, the week had three winners, Montgomerie had ended his sequence of play-off defeats and, 16 years apart, Langer had featured in the two ties in European Tour history. In the 1986 Trophée Lancôme he and Severiano Ballesteros could not carry on after four sudden death holes.

Langer said: "We both played great and both deserved to win."

Montgomerie responded: "It is only appropriate that in the year we have won back The Ryder Cup, we should share this wonderful trophy. I'm delighted."

Mark Garrod

shot of the week

COLIN MONTGOMERIE Scotland

Nobody can discount the part that Lady Luck often plays in golf and she certainly helped Colin Montgomerie when his drive down the 71st hole went into the trees and then came out again. But it is taking advantage of such breaks that matters and after laying up the Scot brought a roar from the crowd with an immaculate pitch over the water and up onto the back shelf to three feet. The birdie to go ahead of Bernhard Langer again was followed by a bogey to tie, but what a shot at what a moment.

VOLVO MASTERS Andalucia

HOYO	JUGADOR		± PAR	RESULTADO
1 8	MONTGOMERIE	(SCOT)	–	3
1 8	LANGER	(GER)	–	3
1 8	DREDGE	(WAL)	–	1
1 8	CABRERA	(ARG)	+	1
1 8	O'MALLEY	(AUS)	+	1
1 8	SANDELIN	(SWE)	+	2
1 8	SCOTT	(AUS)	+	3
1 8	GARCIA	(SP)	+	3

the course

Valderrama is known the world over for the immaculate condition it is kept in and the demands it makes on even the world's best players. At 6,945 yards it is not long by modern-day standards, but as Colin Montgomerie said: "Every shot is a potential disaster. You can't relax." Of all the holes the 536 yard 17th requires special care. It saw everything from a three to a ten, yet Angel Cabrera reached the green with a drive and seven iron en route to his opening 64.

Phillip Price

Jarmo Sandelin

Bernhard Langer

Bradley Dredge

Colin Montgomerie

final results

Club de Golf · Valderrama · Spain
November 7-10 · 2002 · Par 71 · 6945 yards · 6350 metres

Pos.	Name		Rd1	Rd2	Rd3	Rd4	Total	Par	Prize Money Euro	£
1	Bernhard LANGER	Ger	71	71	72	67	281	-3	435648.42	277775.00
	Colin MONTGOMERIE	Scot	70	69	72	70	281	-3	435648.42	277775.00
3	Bradley DREDGE	Wal	68	71	71	73	283	-1	196357.40	125200.00
4	Peter O'MALLEY	Aus	72	69	75	69	285	1	144915.50	92400.00
	Angel CABRERA	Arg	63	72	76	74	285	1	144915.50	92400.00
6	Jarmo SANDELIN	Swe	69	74	77	66	286	2	109784.50	70000.00
7	Sergio GARCIA	Sp	69	70	75	73	287	3	86259.25	55000.00
	Adam SCOTT	Aus	72	73	70	72	287	3	86259.25	55000.00
9	Robert KARLSSON	Swe	72	67	77	72	288	4	66498.04	42400.00
	Darren CLARKE	N.Ire	73	69	75	71	288	4	66498.04	42400.00
11	Alex CEJKA	Ger	69	75	71	74	289	5	56460.60	36000.00
12	Anders HANSEN	Den	76	70	73	71	290	6	52382.89	33400.00
13	Ian WOOSNAM	Wal	73	72	73	73	291	7	46297.69	29520.00
	Maarten LAFEBER	NL	69	72	75	75	291	7	46297.69	29520.00
	Richard GREEN	Aus	70	74	78	69	291	7	46297.69	29520.00
	Thomas LEVET	Fr	70	75	75	71	291	7	46297.69	29520.00
	Niclas FASTH	Swe	71	77	69	74	291	7	46297.69	29520.00
18	José Maria OLAZÁBAL	Sp	73	69	76	74	292	8	41090.77	26200.00
	Justin ROSE	Eng	71	69	73	79	292	8	41090.77	26200.00
	Ian POULTER	Eng	73	75	73	71	292	8	41090.77	26200.00
21	David GILFORD	Eng	72	71	79	71	293	9	36134.79	23040.00
	Stephen LEANEY	Aus	73	68	77	75	293	9	36134.79	23040.00
	Steen TINNING	Den	68	80	72	73	293	9	36134.79	23040.00
	Thomas BJÖRN	Den	77	74	71	71	293	9	36134.79	23040.00
	Fredrik JACOBSON	Swe	68	72	74	79	293	9	36134.79	23040.00
26	Gary EVANS	Eng	76	74	74	70	294	10	32464.85	20700.00
	Alastair FORSYTH	Scot	75	73	74	72	294	10	32464.85	20700.00
28	Brian DAVIS	Eng	68	81	72	74	295	11	28700.80	18300.00
	Søren HANSEN	Den	71	71	82	71	295	11	28700.80	18300.00
	Jarrod MOSELEY	Aus	71	74	80	70	295	11	28700.80	18300.00
	Joakim HAEGGMAN	Swe	76	74	72	73	295	11	28700.80	18300.00
	Phillip PRICE	Wal	67	73	75	80	295	11	28700.80	18300.00
	Paul LAWRIE	Scot	72	73	79	71	295	11	28700.80	18300.00

Pos.	Name		Rd1	Rd2	Rd3	Rd4	Total	Par	Prize Money Euro	£
34	Sandy LYLE	Scot	76	76	75	69	296	12	24936.77	15900.00
	Retief GOOSEN	SA	73	74	78	71	296	12	24936.77	15900.00
36	Eduardo ROMERO	Arg	71	71	75	80	297	13	22584.24	14400.00
	Padraig HARRINGTON	Ire	74	76	74	73	297	13	22584.24	14400.00
	Carl PETTERSSON	Swe	70	77	73	77	297	13	22584.24	14400.00
39	Henrik BJORNSTAD	Nor	75	72	74	77	298	14	18327.29	11685.71
	Miguel Angel JIMÉNEZ	Sp	81	70	72	75	298	14	18327.29	11685.71
	Richard S JOHNSON	Swe	74	67	79	78	298	14	18327.29	11685.71
	Ignacio GARRIDO	Sp	70	77	76	75	298	14	18327.29	11685.71
	Rolf MUNTZ	NL	75	74	72	77	298	14	18327.29	11685.71
	Greg OWEN	Eng	74	68	79	77	298	14	18327.29	11685.71
	Simon DYSON	Eng	68	74	76	80	298	14	18327.29	11685.71
46	Malcolm MACKENZIE	Eng	71	73	76	79	299	15	15369.83	9800.00
	Barry LANE	Eng	73	73	79	74	299	15	15369.83	9800.00
48	Costantino ROCCA	It	72	73	75	80	300	16	13315.29	8490.00
	Emanuele CANONICA	It	75	71	77	77	300	16	13315.29	8490.00
	Andrew COLTART	Scot	72	78	75	75	300	16	13315.29	8490.00
	John BICKERTON	Eng	75	77	77	71	300	16	13315.29	8490.00
	Tobias DIER	Ger	75	76	77	72	300	16	13315.29	8490.00
53	Peter FOWLER	Aus	77	75	73	76	301	17	11801.83	7525.00
	Trevor IMMELMAN	SA	72	77	77	75	301	17	11801.83	7525.00
55	Jamie SPENCE	Eng	72	76	78	76	302	18	10978.45	7000.00
	Paul CASEY	Eng	81	71	76	74	302	18	10978.45	7000.00
	Graeme MCDOWELL	N.Ire	72	81	69	80	302	18	10978.45	7000.00
58	Carlos RODILES	Sp	73	83	76	71	303	19	10351.11	6600.00
59	Jean-Francois REMESY	Fr	75	73	78	78	304	20	10037.44	6400.00
60	Tony JOHNSTONE	Zim	78	78	71	78	305	21	9143.48	5830.00
	Paul MCGINLEY	Ire	76	77	78	74	305	21	9143.48	5830.00
	Ricardo GONZALEZ	Arg	78	76	79	72	305	21	9143.48	5830.00
	Nick DOUGHERTY	Eng	76	76	76	77	305	21	9143.48	5830.00
	David GLEESON	Aus	74	81	75	75	305	21	9143.48	5830.00
65	Lee WESTWOOD	Eng	76	73	81	78	308	24	8390.67	5350.00
66	Pierre FULKE	Swe	75	WD			75	4	8233.84	5250.00

VOLVO
for life

SOMEBODY'S BEEN WORKING OUT.

ADMIT IT. YOU NOTICED. THE SCULPTED SHOULDERS, THE TRIM MUSCULAR HIPS, THAT OVERWHELMING AIR OF CONFIDENCE. IT'S WHAT SOME CALL MOJO. OTHERS, ESSENCE. AND WHAT THE SWEDES CALL THE VOLVO S60. IT'S SURE TO TURN HEADS IN ANY LANGUAGE. **THE EXPERIENCE CONTINUES AT VOLVOCARS.CO.UK**

S60 range starts from £19,995 otr. Model featured S60 T5 SE manual plus metallic paint £26,795 otr. Fuel consumption in mpg (l/100km): Urban 22.2 (12.7), Extra Urban 38.7 (7.3), Combined 30.4 (9.3). CO2 emissions 222 g/km.

WGC-EMC² World Cup Vista Vallarta · Puerto Vallarta · Mexico

breathtaking tradition

Retief Goosen and Ernie Els

The World Golf Championships – EMC² World Cup, which was first played as the Canada Cup in 1953, has been contested on many of the great courses around the world and in 2002 it was the turn of Mexico to play host to this two man team competition featuring 24 countries. The Nicklaus Course at Vista Vallarta, located in the foothills of the Sierra Madre Mountains with breathtaking views of Puerto Vallarta, provided a wonderful setting with grassy hillsides, dense forests of Palm and giant Ficas trees, natural creeks and arroyos, for the 48th edition of this unique event which has been hosted by no fewer than 23 countries.

The World Cup joined the family of World Golf Championships events in 2000 with EMC² taking over the title sponsorship.

David Duval and Tiger Woods linked together that year at the Buenos Aires Golf Club in Argentina to retain the famous trophy for the United States following the victory of Mark O'Meara and Woods at The Mines Resort & Golf Club in Kuala Lumpur, Malaysia, in 1999.

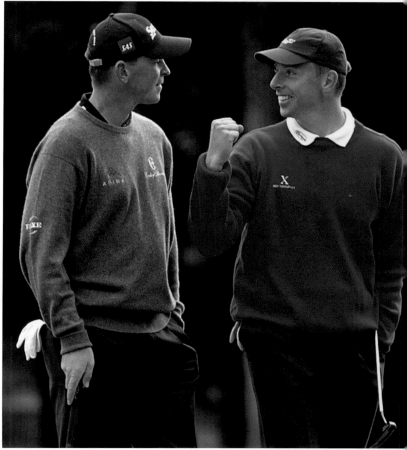

Thomas Björn and Søren Hanse

Then at The Taiheiyo Club, Gotemba, Japan, in 2001, Woods, again in partnership with Duval, gave the Americans the chance of a third successive win, and their 24th triumph in all, when he chipped in for an eagle at the final hole. It meant that Duval and Woods had played the closing four holes in five under par to become the fourth team in a play-off.

Denmark's Thomas Björn and Søren Hansen had set the target, recording the best foursomes round of the week, a superb error free seven under par 65, which meant they had played all 72 holes - two rounds of fourball and two rounds of foursomes - without a single bogey. They were caught on the 24 under par 264 mark first by the South African due of Ernie Els and Retief Goosen, with Els calmly rolling in a putt for an eagle on the last green, then by New Zealand, represented by Michael Campbell and David Smail, and finally by the United States.

Els had tasted victory before, winning the World Cup with Wayne Westner in 1996 at Erinvale Golf Club in his native South Africa, and now he did so again with Goosen, the reigning US Open Champion who would later be voted Asprey Golfer of the Year for 2001, as they overcame Denmark at the second extra hole after New Zealand and the United States had been eliminated at the first.

Unquestionably, the World Golf Championships have become a truly global experience since the launch in February 1999. They feature the game's leading players competing against one another in a variety of formats. The EMC^2 World Cup joined the Accenture Match Play, NEC Invitational and American Express Championship in the World Golf Championships line-up with the

Nick Faldo and David Carter (Winners, 1998)

events rotating through a variety of outstanding venues worldwide. Mexico became the seventh country to have hosted a World Golf Championships event.

Mitchell Platts

Vista Vallarta

global dominance

Wins Around The World

Sergio Garcia

If ever there was an indication that 2002 would prove to be another successful year for European Tour Members competing around the world, it came in the curtain-raising tournament on the US PGA Tour, the Mercedes Championships at the beginning of January, on the beautiful Plantation Course at Kapalua in Maui.

With the cream of American talent assembled behind World Number One Tiger Woods, home supporters waited eagerly for the procession to begin but, come the end of the week, the march to glory was headed by Sergio Garcia.

Garcia, who turned 22 three days after his victory, had given notice that his game was in tip-top condition a month before, a stunning closing 63 pinching the Nedbank Golf Challenge in South Africa from under the nose of Ernie Els. The Spaniard pitched in for victory at the first play-off hole - his stroke of genius on the par three 14th at the Gary Player Country Club bringing cries of 'Seve, Seve' from the galleries.

Comparisons with the great man were equally relevant during Saturday's play at Kapalua. Having opened with an uninspired 73, Garcia had battled his way back with a second round 69 before unleashing the full repertoire of his talents in the desperately difficult conditions foisted on the third round.

While most players signed for scores in the mid 70s, Garcia carded a five under par 68, a score prised from the course thanks to brilliant ball striking and a magical short game. Despite the Herculean effort, he still trailed by four going into the final round but a superb 64 was good enough to draw level with David Toms on 18 under par 274, before yet another birdie putt, this time from eight feet on the revisited 18th green, saw Garcia beat the 2001 US PGA Champion on the first play-off hole.

In 2001, we had to wait until mid-March for a European Tour Member to succeed on the US PGA Tour, when Jesper Parnevik won The Honda Classic, but 2002 proved to be a different story as, barely four weeks after Garcia's triumph, it was the turn of fellow countryman José Maria Olazábal to step into the winners' circle at the beginning of February in the Buick Invitational.

Success for the 1994 and 1999 Masters Champion looked a long way off when he opened with rounds of 71-72 at Torrey Pines in La Jolla to make the cut right on the mark, but over the weekend the 36 year old Spaniard was as hot as the Californian sunshine.

José Maria Olazábal

Ernie Els with his wife Liezl

A third round 67 moved Olazábal back into contention before a superb final round 65 gave him a 13 under par total of 275. Like Garcia four weeks previously, Olazábal was poised for extra holes before the necessity for him to put his spikes back on was removed as J L Lewis three putted the final hole for a 70 to share second place with Mark O'Meara.

The success of European Tour Members at the onset of months on the US PGA Tour continued in the first week of March when Ernie Els captured the Genuity Championship on the Blue Course at the Doral Golf Resort & Spa in Miami.

The name of the course could have not been less appropriate for the mood of the South African if it had tried for the success came in the middle of an incredible run, victories on The European Tour at the Heineken Classic and the Dubai Desert Classic coming either side of the win in Florida.

Els had won only once in 2001 – a one shot victory in the Vodacom Players' Championship in South Africa in December. The win in Florida helped *The Big Easy* to three wins in three weeks and understandable delight, but his pleasure was increased tenfold when he glanced over his shoulder at the player he had relegated to second, namely one Tiger Woods.

Vijay Singh

Retief Goosen

In 2000, Els had finished second to Woods in both the US Open Championship at Pebble Beach and in the 129th Open Golf Championship at St Andrews. The South African had struggled to banish the spectre of the World Number One, but at Doral, he successfully snuffed it out.

Eight shots ahead of Peter Lonard and Woods going into the final round, Els did not produce his best ever scoring round of golf on the Sunday, but in the circumstances it proved perfect to hold off the charging Woods by two shots. Such a performance also helped give the South African the confidence to go on to lift the 131st Open Golf Championship at Muirfield later in the year.

"I felt pretty proud of myself on the back nine, I didn't hit too many loose shots," said Els. "I was tentative over my putting but I guess that's what these kind of leads do to you. You just kind of play a bit too careful and that's what I did on the greens - but I was still pretty aggressive from tee to green."

The success story on the US PGA Tour did not stop there either as in successive weeks at the end of March and the beginning of April, Vijay Singh and Retief Goosen gave The European Tour more cause to celebrate. A casual glance at the leaderboard in the Shell Houston Open would have led observers to believe they were looking at a European Tour event, not one across the Atlantic, such was the dominance of European Tour Members at The Woodlands course in Texas.

Aside from Singh, who recorded his first win in two years in America with a tournament record total of 22 under par 266, second place was claimed by Darren Clarke, the Ulsterman finishing with a highly creditable 16 under par total of 272, while Olazábal took third on 273 and Adam Scott shared sixth on 277.

The following week, there was more European Tour joy as Goosen won for the second time on American shores, his closing 70 at the Sugarloaf course in Duluth, Georgia, for a 16 under par total of 272, good enough for victory in the BellSouth Classic. It was the week before the Masters Tournament and the performance gave the 2001 Volvo Order of Merit winner the impetus to go on to finish second at Augusta National, his best showing in four outings amongst the azaleas.

Singh would sign-off the challenge by European Tour Members on the 2002 US PGA Tour by winning The TOUR Championship presented by Dynegy - incidentally one week before England's Luke Donald gained a maiden win on the US PGA Tour in the Southern Farm Bureau Classic - in some style at East Lake Golf Club in Atlanta, Georgia.

It was not only Stateside that Members flourished, the talents and skills honed across Europe put to good use in all four corners of the globe, nowhere more so than on the Sunshine Tour in South Africa where both Justin Rose and Goosen triumphed in successive weeks in February, three months after Darren Fichardt capped a magnificent 2001 season with victory in the Cabs/Old Mutual Zimbabwe Open.

Fichardt had won the South African Tour Championship earlier in 2001, but the 27 year old from Pretoria admitted his win at the Chapman Golf Club in Zimbabwe had been the most demanding test of his professional career to date.

Justin Rose

"That was easily the hardest victory I've ever had, it was all mental," said Fichardt, who had to grit his teeth to come through a tense opening few holes in the final round before a closing 69 gave him victory at 13 under par 275. "My swing wasn't quite there but I managed to work with it – my short game and my putting got me through."

Three months later, the champagne flowed for Goosen for two reasons, primarily in honour of his three shot victory in the Dimension Data Pro-Am at the Gary Player Country Club in Sun City, but secondly as the success came on the occasion of his 33rd birthday. In the end, his 20 under par total of 268 was eventually good enough to end the brave resistance of Scottish Challenge Tour player Scott Drummond, who had tracked Goosen all week before coming up just short.

The following week it was the turn of Rose to celebrate, a 15 under par total of 265 good enough for victory in the Nashua Masters at the Wild Coast Sun Country Club. It was the 22 year old Englishman's second success in the space of three weeks in South Africa following his maiden European Tour victory in the dunhill championship at Houghton Golf Club in Johannesburg.

James Kingston

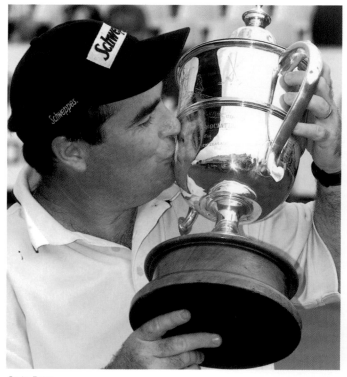

Craig Parry

Rose, of course, went on to enhance his season even further in June with victory in the Victor Chandler British Masters at Woburn Golf and Country Club, but a month before that he proved again how much of a world golfer he had become with an emphatic five stroke win in The Crowns tournament in Japan.

Rose laid the foundations for victory in the Far East with an outstanding opening six under par 64 at the Wago Course at the Nagoya Golf Club before a third round 63 put the issue beyond doubt, cruising home in level par 70 on the final day to keep the title in Europe following the victory in 2001 by Darren Clarke.

Other winners in South Africa during 2001 were Hennie Otto, who won the Limpopo Inustrelek tournament, and James Kingston, who took the title in the Royal Swazi Sun Classic, both tournaments forming part of the Sunshine Tour's winter circuit.

Heading south to Australasia, the success story continued for European Tour Members on the ANZ Tour, Craig Parry holding off fellow Australian Stephen Leaney and local favourites Steve Alker and Michael Campbell by a shot to win the Telstra Hyundai New Zealand Open at the Paraparaumu Beach course.

Also in the field was Tiger Woods who could do no better than sixth as Parry gave himself a belated 36th birthday gift and an early anniversary present for wife Jenny, his 11 under par total of 273 landing him the $NZ110,000 first prize, the richest ever in New Zealand golfing history. Parry, of course, would win the WGC - NEC Invitational later in the year.

Gareth Paddison

adaptability to various conditions, a point conclusively proven by Challenge Tour golfer Roger Beames who won what must have been the strangest tournament in 2002, namely the Drambuie World Ice Golf Championship in Greenland.

In temperatures which often dipped to 25 degrees below zero and on a course flattened out between the snow drifts and icebergs, the 27 year old Scot carded a level par score of 140 over the two round contest to win by a shot from American Jack O'Keefe. "A win is a win wherever it is earned and this is a world championship," said Beames.

One assumes he had no problem in keeping the champagne chilled during a year when, both home and away, there was much for European Tour Members to celebrate.

Scott Crockett

Although Campbell could do no better than a share of second place, there was ample consolation for the 33 year old Kiwi the following week when he was invested as an Officer of the New Zealand Order of Merit for services to golf. He was also named Maori Sportsperson of the Year and Maori Athlete of the Decade.

Other successes Down Under were posted by Challenge Tour Member Gareth Paddison who won the Scenic Circle Hotels Dunedin Classic and Peter O'Malley, whose four sub-70 rounds at the Clearwater Resort Course in Christchurch were good enough to give the 37 year old Australian a 17 under par total of 271 and a five shot win in the Honda Clearwater Classic.

Returning to the Far East, Davidoff Tour success was claimed by Charlie Wi, who posted rounds of 67-69-67-69 for a 16 under par total of 272 to win the SK Telecom Classic at the Lake Side Country Club in Seoul, and by Sergio Garcia, whose rounds of 67-65-66-67 for a 23 under par total of 265 gave him victory in the Kolon Cup Korean Open at Seoul Hanyang Country Club, the Spaniard's first win in Asia.

Finally, European golfers are renowned for their resilience and

Charlie Wi

The European Seniors Tour

simply awesome

The 2002 European Seniors Tour Order of Merit

1 **Seiji EBIHARA** Jpn

2 Denis DURNIAN Eng

3 Delroy CAMBRIDGE Jam

4 John MORGAN Eng

5 Christy O'CONNOR JNR Ire

6 Steve STULL USA

7 John IRWIN Can

8 John CHILLAS Scot

9 Denis O'SULLIVAN Ire

10 Nick JOB Eng

11 Neil COLES Eng

12 Barry VIVIAN NZ

13 Keith MACDONALD Eng

14 Tommy HORTON Eng

15 David GOOD Aus

Seiji Ebihara

The European Seniors Tour

Every now and then the very best golfers tap into a vein of form so rich that it sets them apart from their rivals. Colin Montgomerie went through such a period when he won seven consecutive Volvo Order of Merit titles in the 1990s. More recently, on the US PGA and US LPGA Tours, Tiger Woods and Annika Sorenstam have had spells when they appeared well nigh unbeatable. During 2002 so, too, did Japan's Seiji Ebihara on the European Seniors Tour.

When 52 year old Ebihara arrived in Europe at the start of the 2002 season he was known as one of the Seniors Tour's most consistent performers. He had won twice the season before, at the AIB Irish Seniors Open and the Microlease Jersey Seniors Masters, but even those victories, coupled with his propensity to play aggressive golf no matter what the circumstances, did not prepare his Tour colleagues for what he was about to achieve.

Ebihara wasted little time in getting acclimatised to European conditions. During his first start, he successfully defended his AIB

Irish Seniors Open at the majestic Adare Manor Hotel and Golf Resort in County Limerick and over the next six months he was to win twice more, notching an incredible eight top ten finishes from 12 starts.

The Japanese golfer's second win of the season came at the lucrative Wales Seniors Open, played for the second season in succession at the glorious Royal St David's Golf Club in Harlech. That victory, achieved by three shots over Denis Durnian and Christy O'Connor Jnr, was impressive but he saved his best performance for the De Vere PGA Seniors Championship at the De Vere Carden Park in Cheshire.

On that occasion, Ebihara was simply awesome. In cold and wet conditions, he was a record 21 under par in finishing no less than ten shots ahead of Americans George Burns and Steve Stull. At times, during rounds of 69-67-65 and 66, it was almost as if the Japanese golfer was toying with the excellent Jack Nicklaus design, playing his last 57 holes without dropping a single shot. It was,

Noboru Sugai

Christy O'Connor Jnr

Dragon Taki

Seniors Tour's record for average earnings per tournament. In 2001, Stanley earned an average of 15,106 euro (£9,340) each time he teed up. Twelve months later, while collecting the John Jacobs Trophy for leading the European Seniors Tour Order of Merit, Ebihara collected an average of 27,517 euro (£17,278) per event, a remarkable achievement and one that will take considerable beating.

During 2002 Ebihara dominated proceedings but he did not hog all the headlines. In the height of the summer, for example, his compatriot, Noboru Sugai, created a major slice of history when he became the first Japanese golfer to win the Senior British Open, presented by MasterCard at Royal County Down Golf Club. Then, a fortnight later, Dragon Taki, won the Bad Ragaz PGA Seniors Open in Switzerland, giving Japanese golfers their fourth win in a five tournament stretch.

Sugai and Taki were both first-time winners on the Seniors Tour and they were certainly not alone in that. During 2001, there were a total of eight first-time winners. Twelve months later a similar number emerged. Peter Townsend was the first to achieve that feat when he held off rookie, Guillermo Encina, to win the Royal Westmoreland Barbados Open. Next, the 2001 Seniors Tour Qualifying School medalist, Stull, claimed the inaugural Tobago Plantations Seniors Classic and he was followed by Gary Wintz (Flanders Nippon presents Legends in Golf), Bernard Gallacher (The Mobile Cup), Ray Carrasco (Travis Perkins Senior Masters) and Brian Jones (De Vere Hotels Seniors Classic).

quite simply, a stunning performance, one that prompted several of his rivals to suggest they clubbed together to pay for Seiji and his delightful wife, Toshie, to go on an extended holiday!

Ebihara, of course, resisted all calls to take such a break. Thereafter, he did not win again but did produce two more second place finishes, at the Travis Perkins Senior Masters and the Bovis Lend Lease European Senior Masters, and it was at the first of those that he broke Australian Ian Stanley's previous Seniors Tour money record. By the time he went home, after the Charles Church Scottish Seniors Open, he had accumulated 330,210 euro (£207,339), or 43,185 euro (£29,861) more than Stanley won when he set the previous record in 2001. He also shattered the

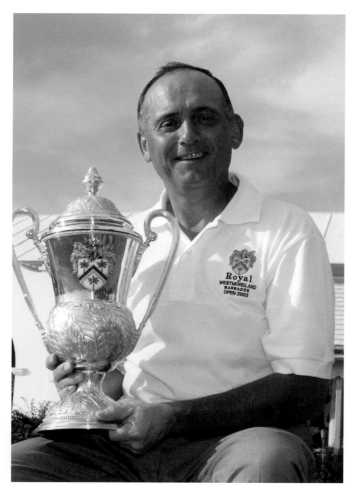

Peter Townsend

It was also a special moment for the European Seniors Tour when Piñero became the latest in a long line of former Ryder Cup golfers to tee-up on the circuit when he swung into action in the GIN Monte Carlo Invitational at the Monte Carlo Golf Club. John Bland was the last player to win on his debut - that was in the London Masters at The London Club in 1995 - and Piñero, who won nine titles on The European Tour International Schedule between 1974 and 1985, did his level best to surge straight past the winning line.

Indeed Piñero played the whole of the tournament without dropping a shot and with a last round of 66 - 15 pars and three birdies - he claimed a share of third place behind Champion Terry Gale of Australia and England's Keith MacDonald, the runner-up. Gale built his victory on a magnificent opening 62, equalling the lowest round in European Seniors Tour history. His opening round was the lowest start by a winner and after two rounds another record had fallen when he and MacDonald set a new record for the first 36 holes of nine under par 129. Gale then moved on to register his second European Seniors Tour victory.

Jones, Stull, Taki and Wintz were all graduates from the 2001 Seniors Tour Qualifying School at Pinta, Portugal, but, in contrast, Carrasco, Gallacher and Townsend had to wait considerably longer before registering their maiden wins. Townsend, in fact, clocked 86 starts before winning for the first time in the Caribbean. Gallacher was making his 59th appearance when he won at Stoke Park and Carrasco was playing his 43rd event when he withstood the challenge at Wentworth Club.

Eamonn Darcy, and his former Ryder Cup colleague, Manuel Piñero, made a big impression when they joined the Seniors Tour towards the end of the season. Darcy made his debut at the Travis Perkins Senior Masters at the superb Wentworth Club. There, on the Edinburgh course, he renewed a whole host of old acquaintances and Carrasco, seeking that first elusive win, was certainly looking over his shoulder as he opened with a 66 and Darcy with a 69. This was to be the week, however, when the 55 year old Californian, who took up the game after watching Roberto de Vicenzo on television, came to the fore. "When I arrived at Wentworth it didn't even cross my mind that I might win," he said. "How did it feel when I had done it? Well, I couldn't begin to tell anyone. It was certainly a very special moment."

John Morgan

Darcy gave ample evidence of making a huge contribution to the European Seniors Tour storybook with a powerful performance at the Bovis Lend Lease European Senior Masters at Woburn Golf and Country Club. He had arrived with stunning credentials following a European Tour career in which he won four titles, accrued almost £2 million in prize money and represented Europe in four Ryder Cup Matches. At Woburn he scored 68-71-70 to tie with Ebihara although both fell short of Jamaican Delroy Cambridge.

Darcy produced another thrilling performance in the Estoril Seniors Tour Championship at Campo de Golfe da Quinta da Marina in Portugal. This time he earned a place in a play-off with Denis Durnian who, Ebihara apart, was the most consistent performer on the 2002 Seniors Tour. The Macclesfield-based golfer finished second on the 2001 European Seniors Tour Order of Merit and he was to duplicate that feat 12 months later, an achievement that brought with it an automatic place in the UBS Warburg Cup at Sea Island Golf Club, Georgia, for the second season in a row.

Durnian was seldom far from the leaderboard. He notched eight top ten finishes in his first 15 starts before he arrived at The Roxburghe in Scotland where he claimed a long overdue second Seniors Tour title in the Charles Church Scottish Seniors Open.

Steve Stull

New Zealand's Bob Charles became the fifth recipient of the European Seniors Tour's Lládro Lifetime Achievement Award, following in the footsteps of Neil Coles, Tommy Horton, Brian Huggett and Gary Player. Bob received the award from Ken Schofield, Executive Director, The European Tour, during the European Seniors Tour's Annual Dinner at Wentworth Club. The left-hander has won 50 titles around the world including the 1963 Open Golf Championship at Royal Lytham & St Annes as well as two Senior British Opens and a total of 24 titles on the US Senior Tour.

Then came the Estoril Seniors Tour Championship where he won at the first extra hole against Darcy.

Cambridge, one of the Seniors Tour's biggest hitters, was an almost ever-present threat. Cambridge won for the second time in his Seniors Tour career when he finished two shots ahead of Tommy Horton and Ian Mosey at the Microlease Jersey Seniors Masters at La Moye Golf Club. Three months later he became only the second repeat winner of the season when he claimed the Bovis Lend Lease European Senior Masters at Woburn Golf and Country Club, and two weeks later he had more reason to celebrate. This time Cambridge emulated Ebihara with a third victory as he claimed The Daily Telegraph/Sodexho Seniors Match Play Championship with a one hole victory over Eddie Polland in the final at Los Flamingos in Spain. The following week Ireland's Denis O'Sullivan captured the Tunisian Seniors Open at Port El Kantaoui Golf Club.

At Woburn Golf and Country Club, one of Cambridge's closest challengers was the indomitable Neil Coles, Chairman of The European Tour Board of Directors, who a couple of months before had produced arguably the most sensational feat of the season when he won the Lawrence Batley Seniors Open at Huddersfield Golf Club at the age of 67.

Michael Rayment from Hardys Wines congratulates Tommy Horton on finishing Number One in the Hardys Super Seniors Order of Merit.

Hardys Super Seniors Final Order of Merit

	Name	Country	Points
1	Tommy Horton	(Eng)	9,375
2	Neil Coles	(Eng)	9,250
3	Bill Hardwick	(Can)	6,375
4	Joe McDermott	(Ire)	5,125
5	Bob Charles	(NZ)	4,750

Ray Carrasco

Bernard Gallacher

When Coles arrived at 'The Batley', as it is affectionately known in honour of its now deceased patron, Lawrence Batley OBE, he already owned the record for being the oldest winner in Seniors golf. He set that record when he won the 2000 Jersey Seniors Open at the age of 65 and 252 days and he was to extend it to 67 and 276 days when he defeated David Creamer and Stull in a play-off. Even by Coles's standards, it was a remarkable achievement. Put in perspective, it means he is now comfortably the oldest winner in worldwide Seniors golf, beating Welshman Brian Huggett, who was 63 and 171 days old when he won the 2000 Beko Classic, and American Mike Fetchick, who holds the record on the US Senior Tour having won the 1985 Hilton Head Seniors Invitational on his 63rd birthday.

Oldest Winners on Tours Around the World

Tour	Player	Age	Year	Event
European Seniors	Neil Coles	67 & 276 days	2002	Lawrence Batley Seniors Open
US Seniors	Mike Fetchick	63	1985	Hilton Head Seniors Invitational
US Tour	Sam Snead	52 & 316 days	1965	Greater Greensboro Open
European Tour	Des Smyth	48 & 34 days	2001	Madeira Island Open

Gary Wintz

Brian Jones

American professional, John Grace, who has won three times on the European Seniors Tour, was one of the first people to put into perspective what Coles had achieved by winning in Huddersfield. "It is hard to believe what Neil is doing here," he said while watching Coles dominate the play-off. "I don't think people understand just how big a gap there is between being 67 and 50. I'm 54 now and, already, I'm beginning to realise how hard it is to compete against the newcomers on this Tour. How Neil does it at his age, I just don't know."

The self-effacing Coles tends to play down his own achievements but his contemporaries have no such qualms.

"He has got a simple swing, good rhythm, a great golfing brain and he's not afraid to hole the five-footers," said BBC commentator Peter Alliss, a man who played on five Great Britain and Ireland

Denis Durnian

Denis O'Sullivan

Delroy Cambridge

Terry Gale

Ryder Cup Teams with Coles in the 1960s. "He also hits the ball every day and still enjoys it which undoubtedly helps as well.

"What Neil has achieved is phenomenal. I was in America when I heard he had won at 'The Batley'. To begin with, I didn't really believe it but then I remembered it was Neil we were talking about and I knew it was true. He's incredible. I wouldn't be at all surprised if he were to win again before he's through."

The last word goes to Huggett. "Nothing that Neil does surprises me," he said. "I have competed against him for over 40 years and in all that time I don't think he has ever changed a thing. His swing is the same. He putts exactly the same and he's still a helluva competitor. As far as I am concerned, he's a one-off. I have the greatest respect for him. We all do, in fact."

Colin Callander

Neil Coles

Ian Stanley

Tony Jacklin

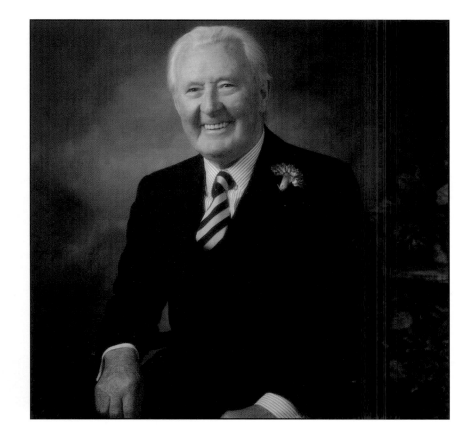

Lawrence Batley OBE

Lawrence Batley OBE, who died peacefully, aged 91, at home in Yorkshire, in August, 2002, was one of the greatest supporters of European golf. Ken Schofield, Executive Director of The European Tour, said: "The European Tour and indeed all of European golf were deeply saddened by Lawrence Batley's passing. For 20 years or so, the Batley Tournaments on, firstly The European Tour and indeed until June of 2002 on the European Seniors Tour, featured Lawrence's inimitable mark and style that also brought him unparalleled success in his pioneering of the UK's Cash and Carry market. Quite simply, Lawrence was irrepressible and he is missed by everyone he touched in his long and wonderful life."

The 2002 European Seniors Tour Order of Merit

Pos.	Name			euro	£		Pos.	Name			euro	£
1	Seiji EBIHARA	(Jpn)	(12)	330,210.95	207,339.49		51	Jeff VAN WAGENEN	(USA)	(18)	35,570.19	22,334.53
2	Denis DURNIAN	(Eng)	(19)	259,982.50	163,243.04		52	Bob SHEARER	(Aus)	(12)	31,819.37	19,979.38
3	Delroy CAMBRIDGE	(Jam)	(19)	184,167.09	115,638.54		53	David HUISH	(Scot)	(15)	31,226.36	19,607.04
4	John MORGAN	(Eng)	(19)	157,216.13	98,716.03		54	Jay HORTON	(USA)	(18)	31,079.14	19,514.60
5	Christy O'CONNOR JNR	(Ire)	(8)	152,319.27	95,641.28		55	Bobby VERWEY	(SA)	(14)	31,022.51	19,479.04
6	Steve STULL	(USA)	(17)	137,468.27	86,316.34		56	Bill HARDWICK	(Can)	(18)	27,773.24	17,438.82
7	John IRWIN	(Can)	(16)	126,127.17	79,195.26		57	Martin GRAY	(Scot)	(7)	27,327.34	17,158.84
8	John CHILLAS	(Scot)	(15)	125,829.57	79,008.40		58	Antonio GARRIDO	(Sp)	(16)	25,135.87	15,782.82
9	Denis O'SULLIVAN	(Ire)	(19)	125,361.75	78,714.65		59	Craig DEFOY	(Wal)	(17)	25,064.44	15,737.97
10	Nick JOB	(Eng)	(19)	122,319.86	76,804.65		60	Peter DAWSON	(Eng)	(15)	24,992.69	15,692.91
11	Neil COLES	(Eng)	(11)	106,798.49	67,058.78		61	Liam HIGGINS	(Ire)	(15)	23,222.34	14,581.31
12	Barry VIVIAN	(NZ)	(13)	103,217.27	64,810.13		62	Mike FERGUSON	(Aus)	(8)	22,267.75	13,981.92
13	Keith MACDONALD	(Eng)	(19)	99,915.14	62,736.73		63	Manuel PIÑERO	(Sp)	(4)	22,117.15	13,887.36
14	Tommy HORTON	(Eng)	(19)	96,574.34	60,639.04		64	Steve WILD	(Eng)	(12)	21,378.85	13,423.78
15	David GOOD	(Aus)	(18)	93,734.27	58,855.76		65	Paul LEONARD	(N.Ire)	(14)	19,900.81	12,495.72
16	Jim RHODES	(Eng)	(19)	91,462.76	57,429.48		66	Hank WOODROME	(USA)	(14)	19,680.20	12,357.20
17	Ian MOSEY	(Eng)	(18)	90,234.83	56,658.46		67	John FOURIE	(SA)	(18)	19,189.09	12,048.83
18	Noel RATCLIFFE	(Aus)	(18)	89,380.55	56,122.06		68	Silvano LOCATELLI	(It)	(9)	16,955.19	10,646.16
19	David CREAMER	(Eng)	(19)	88,768.43	55,737.71		69	David OJALA	(USA)	(14)	16,117.93	10,120.45
20	Malcolm GREGSON	(Eng)	(19)	88,180.76	55,368.71		70	Renato CAMPAGNOLI	(It)	(12)	12,956.49	8,135.38
21	Jerry BRUNER	(USA)	(19)	87,799.52	55,129.33		71	Lawrence FARMER	(Wal)	(5)	12,679.20	7,961.27
22	Ray CARRASCO	(USA)	(14)	87,072.98	54,673.13		72	Norman WOOD	(Scot)	(14)	10,551.13	6,625.05
23	Ian STANLEY	(Aus)	(17)	80,197.74	50,356.17		73	Agim BARDHA	(Alb)	(7)	9,897.76	6,214.80
24	Mike MILLER	(Scot)	(19)	78,604.00	49,355.46		74	Ian RICHARDSON	(Eng)	(6)	8,995.69	5,648.40
25	Guillermo ENCINA	(Chi)	(14)	76,937.38	48,308.99		75	David VAUGHAN	(Wal)	(9)	8,862.45	5,564.73
26	David OAKLEY	(USA)	(19)	76,692.18	48,155.03		76	John BENDA	(USA)	(6)	7,768.84	4,878.05
27	John GRACE	(USA)	(14)	76,330.86	47,928.16		77	Geoff PARSLOW	(Aus)	(3)	7,325.85	4,599.90
28	Bernard GALLACHER	(Scot)	(17)	75,649.60	47,500.39		78	Tommy PRICE	(USA)	(5)	7,077.36	4,443.87
29	Brian JONES	(Aus)	(12)	66,075.58	41,488.87		79	Victor GARCIA	(Sp)	(5)	6,235.36	3,915.18
30	Alberto CROCE	(It)	(16)	65,592.67	41,185.64		80	Jan SONNEVI	(Swe)	(11)	5,679.19	3,565.96
31	Gary WINTZ	(USA)	(18)	65,370.13	41,045.91		81	Brian WAITES	(Eng)	(6)	4,947.49	3,106.53
32	Dragon TAKI	(Jpn)	(12)	64,433.09	40,457.54		82	TR JONES	(USA)	(4)	4,335.34	2,722.16
33	Ross METHERELL	(Aus)	(15)	63,567.31	39,913.92		83	David SNELL	(Eng)	(6)	3,801.87	2,387.19
34	Priscillo DINIZ	(Bra)	(16)	63,234.80	39,705.14		84	Jay DOLAN III	(USA)	(7)	3,667.48	2,302.81
35	Peter TOWNSEND	(Eng)	(18)	62,844.63	39,460.15		85	Kenny STEVENSON	(N.Ire)	(5)	2,695.73	1,692.65
36	Terry GALE	(Aus)	(13)	62,830.04	39,450.99		86	Barry SANDRY	(Eng)	(4)	1,557.40	977.89
37	Eamonn DARCY	(Ire)	(4)	62,754.62	39,403.63		87	Graham BURROUGHS	(Eng)	(2)	1,471.42	923.90
38	Eddie POLLAND	(N.Ire)	(19)	60,654.75	38,085.12		88	Michael MURPHY	(Ire)	(4)	1,040.98	653.63
39	Martin FOSTER	(Eng)	(12)	58,813.78	36,929.18		89	Jan DORRESTEIN	(NL)	(2)	981.13	616.05
40	Alan TAPIE	(USA)	(14)	58,229.22	36,562.14		90	Manuel SANCHEZ	(Sp)	(1)	777.13	487.96
41	John MCTEAR	(Scot)	(15)	57,852.53	36,325.61		91	Kurt COX	(USA)	(2)	777.13	487.96
42	Tony JACKLIN	(Eng)	(12)	55,506.49	34,852.53		92	Manuel BALLESTEROS	(Sp)	(1)	621.70	390.37
43	Russell WEIR	(Scot)	(18)	51,114.60	32,094.86		93	John TURK	(USA)	(2)	578.00	362.93
44	Bill BRASK	(USA)	(12)	50,119.97	31,470.34		94	Antero BABURIN	(Swe)	(1)	466.28	292.78
45	Simon OWEN	(NZ)	(18)	49,577.28	31,129.58		95	Hugh DOLAN	(Aus)	(3)	391.00	245.51
46	Joe MCDERMOTT	(Ire)	(15)	46,475.63	29,182.05		96	Leonard OWENS	(Ire)	(3)	341.00	214.11
47	Maurice BEMBRIDGE	(Eng)	(18)	38,363.88	24,088.68		97	Roberto BERNARDINI	(It)	(1)	255.00	160.11
48	Bob LENDZION	(USA)	(16)	38,093.33	23,918.81		98	Gordon MACDONALD	(Scot)	(2)	255.00	160.11
49	David JONES	(N.Ire)	(9)	36,586.89	22,972.91		99	Roger FIDLER	(Eng)	(1)	225.50	141.59
50	John MASHEGO	(SA)	(14)	36,370.62	22,837.11		100	Deray SIMON	(USA)	(1)	213.00	133.74

The European Challenge Tour

source of inspiration

The 2002
European Challenge
Tour Rankings

1 **Lee S JAMES** Eng

2 Jean-François LUCQUIN Fr

3 Matthew BLACKEY Eng

4 Peter LAWRIE Ire

5 Iain PYMAN Eng

6 Simon HURD Eng

7 Nicolas VANHOOTEGEM Bel

8 John E MORGAN Eng

9 Simon WAKEFIELD Eng

10 Nicolas COLSAERTS Bel

11 Gary BIRCH Jnr Eng

12 Gustavo ROJAS Arg

13 Benn BARHAM Eng

14 Fredrik WIDMARK Swe

15 Julien VAN HAUWE Fr

Lee S James

The European Challenge Tour

Motivation is a key element in the game of golf. It can often be the 15th club in the bag, the crucial factor that lifts one player head and shoulders above the rest either in a certain week or over an entire season.

The dictionary defines motivation as 'incentive or inducement. The process that arouses, sustains and regulates human behaviour.'

There is little doubt that motivation was the major factor in changing the careers of several prominent European Challenge Tour players during 2002, none more so than Lee S James, who finished Number One in the Rankings with three outstanding victories.

Only one year earlier Dorset-based James was at the crossroads of his career. He had enjoyed a highly successful amateur career, winning the 1994 Amateur Championship at Nairn and being capped 32 times by England, before turning professional in 1995 after helping Great Britain and Ireland win the Walker Cup against a Tiger Woods – led United States at Royal Porthcawl. A burgeoning life in the paid ranks beckoned. It did not pan out that way.

James did win the inaugural First Modena Classic Open on the 1996 European Challenge Tour but he still finished 67th in the

Rankings. In 1997 he took 48th place with winnings of only £11,749 from 26 events. If he was seeking motivation then he might have stolen a look at the Rankings that year as, only four places above him, sat Thomas Levet with £14,249 earned from 20 events. Levet, of course, would transform his career by winning the 1998 Cannes Open then the 2001 Victor Chandler British Masters prior to finishing joint runner-up to Ernie Els in the 131st Open Golf Championship.

As it was, James would be the first to admit that pedestrian would be a kind word for his progress. He was 58th in the Rankings in 2000; 49th in 2001. Still, he could also look back over his shoulder and draw motivation from the progress made by team mates from the 1995 winning Walker Cup team like Padraig Harrington and David Howell and, coincidentally at that crossroads, he did find a special source of inspiration from another player with whom he had celebrated at Royal Porthcawl.

Mark Foster had endured a few setbacks of his own since that triumphant time in South Wales. Nevertheless with the assistance of two wins he claimed first place in the 2001 European Challenge Tour Rankings - opening the door to a career on The European Tour. James took another look at the Challenge Tour Rankings for that year - he had earned precisely £15,770 and 65 pence - and then viewed the Volvo Order of Merit where history had been made with the leading 115 players retaining their playing rights for the following season by each earning in excess of £100,000. Foster would join that company in 2002, although James was not to know that when he set out in search of glory, but what he did know was that he wanted to be part of the scene.

James said: "I knew there wasn't a secret formula, and there certainly hasn't been. But I did want to follow Mark onto The European Tour and I knew it would take one thing for sure - hard graft on and off the fairways. I was overweight - around 13 stone - so I went to the gym. I also took a proper interest in my diet. I lost a stone and felt so much better for it. Then I prepared for the new season by spending three weeks in America practising at The Golf Club of Georgia where I'm attached."

It gave him an edge when the season started and he did not have to wait long for success, a final round 64 securing victory in the season's curtain-raising event, the Sameer Kenya Open at Muthaiga Golf Club. James's rekindled confidence brought him further victories in the Clearstream International Luxembourg Open at Kikuoka Country Club and the Talma Finnish Challenge at Golf Talma.

Jean-François Lucquin

That James should spend the best part of the season residing in top spot on the European Challenge Tour Rankings is evidence of his determination to climb even higher. He will celebrate his 30th birthday in the first month of 2003, but if he is looking for further stimulation then he will know that Niclas Fasth and Pierre Fulke both graduated from the Challenge Tour, and made their Ryder Cup debuts in the winning European Ryder Cup Team at The De Vere Belfry in 2002 at the age of 30 and 31 respectively.

Moreover for James, and indeed all 15 of the players to graduate from the 2002 European Challenge Tour, the record books offer further motivation since the total number of wins by former Challenge Tour players on The European Tour International Schedule is in excess of 80 with the victories in 2002 by Thomas Björn, Diego Borrego, Michael Campbell, Alex Cejka, Tobias Dier, Alastair Forsyth, Anders Hansen, Søren Hansen, Richard S Johnson, Stephen Leaney, Adam Mednick, Ian Poulter, Justin Rose, Jarmo Sandelin, Steen Tinning and Miles Tunnicliff.

This will inspire the new boys, many of whom have delivered their games and outlook on a Challenge Tour which annually offers

Iain Pyman

more prize money and increased playing opportunities – Matthew Blackey most certainly slots into this category. He traces his source of motivation to the remarkable finish of Richard Bland, who is a close friend as well as living near to him in Hampshire. Bland changed his career at the Challenge Tour Grand Final at Golf du Médoc in Bordeaux in 2001 when he produced the round of his life – storming home in 29 for a 63 – to secure victory and climb from 44th in the Rankings to tenth. Blackey was intent on following in Bland's footsteps and, perhaps significantly, he made a giant stride in that direction only one week after Bland had rubber-stamped his arrival on The European Tour by finishing sixth in the BMW International Open as he took his Volvo Order of Merit winnings to more than £200,000.

Blackey went out the next week and made his Challenge Tour breakthrough by winning the Formby Hall Challenge with a

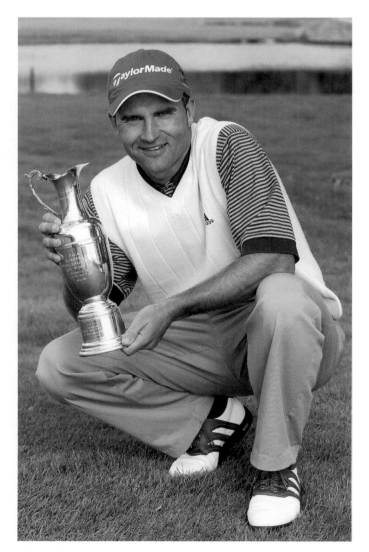

Matthew Blackey

Simon Hurd

Nicolas Vanhootegem

closing 67 on Merseyside and, buoyed by that success, he completed back-to-back wins by capturing the Telia Grand Prix at Ljunghusens in Sweden.

Blackey said: "Blandy's performance in the last two weeks of the 2001 season was awesome. It was a big spur for me. We've been close friends from our amateur days and in the early part of 2002, when I was not winning, I kept thinking of what he had done and where it had taken him."

Other long-term Challenge Tour players to achieve a breakthrough were Simon Hurd, Simon Wakefield and Fredrik Widmark, all of whom earned their cards, and Thomas Norret.

Hurd's long wait for victory which came in the Rolex Trophy at the Golf Club de Genève, was motivated by Ian Poulter's success on The European Tour. The pair were room-mates during several years on the Challenge Tour but that link was broken when Poulter gained his card at the 1999 Qualifying School, since when he has consolidated his position as one of The European Tour's rising stars.

Hurd hoped to follow suit, but he missed gaining a card in 2000, finishing 18th on the Challenge Tour Final Rankings. The progress was not maintained last year, so the 27 year old from Leeds decided to take a different tack.

Last winter he spent three months playing and working on his game in South Africa. "I had to prove to myself and to others that I was a decent player," he said. "Having spent that time working in the sunshine, when it came to the opening event in Kenya I had a head start. I'd played five tournaments, while most of the guys had spent a winter back home.

"I didn't play well in Kenya but still finished sixth, then I was fourth in the Stanbic Zambia Open and sixth again in the Panalpina Banque Commerciale du Maroc Classic. From that moment I felt I could win every week. I never doubted my ability, but you never know when someone else is going to shoot low and that's what invariably happened."

John E Morgan

Peter Lawrie

Gary Birch Jnr

attitude are so much better and I don't lose concentration when things go wrong."

Widmark had made gradual progress over the previous four years and he secured his first title in the Izki Challenge de España at Izki Golf, Vitoria, in Spain in May. The victory followed a five week winter trip to South Africa where he only managed to qualify for one tournament and missed the cut in that. "It probably did me a lot of good although it didn't seem so at the time," he said.

But it all came good in northern Spain when the big-hitting Swede claimed his maiden title with a grandstand finish, running in six birdies in the final eight holes for a 66 and taking his week's haul to 30 birdies, ten in that final round.

Norret's motivation was not wishing to remain a schoolteacher and his victory in the Volvo Finnish Open at Espoo Golf Club ensured that. The 28 year old Dane turned to teaching at the end of 2001, disillusioned with both his form and lack of success. "I played so badly for two years and when you miss ten cuts in a row you can't go on," he said. So, Norret took a job as a schoolteacher to support his wife and two sons.

Hurd did his own bit of low scoring with a closing 65 to win by four strokes in Geneva and galvanise his own career.

Wakefield, from Newcastle-under-Lyme, waited four years for his maiden victory, which came in the Tessali Open del Sud at the Riva dei Tessali Golf Club in Italy with a closing 66. His motivation has been his fiancée Denise - they marry on May 1, 2004 - and sports psychologist, Lee Crombleholme.

"I started seeing Lee before the season started," said Simon. "I had several sessions with him and the difference was amazing. I have been in my own little bubble of concentration on the course and the change could be seen in my results. My temperament and

Simon Wakefield

Gustavo Rojas

Benn Barham

He taught Danish, English and German while keeping his swing in shape by practising in the evenings. However, the lure of the fairways was always there and schoolwork was not what he wanted to do for ever. So he started his comeback in June. Norret said: "I didn't want to teach for the rest of my life, so I took the clubs out again." It proved to be a sound move as he closed with 65 for a one shot success.

Iain Pyman was, perhaps, one man who needed no motivation. Disappointed at losing his European Tour card in 2000, he regained it at the 2001 Qualifying School and in 2002 he produced his best golf on the European Challenge Tour with victories in the Golf Challenge at Brunstorf Golf and Country Club in Hamburg and the BMW Russian Open at Moscow Golf and Country Club.

Markus Brier (Austrian Golf Open), Alex Cejka (Galeria Kaufhof Pokal Challenge), Nicolas Vanhootegem (Aa St Omer Open) and Didier de Vooght (Fortis Bank Challenge Open) ventured onto the Challenge Tour to record important wins; Germany's Wolfgang Huget followed his maiden victory in 2001 with another in the

Nicolas Colsaerts

Julien Van Hauwe

Golf Montecchia - PGA Triveneta Terme Euganee International Open at Golf Club Montecchia in Italy; and Diego Borrego (Madeira Island Open) and Adam Mednick (North West of Ireland Open), were, of course, also successful in tournaments that brought players from The European Tour and the European Challenge Tour together.

If French golfers required motivation then they were not short of this ingredient, inspired as they have been by the performances of compatriots like Gregory Havret, Jean Van de Velde and Levet, and Jean-François Lucquin (Panalpina Banque Commerciale du Maroc Classic) and Thomas Besancenez (Skandia PGA Open) were first time winners as were Zimbabwe's Marc Cayeux (Stanbic Zambia Open), Australia's Ed Stedman (Nykredit Danish Open), America's Scott Kammann (Open des Volcans) and England's John E Morgan (Charles Church Challenge Tour Championship).

In Lucquin's case there was to be ample evidence of his potential

at the Trophée Lancôme later in the year. The 23 year old from Montelimar, playing on home soil against an exceedingly strong field, finished tied third behind Cejka. He will look forward to joining compatriots like Levet on The European Tour as will Julien Van Hauwe. He needed to finish in the top two in the Challenge Tour Grand Final at Golf du Médoc in Bordeaux and he did just that by claiming the runners-up birth with three birdies in this last five holes. Victory in Bordeaux went to Peter Lawrie with which he not only joined the list of first time winners but also became the first Irishman to win on the Challenge Tour since David Higgins won three times in 2000.

Lawrie, who had already secured his European Tour card for 2003, scored a last round of 65 to win by four strokes and by collecting £21,511 he climbed into fourth place on the European Challenge Tour Rankings behind James, Lucquin and Blackey.

The European Challenge Tour continues to provide a platform for

Peter Lawrie

record breaking performances. There were 14 new course records established by Members during the 2002 season and no fewer than 16 holes in one. For England's David Salisbury there was an instant reward on the first morning of the BMW Russian Open at the Moscow Golf and Country Club when he aced the fourth hole with a six iron to win $100,000.

The most tangible reward on offer, however, comes through the European Challenge Tour maturing, over the years, into an integral part of the professional golfing community, continually emphasising the long-term policy of opportunity and incentive operated by The European Tour. There were many individual moments to savour during 2002, and many players were motivated to produce career-best performances, but Lee S James thoroughly deserved his position at the top....motivated, of course, with a little help from a friend.

David Hamilton

Fredrik Widmark

Left to right: Peter Lawrie, Gustavo Rojas, Lee S James, Fredrik Widmark, John E Morgan, Matthew Blackey, Simon Hurd, Benn Barham, Gary Birch Jnr., Iain Pyman, Simon Wakefield, Nicolas Vanhootegem, Jean-François Lucquin, Nicolas Colsaerts, and Julien Van Hauwe.

The 2002 European Challenge Tour Rankings

Pos.	Name			euro	Pos.	Name			euro
1	Lee S JAMES	(Eng)	(19)	121,531.05	51	Richard DINSDALE	(Wal)	(19)	18,972.96
2	Jean-François LUCQUIN	(Fr)	(20)	101,544.31	52	Mattias ELIASSON	(Swe)	(7)	18,643.60
3	Matthew BLACKEY	(Eng)	(19)	94,120.81	53	Sion E BEBB	(Wal)	(17)	17,832.80
4	Peter LAWRIE	(Ire)	(20)	89,072.63	54	Allan HOGH	(Den)	(21)	17,498.97
5	Iain PYMAN	(Eng)	(14)	75,674.10	55	Kariem BARAKA	(Ger)	(20)	17,304.63
6	Simon HURD	(Eng)	(20)	68,788.23	56	Alessandro TADINI	(It)	(12)	17,134.53
7	Nicolas VANHOOTEGEM	(Bel)	(8)	63,823.45	57	James HEPWORTH	(Eng)	(14)	16,755.92
8	John E MORGAN	(Eng)	(15)	62,047.96	58	Michael JONZON	(Swe)	(12)	16,225.79
9	Simon WAKEFIELD	(Eng)	(24)	58,922.31	59	Marc CAYEUX	(Zim)	(13)	16,120.20
10	Nicolas COLSAERTS	(Bel)	(20)	52,247.46	60	Stefano REALE	(It)	(15)	15,999.25
11	Gary BIRCH JNR	(Eng)	(19)	51,219.42	61	Euan LITTLE	(Scot)	(14)	15,246.01
12	Gustavo ROJAS	(Arg)	(10)	50,873.29	62	David RYLES	(Eng)	(6)	14,690.29
13	Benn BARHAM	(Eng)	(18)	50,441.22	63	Martin ERLANDSSON	(Swe)	(17)	13,802.14
14	Fredrik WIDMARK	(Swe)	(19)	50,438.39	64	Gareth PADDISON	(NZ)	(8)	13,751.00
15	Julien VAN HAUWE	(Fr)	(22)	47,472.25	65	Roger WINCHESTER	(Eng)	(6)	13,750.00
16	Andrew RAITT	(Eng)	(17)	47,254.31	66	Adam CRAWFORD	(Aus)	(6)	13,625.44
17	Titch MOORE	(SA)	(19)	46,791.99	67	Kalle BRINK	(Swe)	(17)	13,491.44
18	Didier DE VOOGHT	(Bel)	(9)	46,266.47	68	Joakim RASK	(Swe)	(10)	13,476.51
19	Mark SANDERS	(Eng)	(21)	44,671.23	69	Olivier DAVID	(Fr)	(18)	13,376.55
20	Massimo FLORIOLI	(It)	(23)	43,220.76	70	Dominique NOUAILHAC	(Fr)	(18)	13,258.62
21	Ivo GINER	(Sp)	(19)	38,788.85	71	Pehr MAGNEBRANT	(Swe)	(14)	13,212.41
22	Ed STEDMAN	(Aus)	(14)	38,462.70	72	Garry HOUSTON	(Wal)	(11)	12,622.14
23	David J GEALL	(Eng)	(19)	38,384.12	73	Alberto BINAGHI	(It)	(13)	12,438.21
24	Ben MASON	(Eng)	(22)	37,715.97	74	Kalle VAINOLA	(Fin)	(10)	12,327.67
25	Damien MCGRANE	(Ire)	(13)	37,358.50	75	Knud STORGAARD	(Den)	(18)	12,127.81
26	Jesus Maria ARRUTI	(Sp)	(15)	36,870.53	76	Linus PETERSSON	(Swe)	(9)	12,111.40
27	Wolfgang HUGET	(Ger)	(15)	36,055.91	77	Jean Pierre CIXOUS	(Fr)	(14)	11,587.00
28	Gary MURPHY	(Ire)	(18)	34,747.96	78	Steven O'HARA	(Scot)	(12)	11,362.18
29	Andrew SHERBORNE	(Eng)	(19)	34,548.08	79	Per NYMAN	(Swe)	(6)	11,240.75
30	Richard STERNE	(SA)	(19)	34,537.62	80	Jean Louis GUEPY	(Fr)	(10)	11,114.45
31	Denny LUCAS	(Eng)	(17)	33,487.79	81	Marc PENDARIES	(Fr)	(16)	11,020.47
32	David DIXON	(Eng)	(20)	33,361.26	82	Peter MALMGREN	(Swe)	(14)	10,819.34
33	Paul DWYER	(Eng)	(21)	32,755.13	83	Martin MARITZ	(SA)	(9)	10,809.24
34	Ilya GORONESKOUL	(Fr)	(18)	31,477.87	84	Gianluca BARUFFALDI	(It)	(14)	10,764.88
35	Raimo SJÖBERG	(Swe)	(16)	31,110.63	85	Tuomas TUOVINEN	(Fin)	(7)	10,526.32
36	Guido VAN DER VALK	(NL)	(18)	30,909.44	86	Massimo SCARPA	(It)	(7)	10,392.96
37	Hennie OTTO	(SA)	(17)	29,956.81	87	Regis GUSTAVE	(St.L)	(16)	10,247.38
38	Greig HUTCHEON	(Scot)	(21)	28,356.96	88	Marcel SIEM	(Ger)	(7)	10,049.16
39	Francois DELAMONTAGNE	(Fr)	(20)	27,465.30	89	Carlos QUEVEDO	(Sp)	(10)	10,038.64
40	Scott KAMMANN	(USA)	(12)	27,348.41	90	Federico BISAZZA	(It)	(16)	9,937.53
41	Michael ARCHER	(Eng)	(17)	25,761.29	91	Hampus VON POST	(Swe)	(13)	9,816.96
42	Sam LITTLE	(Eng)	(24)	25,677.02	92	Bjorn PETTERSSON	(Swe)	(15)	9,805.38
43	Hennie WALTERS	(SA)	(20)	24,714.90	93	Frédéric CUPILLARD	(Fr)	(7)	9,535.38
44	Marcello SANTI	(It)	(15)	24,240.86	94	Steven PARRY	(Eng)	(8)	9,400.50
45	Thomas NORRET	(Den)	(15)	23,633.06	95	Van PHILLIPS	(Eng)	(12)	9,216.43
46	Thomas BESANCENEZ	(Fr)	(17)	21,862.00	96	Renaud GUILLARD	(Fr)	(14)	9,192.13
47	Oskar BERGMAN	(Swe)	(12)	21,149.81	97	Charles CHALLEN	(Eng)	(11)	8,862.13
48	Tim MILFORD	(Eng)	(17)	20,030.15	98	Robin BYRD	(USA)	(14)	8,855.60
49	Marco BERNARDINI	(It)	(17)	19,784.66	99	Sebastien BRANGER	(Fr)	(8)	8,832.00
50	Jamie LITTLE	(Eng)	(17)	19,047.66	100	Dennis EDLUND	(Swe)	(8)	8,804.14

Ernie Els wins The European

Tour Shot of the Year

Ernie Els knew as soon as he peered into the cavernous bunker at Muirfield's 13th hole that he faced a make or break shot. The 131st Open Golf Championship was reaching its climax and the South African, playing in the final pairing, was within touching distance of fulfilling his lifetime's ambition.

Such moments require natural talent, a steely nerve and a generous portion of inspiration. The hugely gifted Els didn't disappoint. With a deftness of touch belying his powerful frame, he proceeded to play the most exquisite bunker shot to a matter of inches from the hole – a stroke which not only inspired him to capture the precious Claret Jug, but deservedly secured The 2002 European Tour Shot of the Year.

"I always felt it was my destiny to win the Open at least once in my career," recalled Els. "When I birdied the tenth and 12th that Sunday at Muirfield, I thought I was well on my way to doing just that. However I was caught between clubs and tugged my seven iron just a touch at the 13th. It was my own fault for putting the ball in the bunker.

"I guessed I would be facing a tough shot, but it was only when I got to the green and looked into the bunker that I realised just how tough. The ball was tight against the face of the bunker and just getting it out – never mind close – would be a reasonable result.

"I pulled out my 59 degree sand wedge and at least I had a good stance. I said to my caddie, Ricci (Roberts): 'I'm going to hit this as hard as I can'. I was amazed I got it out and almost holed it. It was a really, really, good save and unquestionably helped me win the Open."

JUSTIN ROSE
January & May

ERNIE ELS
March & July

RETIEF GOOSEN
April

MILES TUNNICLIFF
June

Asprey Golfer of the Month Awards 2002

The Asprey Golfer of the Month Awards
are presented throughout the year
followed by an Annual Award.

PREVIOUS ANNUAL WINNERS

2001 Retief Goosen

2000 Lee Westwood

1999 Colin Montgomerie

1998 Lee Westwood

1997 Colin Montgomerie

1996 Colin Montgomerie

1995 Colin Montgomerie

1994 Ernie Els

1993 Bernhard Langer

1992 Nick Faldo

1991 Severiano Ballesteros

1990 Nick Faldo

1989 Nick Faldo

1988 Severiano Ballesteros

1987 Ian Woosnam

1986 Severiano Ballesteros

1985 Bernhard Langer

GRAEME McDOWELL
August

SAM TORRANCE
September

PADRAIG HARRINGTON
October

*Main Picture: José Maria Olazábal,
Asprey Golfer of the Month in
February, receives his Award from
Edward Asprey, New Business Director
of Asprey, the ultimate authentic
British luxury lifestyle house*

STROKE AVERAGE

1	Padraig HARRINGTON (Ire)	(81)	69.72
2	Ernie ELS (SA)	(59)	70.07
3	Retief GOOSEN (SA)	(80)	70.15
4	Vijay SINGH (Fiji)	(30)	70.27
5	Colin MONTGOMERIE (Scot)	(76)	70.36
	Eduardo ROMERO (Arg)	(77)	70.36
7	Sergio GARCIA (Sp)	(40)	70.43
8	Adam SCOTT (Aus)	(78)	70.54
9	Michael CAMPBELL (NZ)	(71)	70.56
10	Trevor IMMELMAN (SA)	(101)	70.67
11	Thomas BJÖRN (Den)	(78)	70.77
12	Justin ROSE (Eng)	(84)	70.80
13	Bradley DREDGE (Wal)	(93)	70.82
	Alex CEJKA (Ger)	(51)	70.82
15	Ricardo GONZALEZ (Arg)	(75)	70.88
16	Gary EVANS (Eng)	(101)	70.91
17	Joakim HAEGGMAN (Swe)	(81)	70.93
	Angel CABRERA (Arg)	(59)	70.93
19	Des TERBLANCHE (SA)	(32)	70.94
20	Søren HANSEN (Den)	(104)	70.95
21	Stephen LEANEY (Aus)	(74)	70.96
22	Nick O'HERN (Aus)	(84)	70.98
	Anders HANSEN (Den)	(87)	70.98
24	Niclas FASTH (Swe)	(77)	70.99
25	Peter LONARD (Aus)	(40)	71.00
26	Darren CLARKE (N.Ire)	(72)	71.01
	Nick FALDO (Eng)	(70)	71.01
28	Ian POULTER (Eng)	(90)	71.03
29	Mathias GRÖNBERG (Swe)	(48)	71.04
30	Paul LAWRIE (Scot)	(85)	71.05
31	Alastair FORSYTH (Scot)	(86)	71.09
32	Maarten LAFEBER (NL)	(93)	71.12
33	Carl PETTERSSON (Swe)	(103)	71.13
	Barry LANE (Eng)	(104)	71.13
35	Miguel Angel JIMÉNEZ (Sp)	(42)	71.14
36	Bernhard LANGER (Ger)	(52)	71.15
	Paul CASEY (Eng)	(65)	71.15
38	Jarrod MOSELEY (Aus)	(86)	71.16
39	Wei-Tze YEH (C.Tai)	(42)	71.19
40	David HOWELL (Eng)	(73)	71.21
	Steen TINNING (Den)	(77)	71.21
42	Søren KJELDSEN (Den)	(83)	71.22
	Brian DAVIS (Eng)	(87)	71.22
44	Ian WOOSNAM (Wal)	(73)	71.23
45	Fredrik JACOBSON (Swe)	(80)	71.25
	Rolf MUNTZ (NL)	(91)	71.25
47	Robert KARLSSON (Swe)	(78)	71.26
	Peter O'MALLEY (Aus)	(61)	71.26
49	Steve WEBSTER (Eng)	(82)	71.28
50	Ignacio GARRIDO (Sp)	(79)	71.29
	David GILFORD (Eng)	(82)	71.29
52	John BICKERTON (Eng)	(97)	71.31
53	Richard GREEN (Aus)	(80)	71.33
54	Sam TORRANCE (Scot)	(56)	71.34
55	Robert ALLENBY (Aus)	(26)	71.35
	Jean-Francois REMESY (Fr)	(92)	71.35
57	Emanuele CANONICA (It)	(68)	71.37
58	Santiago LUNA (Sp)	(78)	71.38
59	Carlos RODILES (Sp)	(70)	71.41
60	Thomas LEVET (Fr)	(87)	71.43
	José Maria OLAZÁBAL (Sp)	(54)	71.43
62	Jamie DONALDSON (Wal)	(90)	71.49
63	Warren BENNETT (Eng)	(82)	71.52
64	Graeme MCDOWELL (N.Ire)	(40)	71.53
	Mark MCNULTY (Zim)	(47)	71.53
66	Gary ORR (Scot)	(80)	71.54
67	Ian GARBUTT (Eng)	(97)	71.55
	Miles TUNNICLIFF (Eng)	(42)	71.55
	Charlie WI (Kor)	(62)	71.55
70	Pierre FULKE (Swe)	(56)	71.59
71	Peter FOWLER (Aus)	(87)	71.60
	Sandy LYLE (Scot)	(48)	71.60
73	Phillip PRICE (Wal)	(65)	71.65
74	Patrik SJÖLAND (Swe)	(88)	71.66
75	Darren FICHARDT (SA)	(75)	71.67
	Simon DYSON (Eng)	(103)	71.67
77	Greg OWEN (Eng)	(81)	71.70
78	Raphaël JACQUELIN (Fr)	(95)	71.71
	David LYNN (Eng)	(90)	71.71
80	Anthony WALL (Eng)	(90)	71.74
81	Richard S JOHNSON (Swe)	(70)	71.76
	Paul MCGINLEY (Ire)	(68)	71.76
83	Christopher HANELL (Swe)	(85)	71.78
	Greg TURNER (NZ)	(51)	71.78
85	Roger WESSELS (SA)	(85)	71.79
86	Andrew OLDCORN (Scot)	(72)	71.81
	Mark FOSTER (Eng)	(78)	71.81
88	Gordon BRAND JNR. (Scot)	(75)	71.83
	Andrew COLTART (Scot)	(105)	71.83
90	David CARTER (Eng)	(79)	71.84
	Henrik NYSTROM (Swe)	(68)	71.84
92	Jamie SPENCE (Eng)	(86)	71.85
	Martin MARITZ (SA)	(41)	71.85
94	Fredrik ANDERSSON (Swe)	(50)	71.86
	Nick DOUGHERTY (Eng)	(101)	71.86
96	Robert COLES (Eng)	(54)	71.87
97	Henrik BJORNSTAD (Nor)	(81)	71.88
	Mark ROE (Eng)	(75)	71.88
99	Stephen DODD (Wal)	(93)	71.92
	Jonathan LOMAS (Eng)	(93)	71.92

DRIVING ACCURACY (%)

1	Peter O'MALLEY (Aus)	(45)	80.7
2	Richard GREEN (Aus)	(72)	76.9
3	Michele REALE (It)	(36)	76.0
4	Paul EALES (Eng)	(79)	72.2
5	David GILFORD (Eng)	(78)	71.3
6	John BICKERTON (Eng)	(91)	70.6
	Stephen DODD (Wal)	(88)	70.6
8	Ian GARBUTT (Eng)	(90)	70.3
9	Jarrod MOSELEY (Aus)	(78)	70.1
10	Anders HANSEN (Den)	(73)	69.4
11	Diego BORREGO (Sp)	(53)	69.3
12	Darren CLARKE (N.Ire)	(46)	69.2
13	Richard BLAND (Eng)	(75)	69.0
14	Miguel Angel JIMÉNEZ (Sp)	(36)	68.8
15	Pierre FULKE (Swe)	(41)	68.2
16	Jeremy ROBINSON (Eng)	(49)	68.0
	Jamie DONALDSON (Wal)	(86)	68.0
	Gary ORR (Scot)	(76)	68.0
19	Chris GANE (Eng)	(79)	67.7
20	Nicolas VANHOOTEGEM (Bel)	(41)	67.6

DRIVING DISTANCE (YDS)

1	Emanuele CANONICA (It)	(65)	304.9
2	Des TERBLANCHE (SA)	(31)	301.7
3	Ricardo GONZALEZ (Arg)	(61)	300.8
4	Angel CABRERA (Arg)	(33)	300.1
5	Ernie ELS (SA)	(31)	297.4
6	Santiago LUNA (Sp)	(72)	296.0
7	Carl SUNESON (Sp)	(54)	295.9
8	Stephen DODD (Wal)	(88)	295.8
9	Paul CASEY (Eng)	(57)	294.5
10	Michele REALE (It)	(36)	293.6
	Greg OWEN (Eng)	(73)	293.6
12	Bradley DREDGE (Wal)	(86)	293.3
13	Mikko ILONEN (Fin)	(41)	293.1
	Trevor IMMELMAN (SA)	(89)	293.1
15	Rolf MUNTZ (NL)	(87)	293.0
16	Klas ERIKSSON (Swe)	(67)	292.8
	Ignacio GARRIDO (Sp)	(75)	292.8
18	Mark PILKINGTON (Wal)	(97)	292.6
19	Jean HUGO (SA)	(79)	292.2
	José Manuel LARA (Sp)	(38)	292.2
	Niclas FASTH (Swe)	(53)	292.2

Padraig Harrington

Peter O'Malley

Emanuele Canonica

Bernhard Langer

SAND SAVES (%)

1	Bernhard LANGER (Ger)	(28)	81.3
2	Tony JOHNSTONE (Zim)	(50)	72.4
3	Ignacio GARRIDO (Sp)	(75)	71.6
4	Miguel Angel JIMÉNEZ (Sp)	(36)	68.6
5	Justin ROSE (Eng)	(64)	68.1
6	Scott GARDINER (Aus)	(46)	66.7
7	Jamie DONALDSON (Wal)	(86)	66.4
8	Gary EVANS (Eng)	(91)	65.8
9	Anders HANSEN (Den)	(73)	65.6
10	Paul EALES (Eng)	(79)	65.4
11	David DRYSDALE (Scot)	(66)	63.6
12	José Maria OLAZÁBAL (Sp)	(28)	63.3
13	Emanuele CANONICA (It)	(65)	62.5
14	Shaun P WEBSTER (Eng)	(30)	62.2
15	Bradley DREDGE (Wal)	(86)	61.8
16	John BICKERTON (Eng)	(91)	61.7
17	Christopher HANELL (Swe)	(81)	61.5
	Michele REALE (It)	(36)	61.5
	Mark MOULAND (Wal)	(84)	61.5
20	Sebastien DELAGRANGE (Fr)	(70)	61.4

AVERAGE PUTTS PER ROUND

1	Marcel SIEM (Ger)	(45)	27.9
2	Paul CASEY (Eng)	(57)	28.2
	Sam TORRANCE (Scot)	(56)	28.2
4	Ricardo GONZALEZ (Arg)	(61)	28.3
5	Angel CABRERA (Arg)	(33)	28.4
	Olle KARLSSON (Swe)	(56)	28.4
	Pierre FULKE (Swe)	(41)	28.4
	Sandy LYLE (Scot)	(38)	28.4
9	Justin ROSE (Eng)	(64)	28.5
	Jarmo SANDELIN (Swe)	(65)	28.5
11	Dennis EDLUND (Swe)	(34)	28.6
	David HOWELL (Eng)	(65)	28.6
	Shaun P WEBSTER (Eng)	(30)	28.6
	Brian DAVIS (Eng)	(85)	28.6
	Markus BRIER (Aut)	(77)	28.6
	Fredrik JACOBSON (Swe)	(73)	28.6
17	Alastair FORSYTH (Scot)	(83)	28.7
	Ian POULTER (Eng)	(82)	28.7
	Robert KARLSSON (Swe)	(69)	28.7
	Colin MONTGOMERIE (Scot)	(55)	28.7

GREENS IN REGULATION (%)

1	Thomas LEVET (Fr)	(72)	75.8
2	Peter O'MALLEY (Aus)	(45)	74.3
3	Ian GARBUTT (Eng)	(90)	72.7
4	Greg OWEN (Eng)	(73)	72.6
5	Michele REALE (It)	(36)	72.4
6	Richard GREEN (Aus)	(72)	72.2
7	Eduardo ROMERO (Arg)	(61)	72.1
8	Ernie ELS (SA)	(31)	72.0
9	Bernhard LANGER (Ger)	(28)	71.6
10	Alex CEJKA (Ger)	(49)	71.4
11	David LYNN (Eng)	(85)	71.2
12	Gary ORR (Scot)	(76)	71.1
13	Gary EVANS (Eng)	(91)	70.9
14	Des TERBLANCHE (SA)	(31)	70.6
	Michael CAMPBELL (NZ)	(50)	70.6
16	Rolf MUNTZ (NL)	(87)	70.3
17	Maarten LAFEBER (NL)	(89)	70.2
18	Colin MONTGOMERIE (Scot)	(55)	69.8
19	Jarrod MOSELEY (Aus)	(78)	69.7
20	Barry LANE (Eng)	(97)	69.1

PUTTS PER GREEN IN REGULATION

1	Michael CAMPBELL (NZ)	(50)	1.704
2	Sam TORRANCE (Scot)	(56)	1.714
3	Colin MONTGOMERIE (Scot)	(55)	1.716
4	Paul CASEY (Eng)	(57)	1.718
	Marcel SIEM (Ger)	(45)	1.718
6	Retief GOOSEN (SA)	(54)	1.720
7	Justin ROSE (Eng)	(64)	1.727
8	Darren CLARKE (N.Ire)	(46)	1.728
	Fredrik JACOBSON (Swe)	(73)	1.728
10	Ernie ELS (SA)	(31)	1.731
11	Pierre FULKE (Swe)	(41)	1.735
12	Jarmo SANDELIN (Swe)	(65)	1.739
13	Angel CABRERA (Arg)	(33)	1.742
	Steen TINNING (Den)	(74)	1.742
15	Ricardo GONZALEZ (Arg)	(61)	1.744
	Padraig HARRINGTON (Ire)	(53)	1.744
17	Paul LAWRIE (Scot)	(61)	1.745
	Adam SCOTT (Aus)	(58)	1.745
	Sandy LYLE (Scot)	(38)	1.745
20	Ian WOOSNAM (Wal)	(62)	1.750
	Henrik BJORNSTAD (Nor)	(78)	1.750

REUTERS

Performance Data for The 2002 European Tour

Marcel Siem

Thomas Levet

Michael Campbell

EUROPEAN TOUR

OFFICIAL PERFORMANCE DATA

Pos	Name & Country		Total Prize Money	
			euro	£
1	Retief GOOSEN (SA)	(22)	2,360,127.65	1,504,847.55
2	Padraig HARRINGTON (Ire)	(22)	2,334,655.45	1,488,606.15
3	Ernie ELS (SA)	(16)	2,251,708.28	1,435,717.97
4	Colin MONTGOMERIE (Scot)	(23)	1,980,719.95	1,262,932.35
5	Eduardo ROMERO (Arg)	(21)	1,811,329.89	1,154,927.08
6	Sergio GARCIA (Sp)	(11)	1,488,728.30	949,232.19
7	Adam SCOTT (Aus)	(24)	1,361,775.88	868,285.70
8	Michael CAMPBELL (NZ)	(21)	1,325,403.70	845,094.33
9	Justin ROSE (Eng)	(25)	1,323,528.84	843,898.90
10	Paul LAWRIE (Scot)	(25)	1,151,433.91	734,168.97
11	Angel CABRERA (Arg)	(17)	1,128,913.46	719,809.65
12	Thomas BJÖRN (Den)	(22)	1,110,213.17	707,886.10
13	José Maria OLAZÁBAL (Sp)	(16)	1,066,082.90	679,748.08
14	Trevor IMMELMAN (SA)	(30)	1,064,085.05	678,474.22
15	Stephen LEANEY (Aus)	(24)	1,055,029.03	672,699.99
16	Anders HANSEN (Den)	(26)	1,047,920.33	668,167.39
17	Niclas FASTH (Swe)	(23)	982,849.04	626,677.10
18	Bradley DREDGE (Wal)	(26)	961,121.51	612,823.36
19	Bernhard LANGER (Ger)	(15)	947,232.58	603,967.60
20	Søren HANSEN (Den)	(29)	932,789.00	594,758.19
21	Gary EVANS (Eng)	(30)	862,656.79	550,040.99
22	Darren CLARKE (N.Ire)	(20)	848,023.42	540,710.57
23	Alex CEJKA (Ger)	(18)	846,734.23	539,888.56
24	Ian POULTER (Eng)	(27)	832,559.99	530,850.89
25	Thomas LEVET (Fr)	(27)	821,430.29	523,754.45
26	Carl PETTERSSON (Swe)	(29)	806,892.69	514,485.09
27	Nick FALDO (Eng)	(19)	771,471.76	491,900.25
28	Ricardo GONZALEZ (Arg)	(21)	748,354.12	477,160.15
29	John BICKERTON (Eng)	(29)	707,012.40	450,800.14
30	Fredrik JACOBSON (Swe)	(24)	703,400.03	448,496.85
31	Barry LANE (Eng)	(29)	679,966.21	433,555.14
32	Peter O'MALLEY (Aus)	(20)	668,183.41	426,042.28
33	Robert KARLSSON (Swe)	(23)	625,087.92	398,564.04
34	Ian WOOSNAM (Wal)	(21)	598,814.59	381,811.84
35	Pierre FULKE (Swe)	(21)	563,825.75	359,502.50
# 36	Nick DOUGHERTY (Eng)	(32)	562,508.57	358,662.65
37	Greg OWEN (Eng)	(27)	557,654.95	355,567.92
38	Jean-Francois REMESY (Fr)	(30)	549,440.34	350,330.18
39	Brian DAVIS (Eng)	(29)	548,351.95	349,636.21
40	Peter LONARD (Aus)	(11)	523,579.89	333,841.23
41	Steen TINNING (Den)	(24)	519,101.32	330,985.64
42	Alastair FORSYTH (Scot)	(27)	504,442.78	321,639.16
43	Carlos RODILES (Sp)	(23)	492,732.05	314,172.25
44	Malcolm MACKENZIE (Eng)	(28)	486,446.31	310,164.38
45	Jarrod MOSELEY (Aus)	(27)	480,416.43	306,319.65
46	Paul CASEY (Eng)	(19)	475,848.21	303,406.90
47	Jarmo SANDELIN (Swe)	(24)	474,041.75	302,255.08
48	Phillip PRICE (Wal)	(21)	473,096.01	301,652.06
49	Maarten LAFEBER (NL)	(29)	465,943.98	297,091.84
50	David GILFORD (Eng)	(25)	452,157.67	288,301.51
51	Richard GREEN (Aus)	(23)	449,524.09	286,622.31
52	Emanuele CANONICA (It)	(20)	432,406.41	275,707.85
53	Rolf MUNTZ (NL)	(29)	423,767.34	270,199.47
54	Andrew COLTART (Scot)	(31)	414,462.91	264,266.85
55	Jamie SPENCE (Eng)	(27)	414,075.09	264,019.57
56	Graeme MCDOWELL (N.Ire)	(13)	412,203.39	262,826.15
57	Sandy LYLE (Scot)	(16)	407,599.12	259,890.41
58	Paul MCGINLEY (Ire)	(22)	401,597.63	256,063.78
59	Tobias DIER (Ger)	(30)	398,534.65	254,110.78
60	Simon DYSON (Eng)	(33)	397,290.51	253,317.51
61	Henrik BJORNSTAD (Nor)	(25)	388,581.18	247,764.32
62	Joakim HAEGGMAN (Swe)	(25)	386,388.74	246,366.40
# 63	Peter FOWLER (Aus)	(28)	384,737.23	245,313.38
64	Richard S JOHNSON (Swe)	(23)	383,505.29	244,527.87
65	Ignacio GARRIDO (Sp)	(23)	380,108.73	242,362.19
66	Miguel Angel JIMÉNEZ (Sp)	(12)	362,452.62	231,104.42
67	Søren KJELDSEN (Den)	(28)	342,578.41	218,432.37
68	Steve WEBSTER (Eng)	(29)	336,649.82	214,652.23
# 69	Santiago LUNA (Sp)	(21)	325,336.98	207,439.01
70	Roger CHAPMAN (Eng)	(26)	322,283.32	205,491.96
71	Nick O'HERN (Aus)	(25)	321,618.09	205,067.80
72	Raphaël JACQUELIN (Fr)	(29)	319,580.60	203,768.67
~ 73	Richard BLAND (Eng)	(26)	318,773.53	203,254.08
74	David HOWELL (Eng)	(22)	315,409.48	201,109.12
75	Lee WESTWOOD (Eng)	(21)	308,338.70	196,600.70

Pos	Name & Country		Total Prize Money	
			euro	£
76	Raymond RUSSELL (Scot)	(27)	303,749.82	193,674.77
77	Warren BENNETT (Eng)	(28)	298,915.72	190,592.48
78	David LYNN (Eng)	(29)	295,737.78	188,566.19
79	Darren FICHARDT (SA)	(25)	290,509.03	185,232.27
80	Anthony WALL (Eng)	(32)	285,572.43	182,084.63
81	Mark PILKINGTON (Wal)	(33)	283,758.97	180,928.34
82	Ian GARBUTT (Eng)	(30)	281,920.74	179,756.27
83	Jonathan LOMAS (Eng)	(32)	276,028.51	175,999.31
84	Mathias GRÖNBERG (Swe)	(15)	270,977.34	172,778.62
85	Sam TORRANCE (Scot)	(17)	268,770.58	171,371.56
86	Patrik SJÖLAND (Swe)	(28)	255,341.77	162,809.17
87	David CARTER (Eng)	(28)	235,858.88	150,386.63
* 88	Charlie WI (R.Kor)	(17)	234,036.35	149,224.57
# 89	Arjun ATWAL (Ind)	(23)	231,642.74	147,698.37
90	Jamie DONALDSON (Wal)	(30)	229,892.78	146,582.58
91	Roger WESSELS (SA)	(27)	228,055.40	145,411.04
92	Miles TUNNICLIFF (Eng)	(14)	223,170.50	142,296.36
~ 93	Mark FOSTER (Eng)	(29)	220,239.97	140,427.82
94	Henrik NYSTROM (Swe)	(24)	216,222.41	137,866.17
95	Mark ROE (Eng)	(27)	211,859.19	135,084.13
96	Mikael LUNDBERG (Swe)	(27)	207,480.21	132,292.03
97	Stephen GALLACHER (Scot)	(28)	205,607.17	131,097.76
98	Marc FARRY (Fr)	(30)	205,156.38	130,810.33
~ 99	Mårten OLANDER (Swe)	(25)	198,864.71	126,798.68
100	Andrew OLDCORN (Scot)	(24)	198,481.87	126,554.57
101	John DALY (USA)	(11)	194,486.69	124,007.20
102	Diego BORREGO (Sp)	(20)	194,022.43	123,711.18
103	Mikko ILONEN (Fin)	(17)	192,142.89	122,512.76
104	Stephen DODD (Wal)	(30)	189,482.85	120,816.69
$ 105	Martin MARITZ (SA)	(14)	189,399.10	120,763.29
106	Sven STRÜVER (Ger)	(26)	188,996.82	120,506.78
# 107	David PARK (Wal)	(23)	183,671.44	117,111.26
108	Greg TURNER (NZ)	(19)	183,433.98	116,959.85
109	Miguel Angel MARTIN (Sp)	(27)	183,167.58	116,789.99
110	Gary ORR (Scot)	(25)	183,125.34	116,763.05
~ 111	Klas ERIKSSON (Swe)	(26)	182,796.53	116,553.41
# 112	Kenneth FERRIE (Eng)	(20)	182,625.03	116,444.05
# 113	Fredrik ANDERSSON (Swe)	(16)	182,063.96	116,086.31
# 114	David DRYSDALE (Scot)	(22)	178,379.42	113,737.00
115	Paul EALES (Eng)	(30)	176,218.65	112,359.26
116	Gary EMERSON (Eng)	(32)	175,491.92	111,895.89
117	Gordon BRAND JNR. (Scot)	(24)	175,421.78	111,851.17
~ 118	Stuart LITTLE (Eng)	(26)	174,387.39	111,191.63
~ 119	Philip GOLDING (Eng)	(31)	172,713.42	110,124.29
120	Jean HUGO (SA)	(31)	166,660.29	106,264.73
121	Christopher HANELL (Swe)	(29)	166,390.61	106,092.78
# 122	Matthew CORT (Eng)	(22)	166,325.57	106,051.31
123	Anders FORSBRAND (Swe)	(27)	165,250.58	105,365.88
124	Markus BRIER (Aut)	(26)	164,048.93	104,599.69
125	Peter BAKER (Eng)	(31)	159,536.89	101,722.76
126	Mark MCNULTY (Zim)	(17)	154,765.57	98,680.51
# 127	Adam MEDNICK (Swe)	(19)	152,561.94	97,275.44
128	Des SMYTH (Ire)	(21)	152,310.71	97,115.26
$ 129	James KINGSTON (SA)	(14)	151,101.45	96,344.21
130	Lucas PARSONS (Aus)	(29)	149,213.87	95,140.67
# 131	Marcel SIEM (Ger)	(18)	148,197.79	94,492.80
132	Brett RUMFORD (Aus)	(29)	146,704.49	93,540.66
~ 133	Andrew MARSHALL (Eng)	(32)	145,042.11	92,480.70
134	Gregory HAVRET (Fr)	(31)	138,036.51	88,013.85
135	Mark MOULAND (Wal)	(33)	137,664.56	87,776.68
136	Scott GARDINER (Aus)	(17)	137,355.53	87,579.64
137	Stephen SCAHILL (NZ)	(31)	131,954.36	84,135.78
138	Wei-Tze YEH (C.Tai)	(15)	130,204.92	83,020.32
~ 139	Peter HANSON (Swe)	(20)	125,341.81	79,919.54
~ 140	Gary CLARK (Eng)	(32)	121,223.61	77,293.72
141	Paul BROADHURST (Eng)	(23)	119,812.81	76,394.18
# 142	Robert COLES (Eng)	(18)	106,375.74	67,826.53
~ 143	Sebastien DELAGRANGE (Fr)	(28)	103,484.58	65,983.09
144	Jorge BERENDT (Arg)	(25)	98,417.96	62,752.55
$ 145	Jean-François LUCQUIN (Fr)	(3)	97,120.39	61,925.20
~ 146	Chris GANE (Eng)	(30)	95,771.24	61,064.97
147	Des TERBLANCHE (SA)	(9)	92,510.25	58,985.72
# 148	Sam WALKER (Eng)	(20)	92,219.62	58,800.41
~ 149	Robert-Jan DERKSEN (NL)	(29)	88,799.06	56,619.42
# 150	Didier DE VOOGHT (Bel)	(23)	86,026.84	54,851.81

First time winners on The 2002 European Tour International Schedule. From the top right, clockwise; Justin Rose, Kevin Sutherland, Alastair Forsyth, Malcolm Mackenzie, Miles Tunnicliff, Graeme McDowell, Adam Mednick, Rich Beem, Søren Hansen, Anders Hansen, Carl Pettersson, Arjun Atwal, Richard S Johnson and Tim Clark

$ = 2001 Challenge Tour Members • = Affiliated Member # = 2001 Qualifying School Graduates ~ = 2001 Challenge Tour Graduates Figures in parentheses indicate number of events played

The European Tour

(A company limited by guarantee)

BOARD OF DIRECTORS

N C Coles, MBE Chairman

A Gallardo, *Vice Chairman* T A Horton, MBE M Lanner

R Claydon M H James (alternate K J Brown) J E O'Leary

D Cooper D Jones D J Russell

B Gallacher, OBE O Sellberg

Sir Michael F Bonallack, OBE *(Non Executive)*

P A T Davidson *(Non Executive)*

B Nordberg *(Non Executive)*

K S Owen *(Non Executive)*

TOURNAMENT COMMITTEE

M H James (Eng), *Chairman*

M Lanner (Swe), *Vice Chairman*

R Chapman *(Eng)*

D Clarke *(N Ire)*

P Eales *(Eng)*

A Forsbrand *(Swe)*

T Gögele *(Ger)*

B Langer *(Ger)*

R Lee *(Eng)*

C Montgomerie, MBE *(Scot)*

O Sellberg *(Swe)*

J Spence *(Eng)*

S Torrance, MBE *(Scot)*

G Turner *(NZ)*

J Van de Velde *(Fr)*

T Björn (Den) *(co-opted)*

M A Jiménez (Sp) *(co-opted)*

EXECUTIVE MANAGEMENT

Executive Director	K D Schofield, CBE
Deputy Executive Director	G C O'Grady
General Counsel	M D Friend
Assistant to Executive Director and Ryder Cup Director	R G Hills
Director of International Policy	K Waters
Group Marketing Director	S F Kelly
Director of Corporate Affairs and Public Relations	M S Platts
Director of Tour Operations	D W Garland
Assistant Director of Tour Operations	D A Probyn
Chief Referee	J N Paramor
Senior Referee	A N McFee
Managing Director, European Seniors Tour	K A Stubbs
Championship Director, World Golf Championships	P Adams
Director of Challenge Tour	A de Soultrait
Group Company Secretary	M Bray
Senior Tournament Director and Qualifying School Director	M R Stewart
Director of Tournament Services	E Kitson
Director of Tournament Development	J Birkmyre
Chief Financial Officer	J Orr
Director/Special Projects	M MacDiarmid
Director of IT and New Media	M Lichtenhein
Director of Communications	G Simpson
Sales Director	T Shaw

The Contributors

Mike Aitken *(The Scotsman)*
The Barclays Scottish Open

Colin Callander
The European Seniors Tour

Phil Casey *(PA Sport)*
Caltex Singapore Masters

Jeremy Chapman *(Racing Post)*
Victor Chandler British Masters

Bruce Critchley *(Sky Sports)*
Novotel Perrier Open de France

Scott Crockett *(The European Tour)*
Omega Hong Kong Open
The Great North Open
Diageo Scottish PGA Championship
Wins Around the World

Norman Dabell
Algarve Open de Portugal
Volvo Scandinavian Masters
Telefonica Open de Madrid

Bill Elliott *(The Observer / Today's Golfer)*
Volvo Order of Merit Winner
The Year in Retrospect
Volvo PGA Championship
131st Open Golf Championship

Andy Farrell *(The Independent)*
US Open Championship

Mark Garrod *(PA Sport)*
Volvo Masters Andalucia

Tim Glover *(Independent on Sunday)*
The Celtic Manor Resort Wales Open

David Hamilton
The European Challenge Tour

Martin Hardy
The Compass Group English Open

John Hopkins *(The Times)*
WGC – Accenture Match Play

John Huggan *(Golf World US)*
Deutsche Bank – SAP Open TPC of Europe

Renton Laidlaw *(The Golf Channel)*
ANZ Championship
Dubai Desert Classic
Qatar Masters

Derek Lawrenson *(Daily Mail)*
Masters Tournament
US PGA Championship

Jock MacVicar *(Scottish Daily Express)*
dunhill links championship

Lewine Mair *(The Daily Telegraph)*
Benson and Hedges International Open
Omega European Masters

Michael McDonnell
The 34th Ryder Cup Matches

James Mossop *(Sunday Telegraph)*
Heineken Classic

Charlie Mulqueen *(The Examiner)*
WGC – American Express Championship

Graham Otway
Johnnie Walker Classic

Mitchell Platts *(The European Tour)*
BMW Asian Open
WGC – EMC^2 World Cup

Philip Reid *(Irish Times)*
Murphy's Irish Open

Gordon Richardson
Canarias Open de España
The TNT Open
Linde German Masters

Gordon Simpson *(The European Tour)*
Bell's South African Open
dunhill championship
WGC – NEC Invitational
The European Tour Shot of the Year

Colm Smith
The Seve Trophy
Smurfit European Open

Mel Webb *(The Times)*
Madeira Island Open
BMW International Open
Trophée Lancôme
59th Italian Open Telecom Italia

John Whitbread *(Surrey Herald)*
Cisco World Match Play Championship

Roddy Williams *(The European Tour)*
Carlsberg Malaysian Open
North West of Ireland Open

the photographers

Introduction page:
* David Cannon – Getty Images

Opening course photograph:
* Stuart Franklin – Getty Images

The 34th Ryder Cup Matches:
* David Cannon – Getty Images
* Andy Hooper – Daily Mail
* Craig Jones – Getty Images
* Ross Kinnaird – Getty Images
* Bob Martin
* Stephen Munday – Getty Images
* Terry O'Neill – Special Black Tie Picture
* Andrew Redington – Getty Images
* Jamie Squire – Getty Images

Volvo Order of Merit Winner:
* Getty Images

The Year in Retrospect:
* Getty Images
* Terry O'Neill – Special Black Tie Picture

BMW Asian Open:
* Harry How – Getty Images

Omega Hong Kong Open:
* Chris McGrath – Getty Images

Bell's South African Open:
* Andrew Redington – Getty Images

dunhill championship:
* Andrew Redington – Getty Images

Johnnie Walker Classic:
* Nick Wilson – Getty Images

Heineken Classic:
* Nick Wilson – Getty Images

ANZ Championship:
* Nick Wilson – Getty Images

WGC – Accenture Match Play:
* Jeff Gross - Getty Images
* Scott Halleran – Getty Images

Caltex Singapore Masters:
* Warren Little – Getty Images

Carlsberg Malaysian Open:
* Warren Little – Getty Images

Dubai Desert Classic:
* David Cannon – Getty Images
* Ross Kinnaird – Getty Images
* Andrew Redington – Getty Images

Qatar Masters:
* Andrew Redington – Getty Images

Madeira Island Open:
* Ross Kinnaird – Getty Images

Algarve Open de Portugal:
* Stuart Franklin – Getty Images

Masters Tournament:
* AP Photo
* David Cannon – Getty Images
* Harry How – Getty Images
* Craig Jones – Getty Images
* Andrew Redington – Getty Images

The Seve Trophy:
* Ross Kinnaird – Getty Images
* Andrew Redington – Getty Images

Canarias Open de España:
* Stuart Franklin – Getty Images

Novotel Perrier Open de France:
* Stuart Franklin – Getty Images

Benson and Hedges International Open:
* Ross Kinnaird – Getty Images
* Warren Little – Getty Images
* Andrew Redington – Getty Images

Deutsche Bank – SAP Open TPC of Europe:
* Stuart Franklin – Getty Images

Volvo PGA Championship:
* David Cannon – Getty Images
* Stuart Franklin – Getty Images
* Warren Little – Getty Images
* Stephen Munday – Getty Images
* Andrew Redington – Getty Images

Victor Chandler British Masters:
* Warren Little – Getty Images
* Andrew Redington – Getty Images

The Compass Group English Open:
* Stuart Franklin – Getty Images

US Open Championship:
* Andy Lyons – Getty Images
* Donald Miralle – Getty Images
* Stephen Munday – Getty Images
* Ezra Shaw – Getty Images
* Jamie Squire – Getty Images

The Great North Open:
* Warren Little – Getty Images

Murphy's Irish Open:
* Andrew Redington – Getty Images

Smurfit European Open:
* Andrew Redington – Getty Images

The Barclays Scottish Open:
* Stuart Franklin – Getty Images
* Ross Kinnaird – Getty Images
* Warren Little – Getty Images

131st Open Golf Championship:
* David Cannon – Getty Images
* Harry How – Getty Images
* Ross Kinnaird – Getty Images
* Warren Little – Getty Images
* Stephen Munday – Getty Images
* Andrew Redington – Getty Images

The TNT Open:
* Stuart Franklin – Getty Images

Volvo Scandinavian Masters:
* Stuart Franklin – Getty Images

The Celtic Manor Resort Wales Open:
* Andrew Redington – Getty Images

US PGA Championship:
* Harry How – Getty Images
* Craig Jones – Getty Images
* Andrew Redington – Getty Images
* Jamie Squire – Getty Images

North West of Ireland Open:
* Andrew Redington – Getty Images

WGC – NEC Invitational:
* Scott Halleran – Getty Images
* Harry How – Getty Images

Diageo Scottish PGA Championship:
* Ross Kinnaird – Getty Images

BMW International Open:
* Stuart Franklin – Getty Images

Omega European Masters:
* Ross Kinnaird – Getty Images
* Andrew Redington – Getty Images

Linde German Masters:
* Stuart Franklin – Getty Images

WGC – American Express Championship:
* Laurence Griffiths - Getty Images
* Andrew Redington – Getty Images

dunhill links championship:
* David Cannon – Getty Images
* Ross Kinnaird – Getty Images
* Warren Little – Getty Images
* Andrew Redington – Getty Images

Trophée Lancôme:
* Stuart Franklin – Getty Images

Cisco World Match Play Championship:
* David Cannon – Getty Images
* Warren Little – Getty Images
* Andrew Redington – Getty Images

Telefonica Open de Madrid:
* Stuart Franklin – Getty Images

59th Italian Open Telecom Italia:
* Warren Little – Getty Images

Volvo Masters Andalucia:
* Ross Kinnaird – Getty Images
* Andrew Redington – Getty Images

WGC-EMC² World Cup:
* Getty Images

Wins Around the World:
* Getty Images

The European Senior Tour:
* David Cannon - Getty Images
* Phil Inglis – Phil Inglis Photography
* Warren Little – Getty Images

The European Challenge Tour:
* Warren Little – Getty Images
* Stephen Munday – Getty Images
* Andrew Redington – Getty Images

The European Tour Shot of the Year:
* David Cannon — Getty Images

Asprey Golfer of the Month Awards:
* David Cannon - Getty Images
* Andrew Redington – Getty Images